THE PRINCETON REVIEW

CRACKING THE GRE®

BY ADAM ROBINSON AND JOHN KATZMAN

1996 EDITION

Random House, Inc.
New York 1995

ISSN 1062-5534
ISBN 0-679-76136-5

Manufactured in the United States of America

9 8 7 6 5 4 3 2

First 1996 Edition

So you're thinking about graduate school, eh? Maybe you're still in college planning ahead, or maybe you've been out of school for a few years figuring now's a good time to return to get that advanced degree. Anyway, you're going to have to take the GRE, the "SAT" for graduate school.

A lot of people think that because the GRE is so similar to the SAT they don't need to do much preparation. After all, they took the SAT already. How different can the GRE be?

Very different.

While there are many similarities between the two tests, there are also many important differences. As you might have expected, the GRE verbal sections require more advanced vocabulary than the SAT verbal. But perhaps you didn't know that GRE math is actually easier than SAT math. Paradoxically, that makes the math harder! How long ago did you add two fractions, or use the Pythagorean theorem? Did you know that while the SAT penalizes errors, the GRE doesn't? And of course you know that the GRE has two logic sections. Or did you?

Don't kid yourself. While you are older and wiser than you were when you took the SAT, the test is correspondingly more difficult. And you're probably rusty; it's been a while since you had to fill in ovals with a No. 2 pencil.

How is The Princeton Review different from other GRE courses? Well, the bottom line difference is that Princeton Review students improve more than other students. Much more.

How do we do it? Some coaches require you to memorize dozens of math theorems and thousands of words. In short, they get you to learn every little fact that could possibly show up on the GRE, without providing any focus.

The Princeton Review, on the other hand, knows how busy you are. We realize that in a month or two there is simply no way you could master every word and every theorem and every game that could possibly show up on your GRE.

So instead we focus on the concepts that appear the most frequently on the GRE. This information is surprisingly limited. These key concepts can be mastered in a month or two.

And we go a step further. After teaching you the most important material, we teach you how to attack questions when you don't know all the information. For example, Princeton Review students know how to attack an analogy when they don't know all the words. Do you? Princeton Review students know how to attack a geometry question when they can't remember all of their theorems. Do you?

Reading this book is not enough. You'll have to practice our techniques on actual GREs. An indispensable companion to this book is *Practicing to Take the*

GRE, published by the same folks who write the actual test, the Educational Testing Service (ETS). This book is available in some of the larger bookstores, or can be ordered directly from ETS. We'll give you order information in the Orientation chapter.

We use actual GREs in our course. It is very important that you practice our techniques on real GRE questions to convince yourself that they actually work.

When *Cracking the System: The SAT* first appeared in 1986, many people asked us when we'd be coming out with books on other tests and subjects. Since then we've published the book you are reading and over half a dozen other titles including *Word Smart* and *Word Smart II* (vocabulary books that will help you prepare for the GRE, by the way), and guides to the GMAT, LSAT, MCAT, and ACT.

If you have any questions about our course, or about academic matters in general, give us a call at 1-800-995-5585.

Good luck on your GRE!

ACKNOWLEDGMENTS

A successful GRE program is a collaborative effort. We'd especially like to thank our teachers John Sheehan, Mark Sawula, Jim Reynolds, Adam Frank, and Adam Landis for their suggestions and contributions.

We'd like to thank our agent, Julia Coopersmith, for her tireless help and editorial suggestions. To our editor Diane Reverand, our deep appreciation for her patience with our perfectionist delays and for her sponsorship of the entire project. And many thanks to Emily Bestler, and Martha Schueneman—we realize authors aren't always easy to deal with.

Finally we'd like to thank all those who have taught us everything we know about taking tests—our students.

CONTENTS

PART I

Orientation

WHAT IS THE GRADUATE RECORD EXAMINATION?

The Graduate Record Examination (GRE) is a group of standardized, multiple-choice admissions tests intended for applicants to graduate schools. The most important part of the GRE is the General Test, a three-and-a-half-hour "aptitude" test that is divided into seven sections:

1. two 38-question "verbal ability" (vocabulary and reading) sections

2. two 30-question "quantitative ability" (math) sections

3. two 25-question "analytical ability" (word problems and reading) sections

4. one experimental section

Each of these sections lasts thirty minutes. You will receive separate verbal, quantitative, and analytical scores. The experimental section, which will look like a verbal, a quantitative, or an analytical section, won't count toward your score. It is used by the test's publisher to try out new GRE questions and to establish how difficult your GRE is in comparison with GREs given in the past.

The verbal sections of the GRE General Test contain four types of questions:

1. analogies

2. reading comprehensions

3. antonyms

4. sentence completions

The quantitative sections of the GRE General Test contain six types of questions:

1. arithmetic

2. algebra

3. geometry

4. quantitative comparisons

5. discrete quantitatives

6. data interpretations

The analytical sections of the GRE General Test contain two types of questions:

1. analytical reasoning
2. logical reasoning

Each of these question types will be dealt with in detail later in the book.

BEYOND THE GENERAL TESTS

In addition to the General Test, the GRE includes Subject Tests in the following fields:

1. Biology	10. Literature in English
2. Chemistry	11. Mathematics
3. Computer science	12. Music
4. Economics	13. Physics
5. Education	14. Political Science
6. Engineering	15. Psychology
7. French	16. Sociology
8. Geology	17. Spanish
9. History	

If you are applying to a graduate program in one of these areas, you may be required to take the appropriate Subject Test in addition to the General Test.
We'll tell you more about the Subject Tests later, in Part Seven.

WHERE DOES THE GRE COME FROM?

Like most standardized tests in this country, the GRE is published by the Educational Testing Service (ETS), a big, tax-exempt private company in New Jersey. We'll tell you more about ETS in Chapter One. ETS publishes the GRE under the sponsorship of the Graduate Record Examinations Board, which is an organization affiliated with the Association of Graduate Schools and the Council of Graduate Schools in the United States.

HOW IS THE GRE SCORED?

Scores on the GRE General Test are reported on a scale that runs from 200 to 800. For reasons known only to ETS, the scale for each subject test runs from 200 to 980. You will receive only one score for each of the three sections of the General Test and for each Subject Test you take. Do nothing but fill out your name correctly and you will receive anywhere from 200 to 300 points, depending on the section or the subject. For every question you answer (or guess) correctly, you will receive about ten points. (Although virtually all GRE questions are worth ten points, the actual value ranges from zero to twenty points; the number of points is determined *not* by the difficulty of the question but by the number of other questions you have answered correctly.) GRE scores can rise or fall only by multiples of ten. The third digit in a GRE score is thus always a zero. You can't receive a score of 409 or 715 on the GRE.

Your score on each part of the GRE will first be calculated as a "raw score," which is simply the number of questions you answered correctly. (**There is no deduction for incorrect answers on the GRE General Test**. We'll tell you more about this very important fact later in the book.) Raw scores are then converted to the 200-800 scale, according to a formula that takes into account the relative difficulty of your test.

Your scoring report will also contain your "percentile score" for each section of the test. Your percentile score tells you (and graduate-school admissions officers) how many people did better or worse than you did on the test. If your scaled score on the test places you in the 70th percentile, you know that 70 percent of the people who took the test scored lower than you did. So cheer up!

WHAT IS THE PRINCETON REVIEW?

The Princeton Review is the nation's fastest growing test-preparation school. We have branches in dozens of cities all across the country, and our list of locations is constantly expanding. We already prepare more students for the SAT than any other coaching school, and our programs for the GRE, LSAT, and GMAT are growing rapidly. The Princeton Review has the highest average score improvements in the country.

Our teaching methods for the GRE were developed through exhaustive analysis of all available GREs and careful research into the methods by which standardized tests are constructed. Our focus is on the basic concepts that will enable you to attack any problem, strip it down to its essential components, and solve it in as little time as possible. Our approach has been widely imitated, but no one else achieves our results.

A NOTE ABOUT SCORE IMPROVEMENTS

We have found in our courses that students' scores don't improve gradually; instead, they tend to go up in spurts, from one plateau to another. Our students typically achieve score gains of one hundred points or more after mastering the initial concepts of the course. Their scores then level off, only to take another jump a few weeks later when more course material has been assimilated.

If you work steadily through this book, you, too, will feel yourself moving from plateau to plateau. But you will have to work. You won't have one of our teachers standing over you, reminding you to review what you have learned.

A WARNING

Many of our test-taking techniques at first seem to violate common sense. In order to take full advantage of our methods, you will have to trust them enough to make them automatic. **The best way to do this is to practice them on real GREs.**

By "real GREs," we *don't* mean the practice tests in coaching books. The questions on such tests often bear only a superficial resemblance to the questions actually used on the test. Even the questions in this book are not actual GRE questions, although we have designed our questions using the same methods as those used in designing real GREs. **The only source of real GREs is the publisher of the test. We strongly recommend, therefore, that you purchase at least the most recent edition of *Practicing to Take the GRE General Test*, which is published by the Educational Testing Service for the Graduate Record Examinations Board.** This book contains three real GRE General Tests (minus their experimental sections) that were actually administered to test-takers. If you don't find it in your local bookstore, you can order it directly from ETS. To order, send $12 per copy to:

> Graduate Record Examinations
> Educational Testing Service
> Order Services Dept.
> CN 6785
> Princeton, NJ 08541-6785

If you want to practice on more than three tests, request one or two earlier editions as well. These sell for $10 each. If you're in a hurry, you can call the GRE publications office at (609) 771-7243.

IS THE GRE ABOUT TO CHANGE?

You've probably heard that ETS and the College Board made some changes in the SAT in 1994. Antonym questions were dropped from the verbal section, more reading-comprehension questions were added, some quantitative comparison problems in the math section were replaced by a few open-ended problems, and so on.

Will similar changes be made in the GRE? This would seem logical, but so far there has been no indication that a GRE overhaul is in the works. Practice fearlessly! And you can be sure that if changes ever are made in the GRE, we'll be there first to guide you through them.

SHOULD YOU TAKE THE GRE ON A COMPUTER?

No. Taking the optional computerized version of the GRE is a no-win proposition for virtually all test-takers. The computer GRE (referred to by ETS as the CAT, for Computer-Adaptive Testing) is cumbersome and confusing. Even if you love computers, you probably won't do as well on the CAT GRE as you would on the old-fashioned GRE. Hang on to that No. 2 pencil.

If you're determined to take the CAT GRE anyway (or if you want more reasons why you shouldn't) be sure to read Part VI: The GRE CAT and the About Computerized Testing section at the end of this book.

How to Think About the GRE

WHY DOES THE GRE SEEM SO FAMILIAR?

You've already taken the GRE General Test. You took it back in high school, when you took the SAT. The SAT and the GRE are published by the same company. Although there are important differences in levels of difficulty, questions on the two tests are very similar. In many cases, questions for the two tests are written by the same people.

Not all GRE question types are the same as SAT question types. For example, questions in the GRE's analytical-ability sections are instead the same as a question type used on the Law School Admission Test (LSAT).

We'll tell you much more about the differences and similarities between the GRE and the SAT and LSAT later in the book.

WHADJAGET?

Because the GRE and the SAT are so much alike, your old SAT scores can give you some indication of how well you would do on the GRE if you took the test tomorrow, without any help from us. In fact, the correlation between SAT scores and GRE scores is so strong that graduate schools would make virtually the same admissions decisions if they used old SAT scores instead of new GRE scores.

That they don't do this is good news for you. It gives you a chance to push up your scores between now and the time you apply.

WHERE DOES THE GRE COME FROM?

The publisher of the GRE is the Educational Testing Service (ETS). These are the people who publish the SAT, the Graduate Management Admissions Test (GMAT), the Secondary School Admissions Test (SSAT), Advanced Placement tests (AP), the National Teacher Examination (NTE), the National Assessment of Educational Progress (NAEP), and licensing and certification exams in dozens of fields, including hairstyling, plumbing and golf.

ETS uses Princeton, New Jersey, as its return address, implying a connection with the university. But ETS is actually located outside Princeton, in Lawrence Township. It is a private company, not a government agency. Although it pays no taxes, it does earn a lot of money from its testing monopoly. Some of these profits are invested in the company's luxurious four-hundred-acre headquarters, whose amenities include a pond, a swimming pool, jogging trails, tennis courts, and an expensive private hotel.

You've probably taken many ETS tests in your life. Unless you're planning to become a teacher (in which case you'll have to take the NTE) or an investment banker (in which case you'll have to take the GMAT), the GRE may be the last ETS test you'll ever have to take.

WHAT DOES THE GRE MEASURE?

The GRE General Test used to be known as the GRE Aptitude Test. Changing the name was an effort by ETS to distance the GRE from the numerous controversies that have arisen concerning "aptitude" and "intelligence" testing. Even so, admissions officers tend to view GRE scores as measurements of raw mental power. They will use your GRE scores as an "objective" standard against which to judge your college grades. That is, if your grades are high and your scores are low, they'll believe your scores and refer to you as an "overachiever" (rather than an "undertester"). If your scores are below a certain level, an admissions officer may reject you before even looking at your grades.

Despite what ETS says or admissions officers think, the GRE is less a measure of your intelligence than it is a measure of your ability to take ETS tests.

THIS IS *VERY* GOOD NEWS FOR YOU

Fortunately, your ability to take ETS tests can be improved dramatically in a matter of weeks. With proper instruction and sufficient practice, virtually all test-takers can raise their scores, often substantially. You don't need to make yourself smarter in order to do this. You just need to make yourself better at taking ETS tests.

ISN'T THE GRE COACHING-PROOF?

ETS has long claimed that its aptitude tests, including the GRE, are virtually impervious to special preparation. Indeed, this is supposed to be the chief attraction of such tests in the minds of admissions officers. The good news is that all ETS tests can be prepared for.

The first step in doing better on the GRE is developing the proper attitude about aptitude. Before you can raise your score, you must accept the idea that your so-called verbal, quantitative, and analytical abilities can be improved. These abilities are not innate.

You have no trouble accepting this in your ordinary classes. If a professor gives you a disappointing grade on a test, you probably tell yourself, "I need to study more," or "I need to pay more attention in class."

The same is true on the GRE. A low test score doesn't mean you're stupid; it just means you have to work harder at learning to take the test.

Keep in mind that dramatic improvements are possible. Some students actually raise their scores hundreds of points after brief albeit vigorous preparation.

YOU MUST LEARN TO THINK LIKE ETS

Despite what many people believe, the GRE isn't written by distinguished professors, renowned scholars, or graduate-school admissions officers. For the most part, it's written by ordinary ETS employees, sometimes with free-lance help from local graduate students. You don't need to feel intimidated by these people. Indeed, once you learn to view the GRE in the proper light, you will begin to find examples in the test of sloppy writing and confused thinking.

As you become more familiar with the test, you will also develop a sense of what we call "the ETS mentality." This is a predictable kind of institutional thinking that influences nearly every part of nearly every ETS exam. By learning to recognize the ETS mentality, you will enable yourself to earn points even when you aren't certain why an answer is correct. You will do better on the test by learning to think like the people who wrote it.

THE ONLY "CORRECT" ANSWER IS THE
ONE THAT EARNS YOU POINTS

As is true on all ETS multiple-choice tests, the instructions on the GRE tell you to select the "best" answer to each question. ETS talks about "best" answers instead of "correct" answers to protect itself from the complaints of test-takers who might be tempted to quarrel with ETS's judgment or who realize that ETS often gives credit for answers that aren't entirely correct. Your job is not to find the correct answer, therefore, but rather to find the one answer for which ETS gives credit.

To remind you of this, we will speak in this book not of "correct" answers or of "best" answers but of "ETS's answers." ETS's answer to a question is the answer that is worth points.

CRACKING THE SYSTEM

Our emphasis on earning points rather than on finding the "correct" answer may strike you as somewhat cynical, but it is a key to doing well on the GRE. Like all ETS multiple-choice tests, the GRE leaves you no room to make explanations or justifications for your responses. Your paper will be graded by a machine that recognizes one kind of pencil mark. If the space you darken on your answer sheet is different from the one darkened by the question writers at ETS, you'll be out of luck.

When you take the GRE, you will be working under enormous time pressure. If you double-check every answer, your score will suffer. In order to earn the score you deserve, you'll have to work quickly and efficiently, making every effort to maximize the ratio between points earned and time spent.

We teach our students to do better on the GRE and other tests by teaching them to put aside their feelings about *real* education and to surrender themselves to the strange logic of standardized tests. "Cracking the system" is our term for getting inside the minds of the people who write the tests and who, in so doing, help determine where—or whether—you'll attend graduate school. Learning to crack the system puts you on an equal footing with people in a position to decide your educational fate.

ONWARD AND UPWARD

In Chapter Two, we'll teach you the basic principles behind our method for scoring higher on the GRE. Then, in Chapter Three, we'll elaborate on these basic principles and teach you how an imaginary student named Joe Bloggs can help you push your GRE score out of sight.

Cracking the System: Basic Principles

TEST YOUR ETHICS

Shortly before he took the GRE, a student we'll call Johnny X was approached by a stranger who offered to give him a document containing ETS's answer to every single question on the test he was about to take. Johnny X accepted the document.

What would you have done? Would you have told the proctor what had happened? Or would you have taken the document?

Of course you would have taken it. The stranger *was* the proctor and the document was the GRE test booklet. As is true of every multiple-choice test in the world, the answer to every single GRE question is printed right there beneath the question in the test booklet. All you have to do is learn to recognize it.

WHAT'S PI?

Recognizing the answer to a question is vastly simpler than trying to come up with the answer off the top of your head. Here are two math questions that will demonstrate what we mean. Try them both, and see which one is easier to answer:

1. Calculate π to 10 decimal places and write your answer here: _____

2. π calculated to 10 decimal places is

   (A) 5.1828765678
   (B) 4.9387222567
   (C) 3.1415926535
   (D) 2.1760023644
   (E) 1.2099837657

Even if you're a math whiz, you probably found the second question easier than the first. The correct answer to both questions is 3.1415926535, but to answer the first question correctly you would have needed to have all eleven digits memorized and on the tip of your tongue. (Of course, you could also get the correct answer to question 1 by looking ahead to question 2.) All you needed to know to answer the second question correctly, in contrast, was that π is about 3.

THE AMAZING POWER OF POE—PROCESS OF ELIMINATION

In tackling the second question above, you didn't need to know the exact answer ahead of time in order to find it among the choices. Instead, you found it by examining the five possible answers and eliminating the four that you knew to be incorrect. In other words, you used the Process of Elimination.

The Process of Elimination is an extremely powerful tool on the GRE. We refer to it so often in our courses that we call it simply POE.

THE IMPORTANCE OF WRONG ANSWERS

By using POE, you will be able to improve your score on the GRE by looking for *wrong* answers instead of for *right* ones on difficult questions. Why would anyone want to look for wrong answers on a test? Simple. On hard questions, wrong answers are usually easier to find. And once you've found the wrong ones, picking the right one can be a piece of cake.

Incorrect choices on standardized multiple-choice tests are known in the testing industry as "distractors." Their purpose is to distract less knowledgeable students away from correct choices on questions they don't understand. This keeps them from earning points accidentally, by picking the right answer for the wrong reasons.

This simple fact can be an enormous help to you. By learning to recognize these distractors, you can greatly improve your score.

Not surprisingly, some distractors are harder to spot than others. Some are quite obvious, once you know what to look for. By first eliminating the *most obviously incorrect* choices on difficult questions, you can more effectively focus your energies on the smaller number of truly tempting choices.

IMPROVING YOUR ODDS *INDIRECTLY*

Every time you are able to eliminate an incorrect choice on a GRE question, you improve your odds of finding ETS's answer. The more incorrect choices you eliminate, the better your odds.

For this reason, most of our test-taking strategies are aimed at helping you to arrive at ETS's answer *indirectly*. Doing this will make you much more successful at avoiding the traps laid in your path by the people who write the questions. This is because most of the traps are designed to catch unwary test-takers who approach the problems *directly*.

Approaching a problem indirectly is like sneaking into a house through the back door. If you sneak in through the back door, you won't be drenched by the water bucket perched on top of the front door.

POE AND GUESSING

On questions where POE and the techniques based on it don't lead you all the way to ETS's answer, POE will help you substantially improve your chances of earning points by guessing.

If you guessed blindly on a five-choice GRE problem, you would have one chance in five of picking ETS's answer. Eliminate one incorrect choice, and your chances improve to one in four. Eliminate three, and you have a fifty-fifty chance of earning points by guessing.

BUT ISN'T GUESSING DISCOURAGED ON THE GRE?

No. Guessing is an absolute necessity on the GRE. There is no "guessing penalty" on the test. Your score will be based solely on the number of questions you answer correctly, with no deduction or penalty for incorrect answers. *This wasn't true when you took the SAT, but it's true on the GRE.*

Guessing on standardized tests is an issue that produces an enormous amount of confusion among test-takers and their teachers. Should you or shouldn't you? As it happens, guessing *always* works to the advantage of savvy test-takers, even on tests that, like the SAT, deduct points for incorrect answers.

With the GRE, there is no confusion. If you don't mark a choice for *every* question, you will earn fewer points than you should. This is so important that we will state it in the form of a rule:

> You must mark a choice for every question on the GRE, even if you have to mark some of your choices blindly in the final seconds of the testing period.

WHAT GUESSING CAN DO FOR YOUR SCORE

To see how important guessing can be, look at the case of a hypothetical student working on the verbal sections of his GRE.

The two 38-question sections that make up a student's GRE verbal score are timed separately, and you can't move between them. For the sake of this example, though, we'll lump them together.

Let's assume, then, that our student is able to attempt fifty-six of the seventy-six questions and that he selects ETS's answer on forty-two of these. If he stops right now, his forty-two correct choices will translate into a scaled score of about 470, which is roughly the national average.

But let's suppose that instead of leaving twenty questions blank, our hypothetical student guesses blindly on them. The laws of probability say that on average he'll guess correctly on four of the twenty questions. These four additional correct choices will raise his score from 470 to 510, or from the 50th percentile to the 60th.

Now let's assume further that instead of guessing blindly, our student is able to eliminate one obviously incorrect choice from each of the twenty questions before making his guess. We can now expect him to make five correct guesses, raising his scaled score to 520. If he is able to eliminate two obviously incorrect choices on each question—which is quite possible—his expected score rises again, to about 540, or close to the 70th percentile.

Intelligent guessing, in other words, can transform a run-of-the-mill student into one who is far above average.

HOW TO MAKE FOUR MISTAKES AND STILL EARN A PERFECT SCORE

You must be absolutely certain to mark an answer for every question on the test. **But you probably should not *read* every question on the test.** Because of the way the GRE is scored, it is sometimes possible to miss as many as four questions and still earn a perfect score of 800. **Most students would *score higher* if they saved time by ignoring some questions on the test. And we really mean ignoring—that is, spending no time whatsoever on the questions, except the time it takes to mark an answer.**

We'll tell you more about which questions to consider skipping as we go along in the book.

DON'T LISTEN TO WHAT THEY TELL YOU

You should tackle the GRE the same way you put together your new stereo: without reading the instructions. Students who read the instructions during the test are wasting very, very valuable time and costing themselves points.

Memorize the instructions beforehand. Don't even glance at them when you take the test.

USING YOUR TEST BOOKLET

Many test-takers are reluctant to write in their test booklets. Such nice fresh paper—why wreck it up?

But you *must* wreck up your test booklet. By the end of the exam period, your booklet should be filled with pencil marks. Your quantitative and analytical sections should be covered with scratchwork and diagrams. Your verbal sections should be filled with notes and cross-outs.

Students who write in their test booklets sometimes feel ambivalent about doing it. So they make the tiniest, faintest pencil marks they can. When they're finished, they erase what they have written.

This is ridiculous.

YOUR TEST BOOKLET IS JUST GOING TO BE THROWN AWAY

ETS will hang on to your booklet for a while in case anyone accuses you of using it to send messages to the person sitting next to you. After that, your booklet will be thrown away. There is no GRE score for "booklet neatness." No one will know that you couldn't figure out what 2 + 2 equaled without writing it down. You won't get extra credit for solving difficult problems in your head.

THE IMPORTANCE OF BEING A SLOB

Imagine that you're halfway through the math section on a standardized test. Suddenly, the proctor announces, "Five more minutes!" You look at the sea of questions you haven't answered yet, and you lose your train of thought. You jump ahead to the next question. First one choice seems correct. Then another. You start again. Then you panic and jump ahead to another question without marking a choice.

This is five-minute meltdown.

A student who panics on a test can't remember which choices he has eliminated. He runs through the same choices over and over again, making the same calculations and weighing the same considerations. His mind is spinning. He desperately selects choices that two seconds earlier he had decided were incorrect. Before he knows it, the exam period is over and the entire five minutes was wasted.

One of the best ways to prevent five-minute meltdown is to leave your mind uncluttered by doing as much of your work as possible in your test booklet. If you use your test booklet properly, you'll be much less likely to spin out of control in the final minutes of the test. You'll also work much more efficiently in the early part of the exam, before you can think of nothing but the clock.

A FEW RULES

Here are some simple rules that you should follow not only when you take the GRE but also as you work through this book and when you practice on published GREs:

1. When you eliminate an incorrect choice on a question, cross it out in your test booklet.

2. If you are uncertain about a choice, write a clear question mark beside it.

3. If you have trouble with a question that you think you might be able to answer with more work, make your best guess and then clearly circle the entire question in your booklet so that you can go back to it if you have time.

4. When you believe you have found ETS's answer on a question, circle it and write its letter clearly in the margin beside the question. Transfer your answers in blocks at the end of each subsection or the end of each page.

WHY YOU SHOULD CROSS OUT INCORRECT CHOICES

By crossing out a clearly incorrect choice, you permanently eliminate it from consideration. If you don't cross it out, you'll keep reading and rereading it as you make your deliberations. Crossing out incorrect choices can make it significantly easier to find ETS's answer, because there will be fewer places where it can hide. Sometimes, crossing out one or two incorrect choices will make ETS's answer seem to leap right off the page.

WHY YOU SHOULD PLACE QUESTION MARKS BESIDE IFFY CHOICES

Placing a question mark beside a choice that seems possible but not certain is a good way to remind yourself how strongly you feel about that choice. Imagine a difficult question on which you are able to eliminate choices A and D and on which you feel uncertain about C and E. If you have crossed out A and D and placed question marks beside C and E, a single glance at your booklet will be enough to tell you that B is your best guess.

WHY YOU SHOULD MAKE GUESSES AS YOU GO ALONG INSTEAD OF LEAVING BLANKS TO FILL IN LATER

Often on the GRE you will feel that you are tantalizingly close to ETS's answer but that you need more time to work on it than you can afford to spend. Many students in this situation will leave the answer space blank in the hope of coming back to work on the question later.

This is a bad idea.

When you've gone as far as you can go on a question, circle the entire question and *make your best guess then*, even if you plan to come back. (We'll tell you how to mark your best guess later.) By circling the question, you'll make sure you know where to find it later if you do end up with time on your hands. And by making a guess in the meantime, you'll make sure that you don't inadvertently leave the space blank in your hurry to beat the clock.

WHY YOU SHOULD MARK YOUR CHOICES IN YOUR TEST BOOKLET AND TRANSFER THEM IN BLOCKS

Most students mark their answer choices on their answer sheets immediately after answering each question. They read the question, select an answer, and mark it on the sheet.

This is a bad idea.

Constantly moving your eyes and pencil back and forth between a test booklet and an answer sheet is a waste of time. It's also an invitation to disaster. If your concentration falters for a moment, you may mismark an answer or even an entire column of answers. If you mark your answer for question 11 in the space for question 12, you may inadvertently keep mismarking answers until the end of the exam. This happens more often than you might think.

The best way to prevent this sort of careless error is to transfer your answers from your booklet to your answer sheet in blocks. If you are working on the ten questions in an antonym subsection, for example, wait until you have tackled all ten before transferring any of your choices to your answer sheet. When working on subsections that extend over more than one page, you can transfer your answers when you reach the end of each page.

Marking your choices in your booklet and transferring them in blocks has at least three other advantages:

1. Keeping your eyes focused on your test booklet will improve your concentration and make it easier for you to develop a good question-answering rhythm.

2. On certain kinds of GRE questions, such as reading comprehensions, you may find that your feelings about your answer choice on one question are altered by your choice on another. If you haven't transferred your answers yet, you can make the change without making an erasure on your answer sheet. This is important, because erasures and stray marks can trip up ETS's scoring computers and hurt your score.

3. Marking your answer choices in your test booklet gives you a second record of your answers, in addition to the one on your answer sheet. If you do inadvertently mismark your answer sheet by shifting your answers up or down by one place, your test booklet may help you win a rescore or a retest.

SUMMARY

1. Every student who takes the GRE is given all the answers ahead of time; they're printed in every answer book. Your job is to identify them, not to come up with them off the top of your head.

2. The Process of Elimination—POE—is an extremely powerful tool on the GRE. It is the foundation on which we build our techniques.

3. On the GRE, as on all multiple-choice tests, the best way to find the right answer is often to look for wrong answers, which are usually easier to find.

4. If you approach a question *indirectly*, you will sidestep the traps that have been laid for students who approach it *directly*.

5. There is no penalty for guessing on the GRE. You must mark a choice for every question on the test, even if you have to mark some of your choices blindly in the final seconds of the testing period.

6. Intelligent guessing can transform a run-of-the-mill student into one who is far above average.

7. You can make as many as four mistakes on the GRE and still earn a perfect score of 800. Most students would score higher if they didn't read (but did answer anyway) some questions on the test.

8. Learn the instructions before you take the GRE. Don't waste valuable time—and points—by reading them during the test.

9. Your test booklet should be filled with notes and scratchwork by the time you finish the test. You must not be shy about wrecking up your booklet.

10. Doing as much of your work as you can in your test booklet rather than in your head will leave your mind uncluttered and help you avoid five-minute meltdown.

11. When you eliminate an incorrect choice on a question, cross it out in your test booklet.

12. If you are uncertain about a choice, write a clear question mark beside it.

13. If you have trouble with a question that you think you might be able to answer with more work, make your best guess and then circle the entire question clearly so that you can go back to it if you have time.

14. When you believe you have found ETS's choice on a question, circle it and write its letter clearly in the margin beside the question. Transfer your answers in blocks at the end of each subsection or the end of each page.

CHAPTER 3

Cracking the System: Advanced Principles

PUTTING THE BASIC PRINCIPLES TO WORK

As we told you in Chapter Two, POE is a very powerful tool. If you use it to focus on eliminating incorrect choices rather than on finding correct ones, you'll improve your odds of earning a good score on the GRE.

There is, however, more to cracking the system than simply understanding the Process of Elimination. To put our techniques fully to work, you'll need to understand something about how the GRE is made and how you can turn its predictability to your advantage.

ORDER OF DIFFICULTY

One of the single most important facts to know about the GRE is that the questions on it are arranged in order of increasing difficulty. In a nine-item analogy subsection, for example, the first few items are relatively easy, the next few items are somewhat more difficult, and the last few items are quite hard. In fact, the last couple of items in the subsection will be so hard that very few of the people taking the test will be able to answer them correctly. (Questions on the computer-adaptive version of the GRE are not arranged in order of difficulty; see the Appendix.)

With some important exceptions that we'll explain later in the book, this is true of other subsections as well. Questions in each group or subsection on the GRE—as on the SAT and other standardized tests—are presented in order of increasing difficulty: first easy, then medium, then hard. If you're a veteran test-taker, you've probably noticed this yourself.

IS THIS ALWAYS TRUE?

Yes. If the hardest questions were given first, or if the order of difficulty were jumbled, many students would become discouraged and drop out of the test before finding most of the questions they were able to answer. Scores from one administration of the test would be wildly inconsistent with scores from another. Since tests like the GRE are used to compare students who take the test in different versions in different places at different times, consistency is crucial. Maintaining a consistent order of difficulty is a statistical necessity.

Because of this statistical necessity, it is possible to divide every group of questions on the GRE into thirds:

1. *The easy third:* Questions in the first third of each group are easy.

2. *The medium third:* Questions in the second third of each group are medium.

3. *The difficult third:* Questions in the third third of each group are difficult.

HOW DOES ETS KNOW HOW DIFFICULT THE QUESTIONS ARE?

ETS tries out all its GRE questions ahead of time, in pretests. This is the main purpose of the experimental section. Each new question is assigned a difficulty rating, called its *delta*, based on how many students answer it correctly on the pretest. If very few students answer a question correctly, it is judged to be a difficult question and is assigned a high delta; if many students answer it correctly, it is judged to be an easy question and is given a low delta. ETS

constructs new GREs according to an explicit blueprint that dictates where questions of different deltas should be placed.

ETS uses pretests to calculate another statistic, called the *biserial correlation*, for each new question. The biserial correlation is a comparison of how students do on particular questions with how they do on the entire test. On hard questions, for example, ETS wants to be sure that the small number of students selecting ETS's answer are high-scorers, not low-scorers. The biserial correlation tells them if this is so. Questions on which low-scorers do better than high-scorers are eliminated.

KNOWING THE ORDER OF DIFFICULTY CAN HELP YOU IMPROVE YOUR SCORE

Knowing the order of difficulty helps you in several ways. Most obviously, it enables you to make the best possible use of the limited time you are given in which to take the test. Hard questions aren't worth more points than easy ones. Your score will be based solely on your number of correct answers. Ten correct answers on ten easy questions are worth exactly the same number of points as ten correct answers on ten hard questions. To make the most efficient use of your time, answer the easy questions first. If puzzling over a difficult analogy question prevents you from answering an easy antonym question, you're throwing away points.

HERE'S THE RULE

The rule concerning order of difficulty is simple: **Answer easy questions first; save hard questions for last.** Don't start climbing trees until you've picked up all the apples on the ground. In fact, most students could improve their scores by working on *fewer* questions; they waste so much time struggling with items that are too hard for them that they overlook items they could answer with relative ease.

As we go along, we'll give you specific information about how the order of difficulty should affect your approach to each item type on the test.

KNOWING THE ORDER OF DIFFICULTY CAN ALSO HELP YOU FIND ETS'S ANSWERS!

In addition to helping you make the most efficient use of your time, knowing the order of difficulty can actually help you find ETS's answers on questions that you don't understand.

To show you why this is true, we need to tell you something about how most people take standardized tests.

CHOICES THAT "SEEM" RIGHT

What do most people do when they take a multiple-choice test? They work through a problem as far as they can and then select the answer choice that *seems right*, all things considered. On easier questions, they may be completely certain of their choices; on harder questions, they may simply have to trust their hunches.

There's nothing strange or mysterious about this. It's what almost everybody does. Whether they do well or poorly, people select the choices that, for whatever reason, seem right to them. Even *you* select choices that seem right.

WHICH CHOICES *SEEM* RIGHT?

That depends on who the students are and how hard the questions are.
Specifically, here's what happens:

1. On easy questions, ETS's answer seems right to almost everyone: high-scorers, average-scorers, and low-scorers.

2. On medium questions, ETS's answer seems *wrong* to low-scoring students, right to high-scoring students, and sometimes right and sometimes wrong to average-scoring students.

3. On hard questions, ETS's answer seems *right* to high-scoring students and *wrong* to everyone else.

There's nothing tricky about what we've just told you. It's really just common sense. Here's another way to think of it: If ETS's answer on a difficult question *seemed right* to almost everyone, the question wouldn't be difficult, would it? If ETS's answer seemed right to everyone, everyone would pick it, and the question would be an easy one. It would be located in the first third rather than the third third.

To help you remember this important concept, we can state it as a simple rule:

> Easy questions have easy answers; hard questions have hard answers.

COULD IT WORK THE OTHER WAY?

Could there ever be a question on the GRE in which ETS's answer seemed right to low-scoring students and seemed wrong to high-scoring students?

No. ETS uses its biserial correlations to eliminate any such flawed questions from its pool of GRE items. For the average student, an "easy" solution to a hard question will always be wrong.

JOE BLOGGS, THE AVERAGE TEST-TAKER

There isn't much to say about the test-taking behavior of very high-scoring students or very low-scoring students. High-scorers are right almost all the time; low-scorers are wrong almost all the time. But we can say a great deal about, and learn a great deal from, the test-taking behavior of the average-scoring student.

In fact, the average-scoring student is so important that we have a special name for him at The Princeton Review. We call him Joe Bloggs.

Joe Bloggs is exactly average. He's Mr. Fiftieth Percentile. Half the people who take the GRE do better than he does; half the people do worse. He isn't stupid. He isn't brilliant. He's right in the middle.

How can Joe Bloggs help you on the GRE? He can help you by showing you how to recognize the traps that ETS sets for him and for other average students on hard questions on the GRE. Since Joe Bloggs *always* falls into these traps, you can learn to avoid them simply by learning what it is about them that makes them irresistible to Joe.

Learning how Joe Bloggs thinks isn't difficult, because all of us think at least a little like Joe at least some of the time. By honing your sense of Joe's thought processes, you can improve your score on the GRE.

HOW DOES JOE BLOGGS DO ON THE GRE?

Joe Bloggs's performance on the GRE is exactly average, of course. Specifically, here's how he performs:

1. On easy questions, the answers that seem right to Joe really are right.

2. On medium questions, the answers that seem right to Joe are sometimes right and sometimes wrong.

3. On difficult questions, the answers that seem right to Joe are always wrong.

JOE BLOGGS AND YOU

Let's assume you want to earn a high score on the GRE. Could Joe Bloggs, whose scores are just average, be of any help to you?

You may not think so. But you'd be wrong. Joe Bloggs can be an enormous help to you. How? By showing you what *not* to do on difficult questions.

Remember, Joe is always wrong on difficult questions. If you can figure out which choices would appeal to Joe on these questions, you can improve your score simply by doing something else.

Specifically, here's what you're going to do:

1. On the easy third of each group of questions, you're going to do what Joe would do.

2. On the medium third, you're going to be suspicious of what Joe would do.

3. On the difficult third, you're going to figure out what Joe would do and then *do something else*.

WHAT *DOES* JOE DO?

To give you a better idea of how Joe Bloggs thinks on the GRE, let's take a look at a hard math question and see how Joe handles it. Here's the question:

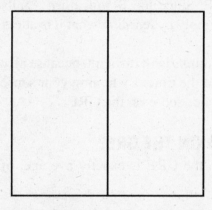

30. What is the greatest number of non-overlapping regions into which a square can be divided with exactly three lines?

(A) 4
(B) 5
(C) 6
(D) 7
(E) 8

This is a hard question, and Joe never gets the hard ones right. Why? Because the answer that seems right to him always turns out to be wrong.

Remember, hard questions have hard answers. But Joe doesn't like hard answers. He looks for easy solutions—answers that *seem right to him*. And the answers that seem right to Joe on hard questions are always wrong. If this weren't true, the question would never have survived its pretest.

Which answer choice seems right to Joe on this problem? To find out, we merely have to look for an easy, obvious solution. What's the easiest, most obvious way to fulfill the requirements of the problem? Think of the drawing as

a pizza with one cut down the middle. What would be the easiest way to make two more cuts? Just like this:

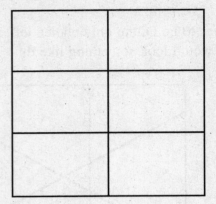

Now we have six pieces of pizza or, in the terms of the problem, six non-overlapping regions. Finding our answer was easy, wasn't it?

It certainly was. In fact, it was *too* easy. If doing what we did were all that was necessary to find ETS's answer, then Joe Bloggs and everyone else would answer this question correctly, and it would be an easy problem instead of a hard one. (Remember, we know it's a hard problem because of its location in the test; its number, 30, shows that it's from the difficult end of a math section.)

Because we were able to produce six regions so easily, we know that answer choice C can't possibly be correct. So we can eliminate it, and cross it out.

We refer to such easy, tempting choices as Joe Bloggs attractors.

Do we know anything else? Yes. Because we have been able to divide the figure into *six* regions, we know that neither five nor four could be the *greatest* number of regions into which the figure can be divided. Six is a greater number than four or five. So we can eliminate choices A and B as well.

Now we're down to two possibilities, D and E. Guessing blindly would give us a 50 percent chance of being right. On a real test, only about 10 percent of the test-takers will answer a question like this correctly. *Twice as many would answer it correctly if they simply guessed wildly from among all five choices.* But with Joe Bloggs's help, we've turned it into a coin toss.

We can even do better than that. As you will learn later in the book, the wording of some GRE questions irresistibly leads some students to select certain incorrect choices. This question contains an example of such irresistible wording—the phrase "greatest number." There are a significant number of low-scoring students who when they see the words "greatest number" invariably select the *greatest number* among the possible choices. The greatest number in this case is 8, choice E. We can eliminate it, because these low-scoring students

are correct even less often than Joe Bloggs is. *A difficult greatest-number question in which the greatest number was ETS's answer would be highly unlikely to survive a pretest, because its biserial correlation would be much too low.*

ETS's answer has to be D, the only choice left. Incidentally, the correctly completed diagram would look something like this:

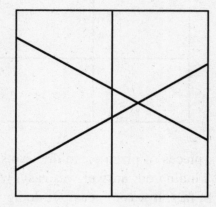

Don't bother trying to figure out this problem mathematically. It isn't really a math question at all. The only way to find ETS's answer (except for our way) is to use sophisticated intuition or time-consuming trial and error.

Notice that on this problem our knowledge of Joe Bloggs enabled us to

1. sidestep all of ETS's traps

2. spend less time on this problem than the high-scoring students who found ETS's answer without Joe's help

3. avoid careless mistakes

4. earn ten points we otherwise would have lost

WHY NOT SIMPLY ELIMINATE *ANY* CHOICE THAT SEEMS CORRECT?

That would be a disaster. Remember, the choices that seem correct to Joe *really are correct* on all of the easy questions and some of the medium questions. That means that on easy questions you want to *pick* the choices that Joe would pick. (On medium questions, you need to be suspicious of Joe's hunches, but they won't always get you into trouble.) It's only on the hard questions that you can safely eliminate any choice that would appeal to Joe.

We'll teach you much more about Joe Bloggs as we go along. As unimpressive as his own score is, he can help you make big gains on the GRE.

COULDN'T ETS GET RID OF THIS PROBLEM
BY CHANGING THE GRE?

There really isn't very much that ETS could do. ETS could make the GRE difficult or impossible to crack if it entirely abandoned the multiple-choice format, but there is no chance that this will happen. ETS and the College Board have recently added a limited number of open-ended, or fill-in-the-blank, questions on the math SAT, but this change was mostly cosmetic. The open-ended questions still require students to darken spaces on their answer sheets with No. 2 pencils. Doing this is very time-consuming. Converting the entire math SAT to this format would not be practical, since such a test would take several hours to complete. And ETS's open-ended format cannot be used on verbal questions.

A test that consists substantially of multiple-choice questions is the only kind of test that can be administered in a reasonable period of time and graded quickly and cheaply. If every GRE required a living, breathing grader, the test would be so expensive that no one could afford to take it.

As long as ETS doesn't switch to a true fill-in-the-blank format, we'll be able to crack the test with relative ease. The multiple-choice format is built around predictable statistical requirements that can all be turned on their heads. The statistical rules by which the test is built are also the keys to cracking it wide open.

SUMMARY

1. Questions on the GRE are arranged in order of increasing difficulty. Groups of questions begin easy and become hard.

2. Easy questions and hard questions are worth the same number of points. You should thus tackle easy questions first and save the hard questions for last.

3. Nearly everyone who takes the GRE approaches questions in the same way: They work out each problem as far as they can, then select the answer that *seems right*.

4. On easy questions, ETS's answer seems right to almost everyone.

5. On medium questions, ETS's answer seems wrong to low-scorers, right to high-scorers, and sometimes right and sometimes wrong to average-scorers.

6. On hard questions, ETS's answer seems right to high-scoring students and wrong to everyone else.

7. In other words, easy questions have easy answers; hard questions have hard answers.

8. For an average-scoring student, an "easy" solution to a hard question will always be wrong.

9. We call the average test-taker Joe Bloggs. He's exactly average. He isn't stupid. He isn't brilliant. He's right in the middle.

10. Because Joe Bloggs always falls into the traps on the GRE, you can learn to avoid the traps by learning what it is about them that makes them irresistible to Joe.

11. Here's how Joe Bloggs does on the GRE:

    • On easy questions, the answers that seem right to Joe Bloggs really are right.

    • On medium questions, the answers that seem right to Joe Bloggs are sometimes right and sometimes wrong.

    • On difficult questions, the answers that seem right to Joe are always wrong.

12. Because Joe Bloggs is so predictable, you can use your understanding of how he thinks to improve your score. Here's how you'll do it:

   - On the easy third of each group of questions, you're going to do what Joe would do.

   - On the medium third, you're going to be suspicious of what Joe would do.

   - On the difficult third, you're going to see what Joe would do and then *do something else*.

13. Joe Bloggs will enable you to

   - sidestep ETS's traps

   - spend less time on hard problems than many high-scoring students who find ETS's answer without Joe's help

   - avoid careless mistakes

   - earn points you otherwise would lose

14. You can't simply eliminate *any* choice that would seem correct to Joe Bloggs. On the easy questions and some of the medium questions, remember, Joe's hunches are correct.

15. ETS can't make significant changes in the way it builds the GRE without abandoning the statistical requirements that govern the construction of all standardized multiple-choice tests.

PART 2

How to Crack the Verbal Sections

GEOGRAPHY OF THE VERBAL SECTIONS

Every GRE contains two scored "verbal-ability" sections. Your test could also contain a third verbal section, as an experimental section. This experimental verbal section would look like the other two verbal sections but would not count toward your score.

Each verbal section on your test will last thirty minutes and contain thirty-eight items, as follows:

- Seven Sentence Completions (items 1–7)

- Nine Analogies (items 8–16)

- Eleven Reading Comprehension questions divided between two reading passages (items 17–27)

- Eleven Antonyms (items 28–38)

The items are arranged this way in each verbal section. Since there are two scored sections, your verbal score will be based on your performance on fourteen sentence completions, eighteen analogies, twenty-two reading comprehension questions, and twenty-two antonyms.

With the exception of the reading comprehension items (as we'll explain in Chapter Five), each group of items is arranged in order of increasing difficulty, as follows:

Item Type	Item Numbers	Difficulty
Sentence Completions	1-2 3-5 6-7	Easy Medium Difficult
Analogies	8-10 11-13 14-16	Easy Medium Difficult
Reading Passage 1 Reading Passage 2	Varies Varies	Varies Varies
Antonyms	28-30 31-35 36-38	Easy Medium Difficult

HAVE YOU EVER SEEN A VERBAL ABILITY?

ETS says that these seventy-six items test "one's ability to reason with words in solving problems." In truth, they mostly test your vocabulary. Even the reading-comprehension items are largely a vocabulary quiz.

You need to get to work on your vocabulary right away, because of the heavy emphasis on vocabulary in the GRE. Most people seem to find that increasing a verbal score is more difficult than increasing a math score. The reason for this is that vocabulary places something of a ceiling on scores. The better the vocabulary, the higher the ceiling and the higher the possible scores.

The best way to build a good vocabulary is to read a wide variety of good books over the course of a lifetime. Since you don't have a lifetime to prepare for the GRE, you should turn ahead to Part Five, Vocabulary for the GRE. It contains a relatively short vocabulary list that consists of the words that are most frequently tested on the GRE. It also contains some solid vocabulary-building advice. Skim through Part Five right now and sketch out a vocabulary-building program for yourself. You should work on your vocabulary a little bit every day while you work through the rest of the book. This will give each new word plenty of time to soak in.

Great aids in your vocabulary work are *Word Smart* and *Word Smart II*, The Princeton Review's guides to building an educated vocabulary. These books contain hundreds of solid vocabulary words and a detailed explanation of our techniques. Ask for them at your bookstore or use the order form at the end of this book to order copies directly from our publisher.

Using your newly strengthened vocabulary as a foundation, you will be able to take full advantage of the powerful techniques we describe in the next four chapters. Our techniques will enable you to get as much mileage as possible from the words you do know.

PRACTICE, PRACTICE

Beyond vocabulary, your score will improve as you learn our techniques for attacking questions with partial knowledge and increasing problem-solving speed. Mastering these techniques is a critical step toward achieving your maximum score on the GRE.

As you work along through this book, be sure to practice on real GREs. Work slowly at first, then increase your speed as you gain confidence in our techniques. Practice will rapidly sharpen your test-taking skills. Unless you trust our techniques, you may be reluctant to use them fully and automatically on a real administration of the GRE. The best way to develop that trust is to practice.

GRE VS. SAT

The verbal GRE is just like the verbal SAT, but with harder vocabulary and more tempting distractors. That doesn't mean you'll necessarily find it harder than you found the SAT back in high school. After all, your vocabulary has grown substantially in college. But the test isn't easy. The GRE's pool of test-takers consists of students who did well enough on the SAT to get into college, and then did well enough in college to make it at least most of the way to graduation. If you studied the Princeton Review method for cracking the SAT back in high school, you'll probably notice that GRE Joe Bloggs is a good bit sharper than SAT Joe Bloggs. You'll have to stay on your toes.

CHAPTER 4

Analogies

Each verbal section of your GRE will contain nine analogy items, numbered 8–16. Items 8–10 will be easy, items 11–13 will be medium, and items 14–16 will be difficult.

In this chapter, analogies will be numbered 1–9 instead. A number 1 will be easy; a number 9 will be hard. We do this to remind you that there are nine analogies arranged from very easy to very difficult. Always pay attention to the item position in answering GRE questions. The item number will help determine which technique or combination of techniques you will use to crack the problem.

LEARN THESE DIRECTIONS

Before we begin, take a moment to read and memorize the following set of directions. These are the directions exactly as they will appear on your GRE. You shouldn't even glance at them when you take the test. If you do, you will waste time and lose points. Here are the directions:

> Directions: In each of the following questions, a related pair of words or phrases is followed by five lettered pairs of words or phrases. Select the lettered pair that best expresses a relationship similar to that expressed in the original pair.

OUR BRILLIANT TECHNIQUES

The Princeton Review's techniques for cracking analogies are very powerful. All are based on POE. Sometimes you will be able to use POE to eliminate all four incorrect choices; you should always be able to eliminate at least one. Eliminating even one incorrect choice will improve your odds of earning points.

Our techniques for cracking analogies will enable you to

1. eliminate incorrect choices

2. improve your guessing odds

3. find ETS's answer even if you don't know the meaning of the words in the original pair

4. find ETS's answer even if you don't know one or more words among the choices

JUST WHAT IS AN ANALOGY, ANYWAY?

ETS isn't terribly clear about what it means by an analogy, so it should be no surprise if you aren't either. Some of the graduate schools to which you are applying may require you to take a peculiar standardized test called the Miller Analogy Test (MAT). Miller analogies are based on a broad factual knowledge of the world, whereas GRE analogies are based almost entirely on vocabulary. Also, Miller analogies are in a different format from GRE analogies, and the kinds of relationships between the words are different. Do not apply our GRE analogy techniques to Miller analogies!

There is only one kind of relationship in GRE analogies. We call this kind of relationship a *clear and necessary* relationship. A clear and necessary relationship is just what it sounds like. It's a tight, solid, logical relationship that is based on the meanings of the words. **A clear and necessary relationship is the kind of relationship that exists between a word and its dictionary definition.**

Here's an example:

SHIP : OCEAN

Is there a clear and necessary relationship between these two words? Yes, there is. A ship travels in an ocean. There is a tight, logical link between the meanings of the words. You don't have to stretch your imagination or suspend your disbelief to see the connection between the words. The connection exists because of what the words mean.

Now here's an unclear and unnecessary relationship:

SHIP : MAGAZINE

How are *ship* and *magazine* related? Well, we once saw a picture of a ship in a magazine.

Clear and necessary?

No. The words are unrelated, except in the strained context we've created. The relationship is neither clear nor necessary, and it has nothing to do with the definitions of the words.

Here's another unclear and unnecessary relationship:

SHIP : SNIP

The two words rhyme and have three of four letters in common. You might find such a pair on the Miller Analogy Test, but you won't find one on the GRE. Don't look for this sort of tricky item on the GRE. ETS plays tricks on the GRE, but not like this.

WHAT YOU HAVE TO DO

On the GRE, your job is to determine the clear and necessary relationship between a given pair of words (printed in capital letters and called the "stem" in ETS lingo) and then select another pair of words, from among the five choices, that has exactly the same relationship. If SHIP:OCEAN were the stem, ETS's answer might be "rocket:space." A rocket travels in space, just as a ship travels in an ocean. That's a GRE analogy.

FORM A SENTENCE TO FIND THE RELATIONSHIP

Your first step in solving a GRE analogy problem is to find the relationship between the stem words. To do this, you will form a simple sentence that links the two words and illustrates their meaning. That's exactly what we did in the SHIP:OCEAN example above. "A ship travels in an ocean" is a simple sentence that links the two words through their definitions. It states the relationship between the two words.

Let's try this approach on an easy question:

1. STONE:SCULPTOR::
   (A) brick:house
   (B) words:poet
   (C) bust:portrait
   (D) scalpel:surgeon
   (E) mine:ore

Here's how to crack it:

First we form a sentence. How about this one: "Stone is the medium in which a sculptor creates his art."

That's the relationship, all right, but the sentence is too wordy. It's important to be as succinct as possible. Here's another try: "Stone is shaped by a sculptor." That's pretty economical. We may have to tinker with it as we go along, but it's good enough for now.

Now that we have our sentence, we plug in the choices:

(A) Is brick shaped by a house? No. Bricks are used to build a house. Eliminate (and cross out).

(B) Are words shaped by a poet? Yes, figuratively speaking. A possibility. Let's check the other choices.

(C) Is a bust shaped by a portrait? No. A bust could be a portrait and made of stone by a sculptor, but the relationship between *bust* and *portrait* is not the same as the relationship between *stone* and *sculptor*. Eliminate.

(D) Is a scalpel shaped by a surgeon? No. A surgeon might wield a scalpel in something like the same way a sculptor wields a chisel, but there's no *chisel* in the stem. Eliminate.

(E) Is a mine shaped by ore? Don't get too clever here. You might stretch matters and say that a mine takes its shape from the removal of ore, but that's not what ETS is looking for. *ETS doesn't get cute with analogies.* Eliminate. ETS's answer must be B, the only choice we haven't eliminated. And it is.

MANY DIFFERENT SENTENCES ARE POSSIBLE

In looking at this item, notice that there are many possible ways to state the relationship between the stem words. We could have said, "Stone is a sculptor's medium," or "A sculptor makes art from stone," or something similar. It doesn't matter which we choose, and you should never waste time on the GRE by trying to find the *perfect* sentence. The only requirement is that you find a sentence that expresses the clear and necessary relationship. The more succinct your sentence is, though, the faster you'll find ETS's answer.

DON'T JUMP TO CONCLUSIONS

You should also notice that even though choice B looked good immediately, and even though this is an easy question, we still went ahead and plugged in all the choices. **You should always check out all the choices on GRE analogies.** Even though one choice may look good immediately, you may very well find a better choice farther down the list. When Joe Bloggs makes mistakes on easy analogies, it's out of carelessness.

There is no excuse for careless mistakes on the GRE.

MAKE YOUR SENTENCE SPECIFIC

When ETS's question writers try out new analogy items, they do the same thing we've told you to do: form a sentence. ETS uses the sentence method to make certain that the new analogies are sound.

You will sometimes find two or more choices that seem to fit your sentence when you plug in an analogy. When this happens, you'll have to go back and make your sentence more specific. Here's an example:

> 7. AVIARY:BIRDS::
>   (A) sanatorium:nurses
>   (B) gallery:paintings
>   (C) library:books
>   (D) penitentiary:inmates
>   (E) dictionary:words

Here's how to crack it:

A possible sentence might be, "An aviary is a place where birds are found." Now plug in the choices:

(A) Is a sanatorium a place where nurses are found? Yes. A possibility.

(B) Is a gallery a place where paintings are found? Yes. A possibility.

(C) Is a library a place where books are found? Yes. A possibility.

(D) Is a penitentiary a place where inmates are found? Yes. A possibility.

(E) Is a dictionary a place where words are found? Yes. A possibility.

We've plugged in all the choices and eliminated none. What did we do wrong?

We didn't make our sentence specific enough. Our sentence was too general or too vague to capture the exact type of relationship that ETS had in mind. We now need to go back and fiddle with it. A better sentence would be "An aviary is where birds are confined." Birds aren't just found in an aviary; they're prevented from leaving. The notion of confinement is the key. What's ETS's answer? Choice D.

PARTS OF SPEECH

If both words in the stem are nouns, both words in each choice will be nouns. If the first stem word is a verb and the second is an adjective, the first word in each choice will be a verb and the second will be an adjective. ETS never violates this principle.

You may sometimes have trouble determining the part of speech in one of the words in the stem. If this happens, look at the first answer choice. ETS uses choice A to "establish the part of speech" when the stem is ambiguous. In other words, if you aren't sure about the words in the stem, check the words in the first choice. The parts of speech should be clear.

TYPES OF RELATIONSHIPS

Many types of relationships are possible in GRE analogies. The stem words may be related by

1. degree (ADMIRE:IDOLIZE)

2. cause and effect (DRUG:CURE)

3. category and example (FRUIT:ORANGE)

4. part and whole (CHAPTER:BOOK)

5. agent and action (BRAIN:THINKING)

6. "to be is not to have" (POOR:MONEY)

You'll notice a few other types as you practice on real GREs. Being familiar with the sorts of relationships that crop up again and again can make it easier for you to form sentences quickly. And the faster you form your sentence, the faster you'll find ETS's answer.

Still, there's no need to memorize these or other specific types. Identifying relationship types is not an end in itself. In fact, you'll lose points if you spend a lot of time trying to classify questions before answering them. Much more important than any particular type of relationship you might find is the one general type of relationship you must always find: the *clear and necessary* relationship based on *the meanings of the words*.

BEWARE OF TRIANGULAR NONRELATIONSHIPS

You will sometimes find answer choices containing two words that seem to be related to each other but that are, in fact, related only to a third word. Here are four examples:

> lemon:orange
> irrigation:fertilizer
> salt:pepper
> weight:age

None of these pairs contains a clear and necessary relationship. Lemons and oranges are related in the sense that they are both fruits, but there is no relationship *between* them. You can't make a good GRE sentence using them: "A lemon is a slightly smaller and yellower orange, sort of " is not a good sentence.

Likewise with the other pairs. All these pairs sound good together, but not one contains a clear and necessary relationship. Irrigation and fertilizer are both related to crops, but not to each other. Salt and pepper are both related to seasoning, but not to each other. Weight and age are both related to measurement, but not to each other.

Choices containing such triangular nonrelationships can always be eliminated.

DRILL 1

Here's a drill that will help you get the hang of creating sentences for GRE analogies. Determine the relationship (if any) between the two words and then write a sentence that expresses it in the space at the side. If a pair of words is not related, write "unrelated" in the space. If you don't know the meaning of one of the two words, you'll have to play it safe with a "?" Be sure to look up any words you don't know. The first four are completed for you. (You can check your answers on page 332.)

1. needle:thread — A needle pulls thread.

2. vernal:spring — Vernal means having to do with spring.

3. breach:dam — A breach is a rift in a dam.

4. dog:cat — Unrelated. (Dogs and cats are both pets, but there is no relationship between them.)

5. vacillate:steadfast — opposites

6. scintilla:miniscule — some

7. calumniate:reputation — ?

8. sedulous:piquancy — _____

9. witty:mordant — _____

10. mendacity:truth — _____

11. apposite:impertinent — _____

12. infraction:felony — one faces a felony for an infraction (degree)

13. door:wall   _a door is in a wall_

14. door:roof   _none " below a roof_

15. sanctuary:protection   _one tried prot. in a sanc._

16. flustered:composure   _a flust. person has no comp._

17. malinger:work   _____

18. timorousness:intrepid   _____

19. plagiarize:murder   _none_____

20. snobbishness:sycophant _____

21. metal:filings   _____

22. inexperience:neophyte   _____

23. gaggle:geese   _a gaggle_____

24. evangelism:serenity   _____

25. fervor:emotion   _____

26. stultify:stupid   _____

27. layer:stratification   _____

28. ineluctable:avoid   _____

29. lethargic:stimulate   _____

30. legal:system   _____

31. fuel:log   _____

32. carapace:turtle   _____

33. stealth:detection   _____

34. promiscuous:chaos   _____

35. fortuitous:planning   _____

36. ruminate:meditation   _____

37. vindictive:revenge   _____

38. coltish:discipline   _____

39. vernacular:language   _____

40. ventral:conclusion   _____

41. arsenal:weapon   _____

42. obscurity:light   _____

43. venal:money   _____

44. tortuous:curves   _____

45. illicit:legality   _____

46. histrionic:dramatic   _____

47. glaze:window   _____

48. voter:election   _____

49. manacle:freedom   _____

50. Fred:Barney   _____

FINDING ETS'S ANSWER WITH YOUR EYES CLOSED

You should now have a good understanding of the sort of relationship that must exist between stem words in ETS analogy items. You've already used this understanding to make sentences linking various stem words. Now we're going to show you how to use the same concept to eliminate incorrect answer choices *even if you don't know the meaning of either of the words in the stem.*

HUH?

How can it be possible to eliminate choices if you don't know the words in the stem? Easy.

You already know two facts about GRE analogies:

1. The words in the stem must be related to each other in a clear and necessary way.

2. The words in ETS's answer must be linked by exactly the same relationship as the words in the stem.

From these two rules, we can easily deduce a third:

3. The words in ETS's answer must be related to each other in a clear and necessary way.

That is, since the relationship in ETS's answer must be identical to the relationship in the stem, the relationship in ETS's answer must also be clear and necessary.

Where does this get us? Everywhere. We can now deduce a fourth rule:

> 4. Any answer choice containing words that are *not* related to each other in a clear and necessary way could not possibly be ETS's answer and can therefore be eliminated.

That's right. Since you know that the stem and ETS's answer must both be based on a clear and necessary relationship, you also know that any choice *not* based on a clear and necessary relationship *must be wrong.*

ELIMINATING UNRELATED PAIRS

Keeping in mind the fourth rule above, try your hand at the following analogy. Notice that we've left out the words in the stem:

9. _____ : _____ ::
   - (A) speculation:factions
   - (B) forestation:grass
   - (C) theorizing:rumors
   - (D) replication:duplicates
   - (E) animation:characters

Here's how to crack it:

Give up? Don't! You already have enough information to find ETS's answer.

As usual, the first thing to do is to try to form a sentence. We need to do it with each of the choices. The point in trying to form a sentence is to see if each pair of words is related in a clear and necessary way. Start with the first pair:

- (A) Is there a clear and necessary relationship between speculation and factions? No. You might try to get tricky and say something like, "Speculation among the delegates led to the formation of factions at the political convention," but this is a very unclear and very unnecessary relationship. We can eliminate this choice.

- (B) There might be grass in a forest, but there's nothing clear or necessary about the relationship between these two words. This is not an ETS relationship. We can eliminate this choice.

- (C) Can you think of a clear, succinct sentence linking theorizing and rumors through their meanings? We can't. We can eliminate this choice.

(D) Replication is the creation of duplicates. This is a clear and necessary relationship based on the meanings of the words. A possibility.

(E) Cartoon characters are sometimes animated, but be careful: There is no other relationship between these words. To animate something is to give life to it. There is no clear and necessary relationship here. Many GRE analogy choices will contain pairs of words that just sort of sound right together, even though they are unrelated. These are traps for Joe Bloggs. We can eliminate this choice.

ETS's answer must be choice D, the only choice we couldn't eliminate. It is. (The missing stem is RAMIFICATION:BRANCHES. Ramification is the process of forming branches, just as replication is the process of forming duplicates.)

DON'T BE TOO CLEVER

GRE analogies are not a test of how clever you are at thinking of bizarre relationships between words. Such a test of creativity might be more interesting than the boring old GRE, but you're stuck with the boring old GRE. Any two words can be twisted and bent into some sort of relationship. That's not the point. This isn't creative writing. It's a vocabulary test. Remember the dictionary and dictionary definitions.

Here's another example of how eliminating unrelated pairs can enable you to zero in on ETS's answer:

6. _____ : _____ ::
    (A) captious:criticism
    (B) kind:admiration
    (C) questionable:response
    (D) reprehensible:censure
    (E) incredible:ecstasy

Here's how to crack it:

Once again, look for unrelated pairs.

(A) A captious person is a carping or critical person. Therefore, our sentence might be, "To be captious is to make criticism." This sentence expresses a clear and necessary relationship. A possibility.

(B) Kind people or kind acts often inspire admiration, but there is *not* a clear and necessary relationship between these two words. The words are not linked through their definitions. We can eliminate this choice.

(C) Questionable and response sort of seem as though they ought to go together. But they don't really. *Question* and response would be clearly and necessarily related, but these two words aren't. We can eliminate this choice.

(D) Reprehensible means "worthy of rebuke or censure," according to the dictionary. These two words are clearly and necessarily related. Our sentence might be, "To be reprehensible is to deserve censure." A possibility.

(E) Incredible means unbelievable. Ecstasy is intense delight or emotion. The two words are not related in a clear and necessary way. We can eliminate this choice.

We've eliminated all choices but A and D. If we guess now, we'll have a fifty-fifty chance of being right—a coin toss. Not bad, considering we still don't know what the question is. (The missing stem was MERITORIOUS:PRAISE. Meritorious means deserving of praise. ETS's answer is choice D.)

In the next section, we'll show you techniques that will often enable you to determine which of the remaining choices is most likely to be ETS's answer.

FEAR THE UNKNOWN

Never initially eliminate a choice if you are uncertain of the meaning of either word in it. You can't be positive that two words are unrelated if you have no idea what one of them means.

WORKING BACKWARD FROM THE CHOICES

Not many difficult GRE analogy problems will contain four easily recognizable unrelated pairs among the answer choices. Some may contain just one, or even none. In all cases where eliminating unrelated pairs alone doesn't take you all the way to ETS's answer, you'll need to use other tools. One of the most powerful of these tools is working backward.

Working backward is especially useful when the meaning of one of the words in the stem is unknown or unclear. It is a method of testing a choice by determining its relationship and then assessing whether the words in the stem could possibly be related in the same way.

Working backward is effective because it takes advantage of our favorite immutable fact about relationships between paired words in GRE analogies: The relationship between the stem words must be exactly the same relationship as the one between the words in ETS's answer.

Let's look at an example. Suppose that we don't know the meaning of the first word in the stem but that by identifying unrelated pairs we have been able to eliminate three choices. Here's what's left:

3. _____ : KNIFE ::
   (A) tune:piano
   (B) [eliminated]
   (C) baste:dryness
   (D) [eliminated]
   (E) [eliminated]

Here's how to crack it:

We will look for ETS's answer by forming a sentence for each of the remaining choices and applying it backward to the stem.

Our sentence for choice A is "To tune a piano improves its quality." Could _____ mean to improve the quality of a knife? Sure. It's easy to imagine that there could be a word for that, like *sharpen*. We don't have to think of the exact word to feel certain that such a word could exist.

Now choice C. Our sentence is "To baste [something] reduces its dryness." Could _____ing something reduce its knife? No. This sentence is nonsense. ETS's answer is A. (The missing word in the stem is HONE.)

IMPROVING THE EFFECTIVENESS OF WORKING BACKWARD: DECODING THE STEM

Working backward is a powerful technique. It becomes even more powerful when used in combination with *decoding*, which is a technique for zeroing in on the meaning of an unknown word in the stem.

Like working backward, decoding is based on the fact that the words in GRE analogies must be related in a clear and necessary way. Since this is true, the number of possible meanings of an unknown word is fairly small. Here's an example:

9. SEMIOTICIAN:SYMBOLS

Semiotician is a very hard word. Our first step in decoding it is to look at the choices to see if by doing so we can determine the unknown word's part of speech. Let's say we do and that the following pair is among the choices:

(B) mathematician:topology

Because mathematician is unambiguously a noun, we can be absolutely certain that SEMIOTICIAN is a noun, too. Remember, ETS is always consistent with parts of speech in analogy problems.

This isn't all we know. Because we know that SEMIOTICIAN and SYMBOLS must be related in a clear and necessary way, we know that the meaning of SEMIOTICIAN can't have anything to do with, say, cooking. Why? Because it's impossible to imagine a clear and necessary relationship between cooking and symbols. The meaning of semiotician must have *something* to do with symbols, even if in a negative way.

Now we can think of some possibilities. Semiotician might mean a group of symbols, the absence of symbols, one who works with symbols, an instance of symbolism—there aren't many other possibilities.

As it happens, a semiotician is someone who studies signs and symbols. Decoding may not have given us the dictionary's exact definition of SEMIOTICIAN, but it certainly put us on the right page. We reduced the range of possibilities from tens of thousands to perhaps half a dozen. Having done this, we can be much more effective in working backward from any choices we were unable to eliminate.

Here's an example:

7. _____ :INSIGHT::
   (A) authoritative:despotism
   (B) audacious:hearing
   (C) torpid:activity
   (D) avaricious:generosity
   (E) zealous:enthusiasm

Here's how to crack it:

Once again, we're assuming that we don't know the meaning of the first word in the stem. What can we do without it? First we can eliminate unrelated pairs.

(A) Are authoritative and despotism related in a clear and necessary way? Well, a despot could be authoritative, or one could believe that being authoritative might possibly lead to despotism, but the relationship between these two words is not necessary. You won't find either word in the dictionary definition of the other. Eliminate.

(B) Audacious means recklessly bold or having audacity. It has nothing to do with hearing. (The similarity in sound between the word audacious and the root *audio-* is a trap for Joe Bloggs.) Eliminate.

(C) Are torpid and activity related? Yes. To be torpid is to be inactive, or to display no activity. A possibility.

(D) Are avaricious and generosity related? Yes. Avaricious means greedy. To be avaricious is to display no generosity. A possibility.

(E) Are zealous and enthusiasm related? Yes. To be zealous is to exhibit great enthusiasm. A possibility.

Our search for unrelated pairs has enabled us to eliminate two choices. Here's what we're left with:

7. _____ : INSIGHT ::
    (C) torpid:activity
    (D) avaricious:generosity
    (E) zealous:enthusiasm

Now we're ready to decode and work backward. The first thing we realize is that the missing stem word, whatever it means, must be an adjective. We also know that whatever the missing adjective means, its meaning must be clearly and necessarily related in some way to the meaning of INSIGHT. Perhaps it means "with insight," or "without insight," or "with great insight." There aren't many other possibilities.

Keeping this in mind, we can work backward from the relationships in the choices we have not eliminated. Here's what we know:

1. If choice C is ETS's answer, the missing word must mean "displaying no insight."

2. If choice D is ETS's answer, we know that the missing word must mean "displaying no insight."

3. If choice E is ETS's answer, we know that the missing word must mean "displaying great insight."

The first thing to notice is that, at least as we have formed our sentences, the words in choice C are related in exactly the same way as the words in choice D. What does this mean? It means that neither can be ETS's answer, because if one of them were ETS's answer then the other would have to be as well, and GRE questions have only one credited answer. We need to be careful, though, because we may have overlooked a nuance.

Even so, we can tell from our remaining choices that the missing stem word must mean either something like "displaying no insight" or "displaying great insight." With this in mind, let's look at the complete stem:

7. PERSPICACIOUS:INSIGHT

Selecting an answer choice is now merely a matter of deciding whether PERSPICACIOUS seems more likely to mean "displaying no insight" or "displaying great insight." This is a vastly simpler task than attempting to guess the definition of a word out of context. Indeed, if you've heard or seen the unknown stem word before, narrowing your possibilities in this way may jog your memory and enable you to select ETS's answer, which is E. You don't need to know the exact definition of a word in order to deduce that definition by decoding and working backward.

THE TICKING CLOCK

Won't it take hours to apply all these techniques? No. With a little practice, you'll make them an automatic part of your thought process on GRE analogies. In fact, they'll save you time by making you much more efficient in your approach to difficult items. You'll spend less time on these items because you'll spend less time spinning your wheels. Using our techniques can enable you to turn a seemingly hopeless situation into ten quick points.

Decoding unknown words in the answer choices can be tricky, since you can't be certain that the words in a choice are clearly and necessarily related. Assuming you know both words in the stem, you can still ask yourself whether *any* word could create a relationship in the choice identical to the relationship in the stem. If not, you can eliminate the choice.

JOE BLOGGS AND GRE ANALOGIES

Whether a question is easy, medium, or difficult, Joe Bloggs finds some answer choices much more appealing than others. Most of all, Joe is attracted to choices containing words that

1. remind him of words in the stem

2. "just seem to go with" the words in the stem

3. are easy to understand

Here's an example:

> 1. WELD:METAL::
>   (A) cater:gala
>   (B) tweak:skin
>   (C) catheterize:fluid
>   (D) nail:wood
>   (E) lash:whip

Here's how to crack it:

Which choice "just seems to go with" the stem? Choice D. Welding metal, nailing wood. Joe Bloggs is definitely attracted to this choice. Should we eliminate it?

No!

Don't forget: on the easy third of a subsection, Joe Bloggs's hunches are correct. This question is a number 1, the easiest in the group. Choice D is ETS's answer.

Now let's look at a hard analogy:

> 9. APOSTATE:FAITH::
>   (A) apostle:leader
>   (B) altruist:literature
>   (C) defector:allegiance
>   (D) potentate:religion
>   (E) patriot:principle

Here's how to crack it:

First, eliminate unrelated pairs:

(A) Is there a clear and necessary relationship between apostle and leader? Yes. An apostle is a leader. A possibility.

(B) How about altruist and literature? No. An altruist is a generous or selfless person. This has nothing to do with literature. Eliminate.

(C) A defector is someone who forsakes an allegiance, such as to a country. Clear and necessary? Yes. A possibility.

(D) Potentate and religion? No. Eliminate.

(E) Is there a clear and necessary relationship between patriot and principle? Be careful. A patriot might have principles, but there is nothing clear or necessary about the relationship between these two words. You would not find either word in the dictionary definition of the other. Eliminate.

We're left with choices A and C. We've already improved our odds on this difficult item to one in two. What do we do now? Look for Joe Bloggs attractors.

Which choices "just seem to go with" the stem? Choice A. Apostle is a religious word; it also sounds like apostate, and Joe likes choices that sound like the stem. Choice A is a Joe Bloggs attractor—so you can eliminate it. Remember, if finding ETS's answer were as easy as Joe thinks it is, this would be an easy question, not a hard one.

ETS's answer is choice C. An *apostate* is one who *forsakes* his faith.

Here's another hard analogy. It's an item we've already looked at.

9. RAMIFICATION:BRANCHES::
    (A) speculation:factions
    (B) forestation:grass
    (C) theorizing:rumors
    (D) replication:duplicates
    (E) animation:characters

Do you see any Joe Bloggs attractors? How about choice B? Branches and grass "just seem to go together" in Joe's mind. You can eliminate this choice immediately.

Here's another item we've looked at already:

7. PERSPICACIOUS:INSIGHT::
    (A) authoritative:despotism
    (B) audacious:hearing
    (C) torpid:activity
    (D) avaricious:generosity
    (E) zealous:enthusiasm

There is one Joe Bloggs attractor among the choices: B. The word hearing reminds Joe of the word INSIGHT. (Joe also thinks that *audacious* has something to do with *audio*.) Eliminate.

BLOGGS FIRST

On the difficult third, eliminate Joe Bloggs attractors before you do anything else. These choices are likely to be the most tempting of the incorrect choices. Getting them out of the way will make it easier for you to find ETS's answer without falling into a trap.

HARD QUESTIONS, HARD ANSWERS

Joe Bloggs is lazy. As a result, he has a powerful tendency to select choices that he understands. That is, he's unlikely to select a choice if it contains words he's never heard of (unless there's something else about the choice that attracts him, such as an easy word that reminds him of the stem). When Joe takes a stab at a question, he tends to pick something familiar.

What does this mean? It means that one of the best places to look for ETS's answer on a hard question is in a hard answer—a choice that Joe doesn't get. When all else fails on a hard question, the best strategy is to eliminate what you can and then simply select the remaining choice with the hardest words. That is, in guessing on harder questions, you want to look for the choice that *seems least likely to seem correct to Joe*.

DRILL 2

Eliminating Joe Bloggs attractors on the difficult third is an important part of our overall strategy. The following drill will give you practice at spotting the kinds of words that Joe Bloggs can't resist. In each question below, assume that the word in capital letters is a stem word from a hard analogy, and circle any attractor or attractors among the five words following it. Some of these quiz items contain no attractors. (You can check your answers on page 333).

1. MATHEMATICS election calender physics sentence frequency

2. ANCHOR coalition constellation electorate ship rectitude

3. OIL energy wheat fortitude correction element

4. PRIEST executive lieutenant bishop master deity

5. FURNITURE manners opinions sensibility mandate fantasy

6. HORSE automobile sheep poultry child furnace

7. ARSON vandalism despotism exile collusion philosophy

8. TREE body mountain cave flower fence

9. LANGUAGE oratory grammar technology art philosophy

10. AXIOM analysis reasoning music compound cadence

PUTTING IT ALL TOGETHER: STRATEGY BY THIRDS

The techniques we have described are the tools you will use to crack GRE analogies. Which tools you use will depend on the difficulty—as determined by its number—of the item you're working on. Here are some tips on how to tailor your approach.

EASY THIRD
(The first three analogies)

1. Joe Bloggs gets these right. Trust your hunches.

2. Don't worry too much about hard words among the choices (Joe doesn't know them either). If you're stuck, go with an obvious choice.

3. Form a sentence and plug in each choice. If you end up with more than one possibility, make your sentence more specific and try again.

4. Eliminate unrelated pairs.

MEDIUM THIRD
(The middle three analogies)

1. Joe Bloggs gets some right, some wrong. Be wary of your hunches.

2. Form a sentence and plug in each choice. It is especially important to try every choice. If you end up with more than one possibility, make your sentence more specific and try again.

3. Eliminate unrelated pairs.

4. If you're stumped by one of the words in the stem, work backward from the choices and decode.

DIFFICULT THIRD
(The last three analogies)

1. Joe Bloggs gets these wrong. Before you do anything else, eliminate the choices that attract him.

2. If you know the words in the stem, form a sentence and plug in.

3. Eliminate unrelated pairs.

4. If you're stumped by one of the words in the stem, work backward from the choices and decode.

5. If you're stumped by both of the words in the stem, and if you have eliminated any unrelated pairs, pick the choice with the hardest words.

SUMMARY

1. The only kind of relationship between words in GRE analogies is a clear and necessary one. This is a tight, solid, logical relationship that is based on the meanings of the words. It is the kind of relationship that exists between a word and its dictionary definition.

2. Don't look for tricky, Miller Analogy-type relationships in GRE analogies. ETS doesn't use them.

3. To find the relationship between the stem words (the words in capital letters), form a simple sentence that links the two words and illustrates their meaning. Then plug in the choices.

4. Try for the shortest, most succinct sentence you can, but don't waste a lot of time honing a masterpiece.

5. You should always plug in all the choices on GRE analogies, even if you're sure you've already found ETS's answer.

6. If more than one of the choices fits your sentence, go back and make your sentence more specific or look for a nuance that you have missed.

7. If both words in the stem are nouns, both words in each choice will be nouns. ETS is always consistent with parts of speech.

8. Make yourself familiar with the most common types of relationships found in GRE analogies, but don't waste time trying to categorize items on your test.

9. You can automatically eliminate any answer choice containing a triangular nonrelationship.

10. You can automatically eliminate any answer choice containing words that are not related in a clear and necessary way.

11. Don't be too clever in looking for relationships between words. You'll get no points for creativity on the GRE.

12. Never initially eliminate a choice if you are uncertain of the meaning of either word in it. You can't be positive that two words are unrelated if you have no idea what one of them means.

13. When you don't know the meaning of one of the words in the stem, work backward from the choices.

14. You can improve the effectiveness of working backward by using information in the problem to decode the unknown word in the stem.

15. If you know both words in the stem, you can sometimes eliminate a choice even if you don't know one of the words, by determining whether *any* word could create a relationship like the stem relationship.

16. Practicing our techniques on real GREs will make them automatic—so practice.

17. On hard analogies, eliminate Joe Bloggs attractors before doing anything else. Joe Bloggs is attracted to choices containing words that

    a. remind him of words in the stem

    b. "just seem to go with" the words in the stem

    c. are easy to understand

18. Don't forget that Joe's hunches are correct on the easy third and sometimes correct on the medium third.

19. Be suspicious if you find more than two Joe Bloggs attractors on a difficult analogy. If clear Joe Bloggs attractors abound, you can be nearly certain that ETS's answer is hidden among them.

20. When all else fails on the difficult third, eliminate what you can and then pick the choice containing the hardest words.

5

Reading Comprehension

Each verbal section of your GRE will contain two reading passages. Each passage will be followed by between three and eight questions. **Reading-comprehension questions are the only ones on the verbal GRE that do not appear in order of difficulty.** We'll explain more about this later in the chapter.

MEMORIZE THESE DIRECTIONS

Before we begin, take a moment to read and learn the following set of directions. These are the directions exactly as they will appear on your GRE. You shouldn't even glance at them when you take the test. If you do, you will waste time and lose points. Here are the directions:

> Directions: Each passage in this group is followed by questions based on its content. After reading a passage, choose the best answer to each question. Answer all questions following a passage on the basis of what is stated or implied in that passage.

ORDER OF DIFFICULTY, LOGICAL ORDER

Reading comp questions are the only ones on the verbal GRE that aren't given in order of difficulty. Instead, they follow the structure of the passage. That is, the first questions will almost always refer to the first part of the passage; the last questions will almost always refer to the end of the passage. A question about information in the second paragraph will come before a question about information in the fourth paragraph. Later in the chapter, we will tell you how to take advantage of this fact in answering questions.

OUR ASTONISHING TECHNIQUES

Nobody likes reading comp. The passages are boring and hard to understand, the questions are either difficult or infuriating, and the whole thing takes too much time. Fortunately, we have solutions to these problems.

Our techniques for cracking reading comp will enable you to:

1. Learn more by doing less

2. read quickly and efficiently

3. improve your guessing odds by eliminating choices that could not possibly be correct

4. take advantage of outside knowledge

5. take advantage of inside knowledge

6. find ETS's answers in some cases without reading the passages

WHY YOU HATE READING COMP

A GRE reading passage is unlike any other text you read. It is presented to you entirely out of context. It is often condensed to the point of incomprehensibility (ETS takes passages from published writings and compresses them to make them dense with information). Any correlation between its topic and your interests is purely accidental (ETS tries to avoid topics that might be of direct interest to particular groups of college students, to prevent some test-takers from gaining an advantage over others through outside knowledge).

Furthermore, GRE reading-comp passages and questions are dreadfully written. Here are three examples:

ETS-speak	English Translation
It can be inferred from the passage that the author views the system of paying all workers equally on time rates as	The author seems to believe that paying everyone the same wage is
The passage suggests that factors contributing to the variation in the amount of ozone above different areas of the Earth's surface include which of the following?	Why isn't ozone spread evenly over the earth?
It can be inferred from the passage that classifying a poet as either conservative or experimental would be of little significance when discussing Black poets of the 1910's and 1920's because	To classify a Black poet of the 1910's and 1920's as either conservative or experimental is beside the point because

ETS's test-makers don't write poorly on purpose. They aren't secretly testing your ability to understand bad prose. They actually try to be graceful, clear, and concise. But the result isn't very impressive.

SAVE READING COMP FOR LAST

Partly because the passages and questions are so poorly written, reading comps are incredibly time-consuming. In fact, answering the eleven reading-comp questions in one of your verbal sections could easily take you more time than answering all twenty-seven other questions in the section. **And yet those eleven reading-comp questions aren't worth any more points than any other eleven questions**. Three hard reading-comp questions, which might take you five or more minutes to answer, are worth exactly the same number of points as three easy antonym questions, which you might be able to answer in a few seconds.

For this reason, you must always save reading comp for last. Don't even peek at a reading-comp passage until you have finished every other item in the verbal section you're working on. When you come to the reading-comp pages in each verbal section, skip over them immediately and answer the eleven antonym questions hidden behind them. **Don't sacrifice 110 points in the hope of earning 30**.

IN FACT, IT WOULD PROBABLY MAKE SENSE FOR YOU TO SKIP SOME READING PASSAGES ENTIRELY

The vast majority of students could score higher on the GRE if they skipped at least one reading-comp passage in each verbal section. Skipping a passage gives you a big chunk of time that you can invest much more profitably in other parts of the test.

Most students don't do well on reading comps anyway. Skipping passages is thus doubly beneficial. What's the point of spending ten or fifteen minutes on reading comps if you're only going to answer a few of the questions correctly?

There will be eleven reading-comp questions in each of your two scored verbal sections. That makes a total of twenty-two reading-comp questions contributing to your verbal score. The laws of probability say that on average you can expect to pick four or five correct answers on those twenty-two questions simply by guessing blindly. *Many students who answer the questions in earnest don't do as well as that.*

WHAT TO SKIP

If you're aiming for a verbal score below 550, you should probably consider skipping *all* the reading comps on your GRE. *That doesn't mean you shouldn't mark answers for the questions, of course.* (Remember, you must always mark a choice for every question on the GRE.) It does mean that you should skip the passages. Blind guessing would give you, on average, four or five of ETS's answers in twenty-two tries.

If you're aiming for a verbal score below 650, you should probably consider skipping *one* reading comp on *each* verbal section. *Once again, this doesn't mean you shouldn't mark choices for the questions; it just means you shouldn't read the passages.*

Even if you're aiming for a score as high as 700, skipping a small passage may make good sense. The time you'll save could enable you to nail down some easier points elsewhere in the test.

Students aiming for scores *above* 700 will need to tackle all four reading comps, but these students should still save these items for last. If you know you've answered all the other items in the section, you'll be able to approach reading comps without distractions.

Of course, if you have an unusual knack for reading comps, as some students do, you should forget about skipping, even if you're only aiming for a score in the 500's or 600's. Some students are just good at reading comps. If you're one of these rare few, don't skip.

Your decision about skipping should be based on how well you do on reading comps when you practice on real GREs. Learn our techniques, try them on timed practice tests, and then make an honest determination of how your limited time can best be spent.

LENGTHS OF PASSAGES

Each of the two verbal sections on your GRE will typically contain one longish passage and one shortish one. The shortish passage may look more appealing, but it will often be denser and harder to understand than the longish one. In a short passage, you may have to read every sentence carefully to figure out what is being said.

In the discussion that follows, we will refer again and again to the sample passage and questions printed on pages 68–70.

It is well-known that termites are blind, but little has been discovered about the other sense organs of these insects or their reactions to various stimuli. Body odors,

Line as well as odors related to sex and to colony, certainly
(5) play a part in the activities of the termite colony. When specimens of eastern subterranean termites are placed in a jar containing a colony of rotten wood termites from the Pacific Coast, the host termites recognize these foreign insects by differences in odor and eventually kill the
(10) invaders. The progress of the chase and kill is very slow, and the larger host termites appear awkward in their efforts to bite and kill their smaller but quicker-moving cousins. Finally, more or less by sheer numbers and by accident, they corner and exterminate the enemy.
(15) Eastern dealated (wingless) termites that manage to survive in the rotten wood termite colony for more than a week, however, are no longer molested. This is noteworthy, since eastern termites of this variety had previously been pursued and killed. Fresh eastern wingless speci-
(20) mens placed in the colony alongside the week-old visitors are immediately attacked, thus indicating that the rotten wood termites have in no way lost their capacity for belligerence.
What else besides odor helps termites interpret the
(25) world around them? The insects have sense or "chorodontal" organs located on the antennae, on the bristles, on the base of the mandibles, and on the legs. These organs apparently enable termites to receive vibrations sent through the air, or, more precisely, aid in
(30) the reception of stimuli sent through the nest material or through air pockets within the nest material. When alarmed, soldier termites exhibit synchronous, convulsive movements that appear to be a method of communication adapted to the chorodontal organ system, although no
(35) sound that is audible to man is produced by these movements. Termite soldiers also strike their heads against wood and other nest materials, producing noises that, after passing through the sounding board formed by the nest material, become rustling and crackling sounds plainly
(40) audible to man's duller and possibly differently attuned perceptions. In fact, soldiers of one termite species, found in the arid regions of California, strike their heads against the dry, dead flower stalks of Spanish bayonets and agave plants with such force that the sound produced can be

(45) heard several feet away. Other types of soldier termites found in the tropics make audible clicking noises with their jaws.

There is a clear correlation between the functioning of the chorodontal system and termite settlement patterns.
(50) Seldom are termites found infesting railroad ties over which there is frequent heavy traffic, or on the woodwork of mill or factory buildings where heavy machinery in motion would cause vibrations. Small-scale tests with a radio speaker and vibrator yielded interesting results
(55) when termites were placed in the speaker and exposed to various frequency vibrations. When the vibrations ranged from 50–100 per second, the termites were thrown about; at vibrations of 100–500, termites set their feet and mandibles and held on with all their power; at 2,000–
(60) 5,000 vibrations per second, the termites crawled about undisturbed.

21. The author's primary concern in the passage is to

   (A) show how little is known of certain organ systems in insects
   (B) describe the termite's method of overcoming blindness
   (C) provide an overview of some termite sensory organs
   (D) relate the termite's sensory perceptions to man's
   (E) describe the termite's aggressive behavior

22. It can be inferred from the passage that dealated eastern termites that have survived a week in a rotten wood termite colony are no longer attacked because they

   (A) have come to resemble the rotten wood termites in most ways
   (B) no longer have an odor provocative to the rotten wood termites
   (C) no longer pose a threat to the host colony
   (D) have learned to resonate at the same frequency as the host group
   (E) have changed the pattern in which they use their mandibles

23. Which of the following statement(s) is (are) supported by the passage?

   I. Termites vary in speed and agility.
   II. Soldier termites frighten intruders by striking their heads against wood and other nest materials.
   III. Termites are found both in North America and outside its boundaries.

   (A) I only
   (B) II only
   (C) I and II only
   (D) I and III only
   (E) I, II, and III

24. According to the passage, the struggle by rotten wood termites against invading wingless termites is

(A) a brutal fight until one of the two colonies is completely destroyed
(B) a lengthy matter with an element of uncertainty
(C) carried out by shaking the invaders from the host nest
(D) usually a short affair since the rotten wood termites are so much larger
—(E) successful if the invading termites are not too large a group

25. It can be inferred from the passage that an insecticide designed to confuse soldier termites would be most effective if it deprived the insect of its

(A) eyes
--(B) ears
(C) bristles
(D) wings
(E) odor

26. According to the passage, a termite's jaw can be important in all of the following EXCEPT

(A) aggression against intruders of other termite species
(B) the reception of vibrations sent by other termites
—(C) stabilization of the insect against physical disturbances
(D) the production of sound made by striking wood or plants
(E) sounding an alert to notify other termites of danger

27. The passage would most likely be followed by

(A) a discussion of the reasons for the blindness of termites
(B) a discussion of how to use the characteristics of the termites' sensory organs to exterminate termites
(C) a discussion of the effects of termites' vibrations on man
—(D) a discussion of the differences between termites found in temperate climates and those found in tropical ones
(E) a list of various structures classified by the government as safe from termite attack

READING THE PASSAGES: FORGET ABOUT COMPREHENSION

There are many different reasons for reading. Sometimes you read for pleasure; sometimes you read for general knowledge; sometimes you read in order to discover a particular piece of information.

On the GRE, you read for one reason only: *to earn points*. If you can accept this simple fact, you'll be far, far ahead of Joe Bloggs.

Your first step is to forget about "reading comprehension." If you actually sat down and tried to *comprehend* a passage on the GRE—by reading and rereading it until you understood it thoroughly and were able to discuss it intelligently—you would have no time for the rest of the test.

GOOD NEWS

Fortunately, reading to earn points is much easier than reading for comprehension. The questions test only a tiny fraction of the boring, hard-to-remember details that are crammed into each passage. All you have to do to maximize your score is learn to identify the important 10 to 20 percent of the passage that is being tested. That's what our techniques are designed to do.

Most students read much too slowly and carefully on reading comps. Trembling with the importance of what they're doing, they circle every other word, underline key phrases, look for hidden meanings, and generally become completely lost. When they reach the end of the passage, they often gulp and realize they have no idea what they have just read.

Our years of experience with ETS reading comps have enabled us to develop a simple and effective approach to reading passages and answering the questions that follow them. We'll outline our approach first, then discuss each step in detail. Here's the outline:

Step 1: Find the main idea of the passage. Don't read the passage. Just spend a minute or two getting a sense of its main idea or theme. We'll tell you exactly how to do this in a moment. When you have a sense of the main idea, jot it down in the margin of your booklet.

Step 2: Find and answer the general questions. General questions are ones that ask about the theme of the passage, or the tone of the passage, or the main idea of the passage, and so on. A general question is broader than a specific question, which might ask you about a single fact. Very often, the very first question will be a general one. In fact, the very first question may well concern the "main idea" that you just spent one or two minutes discovering. General questions are usually the easiest. Answering them will also help you solidify your sense of what the passage is about, making it easier for you to find the answers to specific questions later on.

Step 3: Find and answer the specific questions. Specific questions are ones that concern specific facts in the passage. Before looking at the passage, see if you can eliminate any of the answer choices ahead of time. If you can eliminate a choice, cross it out in your test booklet so that it won't confuse you. Then go to the passage and find ETS's answer. If you don't find it immediately, skim quickly until you locate it.

Don't try to keep more than one question in your mind at a time. Read one question, eliminate any obviously impossible choices, go to the passage, find

ETS's answer, then move to the next. Don't do what many students do and read all the questions before trying to answer any. Reading comp is much easier if you attack it one step at a time. Students who try to do too much at once often end up feeling overwhelmed.

Don't let yourself get in a rut. If you find that your wheels are spinning on one question, eliminate any obviously incorrect choices, mark your best guess, circle the question if you think you'll come back to it, and move on. It may turn out that finding ETS's answer to a later question will clear up your confusion. But don't waste time now.

STEP 1: FIND THE MAIN IDEA OF THE PASSAGE

Most GRE reading passages (and most paragraphs within them) have a similar structure: An idea is expressed, then the idea is supported. That's all there is to it. Support for an idea may take the form of details, examples, counterexamples, or secondary ideas. Some reading comp questions—the general ones—are about the main idea or ideas; other questions—the specific ones—are about the details.

The main idea of the passage is what the passage is *about*. A question that asks you to choose the best title for a passage is really asking you to find its main idea. The main idea may be presented immediately, in the very first sentence—in effect introducing the details that follow. Or the main idea may be presented gradually, in the first sentences of the paragraphs. Or the main idea may come last, as a conclusion to, or summary of, the details or arguments that have been presented.

You may find it helpful to think of a reading passage as a house. The main idea of the passage is like the overall plan of the house. Finding the main idea of the passage is like walking quickly through the house. As you walk, you want to develop a sense of the overall plan of the house: two floors, no basement, big family room, bedrooms upstairs. You don't want to get bogged down in upholstery patterns, the contents of bureau drawers, or other tiny details. Later, if you are asked what is sitting on the kitchen counter, you won't know the answer off the top of your head, but you'll have a pretty good idea of where to find it. And your mind won't be cluttered with a lot of extraneous information—most of which you will have forgotten anyway.

Finding the main idea of a passage is usually pretty easy. Here's all you have to do:

- Read the first sentence of each paragraph.

- Read the last sentence of the passage.

- In the margin of your booklet, jot down three simple words that express the main idea you've found.

If a paragraph is very short, you may find that it makes sense to read more than just the first sentence. But don't spend a lot of time doing this. And don't try to memorize what you are reading, or to learn any of the supporting details. Don't even try to "skim" the entire passage—your eyes will slide over the words, and you'll end up remembering nothing. All you should be doing is looking for a general sense of the overall passage which can be reduced to a few simple words.

Main Ideas and Passage Types

There are two basic types of GRE reading passages: science and nonscience. The science passages may be either specific or general. Knowing a little about the types will help you anticipate the main ideas.

Specific science passages deal with the "hard facts" of science. They are almost always objective or neutral (and often boring) in tone. The sample passage, about "termite senses," is an example of a specific science passage. Other typical themes: how an organism adapts to its environment; a description of an experiment; a discussion of a phenomenon we don't understand; a popular misconception. When dealing with one of these passages, you should avoid looking for a complex theme or a strong point of view. The terminology may be complex (words like *isotopic* or *racemization*), but the main idea or theme will not. Don't be thrown into confusion by big words. You can almost always read around them. If you focus on the main idea, you won't have to worry about the jargon.

General science passages deal with the history of a scientific discovery, the development of a scientific procedure or method, why science fails or succeeds in explaining certain phenomena, and similar "soft" themes. The authors of these passages have a more definite point of view than do the authors of the specific science passages; that is, the tone may not be neutral or objective, and the author may be expressing an opinion. For example, the author may take a side in a disagreement about types of contemporary research, or warn about the possible dangers of a certain avenue of inquiry. The main theme will be whatever point or argument the author is trying to make.

Nonscience passages deal with topics in the humanities (art, literature, philosophy, music, folklore) or social science (history, law, economics). Humanities passages typically take a specific point of view, or compare several views. Typical themes: a particular author's weaknesses and strengths; differences between competing trends, such as abstract and realist painting; pioneering techniques in an art form; a forgotten craft. The language may be abstract and dense.

Social-science passages usually introduce an era or event by focusing on a specific problem, topic, person, or group of persons. The key is usually the relationship between the focus and some larger context. Typical themes: a

revisionist interpretation of an era which arose from the discovery of new evidence; the adaptation of a certain social class to changing conditions; new contributions to a field of study. The tone is likely to be partisan and opinionated, although some social-science passages take the form of a neutral discussion of facts.

Finding the Main Idea: A Test Drive

Let's try this technique on the sample passage that begins on page 65. Remember, all you want to read at this point are the first sentences of the paragraphs and the last sentence of the passage. Here's the first sentence:

> It is well-known that termites are blind, but little has been discovered about the other sense organs of these insects or their reactions to various stimuli.

Having read just this much, what would you say is the main idea? Something to do with "termite senses"? Most likely. (The very first sentence of a passage is the most common hiding place for main ideas.) Let's check the first sentences of the other paragraphs, and the last sentence of the passage, just to make sure.

First sentence, second paragraph:

> Eastern dealated (wingless) termites that manage to survive in the rotten wood termite colony for more than a week, however, are no longer molested.

First sentence, third paragraph:

> What else besides odor helps termites interpret the world around them?

First sentence, fourth paragraph:

> There is a clear correlation between the functioning of the chorodontal system and termite settlement patterns.

Last sentence, passage:

> When the vibrations ranged from 50–100 per second, etc.

There's nothing in these sentence to change our initial impression of the main idea, and some of the sentences directly support it. Good. That means we're on the right track. We scrawl a quick note—"termite senses"—in the margin of our test booklet, and head for the first general question. Total elapsed time: about a minute.

STEP TWO: FIND AND ANSWER THE GENERAL QUESTIONS

Now that you've found the main idea of the passage, you are ready to attack the general questions. There are two main types of general questions: *main idea* and *tone*. We'll cover them one at a time.

Main Idea Questions

A main idea question asks you to find the main idea of the passage. Since you have just done that, a question like this should be a piece of cake. Main idea questions usually come either first or last. They can be phrased in several different ways:

"The author's main purpose is..."

"The main idea of the passage is..."

"Which of the following is the best title for the passage?"

"Which of the following questions does the passage answer?"

All of these are *general* questions; therefore, they will almost always have general answers. That means that you can eliminate any choice that is too specific. (The main idea of a passage will not be "to describe the rate of vibration that causes termites to be thrown about.")

At the same time, ETS's answer won't be a statement that is *so* general that it could be true of virtually any passage. (The main idea will not be "to explain the author's point of view.")

Nor will the main idea of a passage ever be something that could not possibly be accomplished in a few short paragraphs. (The author's purpose in writing a 250-word essay could never be "to explain the meaning of life.")

ETS's answer to one of these questions will be like Baby Bear's porridge: not too hot, not too cold—*just right*. Practicing with real GRE reading passages will help you develop a good sense of the kind of answer ETS invariably looks for.

The incorrect choices on a question like this will likely be statements that are partly true, or are true of part of the passage but not of the whole thing. Or they may be choices that sound almost exactly right, but with one or two teeny differences. Joe Bloggs misses these teeny differences. That's why you need to use POE and cross out incorrect choices as you eliminate them.

Main Idea Questions: A Test Drive

The first question following a GRE reading comp passage is usually a general question and often a main-idea question. That's the case with our sample passage on pages 68–69. Take another look at the first question:

21. The author's primary concern in the passage is to

    (A) show how little is known of certain organ systems in insects
    (B) describe the termite's method of overcoming blindness
    (C) provide an overview of some termite sensory organs
    (D) relate the termite's sensory perceptions to man's
    (E) describe the termite's aggressive behavior

Here's How to Crack It:

A "primary concern" is the same thing as a main idea or main theme or author's purpose. Check out each choice without looking back at the passage. (If possible, you should always answer a main idea question without referring back to the passage. Why? Because the details in the passage may lead you astray. The main idea you found should be enough to lead you to ETS's answer.)

(A) This is a trap for Joe Bloggs. Termites are insects, but the passage is not about insects; it is about termites. This choice can be eliminated for that reason alone. If the main purpose of a passage is to describe a particular person or thing, then that particular person or thing will definitely be mentioned specifically in ETS's answer. If you have a passage about Charles Dickens, its main purpose will not be to "discuss the works of English novelists." Similarly, if the main purpose of a passage is to describe something about termites, then on a main idea question you can eliminate any choice that contains no mention of termites. So eliminate this choice.

(B) For Joe Bloggs only. Common sense alone tells you that termites have no methods of "overcoming blindness" (tiny Seeing-Eye dogs?). Eliminate.

(C) This corresponds closely with the main idea we discovered. Hang on to this choice. It's a possibility.

(D) We can tell from our quick search for the main idea that the author's primary concern is not a comparison between termites and humans. A quick glance back at the passage confirms this. Eliminate.

(E) Sort of possible, although this choice makes no mention of senses. The passage touches on fighting, but not as the main idea. Probably not ETS's answer.

The best choice? Undoubtedly (C)—ETS's answer.

Because you've only read a tiny portion of the passage, you shouldn't always expect ETS's answer to seem obvious to you on your first pass through the questions. But you should be able to eliminate some obviously incorrect choices right off the bat. You must be absolutely certain to cross out these incorrect choices as you eliminate them. The key to doing well on reading comp is to narrow the field as rapidly as possible. With five choices swimming in your head, you'll keep covering the same ground over and over again. Small differences are easier to see once you've swept away the clutter. After eliminating two or three choices, you can look back at the passage quickly to help you zero in. When you look back at the passage, though, keep in mind that you are looking only for enough information to enable you to find ETS's answer and earn points. This is not the time to brush up on your knowledge of termites.

Questions about Tone, Attitude, or Style

This is the second main type of general question. These questions ask you to identify the author's tone, style, or overall point of view. Is the author being critical, neutral, or sympathetic? Is the passage subjective or objective? Like main idea questions, these questions can be phrased in several ways:

"The author's tone is best described as..."

"The author views his subject with..."

"The author's presentation is best characterized as..."

"The passage is most likely from..."

"The author most likely thinks the reader is..."

These questions are usually easy to spot, because they seldom contain many words. In fact, each choice may be just a single word. Almost every GRE will have at least one of these questions.

These questions are also usually easy to answer, because ETS writes them in very predictable ways. Knowing a little about the "ETS mentality"—the very predictable point of view of ETS's test-question writers—will help you find ETS's answer. Here are the main things for you to remember:

- ETS uses only passages and authors that it feels good about. The passages are meant to be thoughtfully conceived, carefully written, and uncontroversial. ETS doesn't use crackpot diatribes, bitter invectives, or scathing harangues. The authors of GRE reading passages are almost always thoughtful, optimistic, reflective, instructive, or something similarly positive. They are never cynical, desperate, hateful, vengeful, or apathetic. As a result, you can eliminate

any choice that is too negative or too extreme. The tone of a science passage will be objective, neutral, unbiased, analytical, or something similar. It will not be careless, dogmatic, ambivalent, or contradictory.

- ETS has great respect for artists, writers, intellectuals, professors, doctors, lawyers, scientists, scholars, and professionals of all kinds. It does not use passages that reflect badly on these people. You will not find a reading passage about dishonest lawyers. Nor will you find one about untalented novelists. If an answer choice says that the purpose of a passage is "to demonstrate the intellectual dishonesty of college professors," you can safely eliminate it without so much as glancing at the passage.

- ETS has no strong emotions; its reading passages have no strong emotions, either. ETS is middle-of-the-road, conservative, responsible, establishment, boring. The tone of a passage would never be scathing. An author's style would never be violent. An author would never be irrational.

- ETS is politically correct. Most GREs contain one reading passage concerning a minority group or its members. Such passages are almost always positive or inspirational in tone. Any negative or politically *incorrect* choices can quickly be eliminated.

STEP THREE: FIND AND ANSWER THE SPECIFIC QUESTIONS

Always attack the specific questions in order, one at a time. If you try to keep two or more questions in your mind at once, you'll become confused and waste time. Remember that the order of the questions follows the structure of the passage. After reading a question, look back to the passage and skim quickly till you find the information you are looking for. Use POE to eliminate two or three choices quickly, then zero in on ETS's answer.

Don't waste time. If you find yourself in a rut, eliminate what you can, mark an answer, and move on. You can circle the question if you think you'll have time to return to it for another look, but coming back to reading comp questions is usually a waste of time. (You won't remember what the passage was about or where to look for ETS's answer; any remaining time at the end of the period would probably be better spent on other item types.)

The following techniques will help you use POE to eliminate incorrect answer choices and zero in on ETS's answer.

TECHNIQUE 1: USE COMMON SENSE

ETS takes its reading passages from textbooks, collections of essays, works of scholarship, and other sources of serious reading matter. You won't find a passage arguing that literature is stupid, or that history doesn't matter, or that the moon is made of green cheese. As a result, you will often be able to eliminate answer choices simply because the facts or opinions they represent couldn't possibly be found in ETS reading passages.

Here's an example. You don't need to see the reading passage it refers to. Which choices can you eliminate?

25. The author argues that poetry

    (A) has no place in a modern curriculum, because it is irrelevant to most students' lives.
    (B) is often slighted at the secondary level, because teachers are not trained to overcome the resistance of their pupils.
    (C) will become more important as modern life becomes more complex.
    (D) is the cornerstone of a classical education.
    (E) should not be taught because it is more difficult for most students to understand than prose.

Here's how to crack it:

Even without the passage, you should be able to see that some of these choices couldn't possibly be ETS's answer. Let's look at each one:

(A) Would any reputable essayist or scholar—the likely sources of the reading passage—argue that poetry has no place in a curriculum? No. Eliminate.

(B) Nothing screwy here. This could be ETS's answer.

(C) This isn't as off-the-wall as choice A, but it's a bit dumb. Unlikely.

(D) A possibility.

(E) Easy to eliminate, for the same reason we eliminated choice A.

Here's another example:

27. The author's attitude toward scientists who first test experimental vaccines by injecting them into themselves can best be described as one of

    (A) apathy
    (B) skepticism
    (C) admiration
    (D) confusion
    (E) consternation

Here's how to crack it:

Any scientist who injected an experimental vaccine into himself before trying it on other people would have to be pretty brave, right? So what would the author's attitude in all likelihood be? It would be admiration, choice C. The other choices just don't make sense.

TECHNIQUE 2: USE OUTSIDE KNOWLEDGE

ETS says to answer questions based only on "what is *stated or implied*" in the passage. In other words, don't use outside knowledge. But this is bad advice. Outside knowledge can be very helpful in answering reading-comp questions. It can enable you to eliminate incorrect answer choices and even to find ETS's answer. Although ETS does not use reading comp to test your knowledge of biology, history, or other topics, its answers will not contradict established fact. This means that you can be quite confident in eliminating choices that *do* contradict established fact. Here's an example:

18. In the text, a "true vacuum" is

    (A) empty space with ether in it
    (B) an indivisible unit of matter
    (C) empty space with nothing in it
    (D) empty space filled only by air
    (E) the space between planets

Here's how to crack it:

If you were even halfway awake in sixth-grade science, you should be able to find ETS's answer to this question without reading the passage. It has to be choice C. None of the other choices describes a vacuum.

TECHNIQUE 3: ATTACK DISPUTABLE STATEMENTS

ETS doesn't want to spend all its time defending its answer choices to grumpy test-takers. If even one percent of the people taking the GRE decided to quibble with an answer, ETS would be deluged with angry phone calls. To keep this from happening, ETS tries very hard to construct correct answer choices that cannot be disputed.

What makes a choice indisputable? Take a look at the following example:

(A) Picasso had many admirers.
(B) Everyone loved Picasso.

Analysis:

Which choice is indisputable? Choice A. Choice B contains the highly disputable word *everyone*. Did *everyone* really love Picasso? Wasn't there even one person somewhere who didn't think all that much of him? Of course there was. Choice A is complaint-proof (who can say how many *many* is?). Choice B could never be ETS's answer.

Since ETS will always prefer an indisputable answer to a disputable one, you should focus your attention on the *most disputable* choice that you have not yet eliminated. If you can find any reason to doubt the choice, you should eliminate it. In the example above, you only need to find one person who didn't like Picasso to prove choice B false; to prove choice A wrong, you'd have to poll everybody in the world.

What makes a choice disputable? Specificity. The more specific a choice is, the easier it is to dispute and the less likely it is to be ETS's answer. Here's another example:

(A) The population of the world is 4,230,591,306.
(B) The population of the world is very large.

Analysis:

If the number in choice A is correct now, it won't be correct one second from now. This choice is much too specific to be ETS's answer. Eliminate. The statement in choice B, on the other hand, is so general that it is impossible to dispute. It has to be ETS's answer.

Certain words make choices highly specific and therefore easy to dispute. Here are a few of these specific words:

must	*will*
each	*totally*
every	*always*
all	*no*

You don't want to automatically eliminate a choice containing one of these words, but you want to turn your attention to it immediately and attack it vigorously. If you can find even one exception, you can eliminate that choice.

Other words make choices vague and general and therefore hard to dispute. Here are a few of these general words:

may	*most*
can	*sometimes*
some	

Vague, general choices won't always be ETS's answer, but ETS's answer will always be indisputable. If a statement says that something is *sometimes* true, you only need to find one example to prove it correct.

Now look at a complete example:

18. The author implies that the founding fathers
    (A) could resolve contemporary questions were they alive
    (B) were completely unaware of the ethical implications of slavery
    (C) avoided the issue of slavery as it pertained to human rights
    (D) had no understanding of social problems
    (E) originally thought slavery was a just institution

Here's how to crack it:

Which choices are easiest to dispute? Choices B and D. What makes them disputable? The words *completely* and *no*. ETS's answer will most likely be found among the other three choices.

Where Disputable Choices Come From

Very often on the GRE, the words that make a choice disputable (*totally*, *never*, etc.) were inserted into the choices *specifically in order to make those choices incorrect*. All GRE questions undergo reviews at ETS. If a reviewer finds a distractor for which he thinks a test-taker could make a case, he or the test's assembler will edit it in an effort to make it indisputably wrong. If you make yourself familiar with these words, they'll jump off the page at you when you take the test.

TECHNIQUE 4: AVOID DIRECT REPETITIONS

Joe Bloggs's favorite guesses on reading comps are choices that repeat significant portions of the passage. The more a choice sounds like the passage, the more that choice will seem right to Joe Bloggs.

This means that you should be very wary of choices that exactly reproduce the wording of the passage. ETS's answer will almost always be a paraphrase, not a direct repetition.

Here's an example of what we mean:

> **Passage Excerpt:** The Molniya orbit looks peculiar on a map. Its perigee, or lowest point, is just 600 kilometers above a spot in the Southern Hemisphere, and its apogee, or highest point, is more than 40,000 kilometers above Hudson Bay. Because each Molniya satellite takes twelve hours to travel around the earth—half the time it takes the earth to turn on its axis—it actually makes two loops each day. Twelve hours after the Hudson Bay apogee it reaches another one, over central Siberia. Only the Hudson Bay apogee is used for television transmission; the Soviets use the Siberian one for voice and data transmission.
>
> **Question:** The author of the passage implies that which of the following is the primary reason for the peculiar appearance of the Molniya orbit?
>
> (A) Its apogee is more than 40,000 kilometers above Hudson Bay.
> (B) The satellite is required to be used for voice and data transmission.
> (C) The difference in altitude between the high and low points of the orbit is so dramatic.
> (D) The satellite requires only twelve hours to travel around the earth.
> (E) The Soviets are incapable of placing a satellite in a normal orbit.

Here's how to crack it:

Three of the choices contain verbatim repetitions of significant chunks of the passage: A, B, and D. These are, therefore, Joe Bloggs attractors and highly unlikely to be ETS's answer. (Also notice that outside knowledge tells us that choice E is factually incorrect and can be eliminated, even though we haven't been shown the part of the passage to which it refers.) ETS's answer is choice C.

Of course, ETS will often have to use *some* words from the passage in its answer. But the general rule is a good one:

> *The more closely a choice resembles a substantial part of the passage, the less likely the choice is to be ETS's answer.*

TECHNIQUE 5: LINE NUMBER QUESTIONS

These questions ask you to interpret the meaning of a certain word or phrase in the context of the passage. You will usually be referred to a specific line number in the text. These questions can be phrased in a number of ways:

> The 'great conversation' (line 29) is used as a metaphor for . . .
>
> Which of the following words would be the best substitute for the word 'adopted' (line 11) . . .
>
> The author uses the term 'indigenous labor' (line 40) to mean . . .
>
> The author quotes Richard Hofstadter in order to . . .

Strategy:

Joe Bloggs loves these questions, because he thinks they tell him exactly where to find ETS's answer. Therefore, you will generally *not* find ETS's answer in the exact line referred to. **Read the five lines before it and the five lines after it as well.**

The answer to a line number question will *not* be the general theme of the essay. Make certain you understand exactly what the question is asking for.

Beware of choices containing substantial repetitions from the passage. ETS's answer will most likely be a paraphrase.

TECHNIQUE 6: LEAST/EXCEPT/NOT QUESTIONS

Lots of careless errors are made on these questions. To keep from making them yourself, you need to keep reminding yourself that ETS's answer will be the choice that is *wrong*. Here are some of the ways these questions are phrased:

> Which of the following statements would the author be LEAST likely to agree with?
>
> According to the passage, all of the following are true EXCEPT . . .
>
> Which of the following does NOT support the author's argument that the best offense is a good defense?

Strategy:

Circle the word LEAST, EXCEPT, or NOT. That way you'll be less likely to forget it's there.

ETS's answer will be the dumb choice, the wrong choice, the crazy choice.

Look for "correct" answers—and eliminate them. That is, refer back to the passage with each uneliminated choice and see if the passage supports it. If it does, cross it out. You're looking for the one choice that doesn't make sense.

TECHNIQUE 7: TRIPLE TRUE/FALSE QUESTIONS

These time-consuming clunkers—in which you are asked to analyze three statements identified with Roman numerals—really contain three true-false questions. Unfortunately, you have to get all three right to receive credit.

Strategy:

Triple true/false questions are very time-consuming; save them for last.

Although time-consuming, these questions are a good place to use POE: Start with the shortest of the Roman-numeral statements. Go back to the passage to find out if it's true or false.

When you find a false statement, be sure to eliminate all appropriate answer choices. When you find a true statement, eliminate any answer choice that does not include it. See our analysis of question 22 on page 87.

Don't do more work than you have to.

> *You'll often be able to find ETS's answer by checking out just two of the Roman-numeral statements.*

Now you can gather up all your techniques and strategies and throw them at the specific questions following the sample passage back on pages 68–69.

Here is the first specific question:

22. It can be inferred from the passage that dealated eastern termites that have survived a week in a rotten wood termite colony are no longer attacked because they

(A) have come to resemble the rotten wood termites in most ways
(B) no longer have an odor provocative to the rotten wood termites
(C) no longer pose a threat to the host colony
(D) have learned to resonate at the same frequency as the host group
(E) have changed the pattern in which they use their mandibles

Here's how to crack it:

This is just the second question, and the first specific one, so it must refer back to a very early part of the passage. It does. "Dealated" termites are first mentioned in the first sentence of the second paragraph; by skimming that paragraph, and a few sentences in the previous one, you can zero in on ETS's answer. As you do, eliminate as many choices as you can. Here are the choices:

(A) This is an absurd statement that is nowhere supported in the passage. While it may be true that the alien termites have come to resemble the hosts in *one* way, there is nothing in the passage to suggest that they have come to resemble them in *most* ways. Eliminate.

(B) This sounds like just what we're looking for. A good possibility.

(C) Tempting to Joe Bloggs, but not likely to be ETS's answer. The annihilated termites didn't pose a threat in the first place; all they really did was smell funny. Eliminate.

(D) Making sounds has not yet been mentioned in the passage. Eliminate.

(E) A nutty choice, unsupported by the passage. Eliminate.

ETS's answer is choice B.

The next question is a triple true/false, so we circle it and move on to 24:

24. According to the passage, the struggle by rotten wood termites against invading wingless termites is

   (A) a brutal fight until one of the two colonies is completely destroyed
   (B) a lengthy matter with an element of uncertainty
   (C) carried out by shaking the invaders from the host nest
   (D) usually a short affair since the rotten wood termites are so much larger
   (E) successful if the invading termites are not too large a group

Here's how to crack it:

Since we had to read the sentences about the termite attack to answer question 22, answering this question should be easy. You can probably answer it without referring back to the passage:

   (A) The big termites invariably win, so the phrase "one of the two colonies" doesn't make any sense. Eliminate.
   (B) This vague, indisputable sentence neatly describes what the passage says happens. A good possibility.
   (C) No mention of shaking in the passage. Eliminate.
   (D) The rotten wood termites are larger, but the passage says that killing off the little termites takes a long time. Eliminate.
   (E) This seems plausible, but saying it would require us to draw an inference. Eliminate.

ETS's answer is choice B.

The next question is nice and short. Here it is:

25. It can be inferred from the passage that an insecticide designed to confuse soldier termites would be most effective if it deprived the insect of its

   (A) eyes
   (B) ears
   (C) bristles
   (D) wings
   (E) odor

Here's how to crack it:

Another inference question. Go back and look for the answer. Soldier termites are mentioned in the third paragraph. Then check the choices:

   (A) Termites are blind. Eliminate.
   (B) There's no mention of ears in the passage. For all we know, termites don't have them. Eliminate.
   (C) Bristles are part of a termite's chorodontal system. A possibility.

(D)   No mention of wings, which have nothing to do with senses. Eliminate.

(E)   We've just been talking about odor. Could this be ETS's answer? Odorless termites might confuse soldier termites. But why would depriving a soldier termite of its own odor confuse it? Choice C seems a better choice. Eliminate E.

ETS's answer is choice C.

The next question is an EXCEPT question. This means that ETS's answer will be the one *incorrect* statement among the choices. Here's the question:

26.   According to the passage, a termite's jaw can be important in all of the following EXCEPT

(A)   aggression against intruders of other termite species
(B)   the reception of vibrations sent by other termites
(C)   stabilization of the insect against physical disturbances
(D)   the production of sound made by striking wood or plants
(E)   sounding an alert to notify other termites of danger

Here's how to crack it:

Check each choice, eliminating those that hold up.

(A)   The first paragraph says that termites kill intruders by biting them. This statement is correct. Eliminate.

(B)   The second sentence in the third paragraph says that some of a termite's chorodontal organs are located on its mandibles, or jaws. This statement is correct. Eliminate.

(C)   The final sentence of the passage says that termites "set their. . .mandibles" when subjected to certain physical disturbances. This statement is correct. Eliminate.

(D)   Termites strike wood and plants with their heads, not their jaws. This statement appears to be incorrect. It is therefore a possibility.

(E)   The final sentence of the third paragraph describes termites making a sound with their jaws. This sentence is part of a discussion of how termites communicate with other termites "when alarmed." This statement is correct. Eliminate.

ETS's answer is choice D.

The next question is an inference question. It requires us to make a judgment about what sort of paragraph might follow the last paragraph in the passage.

Here's the question:

27. The passage would most likely be followed by

   (A) a discussion of the reasons for the blindness of
        termites
   (B) a discussion of how to use the characteristics of the
        termites' sensory organs to exterminate termites
   (C) a discussion of the effects of termites' vibrations on man
   (D) a discussion of the differences between termites
        found in temperate climates and those found in
        tropical ones
   (E) a list of various structures classified as safe from
        termite attack

Here's how to crack it:

We have to be careful, since inference questions require us to use judgment.
Check each choice carefully:

(A) The blindness of termites is mentioned in the first sentence
     of the passage and then never discussed again. There's
     nothing in the passage to indicate that the author is about to
     return to this subject. Eliminate.

(B) Termites are pests. The final paragraph discusses the aver-
     sion of termites to certain kinds of vibrations. A paragraph
     discussing how this knowledge might be used to keep
     termites away from other structures could logically follow
     this paragraph. A possibility.

(C) This is a dumb choice. Termite vibrations have no effect on
     man. Eliminate.

(D) There undoubtedly are differences, but there is nothing in
     the final paragraph or in the rest of the passage to indicate
     that such a discussion is coming. Eliminate.

(E) Why would the author suddenly append such a list to this
     essay? The final paragraph does mention some structures that
     are seldom infested with termites, but we have no reason to
     believe that a list of other such structures is coming. Eliminate.

ETS's answer is B.

Now we're ready for the triple true/false question we skipped earlier. Here it is:

23. Which of the following statement(s) is (are) supported by the passage?

    I. Termites vary in speed and agility.
    II. Soldier termites frighten intruders by striking their heads against wood and other nest materials.
    III. Termites are found both in North America and outside its boundaries.

(A) I only
(B) II only
(C) I and II only
(D) I and III only
(E) I, II, and III

Here's how to crack it:

The main question here is an inference question ("supported by the passage"). Our strategy, remember, is to start with the shortest of the three Roman-numeral statements. That's statement I. Is it true or false that such an inference could be drawn from the passage? Clearly, it's true. The next-to-last sentence of the first paragraph mentions "smaller but quicker-moving cousins."

Statement I, therefore, is true. This means we can eliminate choice B.

The next shortest statement is statement III. Does the passage suggest that termites are found both in North America and outside its borders? Yes. The last sentence of the third paragraph mentions termites in the tropics.

Statement III is true. Knowing this, can we eliminate any other choices? Yes. We can eliminate choices A and C.

Now we have to deal with statement II. Is there anything in the passage to suggest that termites strike their heads in order to *frighten intruders*, rather than to communicate with other termites in their colonies? There is not. This statement is not supported by the passage. Eliminate choice E.

ETS's answer is choice D.

SUMMARY

1. There are a total of four reading passages in the two scored verbal sections of a GRE. Each passage is followed by between three and eight questions. There are twenty-two reading-comprehension questions altogether in the scored verbal sections of a GRE.

2. Reading-comprehension questions are the only items on the GRE that are not presented in order of difficulty. Instead, their order tends to follow the structure of the passage.

3. GRE reading comprehension is unlike any other reading you do. Therefore, you should not approach it in the way you approach other reading.

4. ETS reading passages are poorly written, but not on purpose. Don't look for hidden meanings in grammatical and stylistic errors.

5. Because reading comp is so time-consuming, you must always save it for last.

6. The vast majority of students could score higher on the GRE if they skipped at least one reading passage in each verbal section and used the extra time to work on other types of items.

7. If you're aiming for a verbal score below 550, you should probably consider skipping *all* the reading comps on your GRE. (Don't forget to mark answers, though.)

8. If you're aiming for a score below 650, you should probably consider skipping *one* reading comp on *each* verbal section.

9. Even if you're aiming for a score as high as 700, skipping a passage may make good sense. The time you'll save could enable you to nail down some easier points elsewhere in the test.

10. Students aiming for scores *above* 700 will need to tackle all four reading comps, but these students should still save these items for last.

11. Some students are just good at reading comps. If you're one of those peculiar few, don't skip.

12. Forget about "comprehension." On the GRE, you read for one reason only: to earn points. If you can accept this simple fact, you'll be far, far ahead of Joe Bloggs.

13. We have a step-by-step approach to earning points on GRE reading comp:

Step 1: Find the main idea of the passage.

Step 2: Find and answer the general questions.

Step 3: Find and answer the specific questions.

14. Don't try to keep more than one question in your mind at a time.

15. If you find that you are spinning your wheels on one question, eliminate any obviously incorrect choices, mark your best guess, circle the question if you think you'll come back to it, and move on.

16. To find the main idea of a passage:

- Read the first sentence of each paragraph

- Read the last sentence of the passage

- Jot down three simple words that express the main idea you've found

17. There are two basic types of GRE reading passages:science and nonscience.

18. Science passages may deal with either the "hard facts" of some particular science, or with a "soft" topic, such as the history of science.

19. Nonscience passages will deal with either a topic related to the humanities or a topic related to the social sciences.

20. General questions have general answers. On a main idea question, you can eliminate any choice that is too specific.

21. ETS's answer to a general question will not be so general that it could be true of virtually any passage.

22. The main idea or author's purpose will never be something that could not possibly be accomplished in a few short paragraphs.

23. The incorrect choices on a general question will likely be statements that are partly true, or are true of part of the passage but not of the whole thing.

24. Questions about tone, attitude, or style are usually short and usually easy to answer.

25. ETS writes questions in very predictable ways. An understanding of the "ETS mentality" will help you find ETS's answers.

26. ETS uses only passages and authors that it feels good about. The authors are almost always thoughtful, optimistic, reflective, instructive, or something similarly positive. They are never cynical, desperate, hateful, vengeful, or apathetic.

27. ETS has great respect for artists, writers, intellectuals, professors, doctors, lawyers, scientists, scholars, and professionals of all kinds. It does not use passages that reflect badly on these people.

28. ETS has no strong emotions; its reading passages have no strong emotions, either.

29. ETS is politically correct. Most GREs contain one reading passage concerning a minority group or its members. Such passages are almost always positive or inspirational in tone.

30. Use common sense. You won't find a passage arguing that literature is stupid, or that history doesn't matter, or that the moon is made of green cheese. As a result, you will often be able to eliminate answer choices simply because the facts or opinions they represent couldn't possibly be found in ETS reading passages.

31. Use outside knowledge. You can be quite confident in eliminating choices that contradict established fact.

32. Attack disputable statements. ETS's answer will be indisputable. The easiest way to find this answer is to focus your attention on disputable choices and use POE aggressively to eliminate as many of them as possible.

33. Certain words make choices highly specific and therefore easy to dispute: *must, each, every, all, will, totally, always, no*.

34. Certain words make choices very general and therefore difficult to dispute: *may, can, some, most, sometimes*.

35. Vague, general choices won't always be ETS's answer, but ETS's answer will always be indisputable. If a statement says that something is *sometimes* true, you only need to find one example to prove it correct.

36. Avoid direct repetitions. Joe Bloggs's favorite guesses on reading comps are choices that repeat significant portions of the text. ETS's answer will almost always be a paraphrase, not a direct repetition.

37. The more closely a choice resembles a substantial part of the passage, the less likely the choice is to be ETS's answer.

38. On line-number questions, you will generally not find ETS's answer in the line referred to. Read the five lines before it and the five lines after it as well.

39. Many, many students make careless mistakes on LEAST/EXCEPT/NOT questions. Be careful. Remember, you're looking for the one *dumb* answer among the choices.

40. Triple true/false questions are time-consuming and should be saved for last. POE will improve your guessing odds dramatically, but don't be afraid to skip these if you're short on time.

Antonyms

Each verbal section of your GRE will contain eleven antonym items, numbered 28–38. Items 28–30 will be easy, items 31–35 will be medium, and items 36–38 will be difficult.

In this chapter, antonyms will be numbered 1–11 instead. A number 1 will be easy; a number 11 will be hard. Always pay attention to the item position in answering GRE questions. The item number will help determine which technique or combination of techniques you will use to crack the problem.

LEARN THESE DIRECTIONS

Before we begin, take a moment to read and learn the following set of directions. These are the directions exactly as they will appear on your GRE. You shouldn't even glance at them when you take the test. If you do, you will waste time and lose points. Here are the directions:

> <u>Directions</u>: Each question below consists of a word printed in capital letters, followed by five lettered words or phrases. Choose the lettered word or phrase that is most nearly <u>opposite</u> in meaning to the word in capital letters. Since some of the questions require you to distinguish fine shades of meaning, be sure to consider all the choices before deciding which one is best.

OUR BREATHTAKING TECHNIQUES

Antonym items are straightforward. As a result, they're hard to crack. If you have a big vocabulary, you'll do well. If you have a tiny vocabulary, you'll have trouble. The best way to improve your antonym score is to improve your GRE vocabulary. Can you give a solid, dictionary-type definition for *corpulent* and *opprobrium*? Try, then look them up. And if you haven't begun studying our GRE Hit Parade (see Part Five), do so now.

Even though antonyms are hard to crack, we do have techniques that can enable you to squeeze the maximum number of points out of your vocabulary. These techniques are based on POE. *They are also closely geared to the difficulty of the items.* So pay careful attention to item numbers.

We'll describe our antonym techniques first, then tie them together in an overall strategy geared to the different thirds.

JOE BLOGGS ON ANTONYMS

As usual, Joe sails through the easies, does so-so on the mediums, and bombs on the difficults. You need to interpret your own hunches accordingly.

Joe Bloggs does very well on the easy third. You should therefore trust your hunches on the first few items, even if you aren't entirely certain about the meaning of the word in capital letters.

The only real trap for Joe Bloggs in the easy third is carelessness. *You must never mark an answer without reading all the choices.* If your grasp of the meaning of the word in capital letters is shaky, incorrect choices can seem more tempting than they should. Check everything to be sure, and cross out choices you are able to eliminate. Crossing out incorrect choices is your most important weapon against carelessness.

On the medium third, you need to be extra careful, because Joe's hunches here are beginning to lead him astray. Some of his errors are careless ones. Pay attention and cross out incorrect answer choices to avoid careless errors.

On the difficult third, Joe becomes lost. You may find that you don't have a clue, even to what Joe is thinking. Don't waste time on real brainteasers. Just mark a choice and go on.

EASY QUESTIONS HAVE EASY ANSWERS

Don't be alarmed if you don't know the meaning of one or more of the *choices* on an antonym item in the easy third. Joe Bloggs avoids words he doesn't understand. This means that easy questions have to have easy answers, which means that on the easy third you can simply eliminate choices that Joe Bloggs doesn't understand. Here's an example:

3. NEFARIOUS:
   (A) angelic
   (B) germinal
   (C) repellent
   (D) inferior
   (E) salutary

Here's how to crack it:

Don't know what germinal and salutary mean? Don't worry. Joe Bloggs doesn't either. Joe finds ETS's answer, choice A, anyway.

BE CAREFUL: HARD QUESTIONS OFTEN HAVE EASY ANSWERS, TOO

Back in the chapter on analogies, we told you that hard items tend to have hard answers. That was true for analogies. It's also true on sentence completions. It's often *not* true on antonyms. Simply picking the hardest choice on a difficult antonym is *not* a dependable strategy.

POSITIVE OR NEGATIVE

There will be times when you don't know the meaning of the word in capital letters but do have some sense of whether it has positive connotations or negative connotations. Suppose, for example, that you've heard the word *contumely* before and know that it means something negative or unfavorable, but you can't quite recall exactly what it means. You may be able to eliminate a choice or two simply on the basis of your vague impression:

10. CONTUMELY:
    (A) reluctance
    (B) chivalrousness
    (C) ardor
    (D) steadfastness
    (E) melancholy

Here's how to crack it:

Our assumption is that we know that *contumely* is a negative word, which means we can eliminate negative choices. Are there any? Yes, choices A and E. In fact, choice E is a triple Joe Bloggs attractor: It's negative; it has the same ending as the word in capital letters; the word in capital letters makes Joe think of the adjective *content*, the opposite of the adjective *melancholy*.

ETS's answer is choice B. Contumely means rudeness or contempt.

WORKING BACKWARD FROM THE CHOICES

Even in the easy third, you may occasionally find that you aren't entirely certain of the meaning of the word in capital letters. In such cases, you can often spur your memory, or at least improve your odds, by working backward from the choices. You can do this by taking each choice, turning it into its opposite, and comparing it with the word in capital letters. Here's an example:

> 3. GARISH:
>   (A) adaptable
>   (B) understated
>   (C) explicable
>   (D) generous
>   (E) nonchalant

Here's how to crack it:

Let's assume you aren't sure what garish means, and that reading the choices doesn't make its meaning pop into your head. Don't give up. Turn each choice into its opposite and see what you have:

(A) unadaptable

(B) overstated

(C) inexplicable

(D) stingy

(E) Joe's a little shaky on this word, but don't worry; this is the easy third, so you can probably just eliminate it.

As you turn each word into its opposite, you want to hold it up to the capitalized word and determine whether it could mean the same thing.

Could garish mean unadaptable?

Could garish mean overstated?

Could garish mean inexplicable?

Could garish mean stingy?

Could garish mean whatever? (Just eliminate this choice.)

If no choice presents itself yet, eliminate the least likely choices, one at a time, and try to zero in on ETS's answer. On the easy third, you'll probably find it. Simply spending a few extra seconds on the item often makes something click in your mind, showing you what ETS is up to. (ETS's answer on this item is choice B. Look it up.)

Working backward is also a powerful tool on the medium and difficult thirds. ETS's answers on these items are seldom exact opposites. You'll often have to turn the words over in your mind for a while to find ETS's wavelength.

Keep in mind, though, that the harder the question is, the less ambitious you can be. On the difficult third, you should feel happy if working backward enables you to eliminate even one choice, thus boosting your odds of guessing ETS's answer.

IN WORKING BACKWARD, ELIMINATE CHOICES THAT HAVE NO OPPOSITES

What's the opposite of cake? What's the opposite of baritone? What's the opposite of calligraphy?

These words have no clear opposites. If they were choices on an antonym item on the GRE, you could eliminate them automatically, even if you didn't know the meaning of the word in capital letters. Why? Because if a choice has no opposite, the capitalized word can't possibly *be* its opposite.

Here's an example:

9. EXHUME:
   (A) breathe
   (B) inter
   (C) approve
   (D) assess
   (E) facilitate

Here's how to crack it:

Let's assume we don't know the meaning of exhume. Work through the choices, turning each into its opposite:

(A) stop breathing—suffocate?

(B) Joe doesn't know this word

(C) disapprove

(D) no clear opposite

(E) make difficult

We can probably eliminate choice D, since it seems to have no opposite. Doing this improves our guessing odds to one in four.

What about the other choices? Exhume reminds Joe Bloggs of exhale, which will make Joe think that A is ETS's answer. For this reason, we can eliminate choice A. That improves our chances to one in three.

Our chances of finding ETS's answer now depend on whether narrowing down our choices has made anything click in our minds. ETS's answer is B; inter means bury, exhume means dig up.

BEWARE OF PSEUDO-ROOTS

A knowledge of roots and prefixes can help you on the GRE, but you must be very, very careful. "Deciphering" hard words is one of Joe Bloggs's favorite techniques. This means that on medium and difficult items, syllables that *look* like common roots very often are not. (On the easy third, though, an obvious-looking root will typically lead you to ETS's answer.)

Here's an example of a difficult antonym item containing a pseudo-root that fools Joe Bloggs:

10. NUMINOUS:
    (A) mundane
    (B) gloomy
    (C) single
    (D) lackluster
    (E) piebald

Here's how to crack it:

Joe Bloggs doesn't know what numinous means, but his passing knowledge of etymology tells him that it has something to do with numbers. His eye falls immediately on choice C. Does he win points for this answer? No, of course not. *Num* in this case is a pseudo-root. Numinous means spiritually elevated. The numen of a place, object, or person is its apparent spirit. To be numinous is to give evidence of this inner spirit—to project an aura. ETS's answer to this difficult question is choice A.

Other Joe Bloggs attractors on this item are choices B and D. Numinous sounds like luminous, which makes lackluster and gloomy seem appealing to Joe.

IN THE MEDIUM AND DIFFICULT THIRDS, BEWARE OF CHOICES THAT SOUND LIKE THE WORD IN CAPITAL LETTERS

Joe Bloggs loves rhymes and similar endings. When he doesn't know what else to do, he's likely to be attracted to a choice that looks or sounds like the word in capital letters. This tendency helps him on the easy third, but hurts him on the medium and difficult thirds. Here's an example from the difficult third:

10. PRECOCIOUS:
    (A) stunted
    (B) insensitive
    (C) capricious
    (D) destructive
    (E) ignorant

Here's how to crack it:

On this item, Joe's eye falls immediately on choice C. Since it's a difficult item, we can eliminate it.

On the difficult third, can you eliminate *any* choice that has the same ending as the word in capital letters? No. If three or more of the choices have the same ending as the word in capital letters, you should select your answer from among those similar-sounding choices.

It's easy to understand the reason for this. Since Joe is naturally attracted to choices with similar endings, the only way to hide ETS's answer from him, if ETS's answer has a similar ending, is to offer several such choices. ETS's answer *must* be hidden from Joe on the difficult third; one way to do this is to

make it part of a crowd. When you see such a crowd, you can assume that ETS's answer is in it. The correct answer to this item is A.

11. PERFIDY:
    (A) flippancy
    (B) optimism
    (C) aptitude
    (D) loyalty
    (E) humility

Here's how to crack it:

Three of the choices have the same ending as the word in capital letters: A, D, and E. Because there are three such similar-sounding choices, we can assume that ETS's answer is to be found among them. We can therefore eliminate choices B and C.

ETS's answer is choice D; perfidy means treachery or disloyalty. Note that loyalty is the easiest word among the choices—proof that hard antonym items don't always have hard answers.

On the medium third, you can eliminate a similar-ending choice if there's only one, but you should select your answer from among such choices if there are two or more. The same reasoning applies. Rhyming and similar-sounding choices are *always* attractive to Joe; how attractive these choices should be to *you* depends on where you find them in the group.

Here's a summary of our rules on rhyming choices:

1. On the medium third, if only *one* choice has the same ending as the word in capital letters, you can eliminate that choice.

2. On the difficult third, if only *one or two* choices have the same ending as the word in capital letters, you can eliminate that choice or those choices.

3. On the medium third, if *two or more* choices have the same ending as the word in capital letters, you should select your answer from among those choices.

4. On the difficult third, if *three or more* choices have the same ending as the word in capital letters, you should select your answer from among those choices.

KNOW WHEN TO BAG IT

Hard antonym items can be *really* hard. Do what you can, but don't be afraid to guess and move on. Save your energy for analogies and sentence completions, which are easier to crack.

PUTTING IT ALL TOGETHER: STRATEGY BY THIRDS

The techniques we have described are the tools you will use to crack GRE antonyms. Which tools you use will depend on the difficulty—as determined by its number—of the item you're working on. Here are some tips on how to tailor your approach:

EASY THIRD
(The first three or four antonyms)

1. Joe Bloggs gets these right. Trust your hunches.

2. Don't worry too much about hard words among the choices (Joe doesn't know them either).

3. If you stumble over the word in capital letters, work backward from the choices.

4. As you work backward, eliminate choices that have no clear opposites.

MEDIUM THIRD
(The next three or four antonyms)

1. Joe Bloggs is sometimes right and sometimes wrong. Be careful.

2. If you stumble over the word in capital letters, work backward from the choices.

3. As you work backward, eliminate choices that have no clear opposites.

4. Beware of pseudo-roots.

5. Beware of choices that rhyme with or otherwise sound like the word in capital letters. If one of the choices has the same ending as the word in capital letters, eliminate it; if two or more do, look for ETS's answer among them.

6. Positive words have negative antonyms; negative words have positive antonyms. Eliminate accordingly.

DIFFICULT THIRD
(The last three or four antonyms)

1. Joe Bloggs gets these questions wrong. Don't do what he would do.

2. Hard antonyms often have easy answers; don't pick a choice simply because you don't know what it means.

3. Positive words have negative antonyms; negative words have positive antonyms. Eliminate accordingly.

4. If you don't know the meaning of the word in capital letters, try to work backward from the choices.

5. In working backward, eliminate choices that have no opposites.

6. Beware of pseudo-roots. Joe Bloggs loves to decipher words he doesn't know. On the difficult third, he's always wrong.

7. If one or two choices have the same ending as the word in capital letters, eliminate them. If three or more choices have the same ending, look for ETS's answer among them.

8. Don't waste time on hard antonyms. If you're stumped, guess and go on.

SUMMARY

1. Each verbal section of your GRE will contain eleven antonym items, numbered 28–38. Items 28–30 will be easy, items 31–35 will be medium, and items 36–38 will be difficult.

2. If you have a big vocabulary, you'll do well on antonyms. If you have a tiny vocabulary, you'll have trouble. Our techniques can help you, but the size and strength of your GRE vocabulary is the main factor on antonyms. Get to work on it.

3. As usual, Joe Bloggs does well on the easies, so-so on the mediums, and poorly on the hards.

4. You must never mark an answer without reading all the choices.

5. Easy antonyms have easy answers. Don't fret over difficult choices in the easy third. But beware: Hard antonyms often have easy answers, too.

6. If you don't know the meaning of the word in capital letters but do have some sense of whether it has positive connotations or negative connotations, you can eliminate similarly positive or negative words among the choices.

7. When you are uncertain about the meaning of the word in capital letters, work backward from the choices by turning each one into its opposite.

8. When working backward, eliminate choices that have no opposites.

9. Beware of pseudo-roots. Joe Bloggs loves to decipher words. Doing this on the difficult third leads to catastrophe.

10. On the medium third, if only *one* choice has the same ending as the word in capital letters, you can eliminate that choice.

11. On the difficult third, if only *one or two* choices have the same ending as the word in capital letters, you can eliminate that choice or those choices.

12. On the medium third, if *two or more* choices have the same ending as the word in capital letters, you should select your answer from among those choices.

13. On the difficult third, if *three or more* choices have the same ending as the word in capital letters, you should select your answer from among those choices.

14. Don't spin your wheels on hard antonyms. If you run out of ideas, guess and go on.

Sentence Completions

Each verbal section of your GRE will contain seven sentence completion items, numbered 1 through 7. Items 1 and 2 will be easy, items 3–5 will be medium, and items 6 and 7 will be difficult.

In this chapter, sentence completions will also be numbered 1–7. A number 1 will be easy; a number 7 will be hard. Always pay attention to the item position in answering GRE questions. The item number will help determine the technique or combination of techniques you will use to crack it.

LEARN THESE DIRECTIONS

Before we begin, take a moment to read and learn the following set of directions. These are the directions exactly as they will appear on your GRE. You shouldn't even glance at them when you take the test. If you do, you will waste time and lose points. Here are the directions:

> Directions: Each sentence below has one or two blanks, each blank indicating that something has been omitted. Beneath the sentence are five lettered words or sets of words. Choose the word or set of words for each blank that best fits the meaning of the sentence as a whole.

OUR STUNNING TECHNIQUES

The Princeton Review's techniques for cracking sentence completions are very powerful. All are based on POE. Sometimes you will be able to use POE to eliminate all four incorrect choices. In any event, you should always be able to eliminate at least one. **Eliminating even one incorrect choice will improve your odds of earning points**.

Our techniques for sentence completions will enable you to

1. zero in on ETS's answer by understanding how the items were written

2. use contextual clues to anticipate ETS's answer

3. use structural clues

4. eliminate Joe Bloggs attractors

LEARNING TO LOVE SENTENCE COMPLETIONS

Sentence completions—which you've known since kindergarten under the less ominous title of "fill in the blanks"—are among the most crackable items on the entire test. You'll soon be wishing there were more than seven of them in each verbal section.

FINDING THE DOCTOR IN GRE SENTENCE COMPLETIONS

Take a look at this simple sentence completion:

1. The woman told the man, "You are very _____ ."

    (A) handsome
    (B) sick
    (C) smart
    (D) rich
    (E) nice

Here's how to crack it:

What's ETS's answer? We have no way of knowing. Each of the five choices makes a plausible sentence; there is no reason for preferring one to another.

Now let's change one word and look at the same question again:

1. The doctor told the man, "You are very _____ ."

    (A) handsome
    (B) sick
    (C) smart
    (D) rich
    (E) nice

Here's how to crack it:

What's ETS's answer now? It has to be B. Of the five possible statements, "You are very sick" is the one that seems most likely to have been made by a doctor. In answering this item, we made use of a very important clue. What was that clue? It was the word *doctor*. Even though a doctor might call a man *handsome*, *smart*, *rich*, or *nice*, the only choice that fits well into the context of the sentence is *sick*.

Every GRE sentence completion will contain a clue like the one in our simple sentence. In approaching each new item, you need to look for this clue. We call this "finding the doctor." As you read each item you should ask yourself, "Where's the doctor? Where's the key to the solution?" The "doctor" in each sentence completion is the word or phrase that reveals which answer choice ETS is looking for.

HIDING THE DOCTOR:
HOW ETS WRITES SENTENCE COMPLETION ITEMS

Let's pretend that we've flunked out of law school, been dishonorably discharged from the Marine Corps, and escaped from federal prison, where we were serving a life sentence. Defeated, disgraced, and on the run, we have no

choice but to take a job writing test questions at ETS. Our first assignment is to create a sentence completion item for the GRE. Here's our rough draft:

Museums are good resources for students of _____ .

(A) art
(B) science
(C) human nature
(D) dichotomy
(E) philanthropy

Here's how to crack it:

As we've written it, this question is unanswerable. Almost any choice could be defended. We couldn't use this question on a real test, because students would justly complain that none of the choices is much better than any of the others.

To make this into a real GRE question, we'll have to change the sentence in such a way that only one of the answer choices can be defended. Here's another try:

Museums, which house many paintings and sculptures,
are good resources for students of _____ .

(A) art
(B) science
(C) human nature
(D) dichotomy
(E) philanthropy

Here's how to crack it:

Now there's only one solid answer: choice A. The clause we added to our original sentence makes this obvious. This clause—containing the words *paintings and sculptures*—is "the doctor." Our finished question is very easy. Joe Bloggs will have no problem with it. Let's call it a number 1—a very easy item.

But suppose that the verbal section we're writing already has a number 1 sentence completion. Suppose that what we really need is a number 4—a medium. Could we turn our item into a medium? Certainly. We'll do it by inserting a harder "doctor"—by throwing in some moderately difficult vocabulary words:

4. Museums, which often house elaborate reliquaries,
talismans, and altarpieces, are good resources for students
of _____ .

(A) religion
(B) science
(C) human nature
(D) dichotomy
(E) philanthropy

Here's how to crack it:

ETS's answer is choice A. To find it, you need to know that reliquaries, talismans, and altarpieces are religious articles.

We might also have created a medium question by complicating the sentence structure:

4. Because the paintings in their collections sometimes
    illustrate changing perceptions of
    the workings of the physical world, museums
    can be good resources for students of the
    history of _____.

    (A) art
    (B) science
    (C) human nature
    (D) dichotomy
    (E) philanthropy

Here's how to crack it:

Here, ETS's answer is choice B. Choice A, art, would be too simple an answer for a medium question that mentioned both paintings and museums. Choices D and E are simply too peculiar to be ETS's answer on a medium. Joe Bloggs has been to a science museum before, and if he isn't careless, he may pick ETS's answer on the item, even if only by accident. That's just what we would expect of Joe—his performance on mediums is always so-so.

On a hard question, ETS's answer *will* be peculiar, and Joe Bloggs won't be able to find it, even by accident. Let's rewrite our item once again to make it a number 7:

7. Because the paintings and sculptures in their collections
    tend to reflect the shifting tastes of that class of privileged
    individuals capable of turning private means to public
    ends, museums are interesting resources for students of
    trends in _____.

    (A) art
    (B) history
    (C) religion
    (D) dichotomy
    (E) philanthropy

Here's how to crack it:

Here ETS's answer is choice E. Joe Bloggs doesn't pick it, because *philanthropy* is a hard word and he doesn't associate it with museums. Also, the sentence is long and impossible for Joe to decipher. Joe Bloggs has heard of art museums and history museums, and as a result he's strongly attracted to both those choices. ETS's answer has to be something that doesn't occur to him.

USING THE DOCTOR TO ANTICIPATE ETS'S ANSWER

In each of the sentence completions above, we changed ETS's answer by changing *the doctor*—by inserting words that restricted the possible meaning of the sentence in such a way that only one of the answer choices could plausibly be defended as correct.

Knowing that this was how the items were constructed, we can do the same thing in reverse to take them apart. By finding the doctor, we can tune in to ETS's wavelength. Doing this will enable us to anticipate ETS's answer, even before we look at the choices. Here's an example of what we mean:

1. Only when one actually visits the ancient ruins of bygone civilizations does one truly appreciate the sad _____ of human greatness.

Here's how to crack it:

Where's the doctor? It's the word *sad*. Without it, any number of different words could plausibly fill in the blank. Without *sad*, we might have said, "Only when one actually visits the ancient ruins of bygone civilizations does one truly appreciate the dimensions/history/antiquity/magnificence/decline/impermanence/scope/nature of human greatness." There are other possibilities as well. But the inclusion of the word *sad* tells us that ETS is looking for something like *impermanence* or *decline*. Finding the doctor, in other words, lets us anticipate ETS's answer. Now take a look at the complete item:

1. Only when one actually visits the ancient ruins of bygone civilizations does one truly appreciate the sad _____ of human greatness.

   (A) scope
   (B) magnitude
   (C) artistry
   (D) transience
   (E) innovation

Here's how to crack it:

Are any of the choices similar to the ones we anticipated? Yes, choice D. This is ETS's answer. There would be nothing sad about the scope, magnitude, artistry, or innovation of bygone civilizations.

DRILL 1

In each of the following sentences, find the doctor and circle it. Then see if you can anticipate ETS's answer. Try to think of three possible choices for each blank. It doesn't matter if your guesses are awkward or wordy. All you need to do is capture the general idea. (You can check your answers on page 334.)

1. Most students found Dr. Schwartz's lecture on art excessively detailed and academic; some thought his display of _____ exasperating.

   _____

   _____

   _____

   _____

2. Despite the apparent _____ of the demands, the
   negotiations dragged on for over a year.

   _____
   _____
   _____

3. The _____ of foreign pronunciations makes one
   overlook the common heritage of many languages, whose
   bond becomes obvious when one discovers the countless
   spelling _____.

   _____   _____
   _____   _____
   _____   _____

4. In retrospect, Jerry considered the unequal allocation of
   his estate _____ , as it caused _____ in what had been a
   harmonious family life.

   _____   _____
   _____   _____
   _____   _____

DRILL 2

Now that you've anticipated ETS's answers, look at the same four questions
again, this time with the choices provided. See if you can use your notes above
to find ETS's answer. (You can check your answers on page 334.)

1. Most students found Dr. Schwartz's lecture on art
   excessively detailed and academic; some thought his
   display of _____ exasperating.

   (A) pedantry
   (B) logic
   (C) aesthetics
   (D) erudition
   (E) literalism

2. Despite the apparent _____ of the demands, the
   negotiations dragged on for over a year.

   (A) hastiness
   (B) intolerance
   (C) publicity
   (D) modesty
   (E) desirability

3. The _____ of foreign pronunciations makes one overlook the common heritage of many languages, whose bond becomes obvious when one discovers the countless spelling _____.

   (A) difficulties . . irregularities
   (B) heterogeneity . . similarities
   (C) range . . corrections
   (D) diversity . . intricacies
   (E) essence . . variations

4. In retrospect, Jerry considered the unequal allocation of his estate _____, as it caused _____ in what had been a harmonious family life.

   (A) biased . . cacophony
   (B) pragmatic . . dissonance
   (C) deleterious . . adversity
   (D) impartial . . discord
   (E) improvident . . dissension

LOOK BEFORE YOU LEAP

In approaching GRE sentence completions, read the sentence, then find the doctor, then anticipate ETS's answer. This is easy to understand, but sometimes hard to do. Many students read sentence completions quickly, then go immediately to the choices and begin plugging them in. This approach may work on easy items, but it will only confuse you on difficult ones. If you take the time to understand what ETS is up to, you'll have a much easier time selecting ETS's answer from among the choices.

MR. BLOGGS, I PRESUME?

As usual, Joe Bloggs is attracted to easy answer choices that remind him of the question. Having read the word *poison* in a sentence, his eye falls quickly on the choice that contains the word *antidote*. On difficult questions, this choice will be wrong.

Here's an example of what we mean:

7. Although bound to impose the law, a judge is free to use her discretion to _____ the anachronistic _____ of some criminal penalties.

   (A) enforce . . judiciousness
   (B) impose . . legality
   (C) exacerbate . . severity
   (D) mitigate . . barbarity
   (E) restore . . impartiality

Here's how to crack it:

This is a number 7—a difficult item. Joe doesn't pick ETS's answer. Which choices does he pick? His top guesses are choices A and B, because *judiciousness* and *legality* make him think of judges and the law. *Therefore, these choices cannot possibly be correct.* Eliminate them before considering any other choices. (ETS's answer is choice D.)

On difficult questions, you should always eliminate Joe Bloggs attractors before you begin to mull over the choices. By ruling out Joe's answers at the outset, you'll sidestep most of the traps that ETS has laid for you.

Be careful, though, that you don't eliminate a choice unless you are dictionary-sure of its definition. Never eliminate a choice simply because it "doesn't sound right" or "doesn't seem to fit" with the other choices. This is what Joe Bloggs does, and Joe Bloggs is not a good role model. (Except, of course, on the easy third, where you *should* eliminate choices containing words that are too hard. We'll tell you more about this shortly.)

THE GOOD, THE BAD, AND THE INDIFFERENT

When you find that you are unable to anticipate ETS's answer, you may be able to zero in on it by making some general guesses about the missing word or words. For example, you may be able to tell from the context of the sentence whether the word in the blank will be a "good" word or a "bad" word—that is, you may be able to tell whether it will have positive or negative connotations. Here's an example:

> 3. Trembling with anger, the belligerent colonel ordered his
>   men to_____ the civilians.

Here's how to crack it:

Is the missing word a "good" word or a "bad" word? It's a "bad" word, isn't it? The colonel is clearly going to do something nasty to the civilians. Now look at the answer choices and see which ones are good words and can therefore be eliminated:

> (A) congratulate
> (B) promote
> (C) reward
> (D) attack
> (E) worship

Here's how to crack it:

Choices A, B, C, and E are all positive words. All, therefore, can be eliminated. ETS's answer is choice D, the only negative word among the choices.

Looking for good words and bad words is especially useful on two-blank sentence completions. Imagine a two-blank question in which you know the first missing word has positive connotations and the second missing word has negative connotations. Using this piece of information, you can confidently eliminate any choice with a different arrangement. This is a useful POE technique even on items in which you feel confident you have anticipated ETS's answer. Crossing out choices that don't fit the pattern will make you less likely to make a careless error.

MORE ON TWO-BLANK QUESTIONS

Most of the hardest sentence completions will have two blanks instead of one. Does this mean that two-blank sentence completions are harder than one-blank sentence completions? Many students feel this way, but they shouldn't. *Two-blank sentence completions are harder than one-blank sentence completions only if you insist on trying to fill in both blanks at the same time.* You'll do much better if you concentrate on just one of the blanks at a time. Remember, a two-blank answer choice can be ETS's answer only if it works for *both* of the blanks; if you can determine that one of the words in the choice doesn't work in its blank, you can eliminate the choice without testing the other word.

Which blank should you concentrate on? The easier one, of course. Usually, this will be the second blank (the one Joe Bloggs never gets to).

Once you've decided which blank is easier, anticipate what sort of word should fit into it, then go to the answer choices and look only at the ones provided for that blank. Then *eliminate* any choice that doesn't work for that blank.

Here's an example of how you can crack a hard two-blank sentence completion by tackling it one blank at a time:

6. A growing number of heretical scientists are claiming the once _____ theory of evolution must be _____, if not actually shelved.

Here's how to crack it:

Ignoring the first blank, which looks more difficult, we reduce the sentence to this: "The theory of evolution must be _____, if not actually shelved." You ought to be able to anticipate roughly what this blank must mean. It must mean something like "*almost* shelved," or "changed in some basically negative way."

Now look at the choices, paying attention only to the second word in each:

(A) _____ . . postulated
(B) _____ . . popularized
(C) _____ . . reexamined
(D) _____ . . modified
(E) _____ . . promulgated

Here's how to crack it:
Do any of these words fit the rough restriction we've anticipated for the second blank? How about choices C and D? To reexamine or modify a theory is to do something negative to it that falls short of actually throwing it out. Now look at the first word in each of these choices:

(C) sacrosanct . . reexamined
(D) modern . . modified

Here's how to crack it:
The word *modern* doesn't make any sense in the first blank, so ETS's answer must be choice C. It is.

TRIGGER WORDS

Certain words signal changes in the meaning of sentence completions. We call them trigger words. They provide important clues about the meaning of the sentence, and—because they confuse Joe Bloggs—they are often the key to finding ETS's answer.

Here are the most important sentence completion trigger words, in order of their importance:

but	*while*
although (though, even though)	*however*
unless	*unfortunately*
rather	*in contrast*
yet	*similarly*
despite	*heretofore*
thus	*previously*

Especially in hard items (where they appear most frequently) trigger words go a long way toward determining the meaning of the sentence. If you ignore trigger words in the difficult third, you will lose points.

To see how these words can provide clues to ETS's answer, fill in the blanks in the following pair of simple sentences:

A fair *and* _____ judge.

A fair *but* _____ judge.

Now here's an example of a full sentence completion in which finding ETS's answer turns on understanding the function of a trigger word:

7. Although he was usually _____ and _____, his illness
   blunted both his appetite and his temper.

   (A) gluttonous . . contentious
   (B) sated . . belligerent
   (C) avaricious . . responsive
   (D) eloquent . . reflective
   (E) ravenous . . reticent

Here's how to crack it:

To see what's going on in this sentence, replace it with a simpler one that follows the same general blueprint:

Although he was usually [something], his illness made
him [something else].

Although he was usually happy, his illness made him sad. Although he was usually stupid, his illness made him intelligent. Although he was usually eager, his illness made him lazy. It's easy to think of many possibilities.

In each case, the trigger word, *although*, tells us that the two halves of the sentence are in opposition to each other. The [something] at the end of the first clause means roughly the opposite of the [something else] at the end of the second.

Now look back at the original test sentence:

> Although he was usually _____ and _____, his illness blunted both his appetite and his temper.

Working on the same model we found in our simplified sentences, we can say, roughly:

> Although he was usually [*un*blunted in his appetite] and [*un*blunted in his temper], his illness blunted both his appetite and his temper.

Now look through the choices for a pair that means, roughly, [unblunted in appetite] . . [unblunted in temper]:

(A) gluttonous . . contentious
(B) sated . . belligerent
(C) avaricious . . responsive
(D) eloquent . . reflective
(E) ravenous . . reticent

ETS's answer is choice A.

EASY QUESTIONS HAVE EASY ANSWERS; HARD QUESTIONS HAVE HARD ANSWERS

The general rule on the GRE is that easy questions have easy answers and hard questions have hard answers. This is because Joe Bloggs has a strong preference for easy answers that remind him of the question. The only exception to this rule that we have encountered so far is with antonyms, where hard questions often do have easy answers (which nonetheless look wrong to Joe).

On sentence completions, the general rule again applies. On easy questions, ETS's answer will consist of easy words that Joe Bloggs understands and that remind him of the question; on hard questions, ETS's answer will usually consist of hard words that Joe has never heard of. This means that on the difficult third you can usually just eliminate choices containing words that are too easy and focus your attention on the choices containing the toughest words.

Take another look at an item we've already discussed:

7. Although bound to impose the law, a judge is free to use her discretion to _____ the anachronistic _____ of some criminal penalties.

   (A) enforce . . judiciousness
   (B) impose . . legality
   (C) exacerbate . . severity
   (D) mitigate . . barbarity
   (E) restore . . impartiality

Here's how to crack it:

Note that ETS's answer, choice D, contains the hardest of the ten words among the answer choices. Joe Bloggs has no idea what mitigate means (and isn't at all certain what barbarity means). This means he won't pick this choice, which makes it a strong candidate for being ETS's answer.

Here's another example:

6. While many people enjoy observing rituals and customs not _____ their culture, they _____ participating in them.

   (A) sanctioned by . . discourage
   (B) endemic to . . eschew
   (C) upheld in . . condone
   (D) central to . . relish
   (E) relevant to . . avoid

Here's how to crack it:

What are the hardest words among the answer choices? Endemic and eschew. What is ETS's answer? Choice B.

Similarly, easy sentence completions will tend to have easy answers. This means that choices containing difficult words can be eliminated. *Don't fret over hard words in the easy third.* Joe Bloggs, who answers easy questions correctly, simply ignores words he doesn't understand.

BAILING OUT

When all else fails on the difficult third, simply select the answer choice containing the hardest words.

> We have found that this strategy alone leads to ETS's answer in the difficult third roughly 75 percent of the time; Joe Bloggs, in contrast, finds ETS's answer in the difficult third roughly 0 percent of the time.

You should also use this knowledge to check your answer choices on the difficult third. If your choice is other than the hardest one, be very certain you have a good reason for picking it.

PUTTING IT ALL TOGETHER: STRATEGY BY THIRDS

EASY THIRD
(Items 1 and 2)

1. Read the sentence, find the doctor, and anticipate ETS's answer.

2. Don't fret about hard words among the answer choices; easy questions have easy answers.

3. Trust your hunches, but don't get careless. Joe Bloggs gets these questions right.

4. If you feel puzzled, determine whether the missing word is a "good" word or a "bad" word and eliminate accordingly.

5. On two-blank sentences, eliminate careless errors by tackling one blank at a time, the easier one first.

6. Pay attention to trigger words.

MEDIUM THIRD
(Items 3–5)

1. Read the sentence, find the doctor, and anticipate ETS's answer.

2. If you feel puzzled, determine whether the missing word is a "good" word or a "bad" word and eliminate accordingly.

3. On two-blank sentences, tackle one blank at a time, the easier one first. The easier blank will usually be the second one.

4. Pay attention to trigger words. Use them to find clues to the meaning of the missing word or words.

DIFFICULT THIRD
(Items 6 and 7)

1. Read the sentence, find the doctor, and anticipate ETS's answer.

2. Don't be tempted by answer choices containing easy words; hard sentence completions have hard answers. Eliminate easy choices that remind Joe Bloggs of the question.

3. If you feel puzzled, determine whether the missing word is a "good" word or a "bad" word and eliminate accordingly.

4. On two-blank sentences, tackle one blank at a time, the easier one first. The easier blank will almost always be the second one, although it may still be relatively hard.

5. Pay very careful attention to trigger words. Use them to find clues to the meaning of the missing word or words.

6. When all else fails, select the choice that contains the hardest words.

SUMMARY

1. Each verbal section of your GRE will contain seven sentence-completion items, numbered 1–7. Items 1 and 2 will be easy, items 3–5 will be medium, and items 6 and 7 will be difficult.

2. Sentence completions are among the most crackable items on the entire test.

3. As you read each sentence, look for the doctor—the word or phrase that captures the essence of the meaning of the sentence and thus holds the key to its solution.

4. When you have found the doctor, use it to anticipate ETS's answer *before* you look at the answer choices.

5. Joe Bloggs is attracted to easy choices that remind him of the question. You must therefore avoid such choices on difficult items.

6. On difficult questions, eliminate Joe Bloggs attractors before you begin to analyze or plug in the choices. By ruling out Joe's answers at the outset, you'll sidestep most of the traps that ETS has laid for you.

7. Don't eliminate a choice unless you are dictionary-sure of its definition (except on the easy third).

8. When you find that you are unable to anticipate ETS's answer, you may be able to zero in on it by making some general guesses about whether each missing word has generally negative or generally positive connotations. You can then eliminate accordingly.

9. Two-blank sentence completions are harder than one-blank sentence completions only if you insist on trying to fill in both blanks at the same time. Instead, tackle one blank at a time, beginning with the easier one. On medium and difficult questions, the easier blank is usually the second one.

10. Pay careful attention to the sentence-completion trigger words: *but, although (though, even though, while), rather, yet, despite, however, unfortunately, in contrast, heretofore, previously.* These words provide clues to ETS's answer.

11. Easy questions have easy answers; hard questions have hard answers.

12. When all else fails on the difficult third, simply select the answer choice containing the hardest words.

PART III

How to Crack the Math Sections

GEOGRAPHY OF THE MATH SECTIONS

Every GRE contains two scored "quantitative ability," or math, sections. Your test could also contain a third math section, as an experimental section. This experimental math section would look like the other two math sections but would not count toward your score.

Each math section on your test will last thirty minutes and contain thirty items, as follows:

- Fifteen Quantitative Comparisons (items 1–15)

- Ten Regular Math Questions (items 16–20 and 26–30)

- Five Chart Questions (items 21–25, based on a single chart)

As the item numbers indicate, the quantitative comparisons come first. They are followed by five regular math questions, five chart questions, and five more regular math questions. Each math section will be arranged this way. Since there are two scored sections, your math score will be based on your performance on thirty quantitative comparisons, twenty regular math questions, and ten graph questions.

Each group of items will be arranged in order of increasing difficulty, as follows:

ITEM TYPE	ITEM NOS.	DIFFICULTY
Quant Comp	1–5 6–10 11–15	Easy Medium Difficult
Regular Math	16–18 19–20	Easy Medium
Chart	21 22–23 24–25	Easy Medium Difficult
Regular Math	26–27 28–30	Medium Difficult

A TRIP DOWN MEMORY LANE

ETS says that these sixty items test "ability to reason quantitatively and to solve problems in a quantitative setting." In truth, they mostly test how much you remember from the math courses you took in junior high school. Why is a passing knowledge of eighth-grade algebra important for a future Ph.D. in English literature? Don't ask us. All that matters is that ETS thinks there's a connection.

In the previous section, we told you that the verbal GRE is really just a harder version of the verbal SAT—same questions, harder words. What about the math GRE? Brace yourself: It's an *easier* version of the math SAT.

Why is it easier?

Because most students study little or no math in college. If the GRE tested "college-level" math, everyone but math majors would bomb.

If you're willing to do a little work, this is good news for you. By brushing up on the modest amount of math you need to know for the test, you can make a big difference in your score.

A WORD OF CAUTION

In constructing the math GRE, ETS is limited to the math that nearly everyone has studied: arithmetic, basic algebra, and basic geometry. There's no calculus (or even precalculus), no trigonometry, and no high-tech algebra or geometry.

Because of these limitations, ETS has to resort to sleight of hand in order to create hard problems. Even the most difficult GRE math problems are typically based on relatively simple principles. What makes the problems difficult is that these simple principles are disguised.

Virtually all problems on the GRE can be solved very quickly, assuming you can see through the disguise. ETS's question writers have a strong preference for elegant solutions. This means that in addition to testing your basic knowledge, ETS is testing your ability to spot shortcuts and solve problems in the most efficient way possible. If you spend three minutes laboring over a problem that could have been solved in three seconds, you've missed the point of the question, at least in ETS's eyes. You may finally arrive at ETS's answer, but you'll have cost yourself precious time that could have been spent on other problems.

To do well on the math GRE, you need to sharpen two sets of skills: your junior-high math skills, and your skill at thinking like ETS. The following chapters will help you do both.

A MATTER OF TIME

Since no points are deducted for incorrect answers on the GRE, you must not fail to mark an answer for every problem. Should you try to *solve* every problem? No. The math GRE gives you just sixty minutes to solve sixty problems, some of them quite difficult. You will enjoy yourself more, and score higher, if you spend your time working on the questions you are capable of answering, and ignore the ones that you would answer incorrectly anyway. Take your time: **No one aiming for a score under 700 in math should ever attempt to solve every problem in a math section**.

The only students who need to worry about finishing a math section are those who are shooting for 800. (Even they don't have to worry that much; on some versions of the test, you can make two errors and still receive a "perfect" score.) All other students should worry less about finishing problems than about being more careful on the ones they attempt to solve. The major cause of poor math scores is carelessness, not ignorance.

If you make more than five mistakes on the math part of the GRE, not including items on which you merely guess, then you are working too quickly. You will raise your score by working out fewer questions.

PRACTICE, PRACTICE

As you work through this book, be sure to practice on real GREs. Work slowly at first, then increase your speed as you gain confidence in our techniques. Practice will rapidly sharpen your test-taking skills. Unless you trust our techniques, you may be reluctant to use them fully and automatically on a real administration of the GRE. The best way to develop that trust is to practice.

GRE Mathematics

There's an awful lot of math in the world. Fortunately, only a tiny, tiny part of it is tested on the GRE. Knowing the stuff that isn't tested on the GRE may make you a better person, but it won't help you on the test.

For help on the test, you need us. We've boiled down all of mathematics into the relatively modest handful of principles that are the only ones ETS cares about. We refer to these principles collectively as GRE Mathematics. Learn it and you'll be well on your way to knowing all you need to know to do well on the GRE.

THE BASICS ABOUT THE BASICS

GRE Mathematics is the stuff they tried to teach you in elementary school, along with some tricky concepts thrown in from junior high.

You should master the principles of GRE Mathematics before you even look at the succeeding chapters, which deal with specific GRE problem types. Our techniques will make much more sense to you, and be much more useful, if you've tackled the basic math first.

Quick—what's an integer? Is 0 positive or negative? How many even prime numbers are there? Read on.

WHOLE NUMBERS

Whole numbers are also known as counting numbers: 0, 1, 2, 3, 4, 5, 6, and so on. The whole numbers include 0 but *not* fractions or negative numbers.

INTEGERS

The integers are the whole numbers plus their negative counterparts: –6, –5, –4, –3, –2, –1, 0, 1, 2, 3, 4, 5, 6. Once again, no fractions.

Remember what Joe Bloggs forgets: Positive integers get bigger as they move away from 0 (6 is bigger than 5); negative integers get smaller as they move away from zero (–6 is smaller than –5).

CONSECUTIVE INTEGERS

Consecutive integers are integers listed in order of increasing size without any integers missing in between. Here are some groups of consecutive integers:

$$0, 1, 2, 3, 4, 5$$

$$-6, -5, -4, -3, -2, -1, 0$$

$$-3, -2, -1, 0, 1, 2, 3$$

Here is a group of consecutive even integers:

$$2, 4, 6, 8, 10$$

Here are some groups of *non*-consecutive integers:

$$2, 4, 6, 8, 10$$

$$1, 2, 3, 4, 6$$

$$-1, -2, -3, -4, -5$$

No numbers other than integers can be consecutive.

ZERO

0 is both a whole number and an integer, but it is neither positive nor negative. It's just nothing.

0 is even (see below).

The sum of 0 and any other number is that other number.

The product of 0 and any other number is 0.

DIGITS

There are 10 digits: 0, 1, 2, 3, 4, 5, 6, 7, 8, and 9. All integers are made up of digits. The integer 10,897 has 5 digits: 1, 0, 8, 9, 7. It is therefore called a 5-digit integer. Each of its digits has its own name:

7 is the units digit

9 is the tens digit

8 is the hundreds digit

0 is the thousands digit

1 is the ten thousands digit

POSITIVE OR NEGATIVE

Always remember what happens when you multiply positive and negative numbers:

pos × pos = pos   2 × 2 = 4

neg × neg = pos   –2 × –2 = 4

pos × neg = neg   2 × –2 = –4

ODD OR EVEN

An even number is any integer that can be divided evenly by 2; an odd number is any integer that can't.

Here are some even integers: –4, –2, 0, 2, 4, 6, 8, 10.

Here are some odd integers: –3, –1, 1, 3, 5, 7, 9, 11.

0 is even.

Fractions are neither even nor odd.

Any integer is even if its units digit is even; any integer is odd if its units digit is odd.

Always remember what happens when you add and multiply odd and even integers:

even + even = even   even × even = even

odd + odd = even   odd × odd = odd

even + odd = odd   even × odd = even

Don't confuse odd and even with positive and negative—a major Joe Bloggs error.

DIVISIBILITY

An integer is divisible by 2 if its units digit is divisible by 2. Example: We know just by glancing that 598,467,896 is divisible by 2, because we know that 6 is divisible evenly by 2.

An integer is divisible by 3 if the sum of its digits is divisible by 3. Example: We know that 2,145 is divisible by 3, because 2 + 1 + 4 + 5 = 12, and 12 is divisible by 3.

An integer is divisible by 5 if its units digit is either 0 or 5.

An integer is divisible by 10 if its units digit is 0.

REMAINDERS

The remainder is the number left over when one integer cannot be divided evenly by another.

4 divided by 2 is 2; there is nothing left over, so there is no remainder.

5 divided by 2 is 2 with 1 left over; 1 is the remainder.

PRIME NUMBERS

A prime number is a number that can be divided evenly only by itself and by 1. Here are *all* the prime numbers less than 30:

2, 3, 5, 7, 11, 13, 17, 19, 23, 29

0 is not a prime number.

1 is not a prime number.

2 is the only even prime number.

FACTORS

x is a factor of y if y can be divided by x without leaving a remainder. 1, 2, 3, 4, 6, and 12 are all factors of 12.

MULTIPLES

A multiple of a number is that number multiplied by an integer other than 0. –20, –10, 10, 20, 30, 40, 50, and 60 are all multiples of 10 (10×-2, 10×-1, 10×1, 10×2, 10×3, 10×4, 10×5, and 10×6).

STANDARD SYMBOLS

Here are some standard symbols you can expect to see on the GRE:

Symbol	Meaning
=	is equal to
≠	is not equal to
<	is less than
>	is greater than
≤	is less than or equal to
≥	is greater than or equal to

STANDARD TERMS

Here are some standard terms. You won't see all of them on the GRE, but you'll need to know them to understand this book:

Term	Meaning
sum	the result of addition
difference	the result of subtraction
product	the result of multiplication
quotient	the result of division
numerator	the "upstairs" number in a fraction
denominator	the "downstairs" number in a fraction

DRILL 1

Check your answers on page 334.

1. List three consecutive negative integers.

2. List three consecutive odd integers.

3. What is the least prime number greater than 8?

4. What is the least integer greater than −5.8?

5. What is the greatest integer less than 3.6?

6. If you interchange the first and last digits of 7,845, what is the resulting number?

7. Name a three-digit number whose digits add up to 14.

8. If set A consists of {4, 5, 6, 7}, how many members of set A are odd?

9. What is the remainder when 99 is divided by 5? (Find your answer without performing division.)

10. What is the remainder when 12,345,671 is divided by 10? (Find your answer without performing division.)

11. A multiple of both 3 and 7 is also a multiple of   ?

12. If 34,569 is multiplied by 227, will the result be odd or even?

13. If two even numbers are multiplied together and then the product is multiplied by an odd number, will the result be odd or even?

14. Express 36 as the product of prime numbers.

15. If −2 is multiplied by −345, will the result be positive or negative?

GRE ARITHMETIC

THE SIX ARITHMETIC OPERATIONS

There are only six basic operations that you will need to perform on the GRE:

1. addition: $3 + 3$

2. subtraction: $3 - 3$

3. multiplication: 3×3, $3 \cdot 3$, or $(3)(3)$

4. division: $3 \div 3$

5. raising to a power: 3^3

6. finding a square root, finding a cube root: $\sqrt{3}$, $\sqrt[3]{3}$

ORDER OF OPERATIONS

Many problems require you to perform more than one operation to find ETS's answer. In these cases, it is absolutely necessary that you perform these operations in *exactly* the right order. In many cases, the correct order will be apparent from the way the problem is written. In cases where the correct order is not apparent, you need only remember the following mnemonic:

Please Excuse My Dear Aunt Sally

PEMDAS stands for Parentheses, Exponents, Multiplication, Division, Addition, Subtraction. This is the order in which the operations are to be performed. (Don't worry about exponents yet; we know you don't remember what to do with them.)

Here's an example:

$$10 - (6 - 5) - (3 + 3) - 3 =$$

Here's how to crack it:

Start with the parentheses. The expression inside the first pair of parentheses, 6 − 5, equals 1. The expression inside the second pair equals 6. We can now rewrite the problem as follows:

$$10 - 1 - 6 - 3 =$$
$$9 - 6 - 3 =$$
$$3 - 3 =$$
$$= 0$$

ASSOCIATIVE LAW

There are actually two associative laws, one for addition and one for multiplication. For the sake of simplicity, we've lumped them together. You don't need to remember the name.

The Princeton Review associative law says: *When you are adding a series of numbers or multiplying a series of numbers, you can regroup the numbers in any way you'd like.* Here are some examples:

$$4 + (5 + 8) = (4 + 5) + 8 = (4 + 8) + 5$$

$$(a + b) + (c + d) = a + (b + c + d)$$

$$4 \times (5 \times 8) = (4 \times 5) \times 8 = (4 \times 8) \times 5$$

$$(ab)(cd) = a(bcd)$$

DISTRIBUTIVE LAW

This is one of the most important principles tested on the GRE. You must know it cold. Here's what it looks like:

$$a(b + c) = ab + ac$$

$$a(b - c) = ab - ac$$

This law is so important that you must apply it every chance you get. Very often on the GRE, finding ETS's answer is simply a matter of performing the distributive law in one direction or the other. Here's an example:

27. If $y + 3 = 2x$, then $3y - 6x =$

    (A) −9
    (B) −3
    (C) 0
    (D) 3
    (E) 9

Here's how to crack it:

In math class, you would solve this problem by "solving for y." You would rewrite the first equation as $y = 2x - 3$ and then substitute $(2x - 3)$ for y in the second equation, and so on. It would take forever.

On the GRE, all you have to do is notice that the given expression in the second equation can be factored this way: $3(y - 2x)$.

Now look at the first equation. Notice anything? You should see that the equation can be rewritten as $y - 2x = -3$. Plugging in −3 as the value for $(y - 2x)$, you see that ETS's answer is A.

The lesson is that you must always be on the lookout for opportunities to apply the distributive law. ETS does this again and again and again.

THE DISTRIBUTIVE LAW AND DEAR AUNT SALLY

Earlier in this chapter we told you that you should remember PEMDAS and always perform the operations in parentheses first. The distributive law provides something of an exception to this rule, because it gives you a better way of achieving the same result (better because ETS uses it so often). Here's an example:

Distributive: $7(5 + 4) = 7(5) + 7(4) = 35 + 28 = 63$
PEMDAS: $7(5 + 4) = 7(9) = 63$

ETS *loves* the distributive law.

FACTORING AND UNFACTORING

When you use the distributive law to rewrite the expression $xy + xz$ in the form $x(y + z)$, you are said to be *factoring* the original expression. That is, you take the factor common to both terms of the original expression (x), and "pull it out." This gives you a new, "factored" version of the expression you began with.

When you use the distributive law to rewrite the expression $x(y + z)$ in the form $xy + xz$, we like to say that you are *unfactoring* the original expression.

DRILL 2

Use the distributive law to rewrite the following expressions. Check your answers on page 334.

1. $2(4 + 20) =$

2. $17(46) - 17(12) - 17(99) =$

3. $x(y - z) =$

4. $ab + ac + ad =$

5. $xyz - vwx =$

FRACTIONS

FRACTIONS ARE SHORTHAND FOR DIVISION

The fraction $\frac{2}{3}$ is just another way of writing the division problem $2 \div 3$.

ADDING AND SUBTRACTING FRACTIONS

Adding fractions that have the same denominators is easy: Just add up the numerators and put the sum over one of the denominators. Here's an example:

$$\frac{1}{9} + \frac{2}{9} + \frac{4}{9} = \frac{1 + 2 + 4}{9} = \frac{7}{9}$$

Handle subtraction the same way:

$$\frac{7}{9} - \frac{4}{9} - \frac{2}{9} = \frac{7 - 4 - 2}{9} = \frac{1}{9}$$

When you're asked to add or subtract fractions with *different* denominators, you need to fiddle around with them so that they end up with the *same* denominator. To do this, you need to multiply at least one of the fractions by a number that will change the denominator without changing the value of the fraction. There is only one number that will do this: 1. Here's an example:

$$\frac{3}{4} + \frac{1}{3} =$$

$$\left(\frac{3}{4}\right)\left(\frac{3}{3}\right) + \left(\frac{1}{3}\right)\left(\frac{4}{4}\right) =$$

$$\frac{9}{12} + \frac{4}{12} =$$

$$\frac{13}{12}$$

Analysis:

The fractions $\frac{3}{3}$ and $\frac{4}{4}$ both equal 1. Multiplying the terms of our problem by these fractions doesn't change the value of the terms, but it does put them in a form that's easier to handle.

MULTIPLYING FRACTIONS

There's nothing tricky about multiplying fractions. All you have to do is place the product of the numerators over the product of the denominators. Here's an example:

$$\frac{5}{7} \times \frac{1}{3} = \frac{5}{21}$$

Joe Bloggs forgets that when one fraction is multiplied by another fraction, the product is *smaller* than either of the original fractions. Here's an example:

$$\frac{1}{2} \times \frac{1}{4} = \frac{1}{8}$$

DIVIDING FRACTIONS

Division of fractions is just like multiplication of fractions, with one crucial difference: Turn the second fraction upside down (that is, put its denominator over its numerator) before you multiply. Here's an example:

$$\frac{4}{5} \div \frac{2}{3} = \frac{4}{5} \times \frac{3}{2} = \frac{12}{10} = \frac{6}{5}$$

ETS will sometimes try to send you into a panic by giving you problems involving fractions whose numerators or denominators are themselves fractions. These problems look intimidating, but if you're careful you won't have any trouble with them. All you have to do is remember what we said about a fraction being shorthand for division. Here's an example:

$$\frac{\frac{6}{1}}{\frac{1}{3}} = \frac{\frac{6}{1}}{\frac{1}{3}} = \frac{6}{1} \div \frac{1}{3} = \frac{6}{1} \times \frac{3}{1} = \frac{18}{1} = 18$$

REDUCING FRACTIONS

Adding and multiplying fractions can leave you with unwieldy fractions that are difficult to work with. Most such fractions can be whittled down to more manageable proportions by eliminating factors that are common to both numerator and denominator. This process is known as *reducing*.

To reduce a fraction, simply express the numerator and denominator as the products of their factors. Then cross out, or "cancel," factors that are common to both. Here's an example:

$$\frac{16}{20} = \frac{2 \times 2 \times 2 \times 2}{2 \times 2 \times 5} = \frac{\cancel{2} \times \cancel{2} \times 2 \times 2}{\cancel{2} \times \cancel{2} \times 5} = \frac{2 \times 2}{5} = \frac{4}{5}$$

You can achieve the same result by dividing numerator and denominator by the largest factor that is common to both. In the example you just worked, 4 is a factor of both the numerator and the denominator. That is, both the numerator and the denominator can be divided evenly (without remainder) by 4. Doing this yields the much more manageable fraction $\frac{4}{5}$.

When you confront GRE math problems involving big fractions, always reduce them before doing anything else. Sometimes reduction alone will lead you to ETS's answer.

CONVERTING MIXED NUMBERS INTO FRACTIONS

A mixed number is a number that is represented as a whole number and a fraction, like this: $2\frac{3}{4}$. In most cases on the GRE, you should get rid of mixed fractions by converting them to fractions. How do you do this? By converting the integer to a fraction with the same denominator as the original fraction and then adding the two fractions. To convert the example just given, we rewrite 2 as $\frac{8}{4}$, a fraction that equals 2 and has the same denominator as $\frac{3}{4}$. Then we simply add, as follows:

$$\frac{8}{4} + \frac{3}{4} = \frac{11}{4}$$

Our result, $\frac{11}{4}$, is the same number as $2\frac{3}{4}$. The only difference is that $\frac{11}{4}$ is easier to work with in math problems.

WHICH FRACTION IS LARGER?

ETS loves problems in which you are asked to compare two fractions and decide which is larger. These problems are a snap if you know what to do. Here's an example:

Which of the following fractions is larger?

$$\frac{3}{7} \qquad \frac{7}{14}$$

Here's how to crack it:

The first thing to do is find a common denominator. The easiest one is 14, which equals 2×7. The second fraction already has 14 as its denominator. We can give the first fraction this same denominator by multiplying it by $\frac{2}{2}$, which equals 1.

Multiplying $\frac{3}{7}$ by $\frac{2}{2}$ yields $\frac{6}{14}$. (If you don't see why, go back and read the section on multiplying fractions.) Now take another look at our problem:

Which of the following fractions is larger?

$$\frac{6}{14} \qquad \frac{7}{14}$$

You should have no trouble seeing that the second fraction is larger.

USING CROSS-MULTIPLICATION TO COMPARE FRACTIONS

In the problem we just solved, we could have achieved the same result by employing a shortcut method called cross-multiplication. In cross-multiplication, you multiply the denominator of each fraction by the numerator of the other. Then you compare your two products. Here's the same problem solved through cross-multiplication:

$$42 \nwarrow \qquad \nearrow 49$$
$$\frac{3}{7} \times \frac{7}{14}$$

$$49 > 42 \text{ so } \frac{7}{14} > \frac{3}{7}$$

Analysis:
Multiplying the first denominator by the second numerator gives us 49; multiplying the second denominator by the first numerator gives us 42. Forty-nine is bigger than 42, so the second fraction, $\frac{7}{14}$, is bigger than the first, $\frac{3}{7}$.

In cross-multiplying, always work from bottom to top, in the direction of the arrows in the problem we just solved. Working in the other direction will give you the wrong answer.

COMPARING MORE THAN TWO FRACTIONS

You will sometimes be asked to compare more than two fractions. On such problems, don't waste time trying to find a common denominator for all of them. Simply compare two of the fractions at a time. Here's an example:

Which of the following fractions is smallest?

$$\frac{4}{7} \qquad \frac{5}{8} \qquad \frac{8}{11}$$

Here's how to crack it:
Compare the first two fractions and eliminate the larger one; compare the remaining fraction with the next in line and eliminate the larger one; compare the remaining fraction with the next in line and eliminate the larger, and so on, until you're left with ETS's answer.

In this case, the smallest of the three fractions is $\frac{4}{7}$.

THE SMALLER THE FRACTION, THE BIGGER THE DENOMINATOR

Which is larger, $\frac{2}{21}$ or $\frac{2}{22}$? Joe Bloggs knows that 22 is larger than 21, so he's inclined to say that $\frac{2}{22}$ is larger than $\frac{2}{21}$, especially when he's feeling careless. **Don't make the same mistake.**

BE CAREFUL

The most common source of errors on GRE fraction problems is carelessness. You'll see problems in which finding ETS's answer will require you to perform several of the steps or operations we've described. Keep your wits about you and remember that the goal of all these steps and operations is to *simplify* the fractions.

DRILL 3
Check your answers on page 335.

1. Reduce the following fractions:

   (A) $\frac{5}{20}$ (B) $\frac{18}{24}$ (C) $\frac{12}{36}$ (D) $\frac{45}{30}$ (E) $\frac{78}{48}$ (F) $\frac{4}{9}$

2. Solve the following problems:

   (A) $\frac{1}{6} + \frac{3}{10} =$ (B) $\frac{5}{8} - \frac{3}{4} =$ (C) $\frac{4}{5} \times \frac{5}{8} =$

   (D) $\frac{1}{3} + \frac{6}{8} =$ (E) $\dfrac{\frac{1}{4}}{3}$ (F) $\dfrac{\frac{1}{5}}{\frac{2}{15}}$

3. Which fraction is larger?

   (A) $\frac{8}{9}$ (B) $\frac{7}{8}$

4. Convert $7\frac{1}{3}$ to an unmixed fraction.

5. How many halves are there in the number 6?

DECIMALS

Decimals make some people (Joe Bloggs, for example) feel panicky. Learn what follows and you won't have any trouble.

DECIMALS ARE JUST FRACTIONS

Decimals and fractions are two different ways of expressing the same thing. Every decimal can be written as a fraction; every fraction can be written as a decimal. For example, the decimal .35 can be written as the fraction $\frac{35}{100}$. These two expressions, .35 and $\frac{35}{100}$, have exactly the same value.

To turn a fraction into its decimal equivalent, all you have to do is divide the numerator by the denominator. Here, for example, is how you would find the decimal equivalent of $\frac{3}{4}$:

$$\frac{3}{4} = 3 \div 4 = 4\overline{)3.00} = 0.75$$

$$\begin{array}{r} 0.75 \\ 4\overline{)3.00} \\ \underline{2.8} \\ 20 \\ \underline{20} \end{array}$$

YOU DON'T NEED A DECIMAL POINT TO HAVE A DECIMAL

All the following numbers are decimals:

$$.5 \qquad 12 \qquad 0.8 \qquad -3 \qquad -32.908$$

You may be unaccustomed to thinking of some of these numbers as decimals, but all of them could be written with decimal points. For example, 12 could be written as 12.0; 12 and 12.0 have exactly the same value.

You don't usually need to think about the missing decimal point with a number like 12. But when you add and subtract decimals, you will need to remember where it would go if it were there.

ADDING AND SUBTRACTING DECIMALS

No problem. Simply line up the decimal points and proceed as you would if the decimal points weren't there. If the decimal points are missing from the numbers you need to add or subtract, put them in, at least mentally. If you like, you can make all your numbers line up evenly by adding zeros to the right of the ones

that need them. Here, for example, is how you would add the decimals 34.5, 87, 123.456, and 0.98:

$$
\begin{array}{r}
34.5 \\
87 \\
123.456 \\
+\ \ \ 0.98 \\
\hline
245.936
\end{array}
$$

Here's the same thing again, with zeros added:

$$
\begin{array}{r}
34.500 \\
87.000 \\
123.456 \\
+\ \ \ 0.980 \\
\hline
245.936
\end{array}
$$

Subtraction works the same way:

$$
\begin{array}{r}
17.66 \\
-\ \ \ 3.2 \\
\hline
14.46
\end{array}
$$

MULTIPLYING DECIMALS

The only tricky part is remembering where to put the decimal point. Handle the multiplication as you would with integers. Then position the decimal point according to this simple two-step rule:

1. Count the total number of digits to the right of the decimal points in the numbers you are multiplying. If you are multiplying 3.451 and 8.9, for example, you have a total of four digits to the right of the decimal points.

2. Place the decimal point in your solution so that you have the same number of digits to the right of it. Here's what you get when you multiply the numbers above:

$$
\begin{array}{r}
3.451 \\
\times\ 8.9 \\
\hline
30.7139
\end{array}
$$

Except for placing the decimal point, we did exactly what we would have done if we had been multiplying 3,451 and 89:

$$
\begin{array}{r}
3,451 \\
\times \quad 89 \\
\hline
307,139
\end{array}
$$

DIVIDING DECIMALS

Before you can divide decimals, you have to convert the divisor into a whole number. (In the division problem $10 \div 2 = 5$, the 10 is the dividend, the 2 is the divisor, and the 5 is the quotient.) This is easy to do. All you have to do is move the decimal point all the way to the right. You must then move the decimal point in the dividend the same number of spaces to the right. Here's an example:

Problem:
Divide 24 by 1.25

Here's how to crack it:
First, set up the problem as you would any division problem:

$$1.25\,\overline{)24}$$

Now start moving decimal points. The divisor, 1.25, has two digits to the right of the decimal point. To turn 1.25 into a whole number, therefore, we need to move the decimal point two spaces to the right. Doing so turns 1.25 into 125.

Because we've moved the decimal point in the divisor two places, we also need to move the decimal point in the dividend two places. This turns 24 into 2,400. Here's what we're left with:

$$125\,\overline{)2,400}$$

Now all we have to do to find our answer is complete the division problem.

$$
\begin{array}{r}
19.2 \\
125\,\overline{)2,400.0} \\
-\ 125 \\
\hline
1150 \\
1125 \\
\hline
25.0 \\
25.0 \\
\hline
0 \\
=\ 19.2
\end{array}
$$

The answer is 19.2. The decimal point in the quotient goes directly above the decimal point in the dividend.

COMPARING DECIMALS

Which is larger, 0.00099 or 0.001? ETS loves this sort of problem, and Joe Bloggs hates it. You'll never go wrong, though, if you do what we teach our students to do:

1. Line up the numbers on their decimal points

2. Fill in the missing zeroes.

Here's how to answer the question we just asked. First, line up the two numbers on their decimal points:

$$0.00099$$

$$0.001$$

Now fill in the missing zeros:

$$0.00099$$

$$0.00100$$

Can you tell which number is larger? Of course you can. 0.00100 is larger than 0.00099, just as 100 is larger than 99.

CONVERT DECIMALS TO FRACTIONS

Fractions are often easier to work with than decimals are. When you're stumped on a decimal problem, ask yourself whether finding ETS's answer would be easier if you converted the decimals to fractions. Wouldn't you rather find the square of $\frac{1}{4}$ than the square of 0.25? (If the answer choices are decimals, stick with decimals in your computations.)

DECIMALS AND MONEY

Money is based on the decimal system. $5.98 is a decimal meaning 5 dollars plus $\frac{98}{100}$ of a dollar. What's $0.25? It's a quarter of a dollar, just as 0.25 equals $\frac{1}{4}$. When you find yourself stuck on a decimal problem, reminding yourself of the money connection may help you regain your bearings.

DRILL 4

Check your answers on page 335.

1. Add 1.045 to 5.12

2. Subtract 10.54 from 15.82

3. Multiply 22.65 by 0.5

4. Divide 22.65 by 0.5

5. Reduce $\dfrac{5.76}{3}$

6. What is four one-thousandths plus three tenths?

7. Which is larger, .002 or .0015?

8. Convert $\dfrac{13}{2}$ to a decimal.

9. Convert .125 to a fraction.

10. Approximate $\dfrac{2.00465}{3.98136}$ (Don't use your pencil.)

PERCENTAGES

So far we've said that a fraction is another way of representing division and that a decimal is the same thing as a fraction. Well, a percentage is also another way of representing division and is also the same thing as a fraction and a decimal. A percentage is just a handy way of expressing a fraction whose denominator is 100.

PERCENTAGES, FRACTIONS, AND DECIMALS

Percent means "per 100" or "out of 100" or "divided by 100." If your best friend finds a dollar and gives you 50 cents, your friend has given you 50 cents out of 100, or $\frac{50}{100}$ of a dollar, or 50 percent of a dollar. Here are two more examples:

$$25 \text{ percent} = \frac{25}{100} = 0.25$$

$$0.3 \text{ percent} = \frac{0.3}{100} = 0.003$$

And another example:

Problem:
What is 30 percent of 200?

Here's how to crack it:
To find 30 percent of 200, multiply 200 by 0.3, like this:

$$0.3 \times 200 = 60$$

That's the answer. 30 percent of 200 is 60.

CONVERTING PERCENTAGES TO FRACTIONS

Converting percentages to fractions is easy. Just make the percentage the numerator in a fraction whose denominator is 100, then reduce. Here's an example:

$$40 \text{ percent} = \frac{40}{100} = \frac{4}{10} = \frac{2}{5}$$

CONVERTING FRACTIONS TO PERCENTAGES

This is easy, too. Simply divide the numerator by the denominator and move the decimal point two places to the right. Here's an example:

Problem:
Express $\frac{4}{5}$ as a percentage.

Here's how to crack it:
First, divide 4 by 5:

$$
\begin{array}{r}
0.8 \\
5\overline{)4.0} \\
\underline{4.0} \\
0 \\
= 0.8
\end{array}
$$

Now move the decimal point two places to the right. This turns 0.8 into 80. That's right: $\frac{4}{5} = 0.8 = 80$ percent.

CONVERTING PERCENTAGES TO DECIMALS

No sweat. Move the decimal point two places to the *left*. Thus 80 percent becomes .80 or 0.8. Furthermore: 25 percent is the same as the decimal 0.25; 50 percent is the same as the decimal 0.5; 100 percent is the same as 1.00 or 1.

CONVERTING DECIMALS TO PERCENTAGES

Just move the decimal point two places to the *right*. This turns 0.8 back into 80 percent, and 0.25 back into 25 percent, and 0.5 back into 50 percent, and 1 back into 100 percent.

MEMORIZE THIS

You should memorize these percentage-decimal-fraction equivalents. Knowing them will come in handy on the GRE:

$$0.01 = \frac{1}{100} = 1 \text{ percent}$$

$$0.1 = \frac{1}{10} = 10 \text{ percent}$$

$$0.2 = \frac{1}{5} = 20 \text{ percent}$$

$$0.25 = \frac{1}{4} = 25 \text{ percent}$$

$$0.5 = \frac{1}{2} = 50 \text{ percent}$$

$$0.75 = \frac{3}{4} = 75 \text{ percent}$$

DRILL 5

You can check your answers on page 325.

1. What is 30 percent of 200?

2. 2 is what percent of 4?

3. 2.2 is 20 percent of what number?

4. 10 percent of 24 equals 20 percent of what?

5. 20 percent of 25 percent of x is 10. What is x?

RATIOS

Ratios, like fractions, percentages, and decimals, are just another way of representing division. Don't let them make you nervous.

EVERY FRACTION IS A RATIO, AND VICE VERSA

A fraction is a ratio between its numerator and its denominator. Every ratio, furthermore, can be expressed as a fraction. The ratio 1:2 ("1 to 2") means exactly the same thing as the fraction $\frac{1}{2}$, or 1 divided by 2, or 50 percent, or 0.5.

On the GRE, you'll see ratios expressed in these different ways:

1. $\frac{x}{y}$

2. the ratio of x to y

3. x is to y

4. $x:y$

TREAT A RATIO LIKE A FRACTION

Anything you can do to a fraction you can also do to a ratio. You can cross-multiply, find common denominators, reduce, and so on.

COUNT THE PARTS

If you have 3 coins in your pocket and the ratio of pennies to nickels is 2:1, how many pennies and nickels are there? That's easy. There are 2 pennies and 1 nickel.

If you have 24 coins in your pocket and the ratio of pennies to nickels is 2:1, how many pennies and nickels are there? That's harder. You have 16 pennies and 8 nickels.

How did we find that answer? Easy. We counted "parts." The ratio 2:1 contains 3 parts: there are 2 parts pennies for every 1 part nickels, making 3 parts altogether. To find out how many of our 24 coins were pennies, we simply divided 24 by the number of parts (3) and then multiplied the result by each part of the ratio. Dividing 24 by 3 yields 8. That is, each of the 3 parts in our ratio consists of 8 coins. Two of the parts are pennies; at 8 coins per part, that makes 16 pennies. One of the parts is nickels; that makes 8 nickels.

Here's another example:

18. At a camp for boys and girls, the ratio of the girls to boys is 5:3. If the camp's enrollment is 160, how many of the children are boys?

    (A) 20
    (B) 36
    (C) 45
    (D) 60
    (E) 100

Here's how to crack it:

A ratio of 5:3 means 8 parts. To find out how many children are in each part, we divide the total enrollment by the number of parts. Dividing 160 by 8 yields 20. That means each part is 20 children. Three of the parts are boys, which means there are 60 boys. ETS's answer is choice D.

One reason Joe Bloggs has trouble with this problem is that he doesn't pay attention to which half of the ratio is boys and which half is girls. Don't be careless. ETS often makes subtle changes in wording; the question at the end of a word problem may change the order of the elements that were introduced earlier. Pay attention.

PROPORTIONS

The GRE often contains problems in which you are given two proportional, or equal, ratios from which one piece of information is missing. These questions take a given relationship, or ratio, and project it onto a larger or smaller scale. Here's an example:

8. If 10 baskets contain a total of 50 eggs, how many eggs would 7 baskets contain?

    (A) 10
    (B) 17
    (C) 35
    (D) 40
    (E) 50

Here's how to crack it:

In this problem, you are given two equal ratios, one of which is missing one piece of information. To find ETS's answer, make a quick diagram:

10 (baskets)   7 (baskets)
50 (eggs)   *x* (eggs)

Because you can treat ratios exactly like fractions, you can find the missing element by cross-multiplying:

$$10x \qquad\qquad 350$$
$$\frac{10}{50} \diagdown \frac{7}{x}$$

$$10x = 350$$
$$x = 35$$

ETS's answer is 35. (Note that we could have made our cross-multiplication simpler by reducing $\frac{10}{50}$ to $\frac{1}{5}$ before cross-multiplying.)

DRILL 6

Here's a chart that illustrates how fractions, decimals, and percentages all fit together. You fill in the blanks. Check your answers on page 336.

Fraction	Decimal	Percent	Ratio
$\frac{1}{2}$	0.5	50%	1:2
$\frac{1}{3}$			
			2:3
		25%	
	0.75		
$\frac{1}{5}$			
		40%	
	0.6		
$\frac{4}{5}$			
			1:6
		12.5%	

AVERAGES

The average (arithmetic mean) of a set of numbers is the total value of all the numbers divided by the number of numbers in the set. The average of the set {1, 2, 3, 4, 5, 6, 7} is the total of the numbers ($1 + 2 + 3 + 4 + 5 + 6 + 7$, or 28) divided by the number of numbers in the set (which is 7). Dividing 28 by 7 gives us 4. Thus 4 is the average of the set.

ETS always refers to an average as an "average (arithmetic mean)." This confusing parenthetical remark is meant to keep you from being confused by other kinds of averages, such as medians and modes. You'll be less confused if you simply ignore the parenthetical remark. Medians and modes are never tested on the GRE.

WHAT'S THE TOTAL?

Average problems will require you to do some real math work. Don't try to solve them all at once. Do them piece by piece. The critical formula to keep in mind is this:

$$\text{Average} = \frac{\text{the sum of the numbers being averaged}}{\text{the number of elements}}$$

You are always going to need the sum of the numbers being averaged: the *total* amount, the *total* height, the *total* weight, the *total* number of petals, the *total* of the scores, the *total* distance. Averaging questions are always really about *totals*. In fact, an average is just another way of expressing a total; an average is the total divided by the number of elements.

In averaging problems, you should always find the total first, before you do anything else. For example, suppose that a problem states that the average of 4 test scores is 80. What should you do first? Find the total, which is 4×80, or 320. Now suppose that you are told that two of these scores are 90 and 95. That adds up to 185, which means that the total of the *other* two scores is 135, which means that *their* average is 67.5.

THE DEMOCRACY OF AVERAGES

Every element in an average is just as important as every other, even if two or more of the elements are identical. For example, to find the average of 5, 5, 5, 5, and 20, you add $5 + 5 + 5 + 5 + 20$ (which is 40) and divide by 5 (which yields an average of 8). You *don't* add $5 + 20$ and divide by 2; nor do you add $5 + 20$ and divide by 5.

Joe Bloggs always forgets this. He is especially confused when a new element is added to a set that has already been averaged. For example, suppose

you take 2 tests and earn scores of 70 and 80. What's your average score? It's 75. Now suppose you take a third test and score another 70. Does your average remain 75? No, it does not. The new average is $73\frac{1}{3}$.

Joe Bloggs also forgets to count zero when calculating the average of a set of numbers that includes 0. What's the average of 0, 0, 0, and 4? Joe Bloggs thinks it's 4. It's not; it's 1.

WATCH OUT FOR MISSING INFORMATION

ETS often turns an easy averaging problem into a difficult averaging problem by leaving out certain information. Here's an example:

20. The average test score earned by a group of students is 80. If 40 percent of the students have an average score of 70, what is the average score of the remaining 60 percent?

(A) $70\frac{1}{3}$

(B) 80

(C) $86\frac{2}{3}$

(D) 90

(E) 95

Here's how to crack it:

There's a seemingly important piece of information missing from this problem: the number of students in the "group." Since this value is unknown, many students try to solve the problem by setting up a complex algebraic equation: $80 = (x + y + \ldots)$. That's about how far they get before giving up.

What should you do to solve the problem? Easy: Make something up. That's right, simply decide for yourself how many students are in the group. Because we're dealing with percentages, 100 is an easy number to work with. And because all our percentages are multiples of 10, we can make it even easier by simply using 10. So we'll assume that our group contains 10 students. Four of those 10 (40 percent of 10) students have an average score of 70; we're supposed to determine the average score of the remaining 6.

The first thing we need to do (now that we've turned it back into an easy averaging problem) is to find the total. If the average score of 10 students is 80, what's their total score? It's 800. Four of the students have an average score of 70, which means that their total score is 280. What's the total score of the remaining 6 students? That's easy. It's 800 − 280, or 520. What's their average score (which is what we're looking for)? It's 520 ÷ 6, or $86\frac{2}{3}$. ETS's answer is C.

UP OR DOWN

Averages are very predictable. You should make sure you know automatically what happens to them in certain situations. For example, suppose that you take 3 tests and earn an average score of 90. Now you take a fourth test. What do you know? The following:

1. If the average goes up as a result of the fourth score, then you know that the fourth score was higher than 90.

2. If the average stays the same as a result of the fourth score, then you know that the fourth score was exactly 90.

3. If the average goes down as a result of the fourth score, then you know that the fourth score was less than 90.

DRILL 7

Check your answers on page 336.

1. What is the average (arithmetic mean) of the numbers 24, 24, 26, 28, and 40?

2. If the average of 5 numbers is 20, what is their total?

3. If the average of 5 positive integers is 20, what is the largest that any of the numbers could be?

4. If the average of 11, 17, 15, 28, and x is 19.6, what is the value of x?

5. Sam's average score for 4 math tests was 80 out of a possible 100. If his scores on 2 of the tests were 65 and 70, what is the lowest that either of his other scores could have been?

EXPONENTS AND RADICALS

If you've been avoiding math courses for the last few years, you'll need to brush up on exponents and radicals. They aren't hard, but it's easy to forget the details of how they work. Know them cold and you'll save points on the GRE.

WHAT ARE EXPONENTS?

Many numbers can be expressed as the product of one factor multiplied by itself a number of times. For example, 16 can be expressed as $2 \times 2 \times 2 \times 2$. We can also express the same thing using a sort of mathematical shorthand called exponents. Instead of writing $2 \times 2 \times 2 \times 2$ we can write 2^4. The little 4 is called an exponent and the big 2 is called a base. (You don't need to know these terms except to follow our discussion.) The entire expression, called "2 to the fourth power," refers to the number that is the product of a multiplication in which 2 is a factor 4 times—in other words, 16.

MULTIPLICATION WITH EXPONENTS

There's nothing easier than multiplying two or more numbers with the same base. All you have to do is add up the exponents. For example: $2^2 \times 2^4 = 2^{2+4} = 2^6$. Be careful, though.

Joe Bloggs erroneously thinks that this rule also applies to addition. It does not: $2^2 + 2^4$ *does not equal* 2^6. There's no quick and easy method of adding numbers with exponents.

DIVISION WITH EXPONENTS

Since division is just multiplication in reverse, dividing two or more numbers with the same base is easy, too. All you have to do is subtract the exponents. For example: $2^6 \div 2^2 = 2^{6-2} = 2^4$.

Once again, don't make the Bloggsian error of assuming this same shortcut applies to subtraction of numbers with exponents. It doesn't.

RAISING A POWER TO A POWER

This is easy. Simply multiply the exponents. Here's an example:

$$(4^5)^2 =$$
$$4^{5 \times 2} =$$
$$4^{10}$$

DISTRIBUTE POWERS THROUGH PARENTHESES

In solving problems involving exponents, it's extremely important to pay careful attention to terms within parentheses. When an exponent appears on the outside of a parenthetical expression, you must be very careful to distribute the exponent to every term within the parenthetical expression. For example, $(3x)^2 = 9x^2$, not $3x^2$. Joe Bloggs forgets to square the 3. And don't forget the denominators of fractions within parentheses. $\left(\frac{3}{2}\right)^2 = \frac{9}{4}$, not $\frac{9}{2}$.

THE PECULIAR BEHAVIOR OF EXPONENTS

1. Raising a number greater than 1 to a power greater than 1 results in a *bigger* number. For example, $2^2 = 4$.

2. Raising a fraction between 0 and 1 to a power greater than 1 results in a *smaller* number. For example, $\left(\frac{1}{2}\right)^2 = \frac{1}{4}$.

3. A negative number raised to an even power becomes *positive*. For example, $(-2)^2 = 4$.

4. A negative number raised to an odd power remains *negative*. For example, $(-2)^3 = -8$.

BIG NUMBERS

You should have a rough feel for the relative size of exponential numbers. Those little exponents can deceive you. For example, 2^5 is twice as large as 2^4. And 2^{10} is more than 10 times as large as 10^2.

WHAT, ME WORRY?

Don't worry about negative exponents (for example, 10^{-2}). You won't see them on the GRE.

RADICALS

The sign $\sqrt{}$ indicates the square root of a number. For example, $\sqrt{2}$. The sign $\sqrt[3]{}$ indicates the cube root of a number. For example, $\sqrt[3]{2}$.

If $x^2 = 16$, then $x = \pm 4$. You must be especially careful to remember this on quantitative comparison questions. But when ETS asks you for the value $\sqrt{16}$, or the square root of any number, you are being asked for the *positive* root only. Although squaring -5 will yield 25, just as squaring 5 will, when ETS asks for $\sqrt{25}$, the only answer it is looking for is 5.

KNOW THESE TWO RULES

There are only two rules concerning radicals that you need to know for the GRE:

1. $\sqrt{x}\sqrt{y} = \sqrt{xy}$. For example, $\sqrt{2}\sqrt{3} = \sqrt{6}$

2. $\sqrt{\dfrac{x}{y}} = \dfrac{\sqrt{x}}{\sqrt{y}}$. For example, $\sqrt{\dfrac{5}{16}} = \dfrac{\sqrt{5}}{\sqrt{16}} = \dfrac{\sqrt{5}}{4}$

Rule 1 also works in reverse. That is, a large radical can be broken down into its factors, which may be easier to manipulate. For example, $\sqrt{32} = \sqrt{16}\sqrt{2} = 4\sqrt{2}$.

KNOW THESE FIVE VALUES

To use our techniques, you'll need to have memorized the following values. You should be able to recite them without hestitation:

1. $\sqrt{1} = 1$

2. $\sqrt{2} = 1.4$

3. $\sqrt{3} = 1.7$

4. $\sqrt{4} = 2$

5. $\sqrt{5} = 2.2$

DRILL 8

Check your answers on page 336.

1. $3^4 \cdot 3^2 =$

2. If $x = 3$, what is $(2x)^3$?

3. If $x = 4$, what is $(x^2)^3$?

4. If $4^2 + 3^2 = x^2$, what is x?

5. Approximate $3\sqrt{3}$

GRE ALGEBRA

The GRE requires you to do very little real algebra. When you first look at the test, you will probably think that you will need to do more. You will be wrong. *The algebra methods you learned in junior high school and high school will often mislead you on the GRE.*

You should never try to set up an equation and work through to an answer on the GRE. ETS's scoring machines don't care whether you set up an equation properly. All they care about is which space you blacken on your answer sheet.

So relax. You need to know very little algebra to do well on the GRE. All you will need to know is what we call GRE Algebra, a small group of simple rules and concepts that (in combination with techniques we will teach you later) will enable you to solve even the most difficult "algebra" problems on the GRE.

UNIMPORTANT TERMINOLOGY

You won't need to know these words on the GRE, but you will need to know them to follow this book. After you finish the book, you can forget them:

Variable: A letter that represents a number or numbers.

Term: If you think of an equation as a sentence, a term is the equivalent of a word. The equation $3x^2 + 4y = 6y$, for example, contains three terms: $3x^2$, $4y$, and $6y$.

Coefficient: A number multiplied by a variable. In the term $3x^2$, 3 is the coefficient.

Expression: An expression is the algebraic equivalent of a phrase. It is a combination of terms and mathematical operations. For example, $3x^2 + 4y$ is an expression.

Binomial: An expression containing two terms.

Trinomial: An expression containing three terms.

Polynomial: A binomial, trinomial, or any other expression containing two or more terms.

SIMPLIFYING EXPRESSIONS

ETS is very predictable. **Because of this, we can tell you that on any problem that contains an expression that can be factored, you should always factor that expression.** If, for example, you encounter a problem containing the expression $4x + 4y$, you should immediately factor it, yielding the expression $4(x + y)$.

Similarly, whenever you find an expression that has been factored, you should immediately *un*factor it, by multiplying it out according to the distributive law. In other words, if a problem contains the expression $4(x + y)$, you should unfactor it, yielding the expression $4x + 4y$.

Why this game of musical factors? Because the key to finding ETS's answer on such problems is usually nothing trickier than factoring or unfactoring various expressions. As we have said, ETS isn't up to anything very complicated. And it asks essentially the same questions over and over again, on test after test.

MULTIPLYING POLYNOMIALS

Multiplying polynomials can appear frighteningly complicated, but all you have to do is remember to multiply every term in the first polynomial by every term in the second. (Are you beginning to hear the long-forgotten voice of your ninth-grade algebra teacher?)

Here's an example:

$$(x + 4)(x + 3) = (x + 4)(x + 3)$$
$$= (x \cdot x) + (x \cdot 3) + (4 \cdot x) + (4 \cdot 3)$$
$$= x^2 + 3x + 4x + 12$$
$$= x^2 + 7x + 12$$

KNOW THESE TWO EXPRESSIONS

There are two expressions that appear over and over again on the GRE. You should know them cold, in both their factored and unfactored forms. Here they are:

Expression 1:
   Factored form: $x^2 - y^2$
   Unfactored form: $(x + y)(x - y)$
Expression 2:
   Factored form: $(x + y)^2$
   Unfactored form: $x^2 + 2xy + y^2$

Here's an example of the form in which you might find Expression 1 on the GRE:

$$\frac{4x^2 - 4}{x - 1}$$

Here's how to crack it:
What do you do with this expression? Factor it. Pull a 4 out of the numerator, to give you $4(x^2 - 1)$. Now because we told you to be on the lookout for it, you should realize that the expression $(x^2 - 1)$ follows the form $(x^2 - y^2)$ and can

therefore be written in factored form as follows: $4(x + 1)(x - 1)$. Now go back and rewrite the original expression:

Original	Factored Form
$\dfrac{4x^2 - 4}{x - 1}$	$\dfrac{4(x + 1)(x - 1)}{(x - 1)}$

There's one more thing to do. You can simplify the factored form of our expression by canceling the common factor, $(x - 1)$ in the numerator and denominator. This means that our final, fully factored and simplified form of the original expression is simply $4(x + 1)$.

COMBINE AND CONQUER

You will save yourself a lot of trouble if you simplify complicated algebraic expressions by combining similar terms. Here's an example of a complicated algebraic expression:

$$(4x^2 + 4x + 2) + (3 - 7x) - (5 - 3x)$$

Now that's a big, complicated algebraic expression. But look what happens to it when you combine similar terms:

$$(4x^2 + 4x + 2) + (3 - 7x) - (5 - 3x) =$$
$$4x^2 + 4x + 2 + 3 - 7x - 5 + 3x =$$
$$4x^2 + (4x - 7x + 3x) + (2 + 3 - 5) =$$
$$4x^2$$

Given what we started out with, you can't get much simpler than $4x^2$.

SIMULTANEOUS EQUATIONS

ETS will sometimes give you two equations and ask you to use them to find the value of a given expression. In such situations, you don't need any math-class algebra; all you have to do to find ETS's answer is to add or subtract the two equations.

Here's an example:

Problem:
If $5x + 4y = 6$ and $4x + 3y = 5$, then $x + y = ?$

Here's how to crack it:

In math class you would be expected to do something tricky and algebraic such as "solve for *x*" and "solve for *y*." You'd find ETS's answer eventually, if you didn't make any careless errors.

On the GRE, there's an easier way. All you have to do is add the two equations together or subtract one from the other. Here's what we get when we add them:

$$5x + 4y = 6$$
$$+ 4x + 3y = 5$$
$$\overline{9x + 7y = 11}$$

A dead end. So let's try subtraction:

$$5x + 4y = 6$$
$$- 4x + 3y = 5$$
$$\overline{x + y = 1}$$

Eureka. The value of the expression (x + y) is exactly what we're looking for. We found the answer easily, and we didn't use any algebra.

On the GRE, you will never need to use math-class algebra to solve simultaneous equations. Simply add or subtract them exactly as they are written. We've never seen a simultaneous-equation problem on the GRE that couldn't be solved this way.

EQUATIONS SET TO ZERO

ETS loves 0, because it has so many unique properties. There are more than a few math problems on the GRE whose solutions turn on one of these properties.

One of the most important properties of 0 is its ability to annihilate other numbers. Any number multiplied by 0 equals 0. This fact gives you an important piece of information. For example, if you are told that $ab = 0$, then you know without a doubt that either a or b equals 0. You can use this same fact to solve some equations on the GRE. Here's an example:

Problem:

What are all the values of *y* for which $y(y + 5) = 0$?

Here's how to crack it:

In order for $y(y + 5)$ to equal 0, either *y* or $(y + 5)$, or both of them, has to equal 0. All you need to do to solve this problem, therefore, is to determine what you need to do to each element in order to make it equal 0. What would *y* have to be

for y to equal 0? Why, it would have to be 0, of course. What would y have to be for $(y + 5)$ to equal 0? Why, it would have to be –5, of course. To answer the question, here are all the values of y for which $y(y + 5) = 0$: 0 and –5.

INEQUALITIES

In an equation, one expression equals another. In an inequality, one expression does not equal another. The symbol for an equation is an equal sign. Here are the symbols for inequalities:

$\neq$ is not equal to
$>$ is greater than
$<$ is less than
$\geq$ is greater than or equal to
$\leq$ is less than or equal to

You solve inequalities in virtually the same way you solve equations. You can factor, unfactor, simplify, and so on. There's only one peculiar rule that you have to remember: **If you multiply or divide both sides of an inequality by a negative number, you must remember to change the direction of the inequality symbol.**

It's easy to understand the rationale for this. To see what we mean, take a look at a simple inequality:

$$2 < 4$$

No problem here, right? Now multiply both sides of the inequality by –2. This gives us –4 on the left side and –8 on the right side. Which number is bigger, –4 or –8? You should remember that –4 is bigger. Which gives us the following inequality as the result of multiplying both sides by –2:

$$-4 > -8$$

All we did was multiply both sides by the same number, but because the number by which we multiplied was negative, we also had to switch the direction of the inequality symbol.

FUNCTIONS AND FUNNY-LOOKING SYMBOLS

You probably remember the phrase "f of x" from junior-high-school or high-school algebra. Usually written "$f(x)$," this phrase had to do with functions.

The GRE contains function problems, but you probably won't recognize them. Instead of presenting them in "$f(x)$" form, it disguises them by using

funny-looking symbols, such as ⊕, *, and #. These symbols represent arithmetic operations or series of arithmetic operations. If you remember how functions work, you can solve these problems simply by thinking of functions whenever you see the funny-looking symbols.

If you don't remember much about functions, don't worry. Just do what we tell you to do, and you shouldn't have much trouble.

In funny-looking symbol problems, the funny-looking symbol can be thought of as representing a set of operations or instructions. Here's an example:

Problem:
If $x @ y = \dfrac{x - y}{2}$, what is the value of $\dfrac{1}{3} @ \dfrac{1}{5}$?

Here's how to crack it:
The symbol @ represents a series of operations. Let's call it Bloggs. (You can refer to the funny-looking symbol in any funny-looking symbol problem as Bloggs.) The problem tells us that x Bloggs y equals the difference of x and y divided by 2. What do we do to find ETS's answer? Easy: Substitute $\dfrac{1}{3}$ and $\dfrac{1}{5}$ for x and y. This means we have to subtract $\dfrac{1}{5}$ from $\dfrac{1}{3}$. To do this, we need to find a common denominator for these two fractions; 15 will do nicely. Here's how we work it out:

$$\frac{1}{3} @ \frac{1}{5} = \frac{\dfrac{1}{3} - \dfrac{1}{5}}{2} = \frac{\dfrac{5}{15} - \dfrac{3}{15}}{2} = \frac{\dfrac{2}{15}}{2} = \frac{2}{15} \cdot \frac{1}{2} = \frac{2}{30} = \frac{1}{15}$$

WORD PROBLEMS
Almost everyone hates word problems, but they can be easy if you know how to translate them. Translating a word problem lets you express it as an equation, which is easier to manipulate. Here's a word-problem "dictionary" that will help with your translations:

Word	Equivalent Symbol
is	=
of, times, product	×
what (or any unknown value)	any variable (x, k, b)
more, sum	+
less, difference	−
ratio, quotient	÷

For GRE word problems, you should also be familiar with the following formulas:

1. distance = (rate)(time). (Note that this same formula can be rewritten in terms of any of its elements. For example, here's another way to express the same relationship: time = distance/rate.)

2. total price = (number of items)(cost per item).

3. sale price = (original price) – (% discount)(original price).

DRILL 9
Check your answers on page 337.

1. $(3x + 4)(8x - 2) =$

2. Factor or unfactor the following expressions.
    (A) $4x^2 - 9y^2$
    (B) $(2x + 2y)^2$
    (C) $25x^2 + 50xy + 25y^2$
    (D) $(4x + y)(4x - y)$

3. Simplify the following expression by combining similar terms:

    $(6x^2 + 7x - 7) - 2(3x^2 - 3x + 2) + 9$

4. If $x - y = 7$ and $-x + 2y = 3$, then $y =$

5. If $4ab = 0$, and $a > 1$, then $b =$

6. Multiply both sides of the following inequality by -2: $2x^2 - x < x + 4$

7. If $x @ y = x^2 + 3y$, what is the value of $x^2 @ 3y$?

GRE GEOMETRY

You don't need to know much about actual geometry on the GRE. We've boiled down the handful of bits and pieces that ETS actually tests.

DEGREES AND ANGLES

You should know that:

1. A circle contains 360 degrees.

2. A line (which can be thought of as a perfectly flat angle) is a 180-degree angle.

3. When two lines intersect, four angles are formed, and the sum of the angles is 360 degrees.

4. When two lines are perpendicular to each other, their intersection forms four 90-degree angles. Here is the symbol ETS uses to indicate perpendicularity: ^

5. Ninety-degree angles are also called right angles. A right angle on the GRE is identified by a little box at the intersection of the angle's arms:

FRED'S THEOREM

Fred used to teach one of our courses. Here's his theorem: When two parallel lines are cut by a third line, angles that *look* equal *are* equal. (ETS's symbol for parallel lines is //.) Because diagrams on the GRE are often *not* drawn to scale, you have to be careful in applying Fred's theorem, but the principle is useful and much easier to remember in this form than in the form in which you learned it in math class (". . . corresponding exterior angles and blah blah blah . . ."). Here's an example of a diagram to which Fred's theorem applies:

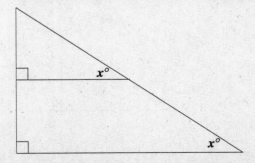

VERTICAL ANGLES

Vertical angles are the angles across from each other that are formed by the intersection of lines. Vertical angles are equal. In the drawing below, angle x is equal to angle y and angle a is equal to angle b.

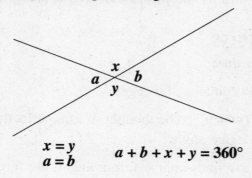

$$x = y$$
$$a = b$$

$$a + b + x + y = 360°$$

DEGREES AND TRIANGLES

Every triangle contains three interior angles, which add up to 180 degrees. You must know this. It applies to every triangle, no matter how skinny, fat, tall, or flat. **Every triangle contains 180 degrees.** Here are some examples:

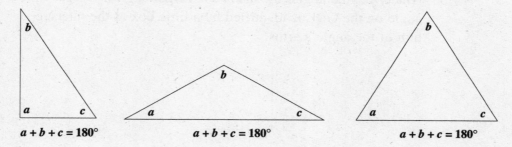

$a + b + c = 180°$ $a + b + c = 180°$ $a + b + c = 180°$

EQUILATERAL TRIANGLES

An equilateral triangle is one in which all three sides are equal in length. Because the sides are all equal, the angles are all equal, too. If they're all equal, how many degrees is each? We certainly hope you said, **Each angle in an equilateral triangle contains 60 degrees.**

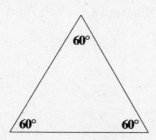

ISOSCELES TRIANGLES

An isosceles triangle is one in which two of the three sides are equal in length. This means that two of the angles are also equal, and that the third angle is not.

If you know the degree measure of any angle in an isosceles triangle, you also know the degree of measures of the other two. If one of the two equal angles measures 40 degrees, then the other one does, too. Two 40-degree angles add up to 80 degrees. Since any triangle contains 180 degrees altogether, the third angle—the only one left—must measure 100 degrees.

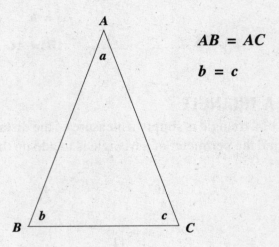

$$AB = AC$$

$$b = c$$

RIGHT TRIANGLES

A right triangle is one in which one of the angles is a right angle—a 90-degree angle. The longest side of a right triangle—the side opposite the 90-degree angle—is called the hypotenuse. On the GRE, a right triangle will always have a little box in the 90-degree corner.

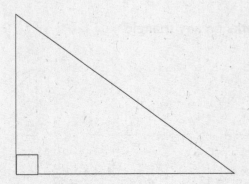

ANGLE/SIDE RELATIONSHIPS IN TRIANGLES

In any triangle, the longest side is opposite the largest interior angle; the shortest side is opposite the smallest interior angle. Furthermore, if two interior angles are equal, so are the lengths of the sides opposite them.

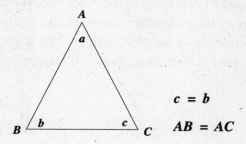

$$c = b$$

$$AB = AC$$

PERIMETER OF A TRIANGLE

The perimeter of a triangle is simply a measure of the distance around it. All you have to do to find the perimeter of a triangle is to add up the lengths of the sides.

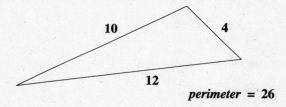

perimeter = 26

AREA OF A TRIANGLE

The area of any triangle is the altitude multiplied by the base, divided by 2:

$$area = \frac{altitude \times base}{2}$$

This formula works on any triangle.

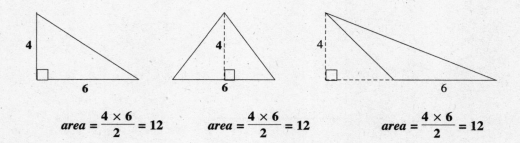

$$area = \frac{4 \times 6}{2} = 12 \qquad area = \frac{4 \times 6}{2} = 12 \qquad area = \frac{4 \times 6}{2} = 12$$

PYTHAGOREAN THEOREM

The Pythagorean theorem is probably the hardest concept you're likely to encounter in a GRE geometry problem. Brush up on what it means and you shouldn't have too much trouble.

The Pythagorean theorem applies only to right triangles, which are triangles containing one 90-degree angle. The theorem states that in such a triangle, the square of the length of the hypotenuse (the longest side—remember?) equals the sum of the squares of the lengths of the two other sides. In the right triangle below, in other words, $c^2 = a^2 + b^2$.

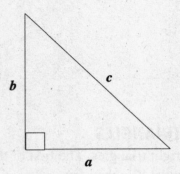

Pythagorean problems on the GRE will often involve right triangles whose sides measure 3, 4, and 5 or multiples of those numbers. Why is this? Because a 3-4-5 right triangle is the smallest one in which measures of the sides are all integers. Here are three examples of right triangles based on ETS's basic 3-4-5 right triangle:

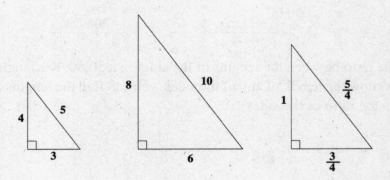

The Pythagorean theorem will sometimes be the key to solving problems where the theorem's application isn't obvious. For example, every rectangle or square contains two right triangles. This means that if you know the length and width of any rectangle or square, you also know the length of the diagonal—it's the shared hypotenuse of the hidden right triangles. Here's an example:

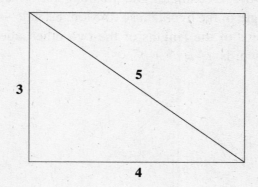

TWO SPECIAL RIGHT TRIANGLES

There are two special right triangles. The first of these is the so-called 30:60:90 right triangle. Here's what it looks like:

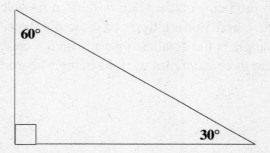

The ratio between the lengths of the sides in a 30:60:90 triangle is constant. If you know the length of any of the sides, you can find the lengths of the others. Here's the ratio of the sides:

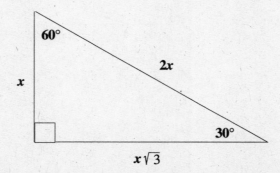

That is, if the shortest side is length *x*, then the hypotenuse is 2*x* and the remaining side is $x\sqrt{3}$. Here are two examples:

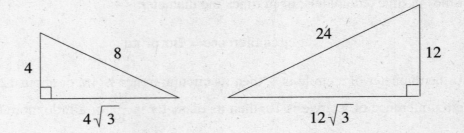

The second special right triangle is the 45:45:90. In such a triangle, the two nonhypotenuse sides are equal. The ratio between the length of either of them and that of the hypotenuse is $1:\sqrt{2}$. That is, if the length of each short leg is *x*, then the length of the hypotenuse is $x\sqrt{2}$. Here are two examples:

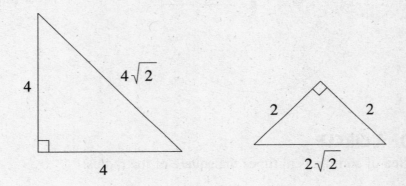

VALUE OF PI

The value of pi (π) is taught in math class as being 3.14 or even 3.14159. On the GRE, $\pi = 3$ is a close enough approximation. You don't need to be any more precise than that in order to find ETS's answer, and 3 is much easier to work with than 3.14 or 3.14159. There will probably be problems on your GRE that you will be able to solve simply by plugging in 3 for each π among the answer choices and comparing the results.

Keep in mind the relationship that π expresses. Pi is the ratio between the circumference of a circle and its diameter. When we say that π is 3, therefore, we're saying that every circle is three times as far around as it is across. **Remember this.**

CIRCUMFERENCE OF A CIRCLE

The circumference of a circle is like the perimeter of a triangle: it's the distance around the outside. The formula for finding the circumference of a circle is 2 times pi times the radius, or pi times the diameter:

$$\text{circumference} = 2\pi r \text{ or } \pi d$$

If the diameter of a circle is 4, then its circumference is 4π, or about 12. If the circumference of a circle is 10, then its diameter is $\dfrac{10}{\pi}$, or a little more than 3.

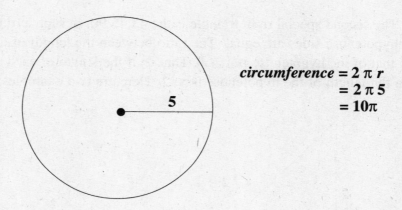

$$\begin{aligned} \textit{circumference} &= 2\,\pi\,r \\ &= 2\,\pi\,5 \\ &= 10\pi \end{aligned}$$

AREA OF A CIRCLE

the area of a circle is pi times the square of the radius:

$$\text{area} = \pi r^2$$

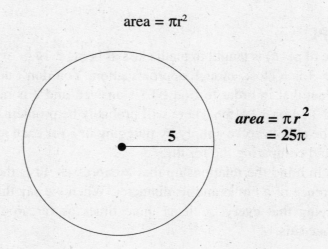

$$\begin{aligned} \textit{area} &= \pi\,r^2 \\ &= 25\pi \end{aligned}$$

PERIMETER OF A RECTANGLE

The perimeter of a rectangle is just the sum of the lengths of the four sides.

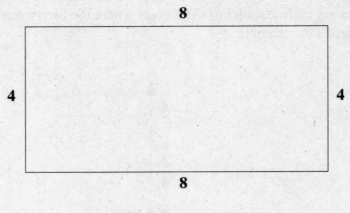

$$perimeter = 4 + 8 + 4 + 8$$
$$area = 8 \times 4$$

AREA OF A RECTANGLE

The area of a rectangle is length times width. The area of the rectangle above is 32.

SQUARES

A square is a rectangle with 4 equal sides. The perimeter of a square, is therefore, 4 times the length of any side. The area is the length of any side times itself, which is to say, the length of any side squared.

VOLUME OF A RECTANGULAR SOLID

You don't have to know how to calculate the volume of any geometric figure except a rectangular solid—that is, a box. The formula is $l \times w \times d$ (length times width times depth).

CARTESIAN GRIDS

A Cartesian grid is shaped like a cross. The horizontal line is called the *X*-axis; the vertical line is called the *Y*-axis. The four areas formed by the intersection of these axes are called quadrants. The point where the axes intersect is called the origin. Here's an example:

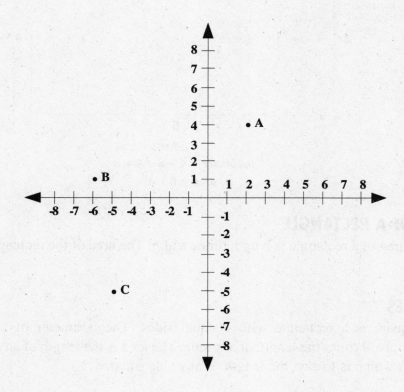

A Cartesian grid is a method of describing the location of any point on the plane on which the Cartesian grid is inscribed. In the diagram above, the marked point above and to the right of the origin can be described by the coordinates (2,4). That is, the point is two spaces to the right and four spaces above the origin. The point above and to the left of the origin can be described by the coordinates (–6,1). That is, it is six spaces to the left and 1 space above the origin. What are the coordinates of the point to the left of and below the origin? (–5,–5)

DRILL 10

Check your answers on page 337.

1. In the figure below, if $l_1 \parallel l_2$, what is the measure of angle b?

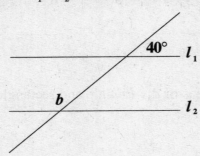

2. In the triangle below, what is the measure of angle c?

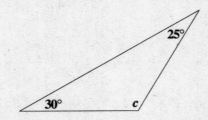

3. In the triangle below, what is the length of side AB?

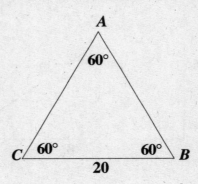

4. In the triangle below, what is the measure of angle c?

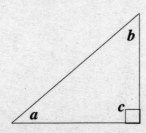

5. What are the perimeters of the triangle and rectangle below?

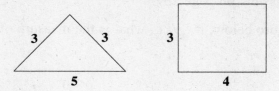

6. What are the areas of the triangle and rectangle below?

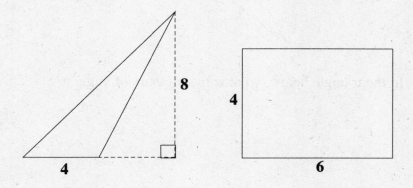

7. What is the length of the third side in the right triangle below?

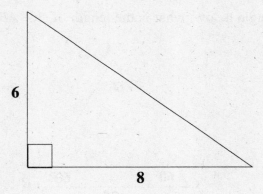

8. What is the approximate circumference of the circle below?

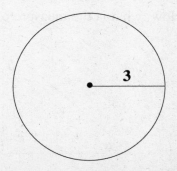

9. What is the approximate area of the circle in problem 8?

10. If a box is 5 inches wide, 10 inches long, and 4 inches deep, what is its volume in cubic inches?

11. Determine the coordinates of points A, B, C and D in the Cartesian grid below:

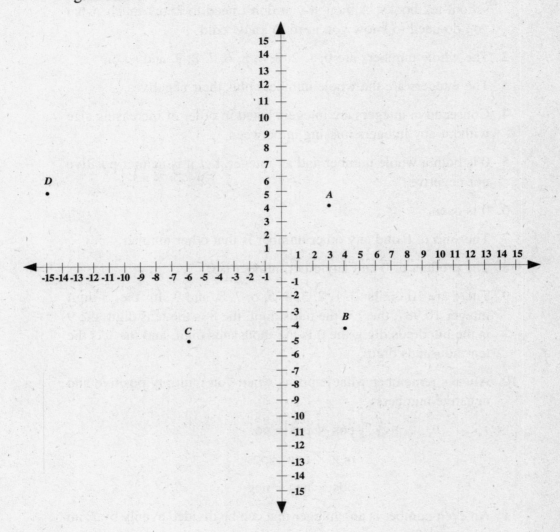

SUMMARY

1. You need very little real math for the GRE. This chapter outlines what you do need. If you have problems following this chapter, consult a basic math book or your old junior-high-school or high-school textbooks. Although you don't need to know much, what you do need to know you need to know cold.

2. The whole numbers are 0, 1, 2, 3, 4, 5, 6, 7, 8, 9, and so on.

3. The integers are the whole numbers plus their negatives.

4. Consecutive integers are integers listed in order of increasing size without any integers missing in between.

5. 0 is both a whole number and an integer, but it is neither positive nor negative.

6. 0 is even.

7. The sum of 0 and any other number is that other number.

8. The product of 0 and any other number is 0.

9. There are 10 digits: 0, 1, 2, 3, 4, 5, 6, 7, 8, and 9. In the 5-digit integer 10,987, the 7 is the units digit, the 8 is the tens digit, the 9 is the hundreds digit, the 0 is the thousands digit, and the 1 is the ten-thousands digit.

10. Always remember what happens when you multiply positive and negative numbers:

$$\text{pos} \times \text{pos} = \text{pos}$$

$$\text{neg} \times \text{neg} = \text{pos}$$

$$\text{pos} \times \text{neg} = \text{neg}$$

11. An even number is any integer that can be divided evenly by 2; an odd number is any integer that can't.

12. Fractions are neither even nor odd.

13. Any integer is even if its units digit is even; any integer is odd if its units digit is odd.

14. Always remember what happens when you add and multiply odd and even integers:

even + even = even	even × even = even
odd + odd = even	odd × odd = odd
even + odd = odd	even × odd = even

15. An integer is divisible by 2 if its units digit is divisible by 2. An integer is divisible by 3 if the sum of its digits is divisible by 3. An integer is divisible by 5 if its units digit is either 0 or 5. An integer is divisible by 10 if its units digit is 0.

16. The remainder is the number left over when one integer cannot be divided evenly by another.

17. A prime number is a number that can be divided evenly only by itself and by 1. Here are *all* the prime numbers less than 30:

$$2, 3, 5, 7, 11, 13, 17, 19, 23, 29$$

18. 0 is not a prime number.

19. 1 is not a prime number.

20. 2 is the only even prime number.

21. x is a factor of y if y can be divided by x without leaving a remainder.

22. A multiple of a number is that number multiplied by an integer other than 0.

23. Here are some standard symbols you can expect to see on the GRE:

Symbol	Meaning
=	is equal to
≠	is not equal to
<	is less than
>	is greater than
≤	is less than or equal to
≥	is greater than or equal to

24. Here are some standard terms. You won't see all of them on the GRE, but you'll need to know them to understand this book:

Term	Meaning
sum	the result of addition
difference	the result of subtraction
product	the result of multiplication
quotient	the result of division
numerator	the "upstairs" number in a fraction
denominator	the "downstairs" number in a fraction

25. There are only six basic operations that you will need to perform on the GRE: addition, subtraction, multiplication, division, raising to a power, and finding a square root.

26. These operations must always be performed in the proper order. You can use the mnemonic **P**lease **E**xcuse **M**y **D**ear **A**unt **S**ally to remind you of this order: Parentheses, Exponents, Multiplication, Division, Addition, and Subtraction.

27. The Princeton Review associative law says: *When you are adding a series of numbers or multiplying a series of numbers, you can regroup the numbers in any way you like.*

28. The distributive law is one of the most important principles tested on the GRE. You must know it cold. Here's what it looks like:

$$a(b + c) = ab + ac$$

$$a(b - c) = ab - ac$$

This is so important that you must do it every chance you get. Very often on the GRE, finding ETS's answer is simply a matter of performing the distributive law in one direction or the other.

29. Fractions are shorthand for division.

30. To add fractions with the same denominator, simply add the numerators and put the sum over one of the denominators.

31. To subtract fractions with the same denominator, simply subtract one numerator from the other and put the result over one of the denominators.

32. To add or subtract fractions with different denominators, first change them so that they have the same denominators.

33. To multiply fractions, place the product of the numerators over the product of the denominators.

34. To divide fractions, turn the second fraction upside down and proceed as in multiplication.

35. Fractions can be reduced and simplified by eliminating factors common to both the numerator and the denominator. This process is commonly called "canceling."

36. Convert mixed numbers to fractions; they're easier to handle in fraction form.

37. To determine whether one fraction is bigger than another, you can cross-multiply. In cross-multiplying, remember that you must always work from bottom to top. If you are at all unclear about this, look back to our discussion earlier in the chapter.

38. When asked to compare more than two fractions, simply compare two at a time.

39. The most common source of errors on GRE fraction problems is carelessness.

40. Every decimal can be written as a fraction; every fraction can be written as a decimal.

41. To turn a fraction into its decimal equivalent, all you have to do is divide the numerator by the denominator.

42. To add or subtract decimals, simply line up the decimal points and proceed as you would if the decimal points weren't there.

43. To multiply decimals, proceed as you would with integers, then count the total number of digits to the right of the decimal points in the numbers you multiplied and place a decimal point in your solution so that you have the same number of digits to the right of it.

44. Before you can divide decimals, you have to convert the divisor into a whole number. Do this by moving the decimal point all the way to the right. Be sure that you also move the decimal point in the dividend the same number of spaces to the right. Then proceed as you would with integers.

45. To prevent careless errors while comparing decimals, line up the numbers on their decimal points, fill in the missing zeros, and compare.

46. Fractions are often easier to work with than decimals are. When you're stumped on a decimal problem, ask yourself whether finding ETS's answer would be easier if you converted the decimals to fractions.

47. Money is based on the decimal system. When you find yourself stuck on a decimal problem, reminding yourself of the money connection may help you regain your bearings.

48. A percentage is just a handy way of expressing a fraction whose denominator is 100.

49. Converting percentages to fractions is easy. Just make the percentage the numerator in a fraction whose denominator is 100, then reduce.

50. Converting fractions to percentages is easy. Just divide the numerator by the denominator and move the decimal point two places to the right.

51. To convert percentages to decimals, just move the decimal point two places to the *left*.

52. Ratios, like fractions, percentages, and decimals, are just another way of representing division.

53. A fraction is a ratio between a numerator and its denominator. Every ratio, furthermore, can be expressed as a fraction.

54. Anything you can do to a fraction you can also do to a ratio.

55. To solve ratio problems, keep track of parts. The ratio 2:1 contains three parts.

56. Proportions are equal ratios. Find missing elements by cross-multiplying.

57. The average (arithmetic mean) of a set of numbers is the total value of all the numbers divided by the number of numbers in the set.

58. Ignore the parenthetical explanation (arithmetic mean) on the GRE.

59. The first step in any GRE average problem is to find the *total* of the numbers being averaged.

60. Every element in an average is just as important as every other, even if two or more of the elements are identical. Don't ignore repeated elements.

61. Exponents are a kind of shorthand for expressing numbers that are the product of the same factor multiplied over and over.

62. When you multiply exponential numbers with the same base, you merely add exponents. (This rule applies only to multiplication. It does not apply to addition, despite what Joe Bloggs may tell you.)

63. When you divide exponential numbers with the same base, you merely subtract exponents. (This rule applies to division, not subtraction.)

64. To raise a power to a power, multiply the exponents.

65. When raising a parenthetical expression to a power, don't forget to distribute the power through every element in the parentheses.

66. Raising a number greater than 1 to a power greater than 1 results in a *bigger* number.

67. Raising a fraction between 0 and 1 to a power greater than 1 results in a *smaller* number.

68. A negative number raised to an even power becomes *positive*.

69. A negative number raised to an odd power remains *negative*.

70. You should have a rough feel for the relative size of exponential numbers.

71. When ETS asks you for the square root of any number, you are being asked for the positive root only.

72. Here are the only two rules regarding radicals that you need to know for the GRE:

   1. $\sqrt{x}\sqrt{y} = \sqrt{xy}$

   2. $\sqrt{\dfrac{x}{y}} = \dfrac{\sqrt{x}}{\sqrt{y}}$

73. Know the following five values:

$\sqrt{1} = 1$

$\sqrt{2} = 1.4$

$\sqrt{3} = 1.7$

$\sqrt{4} = 2$

$\sqrt{5} = 2.2$

74. The algebra methods you learned in junior high school and high school will often mislead you on the GRE. You should never try to set up an equation and work through to an answer. Look for shortcuts instead.

75. If an expression on the GRE can be factored, factor it.

76. If an expression on the GRE can be unfactored, unfactor it.

77. To multiply polynomials, multiply every term in the first polynomial by every term in the second.

78. There are two quadratic expressions that appear over and over again on the GRE. You should know them cold, in both their factored and unfactored forms:

    Expression 1:

    Factored form: $x^2 - y^2$

    Unfactored form: $(x + y)(x - y)$

    Expression 2:

    Factored form: $(x + y)^2$

    Unfactored form: $x^2 + 2xy + y^2$

79. Simplify complicated algebraic expressions by combining similar terms.

80. When ETS gives you a value for one of the variables or terms in an expression and asks you for the value of the entire expression, simply plug in the value ETS gives you.

81. On simultaneous-equation problems on the GRE, simply add or subtract the given equations in the form in which they are given.

82. In problems involving equations set to zero, remember that 0 times any other number is 0.

83. If you multiply or divide both sides of an inequality by a negative number, you must remember to change the direction of the inequality symbol.

84. ETS uses funny-looking symbols to denote functions. If you don't remember how functions work, simply do what the funny-looking symbol tells you to do.

85. To demystify word problems, "translate" them into equations.

86. Know the following formulas:

    1. distance = (rate)(time). (Note that this same formula can be rewritten in terms of any of its elements. For example, here's another way to express the same relationship: time = distance/rate.)

    2. total price = (number of items)(cost per item).

    3. sale price = (original price) − (% discount)(original price).

87. A circle contains 360 degrees.

88. A line is a 180-degree angle.

89. When two lines intersect, four angles are formed, and the sum of the angles is 360 degrees.

90. When two lines are perpendicular to each other, their intersection forms four 90-degree angles, also called right angles. A right angle on the GRE is identified by a little box at the intersection of the angle's arms.

91. Here's Fred's theorem: When two parallel lines are cut by a third line, angles that *look* equal *are* equal.

92. Every triangle contains three interior angles, which add up to 180 degrees.

93. An equilateral triangle is one in which all three sides are equal in length. Each angle in an equilateral triangle contains 60 degrees.

94. An isosceles triangle is one in which two of the three sides are equal in length. This means that two of the angles are also equal, and that the third angle is not.

95. A right triangle is one in which one of the angles is a right angle—a 90-degree angle.

96. The longest side of a right triangle—the side opposite the 90-degree angle—is called the hypotenuse.

97. On the GRE, a right triangle will always have a little box in the 90-degree corner.

98. All you have to do to find the perimeter of a triangle is add up the lengths of the sides.

99. The area of any triangle is the altitude multiplied by the base, divided by 2.

100. The Pythagorean theorem states that in a right triangle, the square of the hypotenuse is equal to the sum of the squares of the other two sides.

101. On Pythagorean–theorem problems, ETS's favorite right triangle has sides measuring 3, 4, and 5 or multiples of those numbers.

102. On the GRE, simply use 3 as the value of pi (π).

103. The formula for finding the circumference of a circle is 2 times pi times the radius ($2\pi r$), or pi times the diameter (πd).

104. The area of a circle is pi times the square of the radius (πr^2).

105. The perimeter of a rectangle is just the sum of the lengths of the four sides.

106. The area of a rectangle is length times width.

107. The formula for the volume of a box is length times width times depth.

108. A Cartesian grid is a method of describing the location of any point on the plane on which the Cartesian grid is inscribed.

Arithmetic, Algebra, and Geometry: Attacking the Problems

Now that you've learned the basics of GRE Mathematics, it's time to move on to specific techniques aimed at cracking the sort of arithmetic, algebra, and geometry problems that you'll actually encounter on the test. Our techniques for solving these problems will enable you to get the maximum possible mileage out of the modest amount of math you need to know. The main idea to keep in mind is that your goal is to score points, not to demonstrate your knowledge of math. Approaching the problems the way your junior-high-school math teacher taught you would take up too much time.

DIRECTIONS

ETS's directions at the beginning of each of the GRE's math sections cover a full page and include four worked quantitative comparison examples. **You shouldn't even peek at these directions on your test.** (We'll tell you about quantitative comparisons in Chapter Eleven.)

ETS's math directions contain some information that applies to all math questions. You should know this information before you take the test. Do not read it in your test booklet. Here's the given information:

- All numbers used are real numbers.

- Position of points, angles, regions, etc., can be assumed to be in the order shown; and angle measures can be assumed to be positive.

- Lines shown as straight can be assumed to be straight.

- Figures can be assumed to lie in a plane unless otherwise indicated.

- Figures that accompany questions are intended to provide information useful in answering the questions. However, unless a note states that a figure is drawn to scale, you should solve these problems NOT by estimating sizes by sight or by measurement, but by using your knowledge of mathematics.

WHAT THIS INFORMATION MEANS

ETS's statements that all numbers on the test are real numbers and that all angles have positive measurements are simply meant to prevent math whizzes from making arguments for peculiar answers. Don't worry about them.

All the other information arises from the fact that the drawings and figures in GRE math problems, unlike those in SAT math problems, are usually not drawn to scale. **This means that you usually can't simply eyeball a drawing and determine whether one side of a triangle is longer than another, and that you can't determine the measure of an angle by "guesstimating," an extremely powerful technique on the SAT.**

Even though GRE math drawings are not usually to scale, some of the information in them can be trusted. This is what ETS means when it tells you that labeled points lie in the order in which they're drawn, and that lines that look straight really are straight, and so on. In other words, everything about a drawing is accurate except its dimensions. We'll tell you more about what this means later in the chapter.

OUR PHENOMENAL TECHNIQUES

Many of our students find it easier to improve their math scores than to improve their verbal scores. If you study our techniques carefully, practice them, and trust them on the test, you should find it possible to improve your GRE math score substantially. Indeed, our techniques can make it possible for you to make short work of problems that would have seemed impossible before.

JOE BLOGGS AND THE MATH GRE

Each math section of your GRE will contain ten regular math questions drawn from arithmetic, algebra, and geometry. (It will also contain fifteen quantitative comparisons and five items based on a chart or graph. We'll discuss these items in succeeding chapters.) The ten regular math questions will be divided into two groups of five items each. The first five-item regular-math group (items 16–20) will come after the quantitative comparisons and before the chart. Of these five items, the first three will be easy and the last two will be medium. The second five-item regular-math group will follow the chart (items 26–30). Of these five items, the first two will be medium and the final three will be difficult.

By now you should know how Joe Bloggs does on these questions. He gets the easy ones right, does so-so on the mediums, and bombs on the difficults. This means you want to trust your hunches on the easy ones, be suspicious on the medium ones, and eliminate choices that attract Joe on the difficult ones.

THE JOE BLOGGS PRINCIPLE: HARD QUESTIONS HAVE HARD ANSWERS

On difficult math problems, Joe Bloggs is attracted to easy solutions arrived at through methods that he understands. This is so important that we'll say it again: **On difficult math problems, Joe Bloggs is attracted to easy solutions arrived at through methods that he understands.** In other words, hard questions have hard answers.

Here's an example:

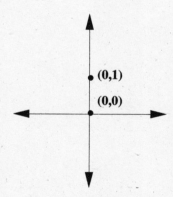

30. How many different positions can there be for a square that must have corners at both (0,1) and (0,0)?

   (A) One
   (B) Two
   (C) Three
   (D) Four
   (E) Five

Here's how to crack it:

What's the easy answer to this difficult question? Joe can easily envision two squares with corners at the marked points. Here are the two squares that Joe sees:

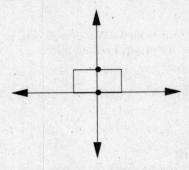

Joe's answer, therefore, is B. Is this ETS's answer as well? Of course not. Joe's answer never wins points on difficult questions. As always, there must be something that Joe has overlooked. Before we look for what Joe missed, we need to cross out his answer. We can also cross out choice A, since we already know that we can find at least two squares. This improves our guessing odds to 1 in 3 on the hardest math question in its section—a queston that only about 8 percent of test-takers can be expected to answer correctly.

What has Joe overlooked? We know that this is a hard question and the ETS's answer can't be easy and straightforward. Is there any *other* way in which the two marked points could serve as corners of a square? Yes, there is. Here's how:

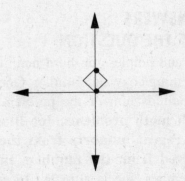

Now we have a total of 3 different positions, which is choice C. This is ETS's answer. Choice D, 4 positions, is an attractor for students who carelessly assume that there could be a square in each of the four quadrants.

Spotting and eliminating the principal Joe Bloggs attractor on this problem was easy. All we had to do was look for a quick, easy solution to this hard problem. Once Joe's answer was out of the way, finding ETS's answer was considerably easier. We knew that there had to be at least one more square than Joe could find, and we knew that finding it couldn't be easy—there had to be something tricky about the solution that Joe wouldn't notice.

JOE BLOGGS LIKES EASY ARITHMETIC

Joe likes to find his answers by using the arithmetic he understands—easy arithmetic. On difficult questions, any such answers can therefore be eliminated. Here's an example:

28. A suit is selling for $100 after a 20 percent discount. What was the original selling price?

    (A) $200
    (B) $125
    (C) $120
    (D) $80
    (E) $75

Here's how to crack it:

Joe sees *$100* and *20 percent discount* and jumps on choice C. After all, isn't $120 twenty percent more than $100? Yes, it is, but that isn't what the question asks for. Eliminate Joe's choice.

You can also eliminate choice D, which is 20 percent *less* than $100. Joe manipulates the numbers he sees in ways he understands. He takes 20 percent more than $100; he takes 20 percent less. Such answer choices can be eliminated.

With choice C out of the way, you should be able to see that the only possible candidate is choice B. This is ETS's answer. Choice A, $200, is much too high; choice E is easy to eliminate, since a suit couldn't cost less before a discount than after.

JOE BLOGGS LIKES ANSWERS THAT REMIND HIM OF THE QUESTION

Joe Bloggs feels lost and helpless on hard math questions. In groping for an answer, he picks something cozy and familiar. One of his favorite guesses is an answer choice that reminds him of the problem. What reminds him of the problem? **On difficult math problems, Joe Bloggs is attracted to answer choices that simply repeat numbers from the problem or that contain numbers easily derived from the numbers in the problem.** On reading comprehensions, remember, Joe is attracted to answer choices that repeated significant chunks of wording from the passages. A similar impulse guides him on math sections. On difficult items, therefore, you should eliminate choices that repeat numbers from the problem.

Here's an example:

28. After 6 gallons of water are transferred from container A to container B, there are 10 gallons more water in container A than in container B. Container A originally had how many more gallons than container B?

    (A) 0 (B) 6 (C) 10 (D) 16 (E) 22

Here's how to crack it:

Any repetitions here? Yes. Joe is attracted to choices B and C, which repeat numbers from the problem. We should therefore simply eliminate these choices. This improves our guessing odds immediately to 1 in 3.

Joe is also attracted to choice D: $6 + 10 = 16$. Eliminate this choice as well. ETS's answer on this problem is choice E.

JOE BLOGGS ON LEAST/GREATEST QUESTIONS

On some difficult problems, you will be asked to find the *least* (or *greatest*) possible value that satisfies the conditions of the problem. On such problems, you can automatically eliminate the least (or greatest) value among the choices. Some low-scoring students—who don't even score at the Joe Bloggs level—are irresistibly attracted to such choices. Because they are, you can eliminate them. Such choices are almost never correct on difficult questions.

JOE BLOGGS AND "IT CANNOT BE DETERMINED"

ETS occasionally offers "It cannot be determined from the information given" as a choice on math problems. (We're not talking here about quantitative comparisons, where "cannot be determined" is choice D on every problem.) When this choice is offered on an easy or medium problem, it has a very good chance of being ETS's answer.

On difficult questions, though, "cannot be determined" is almost never ETS's answer. Why? Because Joe Bloggs, who can *never* determine the answer on these questions, jumps on this choice when it's offered.

The only time you have to be careful is when ETS offers "cannot be determined" as an answer choice on *two* difficult questions in the same math sections, as it occasionally does. **In such cases, you can be certain that one of these choices is ETS's answer.**

BEYOND JOE BLOGGS: WORKING BACKWARD

Working backward is one of the most powerful techniques you can bring to bear on the GRE math sections. The idea is simple: Instead of setting up an equation—which can take forever—you simply try a choice and see if it works. If it works, you have ETS's answer. If it doesn't work, you try another. There are only five choices on regular math problems. One of these choices has to be ETS's answer. You will often find this answer by trying just one or two of the choices. You will never have to try all five.

You will be able to use the working-backward technique on math items in which all five choices are numbers. Here's an example:

20. Which of the following values of a does not satisfy
    $5a - 3 < 3a + 5$?

    (A) –2   (B) 0   (C) 2   (D) 3   (E) 4

Here's how to crack it:

You have been given an inequality with one variable and five possible values for the variable. You're looking for the one that doesn't work. Should you attempt to rewrite the inequality—say, by putting all the a's on one side? No. Simply try each choice. One of them will be correct.

In working backward from the choices, it's usually a good idea to start in the middle and work your way out, beginning with choice C. Why work from the middle? Because GRE answer choices are almost always arranged in order of the size. When working backward, you may be able to tell not only that a particular choice is incorrect but also that it is larger or smaller than ETS's answer. Starting from the middle will save you time in such situations by enabling you to eliminate choices that are clearly too large or too small.

(C)   Plugging in 2 for a gives us $10 - 3 < 6 + 5$, or $7 < 11$. Is this True? Yes. Eliminate.

(B) $0 - 3 < 0 + 5$, or $-3 < 5$. True? Yes. Eliminate.

(D) $15 - 3 < 9 + 5$, or $12 < 14$. True? Yes. Eliminate.

(A) $-10 - 3 < -6 + 5$, or $-13 < -1$. True? Yes. Eliminate.

We now know that ETS's answer must be choice E. Here's how it works out:

(E) $20 - 3 < 12 + 5$, or $17 < 17$. True? No. This is ETS's answer.

Of course, if you realized after trying the first choice that ETS's answer would have to be a number *larger* than 2—as you might have—then you could have tried choice E, or choice D, immediately. But we found ETS's answer anyway, and we didn't even work up a sweat.

Here's another example:

19. The units digit of a 2-digit number is 3 times the tens digit.
    If the digits are reversed, the resulting number is 36 more
    than the original number. What is the original number?

    (A) 13   (B) 26   (C) 36   (D) 62   (E) 93

Here's how to crack it:

There are ninety 2-digit numbers. ETS has already eliminated eighty-five of these. All we have to do is eliminate four more. Should we set up some sort of equation? No, of course not. Let's just try out the choices.

The problem places two conditions on the answer. First, its second digit must be 3 times the first digit. Second, the reversed form of the number must be 36 more than the original number. Since ETS's answer must satisfy *both* conditions, we can eliminate any choice that fails to satisfy either of them. Therefore, we tackle one condition at a time.

Here's how:

(C) Is 6 three times 3? No. Eliminate.
(B) Is 6 three times 2? Yes. A possibility.
(D) Is 2 three times 6? No. Eliminate.
(A) Is 3 three times 1? Yes. A possibility.
(E) Is 3 three times 9? No. Eliminate.

We've narrowed it down to two possibilities, A and B. Now we apply the second condition:

(A) Is 31 equal to 36 more than 13? No.

Eliminate. ETS's answer must be B.

It is. 62 is exactly 36 more than 26.

Working backward can also be used on word problems, especially ones on which your high-school math teacher would have asked you to set up an equation.

BEWARE OF IRRELEVANT INFORMATION

ETS will sometimes make a straightforward problem difficult by introducing information that serves no purpose except to throw you off the trail. Here's an example:

26. A restaurant owner sold 2 dishes to each of his customers at $4 per dish. At the end of the day, he had taken in $180, which included $20 in tips. How many customers did he serve?

(A) 18   (B) 20   (C) 22   (D) 40   (E) 44

Here's how to crack it:

The information about tips is irrelevant. It's only purpose is to cause careless errors and keep lower-scoring students from stumbling over ETS's answer. Before solving this problem, you should eliminate this trap. Simply reduce the day's total by $20—to $160—and pay no more attention to the tips.

What we're left with is a very straightforward problem. If each customer bought 2 four-dollar dishes, then each customer spent $8 on food. Dividing the day's total ($160) by the average check ($8) yields 20 customers. ETS's answer is choice B.

PLUGGING IN

When you work backward, you take the numbers in the answer choices and plug them back into the question. But many problems have variables instead of numbers in the answer choices. On these problems, you can often find a shortcut to ETS's answer by *making up* numbers and plugging them in. Here's what you do:

1. Pick a number for each variable in the problem

2. Solve the problem using your numbers

3. Plug your numbers into the answer choices to see which one of them equals the solution you found in step 2

4. In plugging in, you should work from the outside in, that is, start with A, then do E, B, D, and C.

Here's an example:

20. If $x + y = z$ and $x = y$, then all of the following are true EXCEPT

   (A) $2x + 2y = 2z$
   (B) $x - y = 0$
   (C) $x - z = y - z$
   (D) $x = z/2$
   (E) $x - y = 2z$

Here's how to crack it:

Don't try to solve this problem the way you would in math class. Instead, all you have to do is pick simple values for x, y, and z that are consistent with the two given equations. Let's say that x and y (which we have been told are equal) are both 2. That means that z is 4. Be sure to write down these values in your test booklet, so you don't forget them.

Now we plug these values into the answer choices. Here's what we get:

(A) $2(2) + 2(2) = 2(4)$, or $4 + 4 = 8$. Yes, that's correct. Eliminate. (We're looking for the *wrong* choice, remember? This is an EXCEPT problem.)

(E) $2 - 2 = 2(4)$. This is not correct. It must be ETS's answer.

(B) $2 - 2 = 0$. Correct again. Eliminate.

(D) $2 = \frac{4}{2}$. Correct again. Eliminate.

(C) $2 - 4 = 2 - 4$. Correct again. Eliminate.

You will sometimes have to plug in more than once in order to find ETS's answer. Here's an example:

29. The positive difference between the squares of any two consecutive integers is always:

(A) the square of an integer
(B) a multiple of 5
(C) an even integer
(D) an odd number
(E) a prime number

Here's how to crack it:

The word *always* in the question tells us that all we need to find in order to eliminate a choice is a single instance in which it doesn't work. So let's start by picking two consecutive integers and squaring them. It doesn't matter which consecutive integers we choose. How about 2 and 3? Squaring 2 and 3 gives us 4 and 9. The positive difference between them ($9 - 4$, as opposed to $4 - 9$) is 5. Now look at the choices:

(A) Is 5 the square of an integer? No. Eliminate.
(B) Is 5 a multiple of 5? Yes. A possibility.
(C) Is 5 an even integer? No. Eliminate.
(D) Is 5 an odd integer? Yes. A possibility.
(E) Is 5 a prime number? Yes. A possibility.

We've eliminated choices A and C. That's good. It means that with very little effort we've boosted our guessing odds to 1 in 3 on this very difficult problem. But we can do better than that. Let's pick two more consecutive integers. How about 0 and 1? The squares of 0 and 1 are 0 and 1. The positive difference between them is 1. Now look at the remaining choices:

(B) Is 1 a multiple of 5? No. Eliminate.
(D) Is 1 an odd integer? Yes. A possibility.
(E) Is 1 a prime number? No. Eliminate.

ETS's answer is choice D.

ETS will sometimes give you a value for one of the variables or terms in an expression and then ask you for the value of the entire expression. Nothing could be easier. Simply plug in the value that ETS gives you and see what you come up with. Here's an example:

Problem:

If $3x = -2$, then $(3x - 3)^2 = ?$

Here's how to crack it:

Forget about "algebra"; don't "solve for *x*." Simply plug in –2 for 3*x*. This gives you the following:

$$(3x - 3)^2 = (-2 - 3)^2$$
$$= (-5)^2$$
$$= 25$$

> You should never, never, never try to solve problems like these by "solving for *x*" or "solving for *y*." Plugging in is much easier and faster, and you'll be less likely to make dumb mistakes.

WHICH NUMBERS SHOULD YOU PLUG IN?

You can plug in any numbers you like, as long as they're consistent with any restrictions stated in the problem. But you'll find ETS's answer faster if you use *easy* numbers.

What makes a number easy? That depends on the problem. In most cases, smaller numbers are easier to work with than larger numbers. Especially if the problem requires you to square or cube your plug-ins, you'll want to start small, with 2 or 3, for example. (Avoid 0 and 1 in these situations. Zero and 1 have special properties, about which we'll tell you more later.)

But small numbers aren't always best. In a problem involving percentages, for example, 10 and 100 are good numbers to use. In a problem involving minutes or seconds, 60 may be the easiest number. You should look for clues in the problem itself. Here's an example:

26. A street vendor has just purchased a carton containing 250 hot dogs. If the carton cost *x* dollars, what is the cost in dollars of 10 of the hot dogs?

(A) $\dfrac{x}{25}$ (B) $\dfrac{x}{10}$ (C) $10x$ (D) $\dfrac{10}{x}$ (E) $\dfrac{25}{x}$

Here's how to crack it:

We could plug in anything at all for *x* (how about 199.99?) and still find ETS's answer. But let's pick an easy number. What's easy? How about 250? That means that the hot dogs cost 1 dollar each. In your test booklet write "*x* = 250."

What is the cost of 10 of the hot dogs, given that 250 of them cost $250? That's easy. The cost of 10 hot dogs is $10. That's what ETS wants to know—the cost of 10 hot dogs. Write "10" in your test booklet and circle it. We're now

looking for the answer choice that yields 10 when we plug in 250 for x. Now try the choices:

(A) Plugging in 250 for x, we get 250/25, or 10. This is the number we're looking for. This is ETS's answer.

If you don't believe that plugging in *any* number would lead you to the same answer, try a few more.

Oh, all right. Let's plug in 199.99. If 250 hot dogs cost $199.99, then $x = 199.99$. What is the cost of ten hot dogs? To find that, we divide 199.99 by 25, discovering that ten hot dogs cost $7.9996. We are now looking for the answer choice that yields 7.9996 when we plug in 199.99. Now try the choices.

(A) Plugging in 199.99 for x, we get 199.99/25, or 7.9996. This is the number we are looking for. This is ETS's answer.

Wasn't that easy?

PLUGGING IN ON INEQUALITIES

On some problems, you'll have to plug in several numbers in order to zero in on ETS's answer. On inequalities, in particular, you will find that this is true. But if you work methodically and proceed one step at a time, you shouldn't have any trouble. Here's an example:

29. What are all the values of x such that $x^2 - 3x - 4$ is negative?

    (A) $x < -1$ or $x > 4$
    (B) $x < -4$ or $x > 4$
    (C) $1 < x < 4$
    (D) $-4 < x < 1$
    (E) $-1 < x < 4$

Here's how to crack it:

Joe Bloggs looks at those answer choices and shudders. But you don't need to shudder. Look for one piece of information at a time, and eliminate incorrect choices as you go.

Let's start with choice A. We're going to plug in. But what should we plug in? Choice A describes two different values of x. Since both of them have to work in the given expression if this is to be ETS's answer, we can try them one at a time. If either of them doesn't work, we can eliminate the choice. Because one of these values is contained in both choices A and B—the common value is "$x > 4$"—let's try it. If we can find an x greater than 4 that doesn't work, we can eliminate both A and B.

What's a number greater than 4? How about 5? Plugging 5 into the original expression gives us 25 – 15 – 4, which equals 6. Is 6 negative? No. We can eliminate choices A and B.

If we guess now, we'll have a 1-in-3 shot of earning points on this very difficult question—not a bad return on our investment of a few seconds' worth of plugging in. Let's see if we can eliminate anything else.

Choices C and E overlap; they include values less than 4 and greater than 1. If we can find a value within this range that doesn't work, we can eliminate both choices. Let's try plugging in 3. This gives us 9 – 9 – 4, which equals –4. Is –4 negative? Of course. We can't eliminate either of these choices yet.

But we can eliminate something. What can we eliminate? Choice D. We just proved that 3 works for x, but the range in choice D doesn't include 3. Therefore, the range in choice D can't cover *all* the possible values for x, which is what we've been told to look for. Eliminate.

Now we've narrowed our choice down to C or E. These two choices overlap a great deal. There's just one small area where they don't—the numbers between –1 and 1. What we need to do is pick a number between these two numbers. If it works, ETS's answer must be choice E; if it doesn't work, ETS's answer must be choice C. What should we try? How about 0? This gives us 0 – 0 – 4, which equals –4. The choice works. ETS's answer is choice E.

When plugging in on inequalities, don't forget about 0, 1, fractions, negative fractions, and negative integers, all of which have special properties and are thus useful in eliminating incorrect answer choices.

Sometimes you can avoid plugging in on inequalities merely by simplifying the expressions you have been given. Here's an example:

16. If $-3x + 6 \geq 18$, which of the following is true?

   (A) $x \leq -4$
   (B) $x \leq 6$
   (C) $x \geq -4$
   (D) $x \geq -6$
   (E) $x = 2$

Here's how to crack it:

We could solve this problem by plugging in, but the given inequality is crying out to be simplified. Here's what we get by combining terms and factoring:

$$-3x + 6 \geq 18$$
$$-3x \geq 12$$
$$-x \geq 4$$
$$x \leq -4$$

Thus we can easily see that ETS's answer is choice A.

PLUGGING IN EVEN WHEN YOU DON'T HAVE TO

Sometimes plugging in can help you even when you don't really need to do it. Here's an example:

18. Which of the following is the closest approximation of the value of $\dfrac{0.507(507)}{5.07}$?

(A) 1 (B) 5 (C) 10 (D) 50 (E) 100

Here's how to crack it:

The last thing you want to do on this problem is manipulate these nasty numbers. But you don't have to. We're just looking for an approximation. So why not turn the last two digits of each number into zeros? Here's what we get if we do this:

$$\frac{0.5(500)}{5}$$

In other words, we're being asked for half of 500, divided by 5. Half of 500 is 250; 250 divided by 5 is 50. ETS's answer is choice D.

You can often help yourself by plugging in simpler numbers when the numbers in a problem are just too horrible to deal with. Here's another example:

29. $2^8 - 2^7 =$

(A) 2 (B) $2^{7/8}$ (C) 2^7 (D) 2^8 (E) 2^{15}

Here's how to crack it:

The numbers in this very difficult problem are big and horrible. So let's turn it into an easy problem by using easy numbers instead:

$$2^4 - 2^3 = ?$$

Well, $2^4 = 16$ and $2^3 = 8$. The difference between them is 8, which of course is 2^3. The answer we came up with, in other words, is the same as the second of the two numbers in the problem. Applying the same pattern to the original problem, we select choice C, which is the same as the second number in the original. This, indeed, is ETS's answer.

If you don't believe this works every time, try a few other possibilities. Even 2^1 and 2^0 work.

(Simply studying this problem carefully and calmly would also have given you ETS's answer. The difference between the two big numbers couldn't be bigger than either of the numbers. That eliminates E. Nor could the difference between them be the same as the bigger of the two. That eliminates choice D.

Choices A and B are both Joe Bloggs attractors. Joe always wants to apply the rules concerning the division of exponents to problems involving subtraction. All that's left is choice C. Remember, 2^8 is simply $2(2^7)$, which is another way of saying that $2^7 + 2^7 = 2^8$. Therefore, $2^8 - 2^7 = 2^7$.)

WATCH OUT FOR TRICKY WORDING

Hard math problems are often made harder by tricky wording. If you leave out a step called for by the problem or fail to notice a change in the problem's wording, you will probably find that an incorrect answer choice is waiting to grab you. Be careful. Here's an example:

27. $(PQ)(PQ) = 144$

 If P and Q represent the digits in the two-digit numbers above, the ratio of Q to P is

 (A) 1:2 (B) 1:1 (C) 2:1 (D) 3:1 (E) 12:1

Here's how to crack it:

You can tell by the number that this is a very hard problem. What makes it hard? Let's find out.

You have a big leg up on this problem if you know that the square root of 144 is 12. That is, $(PQ)(PQ) = (12)(12)$, which means that digit P is 1 and digit Q is 2. Pretty easy so far. Now we need the ratio. That looks easy, too. It's 1:2, which means that ETS's answer must be choice A, right?

Wrong. The ratio that ETS asks for is not that of P to Q but that of Q to P. The second half of the question switches the order of the digits. ETS's answer is actually 2:1, or choice C.

Don't get careless! Be sure that the answer you pick really is the answer to the question, and not just an intermediate result along the way.

PLUGGING IN ON GEOMETRY PROBLEMS

On geometry problems, you can plug in values for angles or lengths if the values you plug in don't contradict either the wording of the problem or the laws of geometry (you can't let the interior angles of a triangle add up to anything but 180, for instance).

Here's an example:

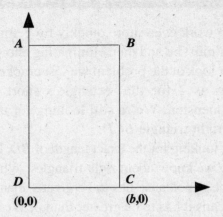

19. The area of the rectangle $ABCD$ is $3b^2$. The coordinates of C and D are given. In terms of b, $BD =$

(A) b (B) $2b$ (C) $b\sqrt{5}$ (D) $3b$ (E) $b\sqrt{10}$

Here's how to crack it:

The distance from D to C is b. Let's plug in a value for b. How about 2? Write "$b = 2$" in your test booklet. Put another 2 by side DC, to remind yourself of the length of that side of the rectangle.

With 2 plugged in for b, we see that the area of the rectangle ($3b^2$) is 12. That means that side BC is 6. Place a 6 on side BC, to remind yourself of the length of that side.

What the problem asks us for is the length of BD, which in addition to being one diagonal of the given rectangle is also the hypotenuse of right triangle BCD. We already know the lengths of the other two sides of right triangle BCD (2 and 6). From the Pythagorean theorem, we know that the square of the length of the hypotenuse is equal to the sum of the squares of 2 and 6. The squares of 2 and 6 are 4 and 36, which means that the square of the hypotenuse is 40. The length of BD therefore, is $\sqrt{40}$, or $2\sqrt{10}$. ($\sqrt{40} = (\sqrt{4})(\sqrt{10}) = \sqrt{10}$.) That means that the length of BD is also $2\sqrt{10}$

Now all we have to do is go to the answer choices, plug in our value for b, and see which one equals the answer we came up with. Choice E fills the bill. It is ETS's answer.

USE COMMON SENSE

You can very often work even more quickly by getting an approximate idea of what ETS's answer must be and then eliminating choices that are far wide of the mark. Take another look at the problem we just cracked. Once again, let's plug in 2 for *b*, giving us 2 for the rectangle's short dimension and 6 for the rectangle's long dimension. We're still looking for the length of *BD*, which is the hypotenuse of right triangle *BCD*.

Now, instead of looking for the exact length of *BD*, let's make a rough estimate based on something we know about right triangles. What do we know? We know that the length of the hypotenuse has to be greater than the length of either of the other sides. That means it has to be greater than 6. We also know that it has to be *less* than the *sum* of the other sides; otherwise, we wouldn't have a triangle. In other words, the number we're looking for is greater than 6 and less than 8.

Now go to the answer choices and plug in 2 for *b*:

- (A) *b* is 2. This is much too small. Eliminate.
- (B) 2*b* would be 4, which is less than 6. Eliminate.
- (C) The square root of 5, as you should remember, is about 2.2. $2\sqrt{5}$ is therefore about 4.4. Eliminate.
- (D) 3*b* is exactly 6. ETS's answer has to be greater than 6. Eliminate.
- (E) You probably don't know the square root of 10 right off the top of your head, but you can easily see that it must be a bit more than 3 (which is the square root of 9). The value of $2\sqrt{10}$ must therefore be a little more than 6. This must be ETS's answer.

Here's another example of how you can use common sense to zero in on ETS's answer:

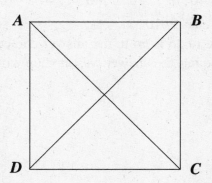

19. In square *ABCD* above, what is the value of $\dfrac{(AD)(AB)}{(AC)(BD)}$?

    (A) $\dfrac{1}{2}$ (B) $\dfrac{\sqrt{2}}{2}$ (C) 1   (D) $\sqrt{2}$ (E) 2

Here's how to crack it:

This problem is similar to the previous one. Once again, we want to plug in some easy numbers to get a rough idea of what ETS's answer is. We can then try to eliminate some choices.

We can tell immediately that $(AD)(AB)$ is going to be smaller than $(AC)(BD)$. (Why? Because the diagonal of a square is larger than any of its sides, which means that the product of two sides has to be smaller than the product of two diagonals.) In other words, the numerator is going to be smaller than the denominator. That means we can eliminate choices C, D, and E.

We've narrowed it down to choices A and B. Plugging in 2 for the side of the square and using the side relationships of a 45:45:90 triangle, we get $(2)(2)/(2\sqrt{2})(2\sqrt{2})$ or $\frac{1}{2}$. ETS's answer is A.

LOOK FOR SHORTCUTS

You will find math problems on the GRE that don't seem to fit any of the patterns we've discussed so far—problems where you don't see a way to plug in or work backward from the answer choices. On such problems, you may be tempted to "solve for x" or perform some other math-class technique.

Don't!

Virtually all GRE math problems can be solved using shortcuts that avoid time-consuming math. Remember: The GRE allows you only about a minute per problem. ETS doesn't expect you to perform a lot of lengthy operations. The test rewards students who cut corners. This is what high-scoring students do intuitively. You can improve your own score by teaching yourself to look for the easy way out.

Here's an example:

20. If $x^2 - 4 = (18)(14)$, then x could be:

(A) 14 (B) 16 (C) 18 (D) 26 (E) 32

Here's how to crack it:

You could solve this the math-class way (by solving for x) or by plugging in (which would require lots and lots of multiplication). But there's an easier way. ETS doesn't just write equations randomly. The equations you do see on the test almost always embody one of the small number of basic principles that ETS tests over and over. In this case, if you've learned your GRE Math, you should immediately notice that the expression on the left side of the equation is in the form $x^2 - y^2$. What should you do with such an expression? Unfactor it! Here's what you get:

$$x^2 - 4 = (x + 2)(x - 2)$$

Now look at our rewritten form of the original equation:

$$(x + 2)(x - 2) = (18)(14)$$

Do you notice anything? If you look for a moment, you should see that $18 = (16 + 2)$ and that $14 = (16 - 2)$. In other words, x could be 16, which is choice B and ETS's answer.

Taking a moment to look for familiar elements in GRE math problems can have a big payoff. If you know what to look for, you can almost always find a shortcut.

SHORTCUTS ON GEOMETRY PROBLEMS

On the SAT, virtually all diagrams on geometry problems are drawn exactly to scale. This means that SAT-takers can often find ETS's answer simply by measuring the diagrams. This is what we teach our SAT students to do.

Geometry problems on the GRE, however, are trickier. GRE diagrams usually are *not* drawn to scale. This means that GRE-takers can't simply "guesstimate" ETS's answer by eyeballing a diagram or by measuring directly—both of which are extremely powerful techniques on the SAT.

But GRE diagrams do still contain a great deal of useful information. If you are very careful, you will often be able to use this information to provide a shortcut to ETS's answer. Here's an example:

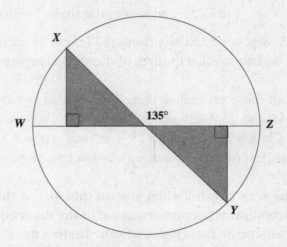

30. If segment *WZ* and segment *XY* are diameters of the circle with length 12, what is the area of the shaded triangles?

(A) 36 (B) 33 (C) 30 (D) 18 (E) 12

Here's how to crack it:

ETS tells you to assume that GRE diagrams are *not* drawn to scale unless you're explicitly told otherwise. But sometimes you can tell from the information given that the drawings really must be drawn to scale, or very nearly so. In this problem, for example, we can tell that the circle really is a circle, and we can see that *WZ* and *XY* really are diameters. We should also be able to tell, just by eyeballing, that the angle marked as 135 degrees really must be roughly, if not exactly, 135 degrees (which is 90 + 45). Taking all of this information into consideration, we can tell that if the drawing is off, it's not off in any significant way. At least for the purposes of estimating a rough answer, we can trust what we have been given.

ETS has also told us that the circle's diameter is 12. This means that its radius is 6, which means that the hypotenuse of each of the two shaded triangles is 6. Based on this, we can tell by eyeballing that the length of each other side of each triangle is, say, somewhere between 4 and 5. We now have enough information to find ETS's answer. Here's how:

First, let's use 4 for the length of each side. This means that the area of each triangle would be $\frac{(4 \times 4)}{2}$, or 8. The area of the shaded region would be twice this number, or 16. Since we actually think the length of each side is probably a little more than 4, we can say that the area of the shaded region must be more than 16.

Now, let's use 5 for the length of each side. This means that the area of each triangle would be $\frac{(5 \times 5)}{2}$, or 12.5. The area of the shaded region would be twice this number, or 25. Since we actually think the length of each side is probably a little less than 5, we can say that the area of the shaded region must be less than 25.

Combining both these estimates, therefore, we can say that ETS's answer must be between 16 and 25. Only one of the answer choices, choice D, fulfills these conditions. Choice D must be ETS's answer. (It is.) This problem is a number 30—the hardest item in its section. And yet we were able to find ETS's answer with relative ease.

You have to be very careful when you do this sort of thing, but you will often find hard problems where information in the diagram will enable you to eliminate at least one or two choices. Some figures are simply impossible to draw out of scale.

We could also have solved the problem above by applying the Pythagorean theorem. Here's how:

We know from the information in the diagram and the problem that the two triangles are right triangles whose hypotenuses measure 6. We've also been given 3 marked angles: a 90-degree angle in each triangle and 135-degree angle in the middle of the circle. Because we remember that every line and every triangle contains 180 degrees, we also know that the unmarked interior angles in the two triangles each measure 45 degrees. Because these angles are equal in measure, the sides opposite them are equal in length. Let's call this length y. The Pythagorean theorem tells us that $y^2 + y^2 = 6^2$, which means that $2(y^2) = 36$, which means that $y^2 = 18$. The area of each triangle is $\frac{y^2}{2}$, or 9. The area of the entire shaded region is thus 18. ETS's answer is choice D.

SUMMARY

1. Each math section of your GRE will contain ten regular math questions drawn from arithmetic, algebra, and geometry. The ten regular math questions will be divided into two groups of five items each. The first five-item regular-math group (items 16–20) will come after the quantitative comparisons and before the chart. Of these five items, the first three will be easy and the last two will be medium. The second five-item regular-math group will follow the chart (items 26–30). Of these five items, the first two will be medium and the final three will be difficult.

2. On difficult math problems, Joe Bloggs is attracted to easy solutions arrived at through methods that he understands.

3. Joe Bloggs likes to find answers by using easy arithmetic. On difficult questions, all such choices can be eliminated.

4. On difficult math problems, Joe Bloggs is attracted to answer choices that simply repeat numbers from the problem.

5. On difficult math problems in which you are asked to find the *least* (or *greatest*) possible value that satisfies the conditions of the problem, you can automatically eliminate the least (or greatest) value among the choices.

6. When "It cannot be determined" is offered as a choice on an easy or medium problem, it has a very good chance of being ETS's answer.

7. When "It cannot be determined" is offered as a choice on a difficult problem, it has almost no chance of being ETS's answer.

8. The only time you have to be careful is when ETS offers "It cannot be determined" as an answer choice on *two* difficult questions in the same math section, as it occasionally does. In such cases, you can be certain that one of these choices is ETS's answer.

9. Work backward instead of setting up an equation—that is, simply try a choice and see if it works.

10. Ignore irrelevant information in otherwise straightforward word problems.

11. When a problem contains variables instead of numbers, you can often find a shortcut to ETS's answer by *making up* numbers and plugging them in. Here's what you do:

    A. Pick a number for each variable in the problem

    B. Solve the problem using your numbers

    C. Plug your numbers into the answer choices to see which one of them equals the solution you found in step 2.

12. You should never, never, never try to solve problems like these by "solving for *x*" or "solving for *y*." Plugging in is much easier and faster, and you'll be less likely to make dumb mistakes.

13. You can plug in any numbers you like, but you'll save time if you use *easy* numbers.

14. When plugging in on inequalities, don't forget about 0, 1, fractions, negative fractions, and negative integers, all of which have special properties and are thus useful in eliminating incorrect answer choices.

15. You can solve problems containing big nasty numbers by plugging in easy numbers.

16. Watch out for tricky wording in GRE word problems.

17. On geometry problems, you can plug in values for angles or lengths if the values you plug in don't contradict either the wording of the problem or the laws of geometry.

18. You can very often work even more quickly by getting a general idea of what ETS's answer must be and then eliminating choices that are far wide of the mark.

19. Virtually all GRE math problems can be solved using shortcuts that avoid time-consuming math.

20. Diagrams on GRE geometry problems usually are *not* drawn to scale. This means that GRE-takers can't simply "guesstimate" ETS's answer by eyeballing a diagram or by measuring directly— both of which are extremely powerful techniques on the SAT.

The Chart

Buried in the middle of every GRE math section is a set of five questions based on a chart or graph (or on a group of charts or graphs). These questions are numbered 21–25. Question 21 is easy, questions 22–23 are medium, and questions 24–25 are difficult.

Always pay attention to the item number in answering GRE questions. The item number will help determine which technique or combination of techniques you will use to crack the problem.

OUR UNBELIEVABLY GREAT TECHNIQUES

The GRE's chart questions test your ability to read charts and graphs. Why ETS thinks this skill has anything to do with your fitness for graduate school is a great mystery. Perhaps ETS thinks that charts make a GRE math section look more graduate school-like than an SAT math section, which it otherwise closely resembles. (For that matter, what does math have to do with anyone's fitness for graduate study in any subject outside of math or science? And why test anyone's fitness for graduate study in math or science with questions drawn mainly from junior high school math?)

Fortunately, the mathematics tested in the chart questions is usually quite simple: percentages, averages, ratios, and so on. If you're on top of your GRE Mathematics, you shouldn't have any trouble.

Where most students do get into trouble is not in making these calculations but in reading the questions and examining the charts. Joe Bloggs reads the questions carelessly and makes his calculations based on the wrong information. Your first step toward improving your performance on charts, therefore, is to slow down and make certain you know exactly what you have been asked to do.

In order to answer these five questions, you'll need to be able to read and understand grid graphs, bar graphs, pie charts, and tables. In this chapter, we'll describe each one and show you how to attack the sorts of questions you can expect to encounter.

CHARTS AND GRAPHS

GRID GRAPHS

If you understand how Cartesian grids work, you understand how grid graphs work. Here's a very simple example. It's a grid graph that depicts the relationship between a person's age and his or her height:

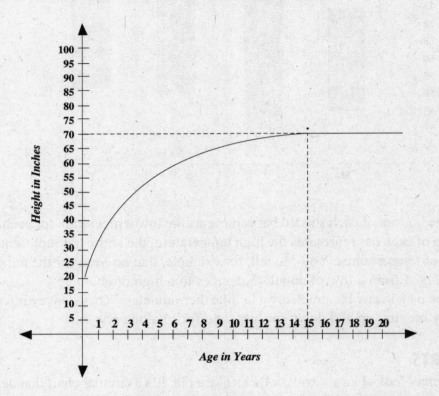

The vertical axis represents height; the horizontal axis represents age; the plotted curve represents the relationship between them. You can use this graph to find the person's height at any age, or age at any height. In the example above, the marked point on the curve shows us that at age 15, the person was 70 inches tall.

BAR GRAPHS

A bar graph is a lot like a grid graph. The following example portrays the range in temperature during four consecutive days:

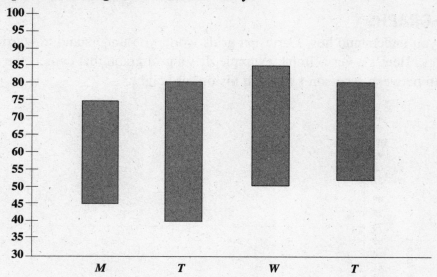

The bottom of each shaded bar represents the low temperature for each day; the top of each bar represents the high temperature; the entire bar represents the range of temperatures. You can tell, for example, that on Monday the temperature ranged from a low of about 45 degrees to a high of about 75.

The bars in any bar graph are a lot like thermometers. They convey information by moving up and down (or back and forth) along one axis.

PIE CHARTS

A pie chart looks like a—well, it looks like a pie. It's a circular chart that depicts fractional parts of whole as wedge-shaped slices. Here's an example that shows how much of a certain blueberry pie was eaten by various members of a family:

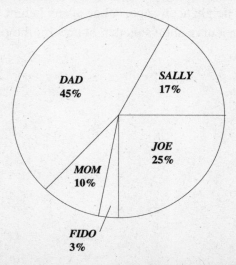

Pie charts are easy to read, if you don't get careless. Just remember that the entire pie stands for 100 percent of whatever is being represented—in the example above, that would be 100 percent of an actual pie. ETS always draws pie charts that are proportionally accurate, so you can often develop a rough idea of what ETS's answer is simply by looking at the graph.

ETS will sometimes make pie charts seem trickier by using a second graph, chart, or table to elaborate on data contained in the pie chart. For example, we could elaborate on the information in the chart above by adding a second pie chart representing just the 45 percent of the pie eaten by Dad:

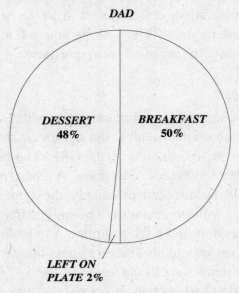

DAD

DESSERT
48%

BREAKFAST
50%

LEFT ON PLATE 2%

Our second pie chart, above, shows when and how Dad consumed his share of the pie. He ate 48 percent for dessert, 50 percent for breakfast the following morning, and left 2 percent on his plate. If you were asked what part of the entire pie Dad ate for breakfast, you would multiply 45 percent (Dad's total share) by 50 percent (the portion of that total share that he ate for breakfast), giving you an answer of 22.5 percent. (Joe Bloggs, reading quickly and carelessly, would answer 50 percent.)

TABLES

A chart is a tool for depicting numerical information as a picture. Instead of simply listing what percentage of the pie each family member ate, for example, a chart shows the same information graphically.

A table, in contrast, conveys the information without the picture. A table is just a list, or lists, of numbers broken down by categories. Some tables on the GRE will stand alone; others will refer to information in other tables or charts.

Here, for example, is a table that conveys exactly the same information as that contained in our original pie chart, above:

The Blueberry Pie: **Who Ate What**
Dad   45%
Joe   25%
Sally   17%
Mom   10%
Fido   3%

Once again, your main concern should be to be absolutely certain you understand what information ETS is asking you to find. If you read quickly and carelessly, you'll miss the point on most questions.

A SAMPLE SECTION

Assuming that you are successful at extracting whatever information ETS has represented in its charts and tables, the questions should pose no more of a problem than other math questions on the GRE. The item types are the same as those used in other arithmetic questions. A chart question that deals with percentages should be attacked in exactly the same way as a regular math question that deals with percentages. The only difference is that some of the information you need to find ETS's solution is to be found outside the question itself. (Most students should also merely guess blindly on items 24 and 25 and get on with easier items later in the test.)

Here's a sample chart section. It consists of two pie charts and five questions. We'll tackle the questions one at a time:

Questions 21–25 refer to the following graphs:

(Fictional) Nationwide survey of people's ice cream preference in 1975 and in 1985, by flavor.

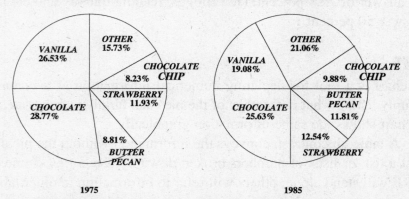

1975   1985

21. To the nearest one percent, what percentage decrease in popularity occured for chocolate from 1975 to 1985?

(A) 9%   (B) 10%   (C) 11%   (D) 89%   (E) 90%

22. What is the ratio of categories that increased in popularity to those that decreased?

(A) 1:2   (B) 1:1   (C) 3:2   (D) 2:1   (E) 5:1

23. In 1985, if 20 percent of the "other" category is Lemon flavor, and 4,212 people surveyed preferred Lemon, then how many people were surveyed?

(A) 1,000   (B) 10,000   (C) 42,120
(D) 100,000   (E) 1,000,000

24. If a percentage-point shift results in annual additional sales of $50,000, how much, in dollars, did combined annual Butter Pecan and Chocolate Chip sales increase between 1975–1985?

(A) $2,325   (B) $4,650   (C) $232,500
(D) $465,000   (E) $23,250,000

25. Which of the following statements can be deduced from the pie graphs?

I. Both the Butter Pecan and Vanilla percentages increased by more than 33 percent between 1975 and 1985.
II. A higher percentage of people chose Butter Pecan and Strawberry in 1975 than chose Butter Pecan and Chocolate Chip in 1985.
III. The total share of Vanilla, Chocolate, and Strawberry decreased by less than 20 percent from 1975 to 1985.

(A) I only   (B) II only   (C) III only
(D) II and III   (E) I, II, and III

ATTACKING THE QUESTIONS

That's what it looks like. Now let's go back and take another look at the first question:

21. To the nearest one percent, what percentage decrease in popularity occured for chocolate from 1975 to 1985?

(A) 9%   (B) 10%   (C) 11%
(D) 89%   (E) 90%

Here's how to crack it:

This is the first question, and therefore the easiest. It's asking you to do something very simple: to find the difference between 28.77 and 25.63 and then determine what percentage of 28.77 that difference is.

(Joe Bloggs gets terribly confused in taking percentages of percentages. Gosh! It sounds like the Twilight Zone! But all you have to do to keep from being confused is to drop the percent sign from the numbers you're taking a percentage of. If you do become confused, put yourself back on track by working a simple problem in your head. For example, 50 percent of 10 is 5; 50 percent of 10 percent is 5 percent.)

First, we need to find the difference between 28.77 (the 1975 figure) and 25.63 (the 1985 figure). The difference is 3.14.

Stop: We've already found ETS's answer. First, you should be able to see at a glance that choices D and E are out of the question. Second–keeping in mind that ETS has asked for an approximate answer ("to the nearest one percent")— you should notice that 3.14 is in the neighborhood of 10 percent of 28.77. Is it exactly 10 percent? No; that means choice B is out. Is it more or less than 10 percent? It's more—exactly 10 percent would be 2.877, and 3.14 is more than 2.877. That means ETS's answer is choice C.

22. What is the ratio of categories that increased in popularity to those that decreased?

    (A) 1:2   (B) 1:1   (C) 3:2   (D) 2:1   (E) 5:1

Here's how to crack it:

In ratio problems, the first step is always to "count the parts." How many parts are there? The same as the number of categories, which is the same as the number of pie slices in *one* of the charts. That's six. Now we need the number of categories that increased between 1975 and 1985, and the number that decreased. Vanilla went down; Other went up; Chocolate Chip went up; Butter Pecan went up; Strawberry went up; Chocolate went down. That is, four of the six parts increased, and two of the six parts decreased. The ratio of increases to decreases, therefore, is 4:2 (not 4:6—be careful). The ratio 4:2 can be simplified to 2:1. That means ETS's answer is choice D.

23. In 1985, if 20 percent of the "other" category is Lemon flavor, and 4,212 people surveyed preferred Lemon, then how many people were surveyed?

    (A) 1,000   (B) 10,000   (C) 42,120
    (D) 100,000   (E) 1,000,000

Here's how to crack it:

The questions are getting tougher, so we have to be careful. First, let's make sure we understand what ETS is looking for.

The first piece of information ETS has given us is a percentage of a percentage. The percentage of people who preferred Lemon in 1985 is equal to 20 percent of 21.06 percent. Make certain you see that before we go on.

Now you should notice that the numbers in ETS's answer choices are very widely separated—they aren't consecutive integers. That means we can be quite rough in our calculations, even if ETS's answer is exact. If we can just get in the ballpark, ETS's answer will be obvious.

We quickly estimate that 20 percent of 21.06 percent is equal to about 4 percent. (A percentage of a percentage again—don't panic.) This means that 4,212 is equal to about 4 percent of the number we have been asked to find. You

should be able to eliminate choices A, B, and C immediately (they're all much too small) and then, after a quick calculation, realize that ETS's answer is choice D.

24. If a percentage-point shift results in annual additional sales of $50,000, how much, in dollars, did combined annual Butter Pecan and Chocolate Chip sales increase between 1975 and 1985?

(A) $2,325 (B) $4,650 (C) $232,500 (D) $465,000
(E) $23,250,000

Here's how to crack it:

The item number tells us that this is a hard problem, but you'll find it easy if you keep your wits about you.

The first thing to keep in mind is that you find a percentage-*point* difference simply by subtracting percentages—you don't have to calculate percentages or multiply percentages times percentages or anything like that. The percentage-*point* decrease between 120 percent and 100 percent is 20; the *percentage* decrease between 120 percent and 100 percent is $16\frac{2}{3}$ percent.

Let's take one thing at a time. What happened to Butter Pecan between 1975 and 1985? It went from 8.81 percent to 11.81 percent. That's a 3 percentage-point increase.

What happened to Chocolate Chip between 1975 and 1985? It went from 8.23 percent to 9.88 percent. That's a 1.65 percentage-point increase.

Once again, the numbers in the answer choices are widely separated, so we don't need to be very exact. The exact combined percentage-point increase between 1975 and 1985 is 4.65, but you could as easily use 4, 4.5, or 5.

To find ETS's answer, simply multiply one of these numbers by 50,000. You get something between 200,000 and 250,000. What's ETS's answer? Choice C.

25. Which of the following statements can be deduced from the pie graphs?

I. Both the Butter Pecan and Vanilla percentages increased by more than 33 percent between 1975 and 1985.
II. A higher percentage of people chose Butter Pecan and Strawberry in 1975 than chose Butter Pecan and Chocolate Chip in 1985.
III. The total share of Vanilla, Chocolate, and Strawberry decreased by less than 20 percent from 1975 to 1985.

(A) I only (B) II only (C) III only
(D) II and III (E) I, II, and III

Here's how to crack it:

This is an enormously time-consuming problem: It's difficult and a triple true/false. Most students would probably be better off guessing on it and moving on. But here's how to solve it.

First, check out the first statement. Did the Butter Pecan percentage increase by more than 33 percent (one-third)? It increased from 8.81 to 11.81. That's a 3-point increase. Is 3 more than one-third of 8.81? Yes. Okay so far. Now check Vanilla. Vanilla went from 26.53 to 19.08. That's a decrease, not an increase. Statement I isn't true. We can eliminate A and E.

Now there are three choices left, B, C, and D. Let's try Statement II. What's the combined percentage for Butter Pecan and Strawberry in 1975? It's 8.81 plus 11.93, or 20.74. What's the combined percentage for Butter Pecan and Chocolate Chip in 1985? It's 11.81 plus 9.88, or 21.69. Statement II is false. We can eliminate choices B and D. ETS's answer is choice C.

SUMMARY

1. The five chart questions on your GRE will be numbered 21–25. Question 21 is easy, questions 22–23 are medium, and questions 24–25 are difficult.

2. The mathematics tested in chart questions is usually quite simple: percentages, averages, ratios, and so on.

3. Where most students get into trouble on chart questions is not in performing the simple calculations required but in reading the questions and examining the charts.

4. There are four main kinds of charts tested on the GRE: grid graphs, bar graphs, pie charts, and tables.

5. A grid graph has two axes, just like a Cartesian grid. It is used to show the relationship between two variable factors, such as height and age.

6. A bar graph is a lot like a grid graph. You can think of each bar as a thermometer; it conveys information by moving up and down (or back and forth) along one axis.

7. A pie chart resembles a pie. Each wedge represents a part of the whole. If the wedges represent percentages, the entire circle, or pie, always represents 100 percent.

8. A table is a list, or lists, of numbers broken down by categories. Some tables on the GRE will stand alone; others will refer to information in other tables or charts.

9. Chart questions don't require special math. A chart question that deals with percentages should be attacked in exactly the same way as a regular math question dealing with percentages. The only difference is that some of the information you need to find ETS's solution is to be found outside the question itself.

Quantitative Comparison

Each math section of your GRE will contain fifteen quantitative comparison items, numbered 1–15. Items 1–5 will be easy, items 6–10 will be medium, and items 11–15 will be hard. Always pay attention to the item number in answering GRE questions. The item number will help determine which technique or combination of techniques you will use to crack the problem.

OUR NUMBING TECHNIQUES

ETS likes quant comps because they're what test-makers call "efficient." That is, they produce roughly the same results as other kinds of math questions but in less time. Joe Bloggs fairly sails through quant comps—no sweat! This means, of course, that you need to be careful.

Fortunately for you, the "efficiency" of quant comps makes them unusually easy to crack. Joe Bloggs sails through them because on hard items the traps seem appealing almost immediately—he doesn't have to waste a lot of time in order to find an incorrect answer. This means that your knowledge of how Joe thinks will be a big help to you on these items.

WHAT IS A QUANTITATIVE COMPARISON?

Here are the directions for quant comps as they will appear on your GRE:

Directions: Each of the Questions 1–15 consists of two quantities, one in Column A and one in Column B. You are to compare the two quantities and choose

A if the quantity in Column A is greater;
B if the quantity in Column B is greater;
C if the quantities are equal;
D if the relationship cannot be determined from the information given

Note: Since there are only four choices, NEVER MARK (E).

Common Information: In a question, information concerning one or both of the quantities to be compared is centered above the two columns. A symbol that appears in both columns represents the same thing in Column A as it does in Column B.

	Column A	Column B	Sample Answers
Example 1:	2×6	$2 + 6$	● Ⓑ Ⓒ Ⓓ Ⓔ

Examples 2-4 refer to $\triangle PQR$.

	Column A	Column B	Sample Answers
Example 2:	PN	NQ	Ⓐ Ⓑ Ⓒ ● Ⓔ

(since equal measures cannot be assumed, even though PN and NQ appear equal)

	Column A	Column B	Sample Answers
Example 3:	x	y	Ⓐ ● Ⓒ Ⓓ Ⓔ

(since N is between P and Q)

	Column A	Column B	Sample Answers
Example 4:	$w + z$	180	Ⓐ Ⓑ ● Ⓓ Ⓔ

(since PQ is a straight line)

OUR OWN DIRECTIONS

Naturally, you shouldn't even glance at ETS's directions when you take the GRE. And for heaven's sake, don't work the sample problems. Pity the poor sub-Bloggs who spends five minutes sweating over four items that don't count.

Usually we tell you to learn ETS's directions. This time we're going to tell you to learn our own directions instead. Why? Because our directions are better than ETS's. They'll keep you out of trouble. Here they are:

> <u>Directions</u>: Each of the Questions 1–15 consists of two quantities, one in Column A and one in Column B. You are to compare the two qua*ntities and choose*
>
> A if the quantity in Column A is <u>always</u> greater
> B if the quantity in Column B is <u>always</u> greater
> C if the quantities are <u>always</u> equal
> D if none of the other choices is <u>always</u> correct

WHAT'S THE DIFFERENCE?

It's not enough to determine that the quantity in Column A is *sometimes* greater than the quantity in Column B. You have to be certain that it *always* is. If you remember this key fact, you'll save points. Here's a simple example:

Column A	Column B
1. $x + 1$	$1 - x$

Here's how to crack it:

Plug in an easy number. How about 1? That gives us 2 as the quantity in Column A and 0 as the quantity in Column B. We know that 2 is greater than 0, so ETS's answer must be choice A, right?

Wrong. Because this isn't *always* true. To see this, try plugging in –1. That gives us 0 in Column A and 2 in Column B—just the reverse of what we had before.

In other words, the relationship between the quantities in the two columns isn't *always* the same. Therefore ETS's answer is choice D.

Remembering the word *always* becomes extremely important on medium and difficult quant comps, when Joe Bloggs gets into trouble. Later in the chapter, we'll tell you more about "testing for always."

NEVER MARK E

Quant comps have only four answer choices. That's great: A blind guess has one chance in four of being correct. Unfortunately, each line on your answer sheet will have five spaces. If you accidentally mark choice E—which is easy to do if you're distracted—your answer will be counted as incorrect. Be careful.

WHERE'S THE MATH?

Quant comps are drawn from the basic arithmetic, algebra, and geometry concepts that constitute GRE Mathematics. In general, then, you'll apply the same techniques you've learned to apply on other types of math questions. Still, quant comps do require a few special techniques of their own. In this chapter, you'll learn about them.

IF A QUANT COMP CONTAINS ONLY NUMBERS, CHOICE D CAN'T BE CORRECT

Any problem containing only numbers must have an exact solution. Therefore, choice D can be eliminated immediately on all such problems. Here's an example:

	Column A	Column B
1.	$\frac{2}{7} - 1$	$\frac{1}{3} - 1$

Here's how to crack it:

Because this problem contains only numbers, you can calculate an exact value for the expression in each column. This means that "cannot be determined" cannot possibly be ETS's answer. Eliminate it.

What *is* ETS's answer on this easy problem? It's choice B. Because −1 appears in both expressions, we can ignore it. That means all we have to decide is whether $\frac{2}{7}$ is bigger than, smaller than, or the same as $\frac{1}{3}$. Of course, it's smaller ($\frac{2}{7}$ is smaller than $\frac{2}{6}$, which is another way of expressing $\frac{1}{3}$).

AVOID COMPUTATION

You will be able to solve some difficult quant comps without putting pencil to paper. Just use common sense to visualize the problem:

	Column A	Column B
14.	Area of a circle with diameter 12	Surface area of a sphere with diameter 12

Here's how to crack it:

This is a difficult item—look at its number. But it's difficult only because Joe Bloggs can't remember whether the formula for surface area of a sphere is pi times radius times pi times whatever . . . But you don't have to know the formula. Just picture a soccer ball and a paper plate. ETS's answer is choice B.

AVOID LENGTHY CALCULATIONS

Quant comps are supposed to be fast. If you find yourself setting up an elaborate calculation (with big numbers or lots of long division), you can be sure you're on the wrong track. As is true on other math questions, you should look for a shortcut. Here's an example:

Column A	Column B
3. $9(3 + 24)$	$(9 \times 3) + (9 \times 24)$

Here's how to crack it:

First of all, you should notice that choice D can't be ETS's answer: There's nothing here but numbers.

Now what? Should you multiply out those numbers? No. ETS isn't testing your ability to multiply. Finding ETS's answer simply depends on your noticing that the expressions in Column A and Column B are simply the factored and unfactored forms of the same number. ETS's answer is choice C.

TREAT THE TWO COLUMNS AS THOUGH THEY WERE THE TWO SIDES OF AN EQUATION

Anything you can do to both sides of an equation, you can also do to the expressions in both columns on a quant comp. You can add the same number to both sides; you can multiply both sides by the same number; you can simplify a single side by multiplying it by some form of 1.

DON'T MULTIPLY OR DIVIDE BOTH SIDES BY A NEGATIVE NUMBER, HOWEVER

Remember what happens to an inequality if you multiply both sides by a negative number? The direction of the inequality symbol changes. That is, if $x > y$, then $-x < -y$. If the quantity in Column A is greater than the quantity in Column B, multiplying or dividing through by a negative number will make Column B greater than Column A. So don't do it.

ALWAYS SIMPLIFY

If you *can* simplify the terms in a quant comp, you should *always* do so. As is so often true on the GRE, finding ETS's answer is frequently merely a matter of simplifying, reducing, factoring, or unfactoring. Here's an example:

Column A	Column B
8. 25×7.39	$\dfrac{739}{4}$

Here's how to crack it:

First of all, you should notice that choice D can't be ETS's answer: There's nothing here but numbers.

What should you do next? Whatever you do, *don't* do the multiplication in the first column and the division in the second. You'd find the answer that way, but it would take forever. Instead, get rid of the fraction in Column B by multiplying *both sides* by 4. Here's what you end up with:

	Column A	Column B
8.	100×7.39	739

Notice anything? You should see immediately that the two quantities are equal. That means ETS's answer is choice C.

PLUGGING IN

The easiest way to solve most quant comps involving variables is to plug in, just as you do on many algebra and geometry problems. Here's an example:

Column A   Column B

$$k < 0$$

2. $((k \times \frac{1}{2}) \div 3) \times 6$ $2(k \times 3) \div 6$

Here's how to crack it:

The expression $k < 0$, you should remember, is a condition that applies to the quantities in both columns.

To solve this problem, simply pick an easy number that satisfies the condition and plug it in. How about −2? (Using it will get rid of the fraction in Column A.) Plugging in −2, we get this for the quantity in Column A:

$$\left(\left(k \times \frac{1}{2}\right) \div 3\right) \times 6 = \left(\left(-2 \times \frac{1}{2}\right) \div 3\right) \times 6$$

$$= \left(\left(\frac{-2}{2}\right) \div 3\right) \times 6$$

$$= (-1 \div 3) \times 6$$

$$= -\frac{1}{3} \times 6$$

$$= -\frac{6}{3}$$

$$= -2$$

Now we plug in the same thing in Column B:

$$2(k \times 3) \div 6 = 2(-2 \times 3) \div 6$$

$$= 2(-6) \div 6$$

$$= -12 \div 6$$

$$= -\frac{12}{6}$$

$$= -2$$

The two quantities are equal. ETS's answer, therefore, is choice C.

TESTING FOR "ALWAYS" WHEN YOU PLUG IN

Unfortunately, plugging in on quant comps isn't always as straightforward as it is on other types of problems. The reason for this is choice D. On quant comps, it's not enough to determine whether one quantity is *sometimes* greater than, less than, or equal to the other; you have to determine whether it *always* is. If it isn't always, then ETS's answer is choice D.

Because of this, you'll have to be a little creative when you plug in. You'll have to find out not just whether a choice *could* be correct but whether it *must* be correct. We call this "testing for always." Here's an example:

Column A	Column B
$x > y$	
10. x^2	y^2

Here's how to crack it:

This is clearly a plug-in problem. Let's say we plug in 3 for x and 2 for y. That satisfies the condition, and it gives us 9 for Column A and 4 for Column B. Column A is bigger, so ETS's answer is A, right?

Not so fast. We know that Column A *can* be bigger, but we haven't proved that it *has* to be bigger. We still have to "test for always." To do this, we need to plug in something different. How about -2 for x and -3 for y? This satisfies the condition, and it gives us 4 for Column A and 9 for Column B. Now Column B is bigger. ETS's answer is choice D.

WHEN YOU TEST FOR ALWAYS, USE *WEIRD* NUMBERS

When you plug in on quant comps, you want to use easy numbers, just as you do on regular math problems. But you also need to use what we call "weird" numbers—numbers with special properties that will reveal any hidden traps or exceptions. Here are the most important weird numbers:

0

1

fractions

negatives

negative fractions

What makes these numbers weird? They all behave in unexpected ways when added, multiplied, and raised to powers. For example:

0 times any number is 0

0^2 is 0

1^2 is 1

$\left(\dfrac{1}{2}\right)^2$ is less than $\dfrac{1}{2}$

$(-2)(-2)$ is 4

a negative number squared is positive

$$\left(-\dfrac{1}{2}\right)^2 \text{ is greater than } -\dfrac{1}{4}$$

When Joe Bloggs plugs in, he usually picks 2 or 3. You'll want to plug in 2 or 3, too, but you'll also need to plug in the numbers that Joe never thinks of—the weird ones. Here's an example:

Column A	Column B
12. $\quad xy$	$x\sqrt{y}$

Here's how to crack it:

First, plug in a pair of easy numbers. Let's try 3 for x and 4 for y. (4 is a good plug-in for y, because $\sqrt{4}$ is an integer.) This gives us 12 for Column A and 6 for Column B. With these plug-ins, choice A looks like ETS's answer.

But before you mark choice A (and lose points by doing it), try a weird number. How about 0 for x and 0 for y? (There's no rule that says x and y have to be different.) That gives us 0 for Column A and 0 for Column B. The two are equal. This means that we can't determine the relationship between the two expressions, and ETS's answer is choice D.

ON MEDIUMS AND DIFFICULTS, ATTACK YOUR HUNCHES

Joe Bloggs begins to fall apart after question 6. After question 10, he's missing everything. So once you've polished off the easy ones, you need to be very suspicious of your hunches. Very often on medium items, and always on difficult ones, answer choices that seem correct immediately (unless you arrived at them by using our techniques) are wrong.

This means that on mediums and difficults you should *attack* easy answers. If a choice seems right to you in a flash, examine it carefully before you mark it on your answer sheet. Plug in some weird numbers, look for exceptions. The higher the item number, the less likely it is that your hunch is correct.

JOE BLOGGS CAN HELP

On items 11 through 15, you should almost always be able to eliminate at least one Joe Bloggs attractor. Remember, on these items, any answer that jumps out at you immediately has to be wrong. To see how this works, take another look at the problem we just discussed:

Column A	Column B
12. xy	$x\sqrt{y}$

Here's how to crack it:

What are the Joe Bloggs attractors on this difficult problem? To find them, simply do what Joe would do and plug in a couple of easy numbers. We used 3 and 4 before. Let's plug them in again. Doing so gives us 12 for the expression in Column A and 6 for the expression in Column B.

What does this tell us? *Everything*. Plugging in the easiest numbers we could think of quickly made A look like ETS's answer. Because this is a difficult item, that means choice A *can't possibly be correct*. If choice A were correct, Joe would get this problem right and it would be an easy, not a medium. So we can eliminate choice A.

Is that all we can do? No. We can also eliminate choices B and C. If the expression in Column A is at least *sometimes* greater than the expression in Column B, then the expression in Column B can't *always* be greater than the expression in Column A. That rules out choice B. Nor can the two *always* be the same. That rules out choice C.

Very quickly, then, we realize that ETS's answer *has* to be choice D. As we already proved, it is.

Here's another example:

Column A	Column B
	$y = x^2 + 1$	
13. xy	x^3

Here's how to crack it:

What are easy (Joe Bloggs) plug-ins? If we plug in 2 for x, we get $y = 4 + 1$, which means that if $x = 2$, $y = 5$. That gives us 10 for Column A and 8 for Column B. That was fast! So, just as fast, we eliminate choices A, B, and C and mark choice D.

To see why this is true, let's plug in a weird number for x. How about -1? That gives us $y = 1 + 1$, which means that if $x = -1$, $y = 2$. This gives us -2 for Column A and -1 for Column B. Once again, ETS's answer must be choice D.

IF THERE'S NO DRAWING ON A GEOMETRY PROBLEM, MAKE ONE YOURSELF

When ETS doesn't include a drawing with a geometry problem, it usually means that the drawing, if supplied, would make ETS's answer obvious. On such problems, therefore, you should supply the drawing yourself. Here's an example:

Column A	Column B
10. On a cube, the number of faces that share an edge	The number of sides of a square with any one face

Here's how to crack it:

There's no reason to visualize this problem in your head. Just make a quick sketch—something like this:

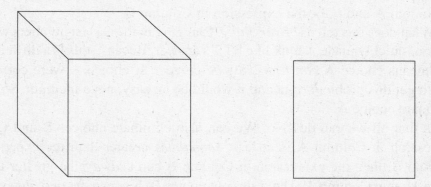

How many faces share an edge with any one face in our drawing of a cube? You should be able to see that each face shares an edge with four other faces. The value of Column A, therefore, is 4. And how about Column B? A square clearly has 4 sides. The values of the two columns are the same. ETS's answer is choice C.

SUMMARY

1. Each math section of your GRE will contain fifteen quantitative comparison items, numbered 1–15. Items 1–5 will be easy, items 6–10 will be medium, and items 11–15 will be hard.

2. Be sure you know The Princeton Review's own directions for quant comps:

   > <u>Directions</u>: Each of the *Questions 1–15* consists of two quantities, one in Column A and one in Column B. You are to compare the two quantities and choose
   >
   > A if the quantity in Column A is <u>always</u> greater
   > B if the quantity in Column B is <u>always</u> greater
   > C if the quantities are <u>always</u> equal
   > D if none of the other choices is <u>always</u> correct

3. Quant comps have only four answer choices. Never mark choice E on your answer sheet.

4. Quant comps are drawn from the basic arithmetic, algebra, and geometry concepts that constitute GRE Mathematics. Virtually all the same techniques apply.

5. On any problem containing only numbers, choice D cannot possibly be correct.

6. Use common sense to avoid computation on quant comps whenever possible.

7. Quant comps are supposed to be fast. If you find yourself setting up an elaborate calculation (with big numbers or lots of long division), you can be sure you're on the wrong track.

8. Anything you can do to both sides of an equation, you can also do to the expressions in both columns on a quant comp. You can add the same number to both sides; you can multiply both sides by the same number; you can simplify a single side by multiplying it by some form of 1.

9. Don't multiply or divide both sides by a negative number, however. You'll get into trouble if you do.

10. If you *can* simplify the terms in a quant comp, you should *always* do so. As is so often true on the GRE, finding ETS's answer is often merely a matter of simplifying, reducing, factoring, or unfactoring.

11. Plugging in is a powerful technique on quant comps with variables, as it is with regular math problems.

12. Remember to "test for always" when you plug in on quant comps. That is, be sure your answer is *always* correct.

13. When you test for always, use both easy numbers and "weird" numbers. Here are the most important weird numbers:

    0

    1

    fractions

    negatives

    negative fractions

14. On medium and difficult problems, attack your hunches.

15. On items 11–15, you should almost always be able to eliminate at least one Joe Bloggs attractor. These are answer choices that jump out at you after you have performed an easy plug-in or calculation.

16. If there's no drawing on a geometry problem, make one yourself.

How to Crack the Logic Sections

GEOGRAPHY OF THE LOGIC SECTIONS

Every GRE contains two scored "analytical ability," or logic, sections. Your test could also contain a third logic section, as an experimental section. This experimental logic section would look like the other two logic sections but would not count toward your score.

Each logic section on your test will last thirty minutes and contain twenty-five items, as follows:

Nineteen "analytical reasoning" questions

Six "logical reasoning" questions

At The Princeton Review, we refer to "analytical reasoning" as *games* and to "logical reasoning" as *arguments*. Each type of question has its own characteristics, which we'll describe in the succeeding chapters. The arrangement of the questions may vary slightly from test to test.

Like the rest of the GRE, the logic sections are arranged in order of increasing difficulty. Each section contains three to four games, each of which is followed by several questions. The first game in each section is easy, the second is easy-medium, the third is medium-difficult or difficult, and the fourth, if there is one, is difficult. The questions accompanying each game are in no particular order.

The argument questions progress in difficulty, too. They appear in two sets of three. The first set is relatively easy and the second set is relatively hard. We say "relatively hard" because most students, especially those who do well on verbal sections, find arguments much easier than games. Even students who do very well on the math sections will find the last game in each section exceedingly difficult.

Here's how the items are arranged in a typical logic section:

Item Analysis	Difficulty
Game 1*	Easy
Three arguments	
Game 2	Medium
Game 3	Medium/Difficult
Game 4	Difficult
Three arguments	

* Each game is followed by three to seven questions.

LAW SCHOOL, ANYONE?

The GRE's logic sections look an awful lot like the Law School Admissions Test (LSAT). Indeed, the question types are identical. The reason for this has less to do with the nature of graduate school than with the economics of the standardized-testing business.

The good news is that the GRE's versions of both these item types are considerably easier than the LSAT's. Many of our LSAT techniques for these item types don't even apply.

THE IMPORTANCE OF PACING YOURSELF

Games questions are sort of a cross between mathematical word problems, brainteasers, and reading comprehension. They can be extremely time-consuming. As is true on much of the rest of the test, you can probably do better by attempting less. You can miss quite a few of these questions and still do very, very well. Unless you're aiming for a score at the very top of the scale, skipping some questions probably makes sense. (You must always mark an answer for every item, of course.)

What should you skip? Virtually all students would benefit from skipping the final game and merely marking guesses for its accompanying questions. Even high-scoring math students would probably find this to their advantage. At the very least—unless you have a supernatural knack for games—you should make certain that you have completed the final three argument questions, which come at the very end of the section, before you even look at the final game. This is especially important if time is running short, as it probably will be.

WHAT ABOUT JOE BLOGGS?

Unfortunately, Joe Bloggs isn't much help on logic questions. Since games questions (as opposed to the games themselves) aren't presented in order of difficulty, you can't be certain whether an attractive choice is a trap or merely an attractive choice. And arguments questions are relatively easy; you simply won't need Joe Bloggs, except as a reminder to be careful. For these reasons, you need to forget about Joe Bloggs most of the time and depend on other techniques.

THE IMPORTANCE OF PRACTICE

As with the other sections, you'll need to practice if you're really serious about improving your score on the logic sections. This is especially true of games. Unless you're familiar with these item types already, they'll take some getting used to. Our techniques will, too. So get to work.

Games

Each logic section of your GRE will contain three or four "analytical reasoning" sets, or games, each of which will be accompanied by between three and seven questions. The games themselves will be presented in order of increasing difficulty, although the questions accompanying them will not. **Since games are so difficult, skipping the hardest one would probably be to your advantage.** At the very least, you should save the more difficult set of games—the second one—for last, after you have completed the set of arguments items that follows it.

OUR SOMEWHAT INCREDIBLE TECHNIQUES

Most students who take the GRE hate games—as well they might. These are tough questions that will probably strike you as being unlike any other test questions you've ever had to tackle, unless you've taken the LSAT.

Games aren't susceptible to a single quick problem-solving technique. Improving your score on games will require practice. Our techniques should help you considerably, but you'll still need to work. The only way you will feel comfortable with games under the pressure of the actual exam room is by practicing them again and again. Our techniques are all aimed at helping you become methodical and efficient in your approach.

Even though they're very hard, games don't have to be drudgery. Many students come to think of them as fun. Think of them as brainteasers—as challenges to your ingenuity.

ETS'S DIRECTIONS

Here are the directions for the logic section as they will appear on your GRE:

Directions: Each question or group of questions is based on a passage or set of conditions. In answering some of the questions, it may be useful to draw a rough diagram. For each question, select the best answer choice given.

OUR OWN DIRECTIONS

Naturally, you shouldn't even glance at ETS's directions when you take the GRE. They won't help you, anyway. Instead, make sure you understand our own directions. They'll give you a much clearer idea of what you're supposed to do on the test. Here they are:

Directions: A GRE game is a puzzle. In each one, you'll be given several clues ("set of conditions" in ETS-speak). You will then be required to use those clues to find the answers to questions. Some questions will contain additional clues; these will apply only to the questions in which they are given. You will almost always want to draw a rough diagram to help you keep track of what you've been told and what you've been able to deduce from it.

The best way to get a feel for GRE games is to work through a simple example. (You'll never really see a game this simple on a real GRE.) Here's the example:

> Tom is older than Dick.
> Dick is older than Harry.

1. Which of the following must be true?

   (A) Tom is younger than Dick.
   (B) Tom is younger than Harry.
   (C) Harry is older than Dick.
   (D) Harry is younger than Tom.
   (E) Dick is older than Tom.

Here's how to crack it:

The initial clues tell us explicitly that Tom is older than Dick and that Dick is older than Harry. These two clues enable us immediately to eliminate choices A, C, and E, each of which directly contradicts the clues we've been given.

This leaves just choices B and D. Assume, for a moment, that you don't instantly see the correct answer (even though we hope you do). How should you proceed? By drawing a diagram. In this case, we'll make a very simple little diagram that uses the clues we've been given to depict the relative ages of Tom, Dick, and Harry. One way to do this is to arrange their ages vertically, placing the initial of someone older over the initial of someone younger. Here's how to diagram the first clue in this way:

T
D

That is, Tom is older than Dick. Now we want to add the information provided in the second clue. Here's what we end up with:

T
D
H

Now look back at the two remaining choices. The first is B, "Tom is younger than Harry." Does the diagram say this is true? No. It shows that it is false. So we know that ETS's answer is choice D.

Sometimes a game question will provide new clues, in addition to the ones given in setting up the game. **Any such additional clues apply only to the**

questions in which they are given. (From now on, we'll refer to the initial clues as the "set-up" clues to distinguish them from the new clues.) Here's an example:

2. If Jane is older than Dick, which of the following could be true?

   (A) Jane is younger than Harry.
   (B) Jane is older than Harry but younger than Dick.
   (C) Jane is older than Tom but younger than Harry.
   (D) Jane is the same age as Harry.
   (E) Jane is the same age as Tom.

Here's how to crack it:

This question introduces Jane and contains the only information we have about her. It tells us that she is older than Dick. We add her to our diagram, like this:

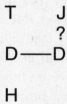

We know that Jane is older than Dick, but we don't know where she stands in relation to Tom. So we place both Jane and Dick off to the side and place a question mark between them. Our diagram now tells us that Jane is older than Dick, who is older than Harry and younger than Tom. That's all we know.

Now we look at the choices closely, looking for the *one* choice that *could* be true:

(A) Could Jane be younger than Harry? No. Our diagram tells us at a glance that Dick is older than Harry, and Jane is older than Dick. Eliminate.

(B) Could Jane be older than Harry but younger than Dick? No. Jane can't be younger than Dick, because we've been told she is older than Dick. Eliminate.

(C) Could Jane be older than Tom but younger than Harry? No. We can easily see that although Jane could indeed be older than Tom, she could not possibly be younger than Harry. Eliminate.

(D) Could Jane be the same age as Harry? No. We know for a fact that she has to be older. Eliminate.

(E) Could Jane be the same age as Tom? Yes, she could. Both Tom and Jane are older than Dick. Though we know nothing else about the relationship between their ages, there is nothing we know that would make this impossible. This must be ETS's answer.

OUR GENERAL STEP-BY-STEP STRATEGY

As we've already told you, we don't have a single, elegantly simple technique for cracking these difficult problems, but we do have a general strategy. We'll outline this strategy first. Then we'll discuss each step in it at greater length. Then we'll show you how the strategy applies to actual games. Here's the outline:

> **Step 1: Read the set-up clues and get the general picture.**
> **Step 2: Draw a diagram based on the set-up clues.**
> **Step 3: Look for the easier questions.**
> **Step 4: Use POE efficiently to eliminate incorrect choices.**

STEP 1: READ THE SET-UP CLUES AND GET THE GENERAL PICTURE

Students often begin to diagram a game before they've read all the set-up clues.

Don't be in such a hurry.

The set-up clues are in no particular order. Sometimes the most revealing clue—the one you'll want to use as the starting point for your diagram—is the last one given. Students who begin diagramming immediately often have to scratch out their initial diagrams and begin again. **Read through *all* the clues before you begin to make your diagram.**

STEP 2: DRAW A DIAGRAM

There isn't a single type of diagram that applies to all GRE games. We'll show you several kinds as we work through the chapter, but you'll want to improvise and look for techniques that make you feel comfortable.

Though every once in a while you will encounter a game that *cannot* be diagrammed, most GRE games can't be solved without a diagram. On virtually all games, you simply won't be able to keep track of the information you're given without symbolizing it on paper.

Your diagram should not merely repeat the information in the set-up clues. That is, it shouldn't simply be shorthand for the clues. The best diagrams are ones that help your thinking and lead you to ETS's answers. The best diagrams are also simple.

Don't spend too much time thinking about which type of diagram to draw. The "ideal" diagram won't be of any use to you if you spend ten minutes figuring out what it is. Don't let yourself become paralyzed. If you get stuck, simply try something.

After you've completed your diagram, don't spend too much time trying to analyze it. If you do, you may be wasting time and making faulty assumptions. Size up your diagram after you've drawn it, but move to the questions as quickly as possible.

STEP 3: LOOK FOR THE EASIER QUESTIONS

As we've already told you, games questions aren't presented in order of difficulty. But this doesn't mean they don't vary in difficulty. Ideally, you'll want to attack the easier questions first. How can you tell which ones are easy and which ones are hard? Here are some general guidelines:

1. Most games include a question that can be answered simply by matching each of the clues against the choices. This question often comes first. Do it first, especially if time is about to be called and you don't have time to draw a diagram.

2. A question that provides new clues is usually easier than one that does not.

3. Questions containing the word *must* are usually easier than questions containing the word *could*. As you'll recall from the chapter on reading comprehension, *must* questions are easier to dispute, and thus easier to solve, than *could* questions.

4. Triple true/false questions (I, II, III questions) are more time-consuming than regular questions. You should save them for later and avoid them when you're short of time.

5. CANNOT and EXCEPT questions can be both time-consuming and confusing. Do easier questions first, and be careful.

6. If you can't answer a question, circle it, mark a choice, and move on to another. Don't waste time if you aren't getting anywhere.

7. Never erase your scratch work. Your solution to an easy question will often provide a key to solving a harder one later on. (Erasing scratch work is a silly waste of time anyway, as we told you at the beginning of the book.)

STEP 4: USE POE EFFICIENTLY TO ELIMINATE INCORRECT CHOICES

POE should always be at the heart of your approach to the GRE: The easiest way to zero in on ETS's answer is to eliminate incorrect choices. This is especially true with games.

When most students first attempt a game, they sit patiently. They want to understand the game. They think, and think some more. The answer doesn't come. So they think some more. Unfortunately, they have at most ninety seconds to read a game question, analyze it, and find ETS's answer.

Smart testers aren't proud. They don't care whether they "understand" a game, and they don't care how they find ETS's answer. All they care about is which choice works—and which choices don't.

Smart testers use POE aggressively and efficiently. Rather than waste time, they try something to see if it works. If it does, they eliminate any choice that conflicts with it. If it doesn't work, they eliminate any choice that permits it.

Here are some POE guidelines:

1. Don't wait to eliminate. If you can eliminate a choice, do it. Get those incorrect choices out of the way, or they'll come back to haunt you.

2. Don't forget what you already know. Answering one question will often give you an insight that you can apply on a later question.

3. Don't sit there thinking—try something! Don't feel you have to "understand" a game before you answer a question. POE will let you earn points by brute force.

4. Don't go overboard. Eliminate only what you need to eliminate in order to find ETS's answer. Don't get so wrapped up in POE that you answer a question without knowing it.

PUTTING THE STRATEGY TO WORK

Here's a relatively simple game, followed by seven questions. Read the game and try your hand at answering the questions (give yourself eight minutes, and be sure to mark your answers in your book or on a sheet of paper).

Then, when you've finished, carefully read our step-by-step implementation of the strategy, which follows the questions. If you picked ETS's answers all by yourself, terrific! If not, our analysis should help you learn from your mistakes.

Here's the sample game and questions: Eight members—P, Q, R, S, T, U, V, and W—are eligible to serve as officers of the Science Fiction Club. The Board of Officers comprises one president, two vice-presidents, and two secretaries. Board members are selected in accordance with the following requirements:

The president must be either P or Q.
Only R, S, and T can serve as vice-president.
Only U, V, and W can serve as secretary.
U cannot serve with W.
T cannot serve with U.
S cannot serve unless Q also serves.

1. Which of the following is an acceptable board?

   (A) P, R, S, V, W
   (B) P, S, T, V, W
   (C) Q, R, S, U, V
   (D) Q, R, S, U, W
   (E) Q, S, T, U, V

2. Which of the following members must serve on the board?

   (A) P   (B) R   (C) S   (D) U   (E) V

3. If R and S serve on the board, which of the following CANNOT be true?

   I. P serves as president.
   II. Both V and W serve as secretaries.
   III. Q serves as president.

   (A) I only
   (B) II only
   (C) III only
   (D) I and II only
   (E) II and III only

4. If P serves on the board, which of the following groups of members can complete the board?

   (A) R, S, U, V
   (B) R, S, V, W
   (C) R, T, U, V
   (D) R, T, V, W
   (E) S, T, V, W

5. If Q, T, and W are chosen for the board, which of the
   following groups of members can complete the board?

     I. R, V
    II. S, V
  ~~III. S, U~~

(A) I only
(B) II only
(C) I and II only
(D) II and III only
(E) I, II, and III

6. If P serves on the board, which of the following members
   CANNOT serve?

(A) R (B) T (C) U (D) V (E) W

7. If R and V serve on the board, all of the following groups
   of members could complete the board EXCEPT

(A) Q, S, U
(B) P, T, W
~~(C) P, Q, U~~
(D) Q, S, W
(E) Q, T, W

READ THE SET-UP CLUES AND GET THE GENERAL PICTURE (STEP 1)

Our first step is to read the set-up clues and get the general picture. At first, these clues may look quite intimidating, but as you read along you should notice a couple of patterns:

1. Although there are a lot of members, there are strict limitations on how they can fill the various positions. P and Q are the only possible presidents; R, S, and T are the only possible vice-presidents; U, V, and W are the only possible secretaries. In other words, instead of 8 members what we really have is just 3 nonoverlapping categories. The key to solving complex games is often to break them down into simpler units and then use POE to eliminate choices.

2. The final 3 clues ("U cannot serve with W," etc.) will probably be extremely useful POE tools, because they place strict limitations on membership on the board. Clues like this are very efficient. Each can be used all by itself to eliminate choices. (The last clue or clues in a game are often the most strictly limited and therefore the most useful. Bear this in mind. Joe Bloggs always begins at the beginning.)

3. You might further notice that U is quite unpopular: U can serve with neither W nor T. U's presence on a board will therefore make that board easy to dispute, since W's or T's presence alone will be sufficient reason for elimination.

DRAW A DIAGRAM (STEP 2)

The best diagram is one that enables you to review all the set-up clues, and the relationships between them, at a glance. Here's a good way to diagram the first three set-up clues:

1 PQ

2 RST

2 UVW

The numbers at the left indicate that we must choose 1 from the first set, 2 from the second set, and 2 from the third set.

The fourth and fifth clues tell us that U cannot work with W or T, which we can indicate something like this:

1 PQ

2 RST

2 UVW

You may prefer to use a different symbol. That's fine. The important thing is that you are able to understand your own diagram.

The sixth clue tells us that if S is on the Board, Q must serve as well. We can indicate this with an arrow:

1 PQ

2 RST

2 UVW

Notice that the arrow points from S to Q. The rule states that if S serves, Q must serve as well, but it does *not* say that S must necessarily serve if Q does. It's always important to read carefully.

We have our diagram. Now on to the questions.

LOOK FOR THE EASIER QUESTIONS (STEP 3)

Which questions are easier? You don't need to be scientific about this, and you certainly shouldn't spend a lot of time weighing the merits of different orders of attack. You should see immediately that questions 3 and 5 are triple true/false questions, and therefore time-consuming. Let's not start with those. Let's also save questions 6 and 7, which are CANNOT/EXCEPT questions. The best place to start, as it often is, is with question 1. As we solve it, we'll be on the lookout for information or insights that may help with other questions.

USE POE EFFICIENTLY TO ELIMINATE INCORRECT CHOICES (STEP 4)

Now it's time to score some points. Here's another look at the first question:

1. Which of the following is an acceptable board?

    (A) P, R, S, V, W
    (B) P, S, T, V, W
    (C) Q, R, S, U, V
    (D) Q, R, S, U, W
    (E) Q, S, T, U, V

Here's how to crack it:

This question can be answered simply by applying the clues to the choices. The last three clues are the most restrictive and hence the most useful for POE. Let's start with the last clue and work our way up.

Always work with one clue at a time, applying it to each of the choices and eliminating choices as you can. Doing this is *much* more efficient than applying all the clues to each choice.

The last clue, clue 6, tells us that if S serves, Q must also serve. That means that if we see an S we can eliminate it if we don't also see a Q. Here's what happens:

    (A) There's an S but no Q. Eliminate.
    (B) There's an S but no Q. Eliminate.
    (C) There's an S and a Q. A possibility.
    (D) There's an S and a Q. A possibility.
    (E) There's an S and a Q. A possibility.

We've eliminated 2 choices already. Be sure to cross them out. We don't even want to glance at them again.

Now we apply the fifth clue, which says that T and U cannot be together:

    (C) There's a U but no T. A possibility.
    (D) There's a U but no T. A possibility.
    (E) There's a U *and* a T. Eliminate.

Now we're ready for the fourth clue, which says that U and W cannot be together:

(C)   There's a U but no W. A possibility.
(D)   There's a U *and* a W. Eliminate.

ETS's answer is choice C.
Now let's move on to question 2:

2. Which of the following members must serve on the board?
(A) P   (B) R   (C) S   (D) U   (E) V

Here's how to crack it:

This question can be answered with the diagram alone. Take another look at the diagram:

We need 2 secretaries, and 2 of the 3 possible candidates can't serve together. That means that the third candidate, V, *has* to be one of the secretaries. ETS's answer is choice E.

Don't worry if you didn't see this in the diagram. Most students don't. Don't sit staring at your diagram, waiting for it to divulge ETS's answer. If you don't see it at a glance, turn to POE. In other words, *try something*. We'll take the answer choices one at a time and see what we can do with them.

(A)   Does P have to be on the board? No. How do we know that? We know that because ETS's answer to question 1 proved that QRSUV is an acceptable board, and QRSUV doesn't contain P. Eliminate choice A.

(B)   Does R have to be on the board? All we have to do to eliminate this choice is to create an acceptable board that doesn't have R on it. Let's start by fiddling with the one acceptable board we've already got, QRSUV. What happens if we remove R? If we remove R, we have to insert T. This gives us QTSUV. Does that work? No, T cannot serve with U. Can we get rid of U? Yes, by inserting W. That gives us our second acceptable board, QTSVW. Eliminate choice B.

Be sure to notice that we can also eliminate choice D. In the course of testing choice B, we got rid of U and still came up with an acceptable board.

All we have left are choices C and E. One of these has to be ETS's answer.

(C)   Does S have to be on the board? We have two acceptable boards to fiddle with. Let's try eliminating S from the first one. With S gone, the vice-presidents have to be T and R. Is QRTUV acceptable? No, T and U can't be together. How about QRTWV? Yes, that works. So S isn't necessary. We can eliminate choice C.

That means that ETS's answer is choice E.

Question 3 is a triple true/false *and* a CANNOT. Let's save it for a while and move to the next relatively easy-looking question, which is number 4:

4. If P serves on the board, which of the following groups of members can complete the board?

(A)   R, S, U, V
(B)   R, S, V, W
(C)   R, T, U, V
(D)   R, T, V, W
(E)   S, T, V, W

Here's how to crack it:

This is a straight POE. Since we're given full boards, we can simply apply the rules to see which ones comply. Since this question supplies information that applies to each of the choices (the information is that P is part of each group) it's probably a good idea to pencil in a P at the beginning of each choice. Doing this won't really help you on this item, but penciling in shared information is a good habit to get into. It will keep you from making careless errors.

Once again, work through the clues from the bottom up (or look at your diagram).

The sixth clue says that if we have S, we must also have Q. This eliminates choices A, B, and E. Not bad!

All we have left is C and D. The fifth rule says that T cannot serve with U. Choice C has a T and a U. That's impossible. ETS's answer is choice D.

What next? All the remaining questions are relatively nasty-looking. Number 3 is probably the nastiest. Question 7 is probably the easiest, but don't waste a lot of time pondering. Here's question 7 again:

7. If R and V serve on the board, all of the following groups of members could complete the board EXCEPT

(A)   Q, S, U
(B)   P, T, W
(C)   P, Q, U
(D)   Q, S, W
(E)   Q, T, W

Here's how to crack it:

First, pencil in the shared information. That is, add R and V to each choice. Here's what the rewritten choices should look like:

(A) Q, S, U, R, V
(B) P, T, W, R, V
(C) P, Q, U, R, V
(D) Q, S, W, R, V
(E) Q, T, W, R, V

Now start with the last clue (or look at your diagram) and eliminate. Remember: ETS's answer on this problem is the *one* choice that *doesn't* work.

The sixth clue says that if we have S, we must also have Q. All the choices satisfy this requirement. The fifth clue says that T and U can't be together. All the choices satisfy this requirement, too. Proceeding through the clues, we finally realize that choice C has two presidents. ETS's answer is choice C.

Now here's question 6:

6. If P serves on the board, which of the following members CANNOT serve?

(A) R   (B) T   (C) U   (D) V   (E) W

Here's how to crack it:

ETS's answer to question 4 showed us that PRTVW is an acceptable board. That means that we can eliminate choices A, B, D, and E. That just leaves choice C, which must be ETS's answer.

Here's question 5:

5. If Q, T, and W are chosen for the board, which of the following groups of members can complete the board?

  I. R, V
 II. S, V
III. S, U

(A) I only
(B) II only
(C) I and II only
(D) II and III only
(E) I, II, and III

Here's how to crack it:

First, pencil in the new clues:

  I. Q, T, W, R, V
 II. Q, T, W, S, V
III. Q, T, W, S, U

Once again, test the boards by applying the clues (or looking at your diagram). Clue six says that S can serve only with Q. All three statements contain Q, so this clue doesn't help.

The fifth clue says that T can't be with U. Statement III violates this clue. Cross it out and eliminate choices D and E.

The fourth clue says that U cannot serve with W. Once again, we can't eliminate anything. Statements I and II must both be true. That means ETS's answer is choice C.

Now here's the question we've been saving for last:

> 3. If R and S serve on the board, which of the following CANNOT be true?
>
>   I. P serves as president.
>   II. Both V and W serve as secretaries.
>   III. Q serves as president.
>
> (A) I only
> (B) II only
> (C) III only
> (D) I and II only
> (E) II and III only

Here's how to crack it:

Test the statements one at a time, always keeping in mind that what we're looking for is a statement or statements that CANNOT be true.

Could there be a board consisting of P, R, S, and two others? If S serves, P cannot be president. This arrangement cannot work, which means that statement I cannot be true. We can therefore eliminate choices B, C, and E.

Now all we have to do is check statement II. Can V and W be secretaries if R and S serve? Yes; the diagram proves it. This statement can be true—which means we can eliminate it.

ETS's answer is choice A. (Remember: We were asked which statement or statements could *not* be true.)

SAMPLE GAME NO. 2

This game is also relatively easy. Give yourself four minutes.

> Six cars—P, Q, R, S, T, and U—are being placed in a parking lot. The parking lot has 6 spaces, numbered 1 through 6. Each car is placed in its own space, according to the following restrictions:
>
> P can park anywhere except in 5 or 6.
> Q can park in 4 or 5 only.
> R can park in 3 or 6 only.
> S can park in 2 or 6 only.
> T can park in 1 or 3 only.
> U can park anywhere except in 1 or 3.
>
> 1. If Q parks in 4, U must park in
>
>   (A) 1   (B) 2   (C) 3   (D) 5   (E) 6

2. If P parks in 3, T must park in

   (A) 1   (B) 2   (C) 4   (D) 5   (E) 6

3. If S parks in 6, which of the following must be true?

   (A) T parks in 1.
   (B) P parks in 2.
   (C) Q parks in 4.
   (D) U parks in 4.
   (E) T parks in 3.

CRACKING SAMPLE GAME NO. 2: STEP 1

We can tell that this game is relatively easy, because it has so many clues. Remember: The more clues you have, the easier the game.

What is the general picture conveyed by the clues? It's quite straightforward: 6 cars, 6 parking places, 6 simple rules. On to the diagram.

CRACKING SAMPLE GAME NO. 2: STEP 2

Several types of diagrams are possible. Here's a table that's easy to read:

	U	T	U		U
T	S	R	Q	U	S
P	P	P	P	Q	R
1	2	3	4	5	6

Each numbered column in the table represents a parking space. The letters above the numbers indicate the cars that *can* park in each space. In the empty columns below the numbers, you have plenty of room to plug in possibilities. This type of diagram is very simple, and it has the advantage of showing at a glance that, for example, there are only two cars that can park in slot 1 and only two that can park in slot 5.

Some students prefer to use such a table to indicate which cars *cannot* park in each space:

				-T	
-U				-S	
-S	-T	-U	-T	-R	-T
-R	-R	-S	-S	-R	-Q
-Q	-Q	-Q	-R	-P	-P
1	2	3	4	5	6

This diagram is the mirror image of the previous one. The minus sign (−) indicates where cars cannot be. For example, the −P above the 5 slot indicates that P can't park there. In this diagram, a car can park anywhere it isn't prohibited.

Some students prefer grids:

	1	2	3	4	5	6
P					×	×
Q	×	×	×			×
R	×	×		×	×	
S	×		×	×	×	
T		×		×	×	×
U	×		×			

The x's indicate the spots where cars cannot go. This type of diagram is easier for some students to read. For example, from left to right it reveals that cars Q, R, S, and T each have only two possible parking places. The disadvantage of this kind of diagram is that it takes a long time to draw and it is cumbersome to use on more than one question.

CRACKING SAMPLE GAME NO. 2: STEP 3

This game has only three questions. There's nothing about any of them that makes any of them look much harder or easier than any other. Just attack them in order.

CRACKING SAMPLE GAME NO. 2: STEP 4

Diagram in hand, we go to the questions. Here's the first one:

1. If Q parks in 4, U must park in
   (A) 1   (B) 2   (C) 3   (D) 5   (E) 6

Here's how to crack it:
Go right to the diagram:

	U	T	U		U
T	S	R	Q	U	S
P	P	P	P	Q	R
1	2	3	4	5	6

Our first step is to eliminate what we can immediately. This question concerns where U can park. We already know from the set-up clues (as represented in the diagram) that U cannot park in 1 or 3. This enables us to eliminate choices A and C.

Now we add our new clue, provided in question 1. This new clue is that (for the purposes of this question) Q is parked in 4. Here's what the revised diagram looks like:

T P	U S P	T R P	U Q P	U Q	U S R
1	2	3	4	5	6
			Q		

Now, if Q is in 4, it can't be anywhere else. That means it can't be in space 5, which in turn means that U *must* be in space 5. This answers the question. ETS's answer is choice D.

Here's the second question:

> 2. If P parks in 3, T must park in
>   (A) 1 (B) 2 (C) 4 (D) 5 (E) 6

Here's how to crack it:

This question is quite similar to the previous one. Before using the new clue, we consult our diagram, which tells us that T cannot park in 2, 4, 5, or 6. This lets us eliminate choices B, C, D, and E. ETS's answer is choice A.

Notice that we didn't even need to resort to the additional clue. Isn't POE great?

Here's the final question:

> 3. If S parks in 6, which of the following must be true?
>   (A) T parks in 1.
>   (B) P parks in 2.
>   (C) Q parks in 4.
>   (D) U parks in 4.
>   (E) T parks in 3.

Here's how to crack it:

Rats! The diagram alone doesn't allow us to eliminate any choices immediately. We'll have to do some work. First, we add the new information to our diagram:

	U	T	U		U
T	S	R	Q	U	S
P	P	P	P	Q	R
1	2	3	4	5	6
			Q	U	
					S

If S parks in 6, neither U nor R can park there. That's not much help with U (which can still park in 2, 3, or 5), but it does tell us that R must park in 3. Add R to the diagram:

	U	T	U		U
T	S	R	Q	U	S
P	P	P	P	Q	R
1	2	3	4	5	6
			Q	U	
		R			S

Have we found ETS's answer? No. "R parks in 3" isn't one of the choices. But we can still eliminate a choice. If R is in 3, nothing else can be there, which means that choice E is impossible. Eliminate choice E.

Also look at what happens to T. If T can't be in 3 (as we've just proved), it can only be in 1. "T parks in 1" is choice A. Choice A is ETS's answer.

> You will find ETS's answer on problems like this by using POE to turn one piece of information into another. Every time you learn something new, every time you eliminate a choice, look for the consequences.

SAMPLE GAME NO. 3

This game is a medium. Give yourself five minutes.

Six books—on history, English, algebra, ceramics, Spanish, and philosophy—are arranged on a shelf, with a bookend at either end.

The history book is next to a bookend.
The English book is next to the algebra book.
At least one book separates the English and ceramics books, or the English and Spanish books.
The ceramics book and the Spanish book are next to each other.
At least two books separate the English and philosophy books.

1. Which of the following books can be next to a bookend?

   I.   philosophy
   II. English
   III. ceramics

   (A) I only
   (B) II only
   (C) I and II only
   (D) II and III only
   (E) I, II, and III

2. The history book CANNOT be next to which of the following books?

   (A) algebra only
   (B) ceramics only
   (C) philosophy only
   (D) English or algebra only
   (E) ceramics or Spanish only

3. If the history book is next to the English book, which of the following must be true?

   (A) The philosophy book is next to a bookend.
   (B) The ceramics book is next to a bookend.
   (C) The Spanish book is next to the algebra book.
   (D) The philosophy book is next to the ceramics book.
   (E) The algebra book is next to the ceramics book.

CRACKING SAMPLE GAME NO. 3: STEP 1

This game provides a fairly large number of clues. It is made somewhat difficult by the fact that several of the clues are complicated and conditional. There isn't really anything else we can deduce from the set-up clues. On to the diagram.

CRACKING SAMPLE GAME NO. 3: STEP 2

Let's start with the "mirror image" version of the table we used as our diagram in the previous game. Here's what we come up with:

	-H	-H	-H	-H	
1	2	3	4	5	6

In other words, the table tells us that H(history) can't be in 2, 3, 4, or 5. That's all that we can conveniently put into our table. So what do we do with the rest of the clues? We symbolize them off to the side. As with diagramming, there are many ways to symbolize. Your goal is to find a way of representing the remaining clues in a way that will let you review them at a glance. Here's one way of doing that:

> ## EA / AE
> ## E_C / C_E or E_S / S_E
> ## CS / SC
> ## E__?P / P__?E

An ugly mess, but it's the best we can do.

CRACKING SAMPLE GAME NO. 3: STEP 3

Once again, there are just three questions. Question 1 is a triple true/false, and question 2 is a CANNOT. So let's begin with question 3, which is wordy but looks straightforward. Then we'll do questions 1 and 2.

CRACKING SAMPLE GAME NO. 3: STEP 4

Here's the question:

3. If the history book is next to the English book, which of the following must be true?

(A) The philosophy book is next to a bookend.
(B) The ceramics book is next to a bookend.
(C) The Spanish book is next to the algebra book.
(D) The philosophy book is next to the ceramics book.
(E) The algebra book is next to the ceramics book.

Here's how to crack it:

The question gives us a clue. Let's fill it in on our diagram. Where should we put it? We know from our diagram that the history book must be in either 1 or 6. Let's try it in 1 and see what happens. With H in 1, E must be in 2 (that's the clue the question gives us). So here's what we have:

	-H	-H	-H	-H	
1	2	3	4	5	6
H	E				

Now look at the symbolized rules. The first one says that we must have either EA or AE. The first choice applies in this case. Put A in slot 3:

	-H	-H	-H	-H	
1	2	3	4	5	6
H	E	A			

The second symbolized clue tells us that slot 4 must be either C or S. Let's put both possibilities on our diagram, by adding a second line:

	-H	-H	-H	-H	
1	2	3	4	5	6
H	E	A	C		
H	E	A	S		

The third symbolized clue tells us that either S must follow C or C must follow S. So we put S in the fifth spot on the first line and C in the fifth spot on the second. That leaves only P for slot 6, so we fill that in, too. Here's what we've got:

	-H	-H	-H	-H	
1	2	3	4	5	6
H	E	A	C	S	P
H	E	A	S	C	P

Now we use POE to go through the choices:

(A) Is the philosophy book next to a bookend? On both our lines, it is. This is a possibility.

(B) Is the ceramics book next to a bookend? No, not on either line. Eliminate.

(C) Is the Spanish book next to the algebra book? It is in the second line but not in the first. We're looking for something that *must* be true, so we eliminate.

(D) Is the philosophy book next to the ceramics book? Not in the first line. Eliminate.

(E) Is the algebra book next to the ceramics book? Not in the second line. Eliminate.

ETS's answer is choice A.

Here's question 1:

1. Which of the following books can be next to a bookend?

    I. philosophy
    II. English
    III. ceramics

    (A) I only
    (B) II only
    (C) I and II only
    (D) II and III only
    (E) I, II, and III

Here's how to crack it:

Our filled-in diagram from question 3 can help us on this question. It proves that the philosophy book can be next to a bookend. That means that statement I is true and that we can eliminate choices B and D.

Now let's test statement III. If we can figure out a way to get the ceramics book next to a bookend, this will be ETS's answer. If we can't, we'll have to test statement II as well. By testing statement III before statement II, there is at least a possibility that we won't have to test statement II.

Start a new line on the diagram, with H at one end and C at the other. We want to see if we can make this work. Here's what we start with:

	-H	-H	-H	-H	
1	2	3	4	5	6
H	E	A	C	S	P
H	E	A	S	C	P
H					C

Now look at the symbolized clues. We see quickly that S has to be next to C, so we put S in slot 5, like this:

	-H	-H	-H	-H	
1	2	3	4	5	6
H	E	A	C	S	P
H	E	A	S	C	P
H				S	C

The first half of the second symbolized clue tells us that slot 4 could be E. The second half of the second clue tells us that slot 3 could be E. Add a new line and show both possibilities, like this:

	-H	-H	-H	-H	
1	2	3	4	5	6
H	E	A	C	S	P
H	E	A	S	C	P
H			E	S	C
H		E		S	C

If E is in 4, then 3 must be A, according to the first clue. So put A in slot 3 on the first line. That means that P would have to be in 2, like this:

	-H	-H	-H	-H	
1	2	3	4	5	6
H	E	A	C	S	P
H	E	A	S	C	P
H	P	A	E	S	C
H		E		S	C

Is this arrangement possible? No, because the last clue says that P and E have to be at least two spaces apart. *Cross out the line.* (Be sure to cross out invalid lines. This will keep you from becoming confused later on.)

If E is in 3, then either 2 or 4 must be A (with P in the remaining slot). Add another line so that both these possibilities are represented:

	-H	-H	-H	-H		
1	2	3	4	5	6
H	E	A	C	S	P
H	E	A	S	C	P
~~H~~	~~P~~	~~A~~	~~E~~	~~S~~	~~C~~
H	A	E		S	C
H		E	A	S	C

Neither of these arrangements is possible, either, because P and E once again aren't far enough apart. In fact, with C and S together at one end, we're never going to have enough room in the middle, because we need at least four spaces for the English and philosophy books. Statement III is false. Cross out the lines and eliminate choice E.

Now we have to test statement II. Can we get the English book next to a bookend? Start a new line on the diagram with H at one end and E at the other:

	-H	-H	-H	-H		
1	2	3	4	5	6
H	E	A	C	S	P
H	E	A	S	C	P
~~H~~	~~P~~	~~A~~	~~E~~	~~S~~	~~C~~
~~H~~	~~A~~	~~E~~	~~P~~	~~S~~	~~C~~
~~H~~	~~P~~	~~E~~	~~A~~	~~S~~	~~C~~
H					E

With E in slot 6, we have to have A in slot 5 and either C or S in slot 4. We add a new line so that we can test both possibilities. Then, following our clues, we put S in the first 3 slot and C in the other. That leaves P for the 2 slot. Here's what we end up with:

1	-H 2	-H 3	-H 4	-H 5	6
H	E	A	C	S	P
H	E	A	S	C	P
H	P	A	E	S	C
H	A	E	P	S	C
H	P	E	A	S	C
H	P	S	C	A	E
H	P	C	S	A	E

Are these valid arrangements? Yes, they are. Statement II is true, and ETS's answer is choice C.

Now we're ready for question 2:

2. The history book CANNOT be next to which of the following books?

   (A) algebra only
   (B) ceramics only
   (C) philosophy only
   (D) English or algebra only
   (E) ceramics or Spanish only

Here's how to crack it:

The first thing to do is check our diagram to see if we can eliminate any choices right off the bat. In previous, valid arrangements, we've had the history book next to the English book and the philosophy book. That means we can eliminate choices C and D.

Time for POE. Ceramics appears in two of the remaining three choices, so let's try it first. If this works (this is a CANNOT question, remember) we'll know that ETS's answer is A, because we'll be able to eliminate both choices B and E. If ceramics doesn't work, we'll be able to eliminate A and only have to test Spanish to find ETS's answer.

We start a new line on the diagram, with ceramics next to history. Then, following the clues, we put S in 3 and E in 4. We can stop right there, because

we can clearly see that there isn't going to be enough room left to put P as far away from E as it needs to be. We cross out the line and eliminate choice A:

	-H	-H	-H	-H		
1	2	3	4	5	6
H	E	A	C	S	P
H	E	A	S	C	P
H	P	A	E	S	C
H	A	E	P	S	C
H	P	E	A	S	C
H	P	S	C	A	E
H	P	C	S	A	E
H	C	S	E		

Now it's time to test Spanish. We start a new line with H in 1 and S in 2. That means we have to have C in 3, like this:

	-H	-H	-H	-H		
1	2	3	4	5	6
H	E	A	C	S	P
H	E	A	S	C	P
H	P	A	E	S	C
H	A	E	P	S	C
H	P	E	A	S	C
H	P	S	C	A	E
H	P	C	S	A	E
H	C	S	E		
H	S	C			

By now we shall have learned that the spacing of P and E is crucial in this game. There are only three spaces left in our line, which means that once again there won't be room for P and E. Spanish doesn't work, which means that ETS's answer is choice E.

SAMPLE GAME NO. 4

This game is medium-difficult. Give yourself nine minutes for the six questions in this set.

Seven passengers—J, K, L, M, N, O, and P—are riding on an elevator that makes four stops. Two passengers get off at every stop except the last, when the final passenger gets off. The following conditions apply:

Neither J nor N gets off with K.
L cannot get off with M.
O must get off with either M or P.

1. Which of the following is an acceptable list of passengers getting off the elevator, from the first stop to the last stop?

    (A) J and N, K and P, L and M, O
    (B) J and N, K and L, O and P, M
    (C) J and K, L and P, N and O, M
    (D) J and L, K and N, M and O, P
    (E) J and P, L and N, K and O, M

2. If L gets off with P, which of the following must be true?

    (A) K gets off with M.
    (B) K gets off with N.
    (C) J gets off with M.
    (D) K gets off last.
    (E) J gets off last.

3. If L gets off last, which of the following passengers must get off with J?

    (A) K   (B) M   (C) N   (D) O   (E) P

4. If K gets off with P, which of the following is a complete and accurate list of those passengers who could get off last?

    (A) J   (B) L   (C) J,L   (D) L,N   (E) J,L,N

5. If J gets off with M, which of the following must be true?

    (A) K gets off last.
    (B) L gets off last.
    (C) N gets off last.
    (D) L gets off with either K or N.
    (E) P gets off with either K or N.

6. If P gets off with N, all of the following could be true EXCEPT

    (A) O gets off with M.
    (B) K gets off with L.
    (C) J gets off last.
    (D) K gets off last.
    (E) L gets off last.

CRACKING SAMPLE GAME NO. 4: STEP 1

This game is relatively difficult, because it provides few clues. The fewer the clues, the less we have to work with and the more difficult our analysis becomes. Since there are so few clues, we can't hope to deduce too much. We should, however, notice that O can't be last. Why? Because the last passenger always gets off alone, and O must always be paired with either M or P. Now let's get to the diagram.

CRACKING SAMPLE GAME NO. 4: STEP 2

We can use a simple diagram representing the four stops of the elevator, like this:

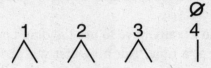

The first three floors have 2 slots, that last floor has only 1. The notation above the fourth floor is a reminder that O can't get off there. If we're neat, we'll be able to use this one drawing for all the questions.

We also need to symbolize the clues. There's no way to do this on the diagram, so we symbolize them beside it. Here's one way to do this:

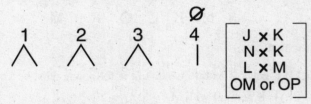

Now we're ready to size up the questions.

CRACKING SAMPLE GAME NO. 4: STEP 3

The only tricky-looking question here is the last one, which is an EXCEPT. We can simply tackle the questions in order. (Question 4 is really a concealed triple true/false question, but we probably wouldn't notice that by simply scanning over the questions.)

CRACKING SAMPLE GAME NO. 4: STEP 4

Here's another look at question 1:

1. Which of the following is an acceptable list of passengers getting off the elevator, from the first stop to the last stop?

   (A) J and N, K and P, L and M, O
   (B) J and N, K and L, O and P, M
   (C) J and K, L and P, N and O, M
   (D) J and L, K and N, M and O, P
   (E) J and P, L and N, K and O, M

Here's how to crack it:

There's nothing to do here but use POE by applying the clues. Here goes:

We can eliminate choice A right away, because it has O getting off last.

The first clue says that J can't get off with K. Skimming quickly, we see that this lets us eliminate choice C.

The first clue also says that N can't get off with K. This lets us eliminate choice D.

We're down to choices B and E. The next clue says that L can't get off with M. This doesn't get us anywhere.

The next clue says that O must get off with M or P. This rules out choice E, where O gets off with K, and choice A, where O gets off alone. ETS's answer is choice B.

Notice that we didn't really have to use the diagram. We simply applied our symbolized clues one at a time. But now that we've found ETS's answer, we may be able to save ourselves some time later on by putting it in the diagram now. The first question has shown us that J and N, K and L, O and P, M is a valid arrangement. That knowledge may come in handy later, so we jot it down:

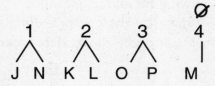

Here's question 2:

2. If L gets off with P, which of the following must be true?

(A) K gets off with M.
(B) K gets off with N.
(C) J gets off with M.
(D) K gets off last.
(E) J gets off last.

Here's how to crack it:

This question adds a clue. Let's start by incorporating the new clue into our diagram and seeing if we can eliminate anything.

If L gets off with P, then O must get off with M, its only other possible partner. We can still leave J and N together at the first floor, which moves K to the fourth floor. Here's what we have so far:

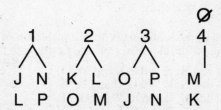

This is a "must" question, so we can eliminate any choice that differs from our diagram. That means we can eliminate choices A, B, C, and E. ETS's answer is choice D.

Notice that this game says next to nothing about the *order* in which passengers must get off. That means that in using POE we can put valid pairs at any of the first three stops. The only important stop, in terms of position, is the last one.

Here's the third question:

> 3. If L gets off last, which of the following passengers must get off with J?
>
>   (A) K (B) M (C) N (D) O (E) P

Here's how to crack it:

Use the clues first. J can't get off with K, which means that we can eliminate choice A. O must get off with M or P, which means it can't get off with J, which means that we can also eliminate choice D.

We're down to choices B, C, or E. Stick L in the last slot on the diagram and see what we come up with. Since this is a "must" question, ETS's answer will be any passenger that works as J's partner in a valid arrangement. We'll just try M, N, and P and see if we can make either of them work.

Let's try M first. We put J and M in the first spot. This uses up M, which means O and P have to be together, so we put O and P in the second spot. The only remaining letters for spot three are N and K. We know from the clues that they can't go together, so we eliminate choice B and cross out this line of our diagram, like this:

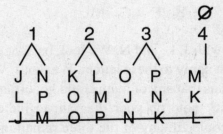

Now we try N. We put J and N in the first spot and L in the last. This leaves us with K, M, O, and P. We know that O has to be with either M or P. Try M. With O and M in the second spot, we have K and P in the third. Here's what our diagram looks like:

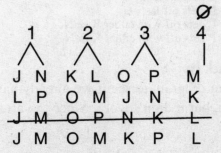

This satisfies all the clues. ETS's answer is choice C. We don't even have to test passenger P.

Here's the next question:

4. If K gets off with P, which of the following is a complete and accurate list of those passengers who could get off last?

(A) J (B) L (C) J,L (D) L,N (E) J,L,N

Here's how to crack it:

Before we do anything else, we look back over our diagram to see if we have already come across a valid arrangement in which K gets off with P. Luckily, we have, in the previous problem. In that problem, L got off last. That means we can eliminate choice A.

Now back to the problem. Our new clue is that K and P are getting off together. We put them in the first spot. If P is off, then O must leave with M, so we put O and M in the second spot. Here's what we have so far:

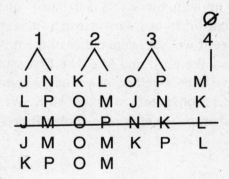

This leaves us with J, L, and N. We look back at our clues to see if we have any restrictions that apply to these letters. We don't. We can put them anywhere we like, which means that any of them could get off last. ETS's answer is choice E. (Also jot a quick note on your diagram to indicate that any of the three remaining letters could fill any of the three remaining places.)

Here's question 5:

5. If J gets off with M, which of the following must be true?

(A) K gets off last.
(B) L gets off last.
(C) N gets off last.
(D) L gets off with either K or N.
(E) P gets off with either K or N.

Here's how to crack it:

First, we look at our diagram to see if we already have an example of J getting off with M. We do, but it didn't work. Since the arrangement wasn't valid, we ignore it.

If J gets off with M, then O must get off with P. So we quickly fill in these letters on our diagram. This leaves us K, L, and N. N and K can't go together, so one of them must be last. We add another line to our diagram and represent both possibilities. Here's what we end up with:

Both of these arrangements are valid. What does that tell us? First it tells us that we can eliminate the first three choices. This is a must question. We've already seen that either N or K can be last, which means that no single letter *must* be last.

ETS's answer is choice D. In our two valid examples, "L gets off with either K or N." That's exactly what we were looking for.

Here's the last question:

6. If P gets off with N, all of the following could be true EXCEPT

(A) O gets off with M.
(B) K gets off with L.
(C) J gets off last.
(D) K gets off last.
(E) L gets off last.

Here's how to crack it:

This is an EXCEPT question, which makes it tricky. We're looking for the choice that doesn't work.

First we scan our diagram for a valid arrangement in which P gets off with N. Unfortunately, we don't have one. Nor do we have any obvious rule violations in the choices alone. We'll have to evaluate all the choices.

Our new clue is that P gets off with N, so we put P and N in the first spot in our diagram. That means O has to get off with M, so we put O and M in the second spot and eliminate choice A. (Remember, proving that a choice *works* means we have to eliminate it.)

We're left with J, K, and L. K and J can't go together, so one of them will have to get off last. This lets us eliminate choices C and D. If K gets off last, L

and J will get off in the third spot; if J gets off last, L and K will get off in the third spot. You may be able to see ETS's answer already. If not, add another line to the diagram so that you can represent both possibilities. Here's how the diagram looks:

Now look at the two remaining choices, B and E. We've just shown that K can get off with L, so we eliminate choice B. ETS's answer is choice E.

SAMPLE GAME NO. 5

This game is difficult. There are only three questions, but you'd better allow yourself seven minutes.

Five students—J, K, L, M, and N—gather for a series of five debates. The debate schedule must conform to the following requirements:

Only two students participate in each debate.

No two students face each other more than once.

Every student debates exactly twice, and no student participates in two consecutive debates.

J will not debate in the third debate.

J will not debate N.

K will not debate M.

1. If L and N participate in the first debate, then which of the following students can debate in the second?

(A) L and N
(B) M and N
(C) K and L
(D) K and N
(E) J and M

2. If J does not participate in the first debate, in which of the following debates must J participate?

    I. the second
   II. the fourth
  III. the fifth

(A) I only
(B) II only
(C) III only
(D) I and II only
(E) I and III only

3. If J and L participate in the first debate, and K and N participate in the second debate, which of the following students must debate in the fourth?

(A) J and K
(B) J and L
(C) L and M
(D) J and M
(E) M and N

CRACKING SAMPLE GAME NO. 5: STEP 1

Once again, we have a shortage of helpful clues. Most of the clues we do have are cumbersome and hard to symbolize. We're going to need help from clues provided in the questions.

CRACKING SAMPLE GAME NO. 5: STEP 2

This game is at least superficially similar to the elevator game, so let's try the same sort of diagram. Here's what we come up with:

The –J above debate 3 indicates J can't debate there. Now we symbolize our clues:

$$J \times N$$
$$K \times M$$

The other two clues are too hard to symbolize, so we simply circle them in our test booklets and hope we remember them.

CRACKING SAMPLE GAME NO. 5: STEP 3

We have three questions. The second is a triple true/false, so we'll save it for last and do the other two in order.

CRACKING SAMPLE GAME NO. 5: STEP 4

Here's the first question:

1. If L and N participate in the first debate, then which of the following students can debate in the second?

   (A) L and N
   (B) M and N
   (C) K and L
   (D) K and N
   (E) J and M

Here's how to crack it:

If L and N participate in the first debate, they can't participate in the second, because the clues say no student can participate in two debates in a row. Because we're looking for the participants in the second debate, we can eliminate any choice containing L or N. That means we can eliminate choices A, B, C, and D. ETS's answer is choice E.

That wasn't bad, was it? We didn't even need to use our diagram. The only trick was in remembering to apply the proper clue.

Here's question 3:

3. If J and L participate in the first debate, and K and N participate in the second debate, which of the following students must debate in the fourth?

   (A) J   (B) K   (C) L   (D) M   (E) N

Here's how to crack it:

This question gives us quite a lot of information, so it may not turn out to be too bad. First, let's fill in what we can in the diagram. We have J and L in the first and K and N in the second. Since K and N are in the second, they can't be in the third. We've been told that J can't be in the third, either, so that means the two participants in the third debate *have* to be L and M. So we put L and M in the third debate. Here's what we have so far:

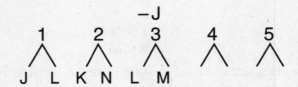

What we're looking for is the participants in the fourth debate. Let's see what we know and what that enables us to eliminate.

One thing we know is that neither L nor M can debate in the fourth, because they debated in the third. (L has also debated twice already.) That means we can eliminate any choice containing L or M, which means that we can eliminate choices B, C, D, and E. ETS's answer is choice A. (Go ahead and add this information to the diagram, in case it turns out to be useful on the next question.

That is, put J and K in spot 4. You don't need to waste time figuring out who would be in debate 5, although you *could* figure it out based on what you know.)

Now here's question 2, the one we skipped:

2. If J does not participate in the first debate, in which of the following debates must J participate?

    I. the second
   II. the fourth
  III. the fifth

(A) I only
(B) II only
(C) III only
(D) I and II only
(E) I and III only

Here's how to crack it:

We already know that J can't be in the third debate. Now we're told that J can't be in the first, either. That leaves only the second, fourth, and fifth—our three choices—as possibilities. We know that J must debate twice. We also know that J can't participate in both the fourth and fifth, because they are consecutive. This means that in any lineup that satisfies the clues, J must participate in either the second and fourth or the second and the fifth. J, in other words, must always be in the second debate. That means we can eliminate choices B and C.

Here's what we have to sort out:

1. If second and fourth can be made to work, then we can eliminate choice E.

2. If second and fifth can be made to work, then we can eliminate choice D.

Can second and fourth be made to work? Let's fiddle around with the partly completed line on our diagram and see what we can come up with. Here's what we have so far:

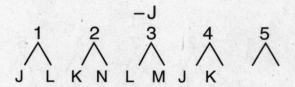

We have J in the first and fourth. Let's switch the participants in the first and second debates and see what happens:

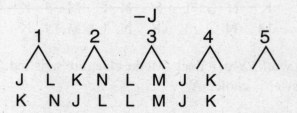

Does that work? No. We have L in consecutive debates, the second and third. Let's see if we can fix that by moving L and M into the empty fifth spot.

We can then fill in the third debate with the two remaining participants, M and N. Here's what we end up with:

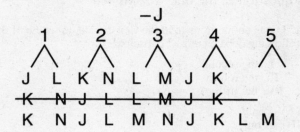

Does that work? Yes, it does. All the rules are satisfied, and we have J in the second and fourth debates. That means we can eliminate choice E.

Now let's see if we can make a valid arrangement with J in the second and fifth. First we'll try simply switching the fourth pair and the fifth pair. Here's what we get:

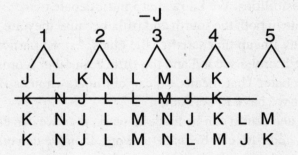

Does that work? No. M is in both the third and fourth. Let's try switching the third with the first, like this:

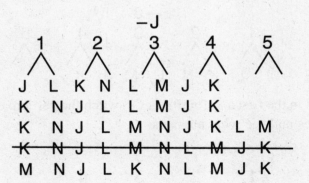

Does that work? Yes, it does. All the clues are satisfied. We eliminate choice D. ETS's answer is choice A.

SUMMARY

1. Each logic section of your GRE will contain three or four games, each of which will be accompanied by between three and seven questions.

2. The games themselves will be presented in order of increasing difficulty, although the questions accompanying them will not.

3. Since games are so difficult, skipping the hardest one would probably be to your advantage. At the very least, you should save the more difficult set of games—the second one—for last, after you have completed the set of arguments items that follows it.

4. You'll have to practice if you want to improve your score on games. Our techniques are helpful, but you will be unlikely to do well unless you feel at ease with this type of item.

5. Learn our directions, not ETS's, and don't even glance at the instructions in your test booklet.

6. The Princeton Review strategy for GRE games has four steps:

   Step 1: Read the set-up clues and get the general picture.

   Step 2: Draw a diagram based on the set-up clues.

   Step 3: Look for the easier questions.

   Step 4: Use POE efficiently to eliminate incorrect choices.

7. Be sure to read all the set-up clues before you begin to work. You should also look for links between clues, which may provide keys to finding ETS's answers.

8. You'll need to draw a diagram to find ETS's answers on the vast majority of games items. On virtually all games, you simply won't be able to keep track of the information you're given without symbolizing it simply on paper.

9. Your diagram should not merely repeat the information in the set-up clues. The best diagrams are ones that help your thinking and lead you to ETS's answers.

10. Don't spend too much time thinking about which type of diagram to draw. If you get stuck, simply try something.

11. Tackle easier questions first, if possible. The first question in a set is usually relatively easy and can often be answered without a diagram.

12. A question that provides new clues is usually easier than one that does not.

13. Questions containing the word *must* are usually easier than questions containing the word *could*.

14. Triple true/false questions (I, II, III questions) are more time-consuming than regular questions.

15. CANNOT and EXCEPT questions can be both time-consuming and confusing.

16. If you can't answer a question, circle it and move on to another. Don't waste time if you aren't getting anywhere.

17. Never erase your scratchwork. Your solution to an easy question will often provide a key to solving a harder one later on.

18. Use POE aggressively and efficiently.

19. If you can eliminate a choice, do it.

20. Answering one question will often give you an insight that you can apply on a later question.

21. Don't sit there thinking—try something!

22. Eliminate only what you need to eliminate in order to find ETS's answer. Don't get so wrapped up in POE that you answer a question without knowing it.

Arguments

Each logic section of your GRE will contain six "logical reasoning" questions, or arguments. Three will be located after the first game and three will be located after the last. The first group of arguments will be relatively easy, and the second group of arguments will be relatively difficult.

OUR EXTRAORDINARY TECHNIQUES

Even the most difficult GRE arguments aren't terribly difficult. Most students don't have much trouble with them. If you study this chapter and practice our techniques, you should be able to use POE to eliminate incorrect choices and zero in on ETS's answer.

ETS'S DIRECTIONS

Here are the directions for the logic section as they will appear on your GRE. ETS intends these directions to apply to both games and arguments. As you may have noticed already, they don't really apply to anything. At any rate, here they are:

> Directions: Each question or group of questions is based on a passage or set of conditions. In answering some of the questions, it may be useful to draw a rough diagram. For each question, select the best answer choice given.

OUR OWN DIRECTIONS

Naturally, you shouldn't even glance at ETS's directions when you take the GRE. They won't help you, anyway. Instead, make sure you understand our own directions. They'll give you a much clearer idea of what you're supposed to do on the test. Here they are:

> Directions: Each GRE argument consists of a brief reading passage followed by a question. The reading passage may be drawn from any of a number of fields, including science, philosophy, literature, and advertising. The question following each reading passage is intended to test your ability to analyze certain information in the passage.

The best way to get a feel for GRE arguments is to work through a simple example. (You'll never see an argument this simple on a real GRE.) Here's the example:

> Alicia told Robert, "Fred is taller than John, so Fred probably weighs more than John."
>
> Alicia was trying to persuade Robert that
>
> (A) Fred is taller than John.
> (B) John is taller than Fred.
> (C) Fred is probably lighter than John.
> (D) John is probably lighter than Fred.
> (E) Fred should lose some weight.

Here's how to crack it:

What is Alicia trying to do? She's trying to persuade Robert that Fred probably weighs more than John. (She's not trying to persuade Robert that Fred is taller than John—that's just her reason for claiming that Fred probably weighs more.) What's ETS's answer? It's choice D, which is just a slightly different way of saying that Fred probably weighs more than John. Here's a similar argument problem, consisting of the same passage but with a different question:

> Alicia told Robert, "Fred is taller than John, so Fred probably weighs more than John."
>
> In making her case to Robert, Alicia assumes that
>
> (A) Fred and John are friends.
> (B) Robert is taller than Alicia.
> (C) A person's height makes no difference.
> (D) There is a strong positive correlation between height and weight.
> (E) John can beat up Fred.

Here's how to crack it:

In this question, we're asked to infer something that isn't directly stated in the passage. We're asked to infer *why* Alicia has said what she has said. ETS's answer is choice D. Alicia has said that Fred is probably heavier than John because she *assumes* that taller people tend to weigh more than shorter people.

These are the sorts of questions you'll be asked in GRE arguments. Sometimes you'll be asked a question that relates directly to the passage; sometimes you'll be asked a question that will require you to draw an inference from the passage. If you read carefully and follow our strategy, you shouldn't have much trouble. You *don't* need to have taken a logic course or, indeed, to know anything at all about formal logic.

SOME PRINCETON REVIEW TERMINOLOGY

Although you don't need to know anything about logic, you do need to know a few simple terms to follow the rest of this chapter. Here's what you need to know:

Conclusion: A conclusion is a claim. In the simple example above, Alicia's conclusion was that Fred probably weighs more than John.

Premise: A premise is a stated reason, a piece of evidence. Alicia's premise in the example above is that Fred is taller than John. This is her reason for thinking that Fred probably weighs more than John.

Assumption: An assumption is an unstated reason. Alicia's assumption is that height is the major determinant of weight.

Argument: An argument is a conclusion supported by premises and assumptions.

In solving GRE argument problems, you'll be asked to find conclusions, test assumptions, identify premises, and perform other kinds of analysis on the passages. Argument problems are really very similar to reading-comprehension problems, although there are important differences. We'll tell you about the similarities and differences as we go along.

JOE BLOGGS AND ARGUMENTS

Joe Bloggs isn't much help on arguments. The questions are mostly straightforward, and there aren't many traps. Of course, on difficult questions you should hesitate before selecting a choice that seems too obvious. For the most part, though, you can approach these questions confidently.

OUR GENERAL STEP-BY-STEP STRATEGY

As with games, we have a general strategy for cracking arguments. We'll outline this strategy first. Then we'll discuss each step in it at greater length. Then we'll show you how the strategy applies to actual arguments. Here's the outline:

- Step 1: Read the question.

- Step 2: Read the argument.

- Step 3: Find the conclusion.

- Step 4: Diagram the argument (if necessary).

- Step 5: Attack the choices using POE.

STEP 1: READ THE QUESTION

You need to read the question first, to get an idea of what you're dealing with. You don't have to *study* the question. If the question is long, just skim it quickly to catch the drift of what ETS is looking for. You shouldn't read the choices. Just read the question to see what you're looking for.

Knowing what kind of question you're dealing with will help you follow the argument and focus on what's important. For example, if the question asks you to identify a weakness in the argument, you can read the argument in that light. If you didn't know the argument *had* a weakness, you might struggle to make sense of it, only to find out later that it was flawed.

Here are the most common types of questions, followed by a brief discussion of each:

Which of the following can be inferred from the statements above? (Which of the following is implied in the passage above?)

You're being asked for something that is missing from the passage— something that can only be inferred.

Which of the following, if true, most weakens (strengthens) the argument above?

This type of question requires you to look for a choice that makes the given conclusion less (more) believable.

Which of the following is an assumption of the argument above?

An assumption, remember, is an unstated reason supporting the author's

conclusion. This kind of question is asking you to find a choice that makes the given conclusion more believable.

If the statements above are true, which of the following statements must also be true? (If the statements above are true, which of the following statements can be concluded?)

This question tells you that the argument doesn't have a conclusion; you're being asked to supply it. Your job is to find the answer choice that follows most logically from what is stated in the argument.

There are a few other types of questions, but these are the most popular. We'll tell you more about them as we go along.

STEP 2: READ THE ARGUMENT

In our chapter on reading comprehension, you learned to read quickly, skimming for important themes. Arguments are different. You need to read each word carefully.

Fortunately, there aren't many words to read in a GRE argument. But every word is important. You can't cut corners here. As you read, keep the question in mind. Try to anticipate ETS's answer.

STEP 3: FIND THE CONCLUSION

Finding the conclusion to an argument is usually the key to finding ETS's answer. In some cases, the question will simply ask you for the conclusion. In others, the conclusion will hold the key to whatever ETS is looking for.

In 95 percent of GRE arguments, the conclusion is very easy to find. It's often in the last sentence; when it's not in the last sentence, it's in the first.

If you can't find the conclusion in either the first or the last sentence, you will almost always be able to find it by asking yourself the following questions: *What is the author trying to prove? What is the author trying to make me believe?* The answer to these questions is the conclusion.

A few GRE arguments won't have conclusions. In most such cases, you'll be asked to supply a conclusion. We'll tell you more about missing-conclusion arguments later on.

STEP 4: DIAGRAM THE ARGUMENT (IF NECESSARY)

Once you've read the question, read the argument, and found the conclusion, you may occasionally find it helpful to draw a diagram. Although making a diagram is a waste of time on most GRE arguments, a few relatively difficult

argument problems will be hard to solve *without* diagrams. Sometimes a diagram will show the connection between premises and a conclusion more clearly than words can.

Take another look at the simple argument we discussed earlier in this chapter:

> Alicia told Robert, "Fred is taller than John, so Fred probably weighs more than John."

There are many possible ways to diagram an argument like this. Here are two of them:

$$F_J \longrightarrow F_J$$

$$F_H > J_H \longrightarrow F_W > J_W$$

We'll tell you more about diagrams later in the chapter.

STEP 5: ATTACK THE CHOICES USING POE

ETS's answers to argument questions tend to be straightforward. Traps are relatively few. The key is to understand what you are looking for. If you're asked to find an assumption, you can eliminate a choice that is an explicit premise or a conclusion.

In our chapter on reading comprehension, we told you to avoid answer choices containing lengthy direct repetitions of the wording in the passage. This rule does *not* apply on arguments. Argument passages are so short that a certain amount of repetition is often unavoidable.

We'll tell you about some specific question-answering techniques as we go along.

PUTTING THE STRATEGY TO WORK

SAMPLE ARGUMENT NO. 1

Practice is the best way to get the hang of GRE arguments. Read the following argument and try your hand at answering the question. Be sure to mark your answer. Then carefully read through our step-by-step implementation of our strategy, which follows.

Here's the sample:

> The Federal Communications Commission (FCC) should not be permitted to regulate the content of television programs. If viewers don't like what they see, they can always change the channel or turn off the set. What offends one viewer may not offend another. People can decide for themselves whether a particular broadcast is offensive.
>
> All of the following, if true, weaken the argument above, EXCEPT
>
> (A) Some people, such as children, are unable to decide matters of offensiveness for themselves.
> (B) The FCC is fully capable of monitoring all the television stations in the country.
> (C) A person encountering offensive broadcast material in a public place might not be able to change the channel.
> (D) The ability to change channels is beside the point if the viewer has already been harmed by offensive material.
> (E) Although standards of decency vary from region to region, there is general agreement on what is grossly offensive.

SAMPLE ARGUMENT NO. 1: STEP 1

The first step is to jump ahead and look at the question. To weaken an argument is to make its conclusion seem less believable. But this is an EXCEPT question. That means that what we are really looking for is a choice that *doesn't* weaken the argument.

SAMPLE ARGUMENT NO. 1: STEPS 2 AND 3

Because we need to find a choice that doesn't weaken the argument's conclusion, we need to make sure that we know what the argument's conclusion *is*. So we read the argument carefully with this in mind.

Reading the argument carefully is easy; there are only four simple sentences. Which one contains the conclusion? The first one. The author's conclusion—the

point of his or her argument—is that the content of television programs should not be regulated.

The other three sentences contain the author's three premises, or reasons. The content of television programs should not be regulated *because* (1) no one is forced to watch, (2) everyone has different standards, and (3) people can make up their own minds.

SAMPLE ARGUMENT NO. 1: STEP 4

There is no need to diagram this relatively simple and straightforward argument.

SAMPLE ARGUMENT NO. 1: STEP 5

Remind yourself what you're looking for: a choice that doesn't make the argument less believable. That means that we can eliminate any choice that weakens the argument, or makes it less believable. Let's look at the choices one at a time:

(A) Does this weaken the argument? Yes, it does, by contradicting one of the premises. Eliminate.

(B) Does this weaken the argument? No. It is irrelevant to the argument. A possibility.

(C) Does this weaken the argument? Yes, it does, by undermining one of the premises. Eliminate.

(D) Does this weaken the argument? Yes, it does, by undermining one of the premises. Eliminate.

(E) Does this weaken the argument? Yes, it does, by contradicting one of the premises. Eliminate.

ETS's answer is choice B.

SPECIAL TECHNIQUE: MISSING CONCLUSIONS

Some GRE arguments don't have conclusions. In most such cases, the question will ask you to supply one. Supply-the-conclusion questions are much like reading-comprehension questions in which you are asked to select the best title for the passage. As with best-title questions, it is not enough for you to select a choice that is *possibly* correct. ETS's answer must follow logically and necessarily from the premises in the argument. There can be no hidden assumptions or missing steps. The argument must prove the conclusion, not merely allow it. Here's an example:

SAMPLE ARGUMENT NO. 2: MISSING CONCLUSION

> Despite dramatically changing economic conditions at home and abroad, exports of Bilco Power Tools increased at an average annual rate of 2.1 percent between 1970 and 1979.
>
> Which of the following conclusions can be validly drawn from the statement above?
>
> (A) Changing economic conditions do not affect Bilco's exports.
> (B) Exports of Bilco Power Tools increased at a constant rate between 1970 and 1979.
> (C) The level of Bilco Power Tools exports was higher in 1979 than it was in 1970.
> (D) Bilco Power Tools exports increased each year between 1970 and 1979.
> (E) The level of Bilco's exports has not changed since 1979.

Here's how to crack it:

The question asks us to supply a conclusion. The argument says (1) economic conditions changed, but (2) exports grew at an average annual rate of 2.1 percent in a particular decade. ETS's answer will be the one choice that follows logically from these simple premises. Once again, there's no need to diagram. Let's go right to the choices:

(A) Does the argument support this conclusion? No, it doesn't. It's possible—indeed, common sense says it's likely—that the changing economic conditions had some effect on Bilco's exports. But it's not necessary. Eliminate.

(B) This is possible but not necessary. Eliminate.

(C) This statement follows clearly and logically from the argument. It is absolutely supported by the premises. This must be ETS's answer.

(D)   This is possible but not necessary. Eliminate.

(E)   This is a silly choice for sleepy test-takers. Eliminate.

ETS's answer is indeed choice C.

SAMPLE ARGUMENT NO. 3: MISSING CONCLUSION

Here's another representative argument to practice on:

> There are freshmen in the German class at Taft High School.
>
> If the statement above is true, which of the following statements must also be true?
>
> (A)   Some freshmen at Taft High School do not study German.
> (B)   At least some of the students who study German at Taft High School are freshmen.
> (C)   If you do not study German at Taft High School, you are not a freshman.
> (D)   All students at Taft High School who study German are freshmen.
> (E)   If you are a freshman at Taft High School, you study German.

Here's how to crack it:

Believe it or not, this is a missing-conclusion question. We've been given a premise—"There are freshmen in the German class at Taft High School"—and asked to draw a conclusion from it. Once again, we can't settle for a choice that is merely *possibly* correct; ETS's answer will be a choice that follows *necessarily* from what we've been told. Look at the choices:

(A)   This is possible but not necessary. For all we know, *all* the freshmen take German. Eliminate.

(B)   This is necessarily true. It's just another way of stating the premise. This must be ETS's answer.

(C)   This is possible, but not necessary. For this conclusion to be true, all the students in the German class would have to be freshmen. That could be true, but we can't tell from the premise. Eliminate.

(D)   This is possible but not necessary, for the same reason as choice C. Eliminate.

(E)   This is possible but not necessary. Eliminate.

ETS's answer is choice B.

SPECIAL TECHNIQUE: ATTACK DISPUTABLE CHOICES

In the chapter on reading comprehension, we told you that the easiest choices to attack are ones that are made highly disputable by the presence of certain disputable words: *only*, *never*, *always*, and so on. Such answer choices are always the easiest to check out. If you find a single exception, you can eliminate.

Attacking disputable choices doesn't necessarily mean eliminating them, but a disputable choice is always the easiest to check. Here's an example:

SAMPLE ARGUMENT NO. 4: ATTACK DISPUTABLE CHOICES

The laws of economics do not always hold. The Phillips Curve is an example. The Phillips Curve depicts an inverse relationship between inflation and unemployment. As unemployment goes down, according to the curve, inflation goes up, and vice versa. According to the Phillips Curve, we are currently experiencing less inflation than we should.

It can be inferred from the passage that

(A) employment is relatively high.
(B) the Phillips Curve was never valid.
(C) inflation is actually good for the economy.
(D) there is no relation between inflation and unemployment.
(E) economics is not a true science.

Here's how to crack it:
This question is asking us to look for an assumption behind the given argument. An assumption, remember, is an unstated premise, and a premise is a statement that strengthens the conclusion.

What's the conclusion? It's in the last sentence: "According to the Phillips Curve, we should be experiencing greater inflation today." If the Phillips Curve suggests that inflation should be higher today than it is, that means that current unemployment must be lower than the Phillips Curve predicts. We're looking for a choice that says this. Go through the choices one at a time:

(A) If employment is high, unemployment is low. This is what we are looking for. This must be ETS's answer.

(B) We can't infer this from what we've been given. Even if the Phillips Curve is inaccurate in this case, it may have been valid at some time in the past. The highly disputable word *never* is a red flag that tells us to attack this choice aggressively, looking for a possible exception. Eliminate.

(C) This choice is appealing to Joe Bloggs, who missed the point of the passage, but it isn't logically connected to what we've been given. Eliminate.

(D) Another highly disputable choice, because of the word *no*. Nothing in the argument rules out the possibility that there could be *some* relationship between inflation and unemployment, even now. Eliminate.

(E) Many people, including some economists, believe this, but it's not what we're looking for. In the context of this question, it's an absurd choice.

ETS's answer is choice A.

SAMPLE ARGUMENT NO. 5: ATTACK DISPUTABLE CHOICES

Britain, Canada, and Australia have all abandoned the English system of measurement in favor of the metric system. And with good reason. Our stubborn refusal to adopt the metric system hurts our exports. When are we going to change over?

All of the following, if true, strengthen the argument above, EXCEPT

(A) The metric system is simpler to use than the English system.
(B) The English system of measurement pervades many aspects of our daily lives.
(C) Most developed countries in the world employ the metric system of measurement.
(D) Britain, Canada, and Australia all experienced increased exports immediately after switching to the metric system.
(E) The cost of switching over to the metric system would be made up in savings during the first year.

Here's how to crack it:

This question is an EXCEPT question. All the choices but one, it tells us, could be premises of the argument above. We are looking for the one choice that isn't—the choice that weakens the argument.

Where's the conclusion? It's contained in the rhetorical question at the end of the argument and can be stated simply as, "We should change over to the metric system." We're looking for the answer choice, therefore, that makes this statement seem *less* compelling; we can eliminate any choice that makes it seem *more* compelling. Let's look at the choices:

(A) Does this weaken the conclusion? No, it strengthens it. Eliminate.
(B) Does this weaken the conclusion? Yes. This is a good reason for not switching over. This must be ETS's answer.
(C) Does this weaken the conclusion? No, it strengthens it. Eliminate.
(D) Does this weaken the conclusion? No, it strengthens it. Eliminate.
(E) Does this weaken the conclusion? No, it strengthens it. Eliminate.

ETS's answer is choice B.

SPECIAL TECHNIQUE: ARGUMENTS THAT LOOK LIKE GAMES

Some arguments are set up almost exactly the way games are. In such cases, you'll want to apply the techniques and approaches you learned in the chapter on games. Most such arguments require diagrams. Here's an example:

SAMPLE ARGUMENT NO. 6: ARGUMENTS THAT LOOK LIKE GAMES

J is older than K, but younger than L.
K and L are each younger than M.
N is older than J.

If the statements above are true, X must be older than J if it is also true that

(A) M is as old as N.
(B) L is as old as N.
(C) X is older than K.
(D) X is older than N.
(E) M is older than X.

Here's how to crack it:

This argument problem could easily have appeared in a games section rather than in an arguments section. The easiest way to deal with it is simply to treat it as though it were a game. The first thing to do is "diagram the set-up clues." Here's one way to do that:

M
L N
  ?
J–J
K

Notice that J appears twice, once in the column on the left and once in the column on the right. We did this because although we know that N is older than J, we don't know how N's age relates to those of L and M. We didn't really need to repeat the J, but doing so is a clear reminder that we aren't quite sure where to put N.

Now we look at the question. We want X to be older than J. One of the choices will make this necessarily true. Let's add X to our diagram and go

through the choices one by one. Here's what our diagram looks like with X in it:

M
L N X
? ?
J–J–J
K

Now we can use POE to sift through the choices:

(A) If M is as old as N, we can put M next to N in our diagram and eliminate the second column. Does that tell us anything about the ages of X and J? No, it doesn't. Eliminate.

(B) If L is as old as N, we can put L next to N in our diagram and eliminate the second column. Does that tell us anything about the ages of X and J? No, it doesn't. Eliminate.

(C) If X is to be older than J, it must also be true that X is older than K. But this by itself isn't enough to establish that X *must* be older than J. Eliminate.

(D) We can see at a glance that N is older than J. If X is older than N, then we can be absolutely positive that X is also older than J. This must be ETS's answer.

(E) If M is older than X, X could still be older than J, but X could also be younger than M and younger than J. Eliminate.

ETS's answer is choice D.

SAMPLE ARGUMENT NO. 7: ARGUMENTS THAT LOOK LIKE GAMES

If Susan drives the Studebaker, George and Melissa will sit in the rear seat.
If the statement above is true, which of the following statements must also be true?
(A) If George and Melissa are sitting in the rear seat, Susan is driving the Studebaker.
(B) If George is sitting in the rear seat, Melissa is also sitting in the rear seat.
(C) If Susan is not driving the Studebaker, George and Melissa are not sitting in the rear seat.
(D) If George is not sitting in the rear seat, Melissa is not sitting in the rear seat.
(E) If Melissa is not sitting in the rear seat, Susan is not driving the Studebaker.

Here's how to crack it:

This argument is very much like Sample Argument No. 3. As with No. 3, we have a condition that works in one direction only. It may help you to think of the clause "If Susan drives the Studebaker" as the premise and the clause "George and Melissa will sit in the rear seat" as the conclusion. Your job is to find another valid argument—one of the choices—that can be derived from this one.

All the usual precautions apply. The key concept is *necessity*. Do George and Melissa *have* to be in the backseat if Susan is driving? Yes. Does Susan have to be driving if George and Melissa are in the backseat? No. The argument doesn't say that. Let's look at the choices:

(A) This is the possibility we just ruled out. Eliminate.

(B) This is possible but not necessary. There is nothing in the original argument that tells us that George and Melissa always sit together. Eliminate.

(C) This is possible but not necessary. Eliminate.

(D) This choice is very much like choice B. It, too, is possible but not necessary. Eliminate.

(E) This is ETS's answer. Since Melissa has to be in the backseat (with George) if Susan is driving, we know with absolute certainty that if Melissa is *not* in the backseat, then Susan cannot be driving.

SAMPLE ARGUMENT NO. 8: ARGUMENTS THAT LOOK LIKE GAMES

Most scientists agree that life requires a planetary body. If so, the possibility of extraterrestrial life has increased dramatically. Astronomers have just discovered an enormous number of possible planetary systems in conjunction with nearby stars. There may be millions or even billions of planets in our galaxy alone.

Which of the following is an assumption of the argument above?

(A) There are an enormous number of planets in our galaxy.

(B) Life will soon be discovered in nearby planetary systems.

(C) Extraterrestrial life does not necessarily require earthlike conditions to exist.

(D) We will recognize extraterrestrial life when we encounter it.

(E) Nearby stars are representative of the galaxy as a whole.

Here's how to crack it:

The question asks us to find an assumption, which is an unstated reason that strengthens the conclusion. Where's the conclusion? In one of its two favorite hiding places, the last sentence: "There may be millions or even billions of planets in our galaxy alone." Now we look through the choices for a statement that, though unstated in the argument, is required by the conclusion.

- (A) This is just another way of stating the conclusion. This isn't what the author is assuming; it's what the author is trying to prove. Eliminate.
- (B) The passage refers to life on other planets, but this statement is entirely unrelated to the conclusion. If life were discovered in nearby planetary systems, would it make you believe that there were millions and billions of planets in the galaxy? No. Eliminate.
- (C) The author doesn't have to assume this. This statement is irrelevant. Eliminate.
- (D) This is entirely irrelevant. Eliminate.
- (E) The author's conclusion about planets in the galaxy is based on observations of a few nearby stars. If the author's conclusion is true, then what is true of nearby stars must be true of the galaxy as a whole. This is ETS's answer.

SPECIAL TECHNIQUE: FIGGERIN'

Some arguments may involve some simple mathematics: You should treat such argument problems as though they were mathematical word problems, applying the appropriate parts of GRE Mathematics. You will seldom have to do any real math. But you will have to be familiar with such basic concepts as averages, percentages, ratios, and so on. Here's an example:

SAMPLE ARGUMENT NO. 9: FIGGERIN'

A New York hospital recently performed a 10-week weight-loss experiment involving men and women. Participants lost an average of 25 pounds. Male participants lost an average of 40 pounds, while female participants lost an average of 20 pounds. Doctors connected with the study attributed the difference to the greater initial starting weights of the male participants.

Which of the following can be concluded from the passage above?

(A) No female participant has a starting weight greater than that of any of the male participants.
(B) Everyone who participated in the study lost weight.
(C) The study included more female than male participants.
(D) Some of the participants did not lose weight.
(E) The average starting weight of the male participants was twice that of the female participants.

Here's how to crack it:

This is a missing-conclusion question in addition to being one that involves some basic math. What we need to find is a choice that follows necessarily from the passage. Let's go through the choices one at a time:

(A) This is possible but not necessary. Eliminate.

(B) This is possible but not necessary. We have only *average* weight-loss figures. Eliminate.

(C) You may think initially that this conclusion cannot be drawn from the information we've been given. But it can. How? The males lost an average of 40 pounds; the females lost an average of 20 pounds. If there had been exactly as many males as females in the study, the average weight loss for the group would have been 30 pounds—not the 25 pounds given in the passage. To account for the 25-pound average, there had to be more females than males. The lower results for the females pulled down the group average. This is ETS's answer.

(D)   This is possible but not necessary. Eliminate.

(E)   This is possible but not necessary. Eliminate.

ETS's answer is choice C. We didn't need to know much math—just a basic understanding of averages—but finding ETS's answer did turn on a mathematical concept.

A FINAL WARNING: READ ALL THE CHOICES

Even if you're sure you've found ETS's answer, you should read any remaining choices, just to make sure. Arguments can be tricky. Sometimes the difference between ETS's answer and an incorrect choice is just a word or two, or a different word order. Especially devious are "flipflops"—choices that are exactly right, except backward. By reading all the choices, you can assure yourself that you haven't overlooked a nuance and lost points due to carelessness.

SUMMARY

1. Each logic section of your GRE will contain six "logical reasoning" questions, or arguments. Three will be located after the first game, and three will be located after the last.

2. The first group of arguments will be relatively easy, and the second group of arguments will be relatively difficult. But even the most difficult GRE arguments aren't terribly difficult.

3. Learn our directions, not ETS's, and don't even glance at the instructions in your test booklet.

4. A conclusion is a claim; a premise is a stated reason or piece of evidence; an assumption is an unstated reason; an argument is a conclusion supported by premises and assumptions.

5. Argument problems are really very similar to reading-comprehension problems, although there are important differences.

6. Joe Bloggs isn't much help on arguments. The questions are mostly straightforward, and there aren't many traps.

7. Here's our general strategy for cracking arguments:

    Step 1: Read the question.

    Step 2: Read the argument.

    Step 3: Find the conclusion.

    Step 4: Diagram the argument (if necessary).

    Step 5: Attack the choices using POE.

8. Reading the question first will help you follow the argument when you read it and focus on what's important.

9. Don't skim and summarize, the way we taught you to do with reading passages. You must read each argument carefully.

10. Finding the conclusion to an argument is usually the key to finding ETS's answer. Read each argument with this in mind.

11. In 95 percent of GRE arguments, the conclusion is very easy to find. It's often in the last sentence; when it's not in the last sentence, it's often in the first.

12. On most GRE arguments, making a diagram is a waste of time. But a few relatively difficult argument problems will be hard to solve *without* diagrams.

13. Do *not* use the reading-comprehension technique of eliminating answer choices that contain lengthy repetitions from the passage. Arguments are so short that repetition is sometimes unavoidable.

14. Practice is the best way to get the hang of GRE arguments. They aren't hard to begin with, but familiarity will make them even less difficult.

15. Some GRE arguments don't have conclusions. In most such cases, the question will ask you to supply one.

16. In supply-the-conclusion questions, ETS's answer must follow logically and necessarily from the premises in the argument.

17. The presence of certain words—*only*, *never*, *always*, and so on— makes answer choices easy to dispute. Attack such choices aggressively. If you find a single exception, you can eliminate.

18. Some arguments are set up almost exactly the way games are. In such cases, you'll want to apply the techniques and approaches you learned in the chapter on games.

19. Some arguments may involve some simple mathematics. You should treat such argument problems as though they were mathematical word problems, applying the appropriate parts of GRE Mathematics. You will seldom have to do any real math.

20. Even if you're sure you've found ETS's answer, you should read any remaining choices, just to make sure.

PART V

Vocabulary for the GRE

THE VERBAL GRE IS A VOCABULARY TEST

Your GRE verbal score will be a close reflection of the size and strength of your vocabulary. If you're an avid reader of good books and publications, your vocabulary is probably in good shape. If your idea of cultural enrichment is watching MTV, you may be in trouble.

Our techniques for cracking the verbal GRE are very powerful, but how helpful they are to you will depend in large measure on the quality of your vocabulary. Our techniques can help you get maximum possible mileage out of the words you do know. The more words you know, the more help we can be.

GET TO WORK

The best way to build a good vocabulary is to absorb it slowly over an entire lifetime. Unfortunately, you don't have an entire lifetime to prepare for the GRE. Since you don't, you need to be as efficient as possible in learning new words. We can help you to do just that.

The most efficient way to learn new words for the GRE would be to learn only those words tested on the edition of the test that you take. Obviously, you won't be able to do exactly that. But you *can* do the next best thing. The Princeton Review has compiled a vocabulary list that contains the most frequently tested words on the GRE. We compiled this list, which we call the Hit Parade, by analyzing released GREs with our computers. The words are listed in order of their importance on the GRE. Words that appear in ETS's answers to questions are weighted more heavily than words that don't.

A great way to reinforce the knowledge you gain from the Hit Parade is to work carefully through *Word Smart* and *Word Smart II,* The Princeton Review's guides to building an educated vocabulary. The *Word Smart* books will help you nail down the meanings of many Hit Parade words. They will also introduce you to other words that may appear on your GRE. Look for *Word Smart* and *Word Smart II* in your bookstore.

THE HIT PARADE

Learning the GRE Hit Parade may be the single most important thing you do in preparation for the exam. Learning these words will give you a solid background in the vocabulary most likely to appear on your test. It will also give you a better idea of the kinds of words that crop up again and again on the GRE. Learning the Hit Parade will give you a feel for the level of vocabulary that ETS likes to test. This in turn will make it easier to spot other possible GRE words in your reading.

Each entry on the Hit Parade is followed by a brief definition. Most of the words on the list have other meanings as well, but the definitions we have given are the ones you are most likely to encounter on the GRE.

Keep in mind as you study the Hit Parade that the words near the top of the list are more important, in terms of the GRE, than words near the bottom.

discrete   separate; distinct

palpable   touchable; obvious

resolute   unyielding; determined

corroborate   to confirm; to back up with evidence

antipathy   firm dislike; hatred

inept   clumsy; incompetent

laconic   using few words, especially to the point of being rude

probity   integrity; honesty

compliant   yielding; submissive

gainsay   to deny; to speak against

frugal   economical; penny-pinching

equivocal   ambiguous; intentionally confusing; capable of being inter-
  preted in more than one way

intractable   hard to control; stubborn

bolster   to support; to prop up

disinterested   unbiased; neutral; impartial

intransigent   unyielding; refusing to compromise

arid   extremely dry; unimaginative; dull

garrulous   extremely talkative or wordy

exonerate   to free completely from blame

manifest   visible; evident

impervious   not allowing anything to pass through; impenetrable

contentious   argumentative; quarrelsome

lament   to mourn

arbiter   one who decides or arbitrates; a judge

allusion   an indirect reference to something else, especially to something in literature; a hint

precipitate   to cause to happen abruptly

inherent part of the essential nature of something; intrinsic

paradox a true statement or phenomenon that nonetheless seems to contradict itself; an untrue statement or phenomenon that nonetheless seems logical

partisan one who supports a particular person, cause, or idea

conventional common; customary; unexceptional

indulgent lenient; yielding to desire

inert inactive; sluggish; not reacting chemically

exposition explication

consensus unanimity or near unanimity

levee an embankment designed to prevent the overflowing of a river

sagacious wise; possessing wisdom derived from experience or learning

pervade to spread throughout

discourse to converse; to speak formally on a topic

conjure to summon or bring into being as if by magic

sanction to authorize or approve; to ratify or confirm

genial cheerful and pleasant; friendly; helpful

cynic one who deeply distrusts human nature; one who believes people are motivated only by selfishness

abstinent abstaining; voluntarily not doing something

placid pleasantly calm; peaceful

exuberant extremely joyful or vigorous; profuse in growth

impede to hinder; to obstruct; to slow (something) down

luminous giving off light; glowing; bright

permeate to spread or seep through; to penetrate

audacity boldness; reckless daring; impertinence

indignant angry, especially as a result of something unjust or unworthy

implicit implied

renascence/renaissance a rebirth or revival

erratic inconsistent; unpredictable; aimless

superfluous extra; unnecessary

vex to annoy; to pester; to confuse

anomaly an aberration; an irregularity; a deviation

genre a distinctive category or class, especially an artistic or literary one

bereave to deprive or leave desolate, especially through death

connoisseur an expert, particularly in matters of art or taste

comprehensive covering or including everything

polemic a powerful argument made in refutation of something

litigate to try in court; to engage in legal proceedings

synthesis the combining of parts to form a whole

forbear to refrain from; to abstain

vindicate to clear from all blame or suspicion

feasible possible

conciliatory making peace; attempting to resolve a dispute through goodwill

squalid filthy; repulsive, wretched; degraded

idyllic charming in a rustic way; naturally peaceful

mandatory required; obligatory

eclectic choosing the best from many sources; drawn from many sources

disseminate to spread or scatter widely; to distribute

pristine pure; uncorrupted; unspoiled; in original condition

palliate to excuse; to cause to seem less serious

prodigy an extremely talented child; an extraordinary accomplishment or occurrence

decorous in good taste; proper

infer to conclude; to deduce

ostentatious   excessively conspicuous; showing off

pathology   the scientific study of disease; any deviation from a healthy, normal condition

frenetic   frantic; frenzied

spurious   bogus; false

subjugate   to subdue and dominate; to enslave

visionary   a dreamer; a person with impractical goals or ideas about the future

reciprocal   mutual; shared; interchangeable

dissonant   disharmonious; in disagreement

plumb   to measure the depth of

debauchery   wild living; intemperance

surreptitious   sneaky; secret

flippant   frivolously shallow and disrespectful

piquant   spicy; pleasantly pungent

satiric   sarcastic; ridiculing

sullen   gloomy; dismal

tacit   implied; not spoken

tractable   easily managed or controlled; obedient

impromptu   unrehearsed; on the spur of the moment

substantive   having substance; solid; substantial

parallel   a similarity between two things

sterile   unimaginative; unfruitful; infertile

deleterious   harmful

fecund   fertile; productive

hermetic   impervious to external influence; airtight

salubrious   promoting good health

judicious   exercising sound judgment

foster   to promote the growth or development of

transitory   not lasting; temporary

goad   to urge forcefully; to prod

cacophony   a harsh-sounding mixture of sounds

turpitude   depravity; shameful wickedness

ingenuous   free from deceit or disguise

maverick   a nonconformist; a rebel

axiom   a self-evident rule of truth; a widely accepted saying

beneficent   kind; doing good

implement   to carry out

capricious   unpredictable; likely to change at any moment

alacrity   eagerness; cheerful readiness

circumlocution   an indirect expression; use of wordy or evasive language

pungent   sharp or biting to taste or smell

savor   to relish; to taste with pleasure; to enjoy

correlate   to establish or show a relationship between two things

malleable   easy to shape or bend

facetious   joking; humorous

allocate   to designate for a purpose; to distribute

petulant   rude; cranky; ill-tempered

rampart   a fortification; a defense

temerity   recklessness; foolish boldness; audacity

truculent   savage; fierce

kinship   a relationship, especially a blood relationship

incisive   cutting right to the heart of the matter

aberration   something not typical; a deviation from the standard

qualify   to modify; to restrict

abstemious   sparing or moderate, especially in eating and drinking

impugn   to attack, especially to attack the truth or integrity of something

beget   to bring into being; to cause to exist

incursion   a hostile invasion

conundrum   a puzzle; a riddle

doggerel   loose, unskillful verse

exorbitant   extravagant; immoderate

invective   insulting or abusive speech

exigent   requiring immediate attention; urgent

placate   to pacify; to appease; to soothe

temperament   disposition or character

baleful   menacing; harmful

antiseptic   free from germs; exceptionally clean

lax   not strict or firm; careless or negligent; slack

accolade   an award or honor; high praise

desiccate   to dry out

erudite   scholarly; deeply learned

debacle   a violent breakdown; a sudden overthrow

flag   to weaken; to slow down

divergent   deviating; differing

effluvium   escaping gas; noxious vapors

impudent   bold; impertinent

evanescent   vanishing or fading; scarcely perceptible

flout   to disregard out of disrespect

ineluctable   inevitable; unavoidable

mellifluous   sweetly flowing

improvident   to fail to provide for the future; careless

oscillate   to swing back and forth; to fluctuate

ossify   to turn to bone; to harden; to become rigid

propinquity   kinship; nearness

proselytize   to convert (someone) from one religion or doctrine to another; to recruit converts to a religion or doctrine

pundit   an expert; a learned person

recondite   hard to understand

brook   to tolerate; to put up with

spendthrift   extravagant or wasteful, especially with money

ribald   indecent; coarse

vacuous   stupid; lacking ideas

sinuous   winding; intricate

coda   a distinct passage that concludes a composition

penchant   a strong liking or leaning

abstruse   hard to understand

cognizant   perceptive; observant

garner   to gather; to collect

obdurate   stubborn; inflexible

chronology   a record of events in order of time; a history

economical   frugal; thrifty

accretion   growth; accumulation; enlargement

panegyric   lofty praise

reprobate   a wicked, depraved person

untoward   unruly; awkward; unfavorable

welter   a confused mass; turmoil

inchoate   just beginning; unformed

hone   to sharpen

timbre   the quality of a sound independent of pitch and loudness

disavow   to deny

saturnine   gloomy or surly in temperament

repugnant   distasteful; offensive

viscous   thick and sticky

veracity   truthfulness

pedagogue   a teacher; a pedantic or dogmatic person

rivet   to attract and hold the attention of

taut   tightly drawn; tense; firm

cajole   to deceptively persuade someone to do something he or she doesn't want to do

fulsome   morally offensive; disgusting

neophyte   a beginner

insolvent   unable to pay one's bills

motility   movement; ability to move

munificent   very generous; lavish

conjoin   to join together

THE PRINCETON REVIEW APPROACH TO LEARNING NEW WORDS

Helping students learn new words is one of the most important things we do at The Princeton Review. Students with big vocabularies simply do better on standardized tests than students with small vocabularies. Since most of our students have little time in which to learn new words, we've given a lot of thought to fast, efficient methods of memorization and retention. That's why we wrote *Word Smart* and *Word Smart II*, our vocabulary guides. (Look for them at your local bookstore.)

To build your vocabulary for the GRE in a hurry, you need to do two things. You need to learn to spot GRE words—the kind of words that ETS tests on the GRE—and you need to find an effective memorization routine that you feel comfortable with. We describe several solid ones in *Word Smart* and *Word Smart II*.

Learning the words on the Hit Parade is an ideal way not only to learn the most important GRE words but also to get a solid feel for the level of vocabulary on the test. Once you've nailed down the Hit Parade, you'll have no trouble spotting other GRE words in your daily reading.

How will you remember all these words? You'll do it by developing a standard routine for learning new words. We suggest that you begin with our method and then tailor it to suit your own preferences. Here's our method:

STEP 1: When you encounter a new word in your reading, try to deduce its meaning from context. That is, treat the unknown word as though it were a blank in a GRE sentence completion and attempt to anticipate what it must mean. You may not be able to tell, and the context may lead you astray, but the mental effort you make will help register the new word in your mind.

STEP 2: Look it up. If you don't have a dictionary handy, write down the new word and look it up later. We tell our students to "look it up" so often that we simply say "LIU." If you have somehow managed to make it through college without owning a dictionary, the time has come for you to make the plunge. Go buy one right now.

STEP 3: When you look up the word, say it out loud, being careful to pronounce it correctly. Saying the word to yourself isn't enough. You'll remember it better if you make a little noise.

STEP 4: When you look up your word in the dictionary, don't assume that the first definition is the one that applies in your case. The first definition may be an archaic one, or one that applies only in a particular context. Scan through all the definitions, looking for the one that fits the context in which you found your word.

STEP 5: If you have time, compare the definition of your new word with the definitions of its synonyms, assuming that it has some. A thesaurus can be helpful for this. Checking the meanings of synonyms can help you nail down the nuances of meaning that distinguish one word from others closely related to it.

STEP 6: Now that you've learned the dictionary's definition of your new word, restate it in your own words. You'll find it much easier to remember a word's meaning if you make it your own. You'll have to be certain, of course, that your definition is consistent with the one in the dictionary.

STEP 7: Use a memory aid, such as a mnemonic or a mental image, to fix the new word in your mind. For example, you might try to help yourself remember the word *conventional* by picturing a "customary" convention of word-memorizers. Or you might remind yourself that *enfranchise* means "to give the right to vote" by picturing people lined up to vote in a McDonald's franchise. The crazier the image, the better. Even if you can't think of a good one, the mental effort you go through in trying to think of one will help etch the word's meaning in your brain.

STEP 8: Keep a vocabulary notebook and use flash cards. We tell our students to carry spiral notebooks in which they can jot down new words and make notes about definitions. Simply having a notebook with you will remind

you to be on the lookout for new words. And using it will help you remember the ones you encounter.

The best way to use a vocabulary notebook is to devote an entire page to each new word. Jot down the word when you find it, note its pronunciation and definition (in your own words) when you LIU, and jot down your mnemonic or mental image. You might also copy the sentence in which you originally found the word, to remind yourself of how the word looks in context.

To nail down the meanings of your new words, you should also make flash cards. Our students usually make theirs out of three-by-five index cards. They write the word on one side and the pronunciation, meaning, and perhaps a mental image on the other. They can then quiz each other or themselves in idle moments through the day. By sticking five or six of your flash cards in your pocket every morning and using them when you can, you'll make surprisingly rapid progress. You can also use your flash cards for review.

STEP 9: Write the new word on your brain. Many students find that writing something down makes it easier to memorize. Use your notebook to write down sentences incorporating your new words.

STEP 10: Use your new word every chance you get. Bore your friends! Infuriate your family! The only sure way to master a word is to make it part of your life. When you're learning a new word, bend over backward to find reasons to use it. Insert it into your speech at every opportunity. A powerful vocabulary requires lots of exercise.

JUST KNOWING THEY'RE THERE

The Hit Parade can help you in more ways than one. Hit Parade words have a marked tendency to turn up in ETS's answers on the GRE. That means that Hit Parade words make very good guesses on items where you have no other reason for preferring one choice to another.

PART VI

The GRE CAT

IN THE BEGINNING

Until 1991, the Graduate Record Exam (GRE) General Test had been available in one format only, the Paper-and-Pencil GRE (or the P&P). This Educational Testing Service (ETS) exam consists of seven half-hour sections: two verbal, two math, two analytical, and one unscored experimental section (it could be math, verbal, or analytical).

Questions on the Paper-and-Pencil GRE are presented in a predictable order of difficulty. With some preparation, you can use this format to your advantage by working the questions in an order that will maximize your score.

YEAR OF THE CAT

In 1991, ETS began offering a new form of the GRE: the Computer-Based Test (CBT). The CBT had the same format as the standard Paper-and-Pencil GRE, except it was on a computer and it included a Computer-Adaptive Test (CAT) for experimental testing purposes.

Like the CBT, the Computer-Adaptive Test asks one question at a time, but unlike the CBT, the CAT adjusts itself to your individual test performance level. For example, if you answer a given question correctly, your next question will usually be harder; if you answer it incorrectly, your next question will usually be easier. Through this process, the CAT quickly zeroes in on your appropriate scoring level (more on this later).

After further testing in 1993, ETS decided to eliminate the CBT and replace it with the CAT. While it plans to continue to make additional changes to the format of the CAT over the next few years, ETS intends to phase out the Paper-and-Pencil GRE by as early as 1997.

CAT FORMAT

The GRE CAT has five sections. Three of these sections—verbal, quantitative, and analytical—count toward your score. These three, along with an adaptive experimental section, are given as the first four sections of the test; you won't know which one of the sections is the experimental, but you'll certainly be aware of an additional verbal, quantitative, or analytical section.

The questions used in each of these sections are the same types that you would see on the paper-and-pencil GRE, but they are presented in no particular order; a verbal section could start with an antonym, move to an analogy, and then move back to another antonym! ETS also requires you to answer a minimum number of questions—roughly 80% of the total (see below)—to guarantee that you do not spend too much time on any individual question. If you fail to answer the minimum number of questions on a section, you receive a grade of NS (no score).

EXPERIMENTAL SECTION

After completing the first four sections, occasionally you'll also be required to complete an unscored research section consisting of additional experimental questions. Fortunately, since you will have completed all scored sections of the test at this point, ETS's use of you as a guinea pig can have no adverse effect on your GRE score. Data obtained from this research section will be used to continue to revise the CAT over the next few years while ETS moves toward discontinuing the traditional Paper-and-Pencil GRE.

Type of Selection	# of Sections	# of Questions Per Section	You Must Answer At Least	Minutes Allowed Per Section
Verbal	1	30	24	30
Quantitative	1	28	23	45
Analytical	1	35	28	60

HOW THE CAT WORKS

CATs use your performance on one question to determine which question you will be asked next. The GRE CAT begins with ETS assuming that you have the average score in a particular category—for example, a 480 in verbal. You'll be asked a question of difficulty appropriate to this score level: if you answer correctly, the computer adjusts your score to a new level, say 550, and your next question is more difficult. If you answer incorrectly, your score will drop and your next question will be less difficult. In addition to adjusting your score, the amount your score will change with each new correct or incorrect answer is reduced as you move further into the test, so by the end the computer will have effectively zeroed in on your GRE score.

TAKING THE GRE CAT

Before the test begins, the computer will run you through a tutorial, which teaches you how to use the program. Take as much time as you need to get comfortable with your surroundings, the mouse, and the test directions; there is no time limit on the tutorial.

Because the CAT format does not allow you to underline, circle, or cross off answers or parts of questions directly on the exam, you will need to be resourceful in your use of scratch paper. Eliminating wrong answers is often critical to finding correct ones, so we suggest that you draw rows of the letters A through E on your scratch paper. You can then cross off these letters when you wish to note that an answer choice is wrong just like you would on a Paper-and-Pencil GRE.

WHAT THIS MEANS FOR YOU

Because of the interactive nature of computer-adaptive testing, taking the GRE CAT will be a completely different experience from taking the Paper-and-Pencil GRE. On the Paper-and-Pencil GRE, most sets of questions begin with the easiest question and end with the hardest. Thus, questions of all difficulty levels are presented to each test-taker.

CATs, on the other hand, do not present this range of difficulty levels. As a result, low-scoring testers will often find CAT questions easier than those on a Paper-and-Pencil test, while high-scoring testers are likely to find the questions more difficult and frustrating.

THE GOOD NEWS

The CAT is technically simple: all testers need to do is to point a mouse arrow at the answer and click, then click a second box to confirm their choice and move to the next question. Other benefits of the CAT include the following:

You receive your scores right after you finish the exam (how's that for immediate gratification?).

Scores go out to schools more quickly.

You may schedule your test any time of the week (during regular business hours only—not so convenient for working people and full-time students). The test has been offered as much as every business day or as little as one week of a month recently.

Because you have scratch paper, your work space is limitless (on the Paper-and-Pencil GRE, you must do all your work in a test booklet, which often provides too little work space).

THE BAD NEWS

The CAT costs almost twice as much as the Paper-and-Pencil GRE ($96 versus $56).

Staring at a computer for roughly four hours can be uncomfortable.

The lack of a test booklet makes it impossible to mark directly on the problems themselves (to cross out incorrect answers, etc.).

You may take the CAT only once every six months.

Almost all practice material available for the GRE was created for the Paper-and- Pencil format (don't worry we have some).

Disclosure—your right to take a look at the test along with your answers— is virtually non-existent for the CAT, whereas most Paper-and-Pencil GREs are disclosed; with the CAT you will never know which questions you missed or how the computer arrived at your final score.

ETS. These people care very little about you or how you react to changes to the test or testing conditions. They have been known to make significant changes without warning students in advance, and have done so a couple of times already with the GRE CAT. Because of this, please check with them if you intend to take the GRE in either format to ensure that no changes have been made since the publication of this document.

If the disadvantages of the CAT worry you, we recommend that you take the Paper-and-Pencil GRE, if possible; the Paper-and-Pencil test will be available at least until 1997.

PREPARING FOR THE GRE CAT

Fortunately, because the questions on the GRE CAT are the same types of questions asked on the Paper-and-Pencil GRE, you can still study for the GRE CAT with a good guide (this book) and copies of actual GRE questions (Practicing to Take the GRE: Warner Books). The Princeton Review offers the only test-preparation software available (PC or MAC) that accurately simulates the CAT. This software, which is used in our courses, will help you become comfortable with the CAT format. And if you've bought the edition of this book tht comes with our software, you're already ahead of the game.

Call (800) 2-REVIEW for more information.

SCHEDULING A CAT SESSION

The easiest way to schedule a test session is to call The Sylvan Technologies National Registration Center at 1-800-967-1100. You may also call your local test center to set up an appointment (a list of centers is available from ETS; most are Sylvan Learning Centers). In either case, you must pay by VISA or Mastercard in order to schedule by phone.

If you prefer paying by check or money order, or if you are submitting a fee waiver certificate, get a copy of the ETS booklet, The New GRE/CAT Service. Inside is a registration form which must be returned with your check. This option will entail a minimum two-to-four week wait. However, because demand for the GRE CAT is relatively small right now, it's possible to walk in without prior registration.

ON TEST DAY

Before you leave home:

Dress in layers, so that you will be comfortable regardless of whether the room is cool or warm.

Make sure to bring two forms of identification, one with a recent photograph, to the test site. Acceptable forms of identification include driver's licenses, photo-bearing employee ID cards, and valid passports.

If you registered by mail, you must also bring the authorization voucher sent to you by ETS.

Because the entire registration process is now computerized, you will be able to complete your pre-test questionnaire on-screen rather than on paper. However, just because the test is now on computer does not mean that you will not need your pencil and some paper. Before the test begins, ask for extra scratch paper. You'll probably need more than you're given, and you don't want to waste time during the test waiting for the proctor to bring you more. You should not fear that your performance will be significantly damaged due to the computer format.

Be forewarned: the test center is monitored by close-circuit television. Don't stress out: just pretend you're at the bank (unless you stress out at banks). Sit back, relax, don't panic, take it one question at a time, and you'll do your best.

PART VII

The GRE Subject Tests

MORE BAD NEWS

In addition to the GRE General Test, many graduate-school departments require or strongly recommend that you take a GRE Subject Test. Check with each of the departments at each of the graduate schools you are applying to for the specific tests you have to take.

SEVENTEEN SUBJECT TESTS

While the GRE purports to measure academic aptitude, the Subject Tests measure what you know. They're not much different from the Achievement Tests you took back in high school, except that they're much more difficult.

Here is a list of the Subject Test areas:

1. Biology
2. Chemistry
3. Computer science
4. Economics
5. Education
6. Engineering
7. French
8. Geology
9. History
10. Literature in English
11. Mathematics
12. Music
13. Physics
14. Political Science
15. Psychology
16. Sociology
17. Spanish

Each Subject Test is two hours and fifty minutes long, but the number of questions varies considerably. The Literature in English Test, for example, has 230 questions. That works out to less than a minute per question. The Engineering Test, however, has 144 questions. That works out to more than a minute a question. Of course, the engineering questions can take a lot longer to work out than the literature questions.

PRACTICE MATERIALS

As with the General Test, the best way to prepare for the Subject Test is with actual tests. Unfortunately, ETS currently offers only one full-length test in fifteen subjects (all except French and Spanish). You can order any of these from ETS or look for them in a college bookstore. Each test is about $10, but prices vary. Here's the address:

Graduate Record Examinations
Educational Testing Service
CN 6014
Princeton, NJ 08541-6014

Free topic outlines and sample questions are available for the other tests. If you're in a hurry, you can call the GRE publications office at (609) 771-7243.

PREPARING FOR A SUBJECT TEST

Lack of practice material is a problem, so you'll have to make do with what's available.

Send away for the Subject Test you'll be taking as soon as you can. If you need a lot of work in certain areas, you want to know this well in advance of the test. If there is no practice test for that particular subject, send away for the free sample questions.

Read the introductory material carefully, especially the outline of the test content. This will tell you the topics covered, and their relative importance. If there is no practice test, do the sample questions carefully. They're all you've got to go on.

If your subject offers a full-length practice test, use it as a diagnostic as soon as you get it.

Step 1: Take the test *timed*. Be sure to use the answer sheet.

Step 2: When the time limit is up, switch to a different-color pen or pencil and attempt any questions you didn't get to.

Step 3: Mark the test. When marking the questions, do *not* put down the correct answer. Simply "x" your errors for now.

Step 4: Score the questions you did during the time limit.

Step 5: Have another go at any questions you got wrong.

Once the test is over, tally your errors according to subject matter. For example, you may be fine in organic chemistry but need to review inorganic chemistry.

SCORING

For some esoteric reason known only to ETS psychometricians, the scaling on the Subject Tests is from 200 to 980. Don't ask us why. The important indicator is your percentile ranking. The scale for percentiles varies from test to test.

Some of the Subject Tests report subscore percentiles. For example, the Psychology Test reports percentiles for two categories: experimental psychology and social psychology. If you take this test, you'll receive an overall score, an overall percentile, and two subscore percentiles.

A more important difference is that unlike the General GRE, the Subject GREs subtract a quarter-question for errors. This means that random guessing probably won't affect your score much one way or the other.

TO GUESS OR NOT TO GUESS

If you lose a quarter-question for each error, when should you guess?

Some students have heard that they should never guess unless they can eliminate three choices and narrow down the selection to two choices. This is incorrect.

The best way to look at guessing is this: if you leave a question blank, you'll lose credit for a full question. If you guess, you have a chance to save that question, while if answering it incorrectly, you only lose another quarter-question. **The bottom line is this: If you can eliminate a single choice on a particular question, the odds favor guessing. Go for it!**

BUT DON'T TRY TO FINISH

The Subject Tests are much tougher than the General GRE. Unless you're scoring in the 99.9th percentile range, you won't have time to analyze every question. (Of course, if you do spend time on a question, you should be prepared to guess.)

Pacing is especially important on these exams. You'd be surprised how quickly 170 minutes can pass. Since you won't have time to analyze each question, where should you spend your time? In other words, which questions should you skip?

You'll have to be the judge. **The questions on the Subject Tests are not in order of difficulty.**

The fourth question on the Education Test might very well be the most difficult question on the test. You have no way of telling, other than by using general considerations. If a question looks longish, or covers a subject you're not familiar with, skip it for now. If you've got time at the end of the test—and you probably won't have much—return to the longer questions.

How many questions can you skip and still do well? It depends on how many questions you get right, but there's a rule of thumb for the Subject Tests: **If you answer two-thirds of the questions correctly, you'll be scoring better than 90 percent of the students taking the test.**

For example, on the Biology Test there are 210 questions. You could leave forty questions blank, get twenty-five questions wrong, and still score in the 90th percentile. Remember that when you're taking the test. Move quickly, but don't panic if you're not finishing.

Answer Key
to Drills

CHAPTER 4

DRILL 1
(pages 45-48)

1. A needle pulls thread.
2. Vernal means having to do with spring.
3. A breach is a rift in a dam.
4. Unrelated. Dogs and cats are both pets, but there is no relationship *between* them.
5. To be steadfast is not to vacillate.
6. A scintilla is a miniscule amount.
7. To calumniate is to ruin the reputation of.
8. Unrelated.
9. To be mordant is to be bitingly witty.
10. Mendacity is not telling the truth.
11. To be impertinent is not to be apposite.
12. A felony is a major infraction.
13. A door is an opening in a wall.
14. Unrelated.
15. A sanctuary provides protection.
16. To be flustered is to lack composure.
17. To malinger is not to work.
18. To have timorousness is not to be intrepid.
19. Unrelated.
20. Unrelated.
21. Filings are small pieces of metal.
22. A neophyte is characterized by inexperience.
23. A gaggle is a group of geese.
24. Unrelated.
25. Fervor is a lot of emotion.
26. To stultify is to make stupid.
27. Stratification is arrangement in layers.
28. What is ineluctable is impossible to avoid.
29. To be lethargic is to be impossible to stimulate.
30. Unrelated.

31. A log is a kind of fuel.

32. A carapace is the shell of a turtle.

33. To do something with stealth is to do it without detection.

34. Unrelated.

35. Something fortuitous happens without planning.

36. To ruminate is to engage in meditation.

37. To be vindictive is to seek revenge.

38. To be coltish is to lack discipline.

39. Vernacular is ordinary language.

40. Unrelated.

41. An arsenal is a store of weapons.

42. Obscurity is absence of light.

43. To be venal is to be corruptible by money.

44. To be tortuous is to have curves.

45. An illicit act is without legality.

46. To be histrionic is to be overly dramatic.

47. To glaze is to put glass in a window.

48. A voter is a participant in an election.

49. A manacle restrains freedom.

50. Fred and Barney are neighbors in Bedrock.

DRILL 2
(pages 58–59)
Here are the Joe Bloggs attractors:

1. physics

2. ship

3. energy

4. bishop, deity

5. No Joe Bloggs attractors

6. sheep, poultry

7. vandalism

8. flower

9. oratory, grammar

10. No Joe Bloggs attractors

CHAPTER 7

DRILL 1
(pages 114–115)

1. The doctor is *excessively detailed and academic.* Here are some words you might have anticipated: *academic detail, pedantry, scholarship.*

2. The doctor: *despite.* Anticipated words: *reasonableness, fairness, mildness.*

3. The doctor: *overlook . . . obvious.* Anticipated words for the first blank: *variety, spectrum, range.* Second blank: *similarities, likenesses, resemblances.*

4. The doctor: *had been a harmonious. . . .* Anticipated words for the first blank: *unfortunate, ill-advised, mistaken.* Second blank: *disharmony, unhappiness, fighting.*

DRILL 2
(pages 115–116)

1. A   2. D   3. B   4. E

CHAPTER 8

DRILL 1
(page 137)

1. For example, –4, –3, –2
2. For example, 3, 5, 7
3. 11
4. –5
5. 3
6. 5,847
7. For example, 347
8. Two: 5 and 7
9. 4 (simply subtract 5 from the other unit's digit)
10. 1
11. 21
12. odd
13. even
14. $2 \times 2 \times 3 \times 3$
15. positive

DRILL 2
(page 140)

1. $(2 \times 4) + (2 \times 20)$
2. $17(46 - 12 - 99)$
3. $xy - xz$
4. $a(b + c + d)$
5. $x(yz - vw)$

DRILL 3
(page 145)

1. (A) $\dfrac{1}{4}$ 2. (A) $\dfrac{7}{15}$ 3. (A) $\dfrac{8}{9}$

   (B) $\dfrac{3}{4}$ (B) $-\dfrac{1}{8}$ 4. $\dfrac{22}{3}$

   (C) $\dfrac{1}{3}$ (C) $\dfrac{1}{2}$ 5. 12

   (D) $\dfrac{3}{2}$ (D) $1\dfrac{1}{12}$

   (E) $\dfrac{13}{8}$ (E) $\dfrac{1}{12}$

   (F) $\dfrac{4}{9}$ (F) $\dfrac{3}{2}$

DRILL 4
(page 150)

1. 6.165   7. .002

2. 5.28   8. 6.5

3. 11.325   9. $\dfrac{1}{8}$

4. 45.3   10. approximately $\dfrac{1}{2}$

5. 19.2

6. 0.304

DRILL 5
(page 153)

1. 60   4. 12

2. 50%   5. 200

3. 11

DRILL 6

(page 157)

Fraction	Decimal	Percent	Ratio
$\frac{1}{2}$	0.5	50%	1:2
$\frac{1}{3}$	0.3333	$33\frac{1}{3}\%$	1:3
$\frac{2}{3}$	0.6666	$66\frac{2}{3}\%$	2:3
$\frac{1}{4}$	0.25	25%	1:4
$\frac{3}{4}$	0.75	75%	3:4
$\frac{1}{5}$	0.2	20%	1:5
$\frac{2}{5}$	0.4	40%	2:5
$\frac{3}{5}$	0.6	60%	3:5
$\frac{4}{5}$	0.8	80%	4:5
$\frac{1}{6}$	0.1666	$16\frac{2}{3}\%$	1:6
$\frac{1}{8}$	0.125	12.5%	1:8

DRILL 7

(page 160)

1. 28.4
2. 100
3. 96
4. 27
5. 85

DRILL 8

(page 163)

1. 3^6, or 729
2. 216
3. 16^3, or 4,096
4. 5 or −5
5. Approximately 5

DRILL 9

(page 170)

1. $24x^2 + 26x - 8$

2. (A) $(2x + 3y)(2x - 3y)$

   (B) $4x^2 + 8xy + 4y^2$

   (C) $(5x + 5y)^2$

   (D) $16x^2 - y^2$

3. $13x - 2$

4. 10

5. 0

6. $-4x^2 + 2x > -2x - 8$

7. $x^4 + 9y$

DRILL 10

(pages 181–183)

1. $b = 140$

2. $c = 125$

3. $AB = 20$

4. $c = 90$

5. triangle $= 11$

   rectangle $= 14$

6. triangle $= 16$

   rectangle $= 24$

7. 10

8. approximately 18

9. approximately 27

10. volume $= 200$ cubic inches

11. $A = (3, 4)$

    $B = (4, -4)$

    $C = (-6, -5)$

    $D = (-15, 5)$

PART IX

The Princeton Review GRE Diagnostic

SECTION 1
Time—30 minutes
30 Questions

Numbers: All numbers used are real numbers.

Figures: Position of points, angles, regions, etc. can be assumed to be in the order shown; and angle measures can be assumed to be positive.

Lines shown as straight can be assumed to be straight.

Figures can be assumed to lie in a plane unless otherwise indicated.

Figures that accompany questions are intended to provide information useful in answering the questions. However, unless a note states that a figure is drawn to scale, you should solve these problems NOT by estimating sizes by sight or by measurement, but by using your knowledge of mathematics (see Example 2 below).

Directions: Each of the Questions 1-15 consists of two quantities, one in Column A and one in Column B. You are to compare the two quantities and choose

A   if the quantity in Column A is greater;
B   if the quantity in Column B is greater;
C   if the two quantities are equal;
D   if the relationship cannot be determined from the information given.

Note: Since there are only four choices, NEVER MARK (E).

Common Information: In a question, information concerning one or both of the quantities to be compared is centered above the two columns. A symbol that appears in both columns represents the same thing in Column A as it does in Column B.

	Column A	Column B	Sample Answers
Example 1:	2×6	$2 + 6$	● Ⓑ Ⓒ Ⓓ Ⓔ

Examples 2-4 refer to $\triangle PQR$.

Example 2:	PN	NQ	Ⓐ Ⓑ Ⓒ ● Ⓔ

(since equal measures cannot be assumed, even though PN and NQ appear equal)

Example 3:	x	y	Ⓐ ● Ⓒ Ⓓ Ⓔ

(since N is between P and Q)

Example 4:	$w + z$	180	Ⓐ Ⓑ ● Ⓓ Ⓔ

(since PQ is a straight line)

GO ON TO THE NEXT PAGE.

A   if the quantity in Column A is greater;
B   if the quantity in Column B is greater;
C   if the two quantities are equal;
D   if the relationship cannot be determined from the information given.

Column A	Column B
1. $4[(3 + 3) + 4]$	45

a and *b* are each greater than 1.

Column A	Column B
2. $3ab$	$(3a)(3b)$

Column A	Column B
3. $\dfrac{5}{9}$	$\dfrac{4}{7}$

Column A	Column B
4. $4(2^6)$	$6(4^2)$

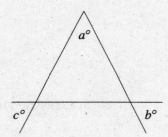

Column A	Column B
5. $b + c$	$180 - a$

Column A	Column B

Mr. Jones purchased a new bedroom set by using an extended payment plan. The regular price of the set was $900, but on the payment plan he paid $300 up front and 9 monthly payments of $69 each.

6. $23	The amount Mr. Jones paid in addition to the regular price of the bedroom set.

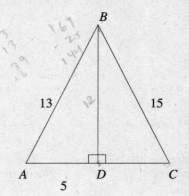

7.   The perimeter of triangle *BCD*   42

8. $\dfrac{1}{5} + \dfrac{1}{7}$	$\dfrac{1}{9} + \dfrac{1}{4}$

GO ON TO THE NEXT PAGE.

A   if the quantity in Column A is greater;
B   if the quantity in Column B is greater;
C   if the two quantities are equal;
D   if the relationship cannot be determined from the information given.

<u>Column A</u>　　　　　　　<u>Column B</u>　　　　　　　　<u>Column A</u>　　　　　　　<u>Column B</u>

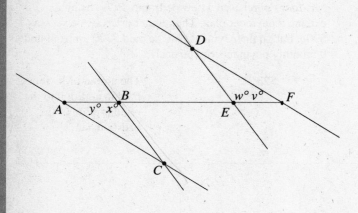

$BC \parallel DE$

9.　　　$x + y$　　　　　　　　　$w + v$

10.　The average (arith-　　　The average (arith-
　　metic mean) of 7, 3,　　　metic mean) of $2a + 5$,
　　4, and 2.　　　　　　　　$4a$, and $7 - 6a$

11.　　$\sqrt{7} + \sqrt{11}$　　　　　　$\sqrt{3} + \sqrt{15}$

<u>Questions 12-13</u> refer to the following number line.

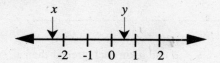

12.　　　$-x$　　　　　　　　　　$2y$

13.　　　$x + 2y$　　　　　　　　$2y - x$

$\sqrt{4r} = 6$ and $s^2 = 81$

14.　　　r　　　　　　　　　　　s

15.　　$7^{15} - 7^{14}$　　　　　　$7^{14}(6)$

GO ON TO THE NEXT PAGE.

Directions: Each of the <u>Questions 16-30</u> has five answer choices. For each of these questions, select the best of the answer choices given.

16. What is the remainder when 117 is divided by 3?

(A) 3 (B) 2 (C) 1 (D) 0 (E) $\frac{1}{3}$

17. The price of a certain stock increased 8 points, then decreased 13 points, and then increased 9 points. If the stock price before the changes was x points, which of the following was the stock price, in points, after the changes?

(A) $x - 5$
(B) $x - 4$
(C) $x + 4$
(D) $x + 5$
(E) $x + 8$

18. If $x = 1$, then $\left(2 - \frac{1}{2-x}\right)\left(2 - \frac{1}{3-x}\right)\left(2 - \frac{1}{4-x}\right) =$

(A) $\frac{1}{6}$ (B) $\frac{5}{2}$ (C) $\frac{10}{3}$ (D) $\frac{7}{2}$ (E) $\frac{5}{6}$

19. If $s = 4r$ and $t = 2s$, then, in terms of r, $3r + 2s + t =$

(A) r (B) $6r$ (C) $7r$ (D) $8r$ (E) $19r$

20. What is the least number r for which $(3r + 2)(r - 3) = 0$?

(A) -3 (B) -2 (C) $-\frac{2}{3}$ (D) $\frac{2}{3}$ (E) 3

GO ON TO THE NEXT PAGE.

343

Questions 21-25 refer to the following chart.

NUMBER OF IMMIGRANTS TO THE UNITED STATES
BY REGION OF LAST RESIDENCE, 1820-1978

(in thousands)

Region	Number of Countries Represented	Total								Percent		
		1820-1978	1951-1960	1961-1970	1974	1975	1976	1977	1978	1820-1978	1961-1970	1971-1978
Europe	21	36,184	1,325.6	1,123.4	80.4	72.8	73.0	74.0	76.2	74.5	33.8	19.2
Asia	12	2,817	153.3	427.8	127.0	129.2	146.7	150.8	243.6	5.8	12.9	33.2
North and South America (excluding United States)	15	9,006	996.9	1,716.4	178.8	174.7	169.2	223.2	266.5	18.6	51.6	45.1
Africa	30	131	14.1	29.0	5.2	5.9	5.7	9.6	11.5	0.3	0.9	1.6
Australia and New Zealand	2	119	11.5	19.6	2.0	1.8	2.1	2.5	2.7	0.2	0.6	0.5
Other Oceania*	3	306	14.0	5.7	1.4	1.8	1.8	2.1	2.2	0.6	0.2	0.4
Total	83	48,563	2,515.4	3,321.9	394.8	386.2	398.5	462.2	602.7	100.0	100.0	100.0

* Consists of the islands of the Central and South Pacific

21. From 1951 to 1960, the third greatest number of immigrants to the United States were from which region?

   (A) Asia
   (B) Africa
   (C) North and South America
   (D) Australia and New Zealand
   (E) Other Oceania

22. In 1974, approximately what was the average (arithmetic mean) number of immigrants to the United States per country of Asia that is represented?

   (A) 1,050   (B) 5,000   (C) 10,500
   (D) 33,000   (E) 130,000

23. From 1951 to 1960, the number of immigrants to the United States from India was 36 thousand. Approximately what percent of the total number of immigrants to the United States from Asia during that decade were from India?

   (A) 10%   (B) 15%   (C) 20%   (D) 25%   (E) 30%

24. From 1951 to 1960, approximately what was the ratio of the number of immigrants to the United States from Africa to the number of immigrants to the United States from Australia and New Zealand?

   (A) $\frac{1}{1}$ (B) $\frac{5}{4}$ (C) $\frac{4}{3}$ (D) $\frac{3}{2}$ (E) $\frac{5}{2}$

25. Which region had the greatest percent change in the number of immigrants to the United States from 1974 to 1975?

   (A) Europe
   (B) Asia
   (C) North and South America
   (D) Africa
   (E) Other Oceania

GO ON TO THE NEXT PAGE.

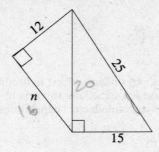

26. What is the value of *n* in the figure above?

   (A) 9
   (B) 15
   (C) 16
   (D) $12\sqrt{3}$
   (E) 20

27. If $2 < r < 8$ and $1 < s < \dfrac{5}{2}$, which of the following expresses all possible values of *rs*?

   (A) $1 < rs < 5$
   (B) $2 < rs < 20$
   (C) $\dfrac{5}{2} < rs < 8$
   (D) $\dfrac{5}{2} < rs < 20$
   (E) $5 < rs < 10$

28. What is the perimeter, in centimeters, of a rectangular newspaper ad 14 centimeters wide that has the same area as a rectangular newspaper ad 52 centimeters long and 28 centimeters wide?

   (A) 80
   (B) 118
   (C) 160
   (D) 208
   (E) 236

29. A pipe of length *x* inches is cut into two segments so that the length of one segment is two inches more than three times the length of the other segment. Which of the following is the length, in inches, of the longer segment?

   (A) $\dfrac{x+4}{3}$
   (B) $\dfrac{3x+2}{3}$
   (C) $\dfrac{x-2}{4}$
   (D) $\dfrac{3x+5}{4}$
   (E) $\dfrac{3x+2}{4}$

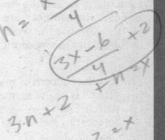

30. For all real numbers x and y, if $x \star y = x(x - y)$, then $x \star (x \star y) =$

   (A) $x^2 - xy$
   (B) $x^2 - 2xy$
   (C) $x^3 - x^2 - xy$
   (D) $x^3 - (xy)^2$
   (E) $x^2 - x^3 + x^2y$

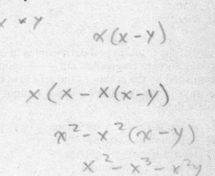

STOP

IF YOU FINISH BEFORE TIME IS CALLED, YOU MAY CHECK YOUR WORK ON THIS SECTION ONLY.
DO NOT WORK ON ANY OTHER SECTION IN THE TEST.

SECTION 2
Time—30 Minutes
38 Questions

Directions: Each sentence below has one or two blanks, each blank indicating that something has been omitted. Beneath the sentence are five lettered words or sets of words. Choose the word or set of words for each blank that best fits the meaning of the sentence as a whole.

1. It is the concern of many ecologists that the "greenhouse effect" is changing many of the Earth's ------- weather patterns into ------- systems, unable to be accurately forecast by those who study them.

    (A) predictable . . erratic
    (B) steady . . growing
    (C) uncertain . . uncanny
    (D) chaotic . . unforeseeable
    (E) weighty . . unbounded

2. Children, after more than a generation of television, have become "hasty viewers"; as a result, if the camera lags, the attention of these young viewers -------.

    (A) expands
    (B) starts
    (C) alternates
    (D) wanes
    (E) clarifies

3. Many of the troubles and deficiencies in otherwise thriving foreign enterprises are ------- ignored or diminished by the author of the article in order to ------- the ways in which other businesses might attempt to imitate them.

    (A) unintentionally . . overstate
    (B) deliberately . . stress
    (C) intermittently . . equalize
    (D) willfully . . confound
    (E) brilliantly . . illustrate

4. Frequently a copyright holder's property, published articles for example, is reproduced repeatedly in the absence of ------- for its reproduction, an action ------- by long-standing practice.

    (A) validation . . provoked
    (B) recognition . . forecast
    (C) payment . . licensed
    (D) accommodation . . instigated
    (E) allowance . . aggravated

5. The ------- of early metaphysicians' efforts to decipher the workings of the universe led some later thinkers to question the ------- of man's intellectual capabilities.

    (A) strain . . roots
    (B) intent . . superiority
    (C) intricacy . . realization
    (D) prevarications . . deceptiveness
    (E) failings . . adeptness

6. Being gracious should not be mistaken for a ------- characteristic of men's personalities; it is instead a fundamental virtue, one whose very state of being is increasingly ------- by the fashionable directive to "say what you feel."

    (A) trivial . . imperiled
    (B) pervading . . undermined
    (C) frivolous . . averted
    (D) superior . . renounced
    (E) immaterial . . influenced

7. While some individuals think that the purpose of sarcastic remarks is to disturb, by turning all communication into -------, other people see sarcastic remarks as a desire for supremacy in miniature over an environment that appears too -------.

    (A) chaos . . perplexed
    (B) equivalence . . confused
    (C) discord . . amiable
    (D) pandemonium . . disorderly
    (E) similarity . . upset

GO ON TO THE NEXT PAGE.

Directions: In each of the following questions, a related pair of words or phrases is followed by five lettered pairs of words or phrases. Select the lettered pair that best expresses a relationship similar to that expressed in the original pair.

8. CHOREOGRAPHER : DANCE ::
   (A) connoisseur : art
   (B) composer : music
   (C) acrobat : height
   (D) athlete : contest
   (E) virtuoso : skill

9. SCOWL : DISPLEASURE ::
   (A) sing : praise
   (B) kiss : affection
   (C) confess : crime
   (D) irritate : anger
   (E) hurl : disgust

10. GOGGLES : EYES ::
   (A) tie : neck
   (B) gloves : hands
   (C) elbow : arm
   (D) braid : hair
   (E) cast : leg

11. DRAWL : SPEAK ::
   (A) spurt : expel
   (B) foster : develop
   (C) scintillate : flash
   (D) pare : trim
   (E) saunter : walk

12. ARBORETUM : TREE ::
   (A) dam : water
   (B) planetarium : star
   (C) apiary : bee
   (D) museum : painting
   (E) forum : speech

13. SUBTERFUGE : DECEIVE ::
   (A) decanter : pour
   (B) interview : hire
   (C) account : save
   (D) outpost : protect
   (E) film : view

14. RATIFY : APPROVAL ::
   (A) mutate : change
   (B) pacify : conquest
   (C) duel : combat
   (D) appeal : authority
   (E) tribulate : opinion

15. SOPORIFIC : SLEEP ::
   (A) conductor : electricity
   (B) syncopation : beat
   (C) provocation : debate
   (D) coagulant : blood
   (E) astringent : pucker

16. METTLESOME : COURAGE ::
   (A) audacious : tenacity
   (B) mediocre : originality
   (C) ludicrous : inanity
   (D) dubious : suspiciousness
   (E) altruistic : donation

GO ON TO THE NEXT PAGE.

347

Directions: Each passage in this group is followed by questions based on its content. After reading a passage, choose the best answer to each question. Answer all questions following a passage on the basis of what is <u>stated</u> or <u>implied</u> in that passage.

In eighteenth-century France and England, reformers rallied around egalitarian ideals, but few reformers advocated higher education for women. Although the
Line public decried women's lack of education, it did not
(5) encourage learning for its own sake for women. In spite of the general prejudice against learned women, there was one place where women could exhibit their erudition: the literary salon. Many writers have defined the woman's role in the salon as that of an intelligent hostess, but the salon
(10) had more than a social function for women. It was an informal university, too, where women exchanged ideas with educated persons, read their own works and heard those of others, and received and gave criticism.

In the 1750's, when salons were firmly established in
(15) France, some English women, who called themselves "Bluestockings," followed the example of the *salonnières* (French salon hostesses) and formed their own salons. Most Bluestockings did not wish to mirror the *salonnières*; they simply desired to adapt a proven formula to their own
(20) purpose—the elevation of women's status through moral and intellectual training. Differences in social orientation and background can account perhaps for differences in the nature of French and English salons. The French salon incorporated aristocratic attitudes that exalted courtly
(25) pleasure and emphasized artistic accomplishments. The English Bluestockings, originating from a more modest background, emphasized learning and work over pleasure. Accustomed to the regimented life of court circles, *salonnières* tended toward formality in their salons. The
(30) English women, though somewhat puritanical, were more casual in their approach.

At first, the Bluestockings did imitate the *salonnières* by including men in their circles. However, as they gained cohesion, the Bluestockings came to regard themselves as
(35) a women's group and to possess a sense of female solidarity lacking in the *salonnières*, who remained isolated from one another by the primacy each held in her own salon. In an atmosphere of mutual support, the Bluestockings went beyond the salon experience. They traveled, studied,
(40) worked, wrote for publication, and by their activities challenged the stereotype of the passive woman. Although the *salonnières* were aware of sexual inequality, the narrow boundaries of their world kept their intellectual pursuits within conventional limits. Many *salonnières*, in
(45) fact, camouflaged their nontraditional activities behind the role of hostess and deferred to men in public.

Though the Bluestockings were trailblazers when compared with the *salonnières*, they were not feminists.

They were too traditional, too hemmed in by their genera-
(50) tion to demand social and political rights. Nonetheless, in their desire for education, their willingness to go beyond the confines of the salon in pursuing their interests, and their championing of unity among women, the Bluestockings began the process of questioning women's role in
(55) society.

17. The primary purpose of the passage is to explain that

(A) the founding of literary salons was a reaction to reformers' insistence that women be granted more extensive rights.

(B) literary salons were initially meant to be a meeting ground for male and female reformers, but gradually became a social forum with limited educational value.

(C) the literary salon provided French and English women with the opportunity to gather and discuss the rationale for free and equal access to higher education.

(D) due to widespread prejudice against higher education for women, the function of the literary salon, in both France and England, was fundamentally social.

(E) for women, who unlike men, did not have free access to higher education, literary salons offered an opportunity to pursue alternative forms of education and a chance to challenge some of society's stereotypes about the "proper" place of women.

18. According to the passage, a significant distinction between the *salonnières* and Bluestockings was in the way each group regarded which of the following?

(A) The value of acquiring knowledge
(B) The role of pleasure in the activities of the literary salon
(C) The desirability of a complete break with societal traditions
(D) The inclusion of women of different backgrounds in the salons
(E) The attainment of full social and political equality with men

GO ON TO THE NEXT PAGE.

19. The author refers to differences in social background between *salonnières* and Bluestockings in order to do which of the following?

    (A) Criticize the view that their choices of activities were significantly influenced by male salon members
    (B) Discuss the reasons why literary salons in France were established before those in England
    (C) Question the importance of the Bluestockings in shaping public attitudes toward educated women
    (D) Refute the argument that the French salons had little influence over the direction the English salons took
    (E) Explain the differences in atmosphere and style in their salons

20. It can be inferred from the passage that which of the following statements most accurately represents the principles of the *salonnières*?

    (A) It is desirable for women to aim to be both well-educated and autonomous.
    (B) Women who have a higher education have a responsibility to be politically active in order to serve as role models for those who are less educated.
    (C) A quest for artistic and aesthetic excellence is justified in itself.
    (D) In establishing a literary salon, content, rather than form, should be the primary focus.
    (E) Only women should be allowed to join groups which seek to establish equal rights for women.

21. According to the passage, which of the following factors most likely lessened the impact that the Bluestockings had on society?

    (A) The rivalry that existed between the various salons.
    (B) The strong emphasis that they placed on fostering individualism.
    (C) The fact that the activities in which they participated were limited in depth.
    (D) The fact that they patterned their own salons after the model provided by the French.
    (E) Their willingness to passively accept many of the conventions of the day.

22. The passage suggests that which of the following could most accurately be characterized as a modern-day counterpart to the literary salons depicted in the passage?

    (A) a literary collective
    (B) a neighborhood center
    (C) a seminar on aesthetics
    (D) a liberal arts study circle
    (E) a forum of political activists

23. To the pronouncement that the Bluestockings could most accurately be characterized as feminists, it can be inferred from the passage that the author would most likely respond with

    (A) blatant disapproval
    (B) limited misgivings
    (C) absolute acceptance
    (D) qualified indifference
    (E) pointed criticism

24. Which of the following titles best describes the content of the passage?

    (A) Eighteenth-Century Egalitarianism
    (B) Feminists of the Eighteenth Century
    (C) Eighteenth-Century Precursors of Feminism
    (D) Intellectual Life in the Eighteenth Century
    (E) Female Education Reform in the Eighteenth Century

GO ON TO THE NEXT PAGE.

When the same parameters and quantitative theory are used to analyze both termite colonies and troops of rhesus macaques, we will have a unified science of sociobiology.
Line Can this ever really happen? As my own studies have
(5) advanced, I have been increasingly impressed with the functional similarities between insect and vertebrate societies and less so with the structural differences that s eem, at first glance, to constitute such an immense gulf between them. Consider for a moment termites and
(10) macaques. Both form cooperative groups that occupy territories. In both kinds of society there is a well-marked division of labor. Members of both groups communicate to each other hunger, alarm, hostility, caste, status or rank, and reproductive status. From the specialist's point of
(15) view, this comparison may at first seem facile—or worse. But it is out of such deliberate oversimplification that the beginnings of a general theory are made.

25. Which of the following statements best expresses the main idea of the passage?

   (A) A unified science of sociobiology cannot be developed if deliberate oversimplification in the field continues.
   (B) A unified science of sociobiology requires specialized knowledge of both insect and vertebrate societies.
   (C) Human societies offer the most appropriate models for understanding insect and vertebrate societies.
   (D) Most insect and vertebrate societies can best be understood if research continues on termites and rhesus macaques.
   (E) A general theory of sociobiology could begin from a study of the functional similarities between insect societies and vertebrate societies.

26. The author regards the possibility of a unified science of sociobiology with

   (A) qualified optimism
   (B) unreserved excitement
   (C) neutral distance
   (D) dismission
   (E) displeasure

27. The passage implies which of the following about insect and vertebrate societies?

   (A) A well-marked division of labor is a distinctive feature of most insect and vertebrate societies.
   (B) Insect societies have caste structures similar to those found in vertebrate societies.
   (C) Cooperative groups of termites and macaques are formed for the purpose of occupying territories.
   (D) Members of insect societies are able to communicate with members of vertebrate societies.
   (E) There are some important structural differences between insect and vertebrate societies.

GO ON TO THE NEXT PAGE.

Directions: Each question below consists of a word printed in capital letters, followed by five lettered words or phrases. Choose the lettered word or phrase that is most nearly opposite in meaning to the word in capital letters.

Since some of the questions require you to distinguish fine shades of meaning, be sure to consider all the choices before deciding which one is best.

28. SLUR:
    (A) honor agreements
    (B) settle disputes
    (C) pronounce clearly
    (D) criticize directly
    (E) exclude purposefully

29. MORATORIUM:
    (A) lack of emotion
    (B) discouragement
    (C) savings
    (D) brilliance
    (E) period of activity

30. DIFFUSE:
    (A) compare
    (B) chill
    (C) concentrate
    (D) blemish
    (E) oscillate

31. THWART:
    (A) aid
    (B) beseech
    (C) dislocate
    (D) assign
    (E) allege

32. AGITATE:
    (A) relieve
    (B) satisfy
    (C) reject
    (D) condense
    (E) confirm

33. AUTHENTICATE:
    (A) sentence
    (B) disseminate
    (C) scrutinize
    (D) theorize
    (E) discredit

34. ACCLIMATION:
    (A) alienation
    (B) adoration
    (C) facilitation
    (D) invigoration
    (E) exaltation

35. TENUOUSLY:
    (A) having a strong basis
    (B) following a formal procedure
    (C) having overall consensus
    (D) with evil intent
    (E) under loose supervision

36. FLORID:
    (A) pallid
    (B) vapid
    (C) lucid
    (D) rancid
    (E) candid

37. FACTIOUS:
    (A) totally generic
    (B) openly welcomed
    (C) closely observable
    (D) seriously rejected
    (E) given to agreement

38. MISCIBLE:
    (A) likely to agree
    (B) hard to please
    (C) generous
    (D) desirable
    (E) not capable of being mixed

STOP

IF YOU FINISH BEFORE TIME IS CALLED, YOU MAY CHECK YOUR WORK ON THIS SECTION ONLY.
DO NOT WORK ON ANY OTHER SECTION IN THE TEST.

SECTION 3
Time—30 Minutes
25 Questions

Directions: Each question or group of questions is based on a passage or set of conditions. In answering some of the questions, it may be useful to draw a rough diagram. For each question, select the best answer choice given.

Questions 1-5

A two way messenger system exists between the following departments in a corporation:

F and G, F and H, H and K, K and M,
K and N, M and J, and J and L.

There is also a one-way messenger system between department J and department G; the possible direction of transit is from J to G.

None of these messenger routes intersect each other except at the departments.

There are no other departments or messenger routes in the corporation.

Messengers must follow the direction established for transit between departments.

1. To send a message from L to G by messenger, it is necessary for the messenger to travel through department

   (A) F
   (B) J
   (C) K
   (D) M
   (E) N

2. If a broken elevator temporarily makes the route between H and K unusable, then in order to send a message to F by messenger from N, a messenger would have to go through how many other departments besides F and N?

   (A) 2
   (B) 3
   (C) 4
   (D) 5
   (E) 6

3. If the hallway between H and K is being resurfaced, making the route unusable, a messenger would NOT be able to travel from

   (A) G to F
   (B) G to L
   (C) J to M
   (D) J to L
   (E) K to F

4. If a broken elevator affects the route from K to M, making it possible for a messenger to travel in only one direction from K to M, it will still be possible for a messenger to travel from J to

   (A) G and/or L but not to F, H, K, M, or N
   (B) G, L, and/or M but not to F, H, K, or N
   (C) F, G, H, and/or M but not to L, K, or N
   (D) F, H, K, L and/or M but not to G or N
   (E) F, G, H, K, L, M, and/or N

5. Assume that building repairs make it possible for a messenger to travel from K to H, but not from H to K. It will then be possible for a messenger to travel between departments F, G, H, J, K, L, M, and N if which of the following temporary routes is erected?

   (A) From F to N
   (B) From J to K
   (C) From L to K
   (D) From L to N
   (E) From M to N

6. For five years, while remodeling the town zoo, the Littleton parks commission has been transferring a large number of animals from the city of Littleton to both the Wambek and Starr King Zoos in the city of Jefferson. It follows that when Littleton's zoo reopens next year, either Wambek or Starr King will have to be closed and their animal populations consolidated.

   The author of the statements above assumes that

   (A) The removal of the Littleton animals from the Wambek and Starr King zoos will leave one or both of these zoos considerably underpopulated.
   (B) Littleton's remodeled zoo will not be large enough for the prospective animal population.
   (C) The Littleton animals comprise only a small part of the total animal populations at both the Wambek and Starr King zoos.
   (D) Incorporation of extra animals from Littleton has placed a tremendous burden on the resources of both the Wambek and Starr King zoos.
   (E) Animals will not be sent between the Wambek and Starr King zoos in the next year.

GO ON TO THE NEXT PAGE.

7. A man-made plant hormone has been added to a section of a garden in order to ward off insect infestation. The designer of the hormone has asserted that the recent dearth of insects in that section of the garden demonstrates that the man-made plant hormone wards off insect infestation.

Which of the following, if true, would cast the greatest doubt on the designer's assertion?

(A) The recent dearth of insects in that section of the garden was not as complete as had been expected given the results derived in controlled experiments.

(B) Because the man-made plant hormone would ultimately be neutralized by soil erosion, more man-made plant hormones would need to be added to the garden every three months.

(C) A man-made plant hormone produced from different chemicals which had been developed by the designer at an earlier period was ineffective in warding off insect infestation.

(D) The recent dearth of insects in that section of the garden is the same as the recent dearth of insects in otherwise very similar sections of the garden without the man-made plant hormone.

(E) The recent dearth of insects in that section of the garden, even though substantial, is not yet sufficient to compensate for the plant loss in that section of the garden in the last year.

8. A higher level of safety in automotive braking mechanisms depends upon control by internal computer monitoring systems.

Automotive braking mechanisms, to be safe, would have to pump in intervals, and determining that the brakes would compensate for all situations is impossible.

Despite technological advances, every internal computer monitoring system has on use proved to have serious weaknesses which in certain circumstances would bring about significant failure.

Which of the following can be inferred from the statements above?

(A) If designers are diligent in planning the internal computer monitoring system to be used for automotive braking mechanisms, there is an exceptionally good chance that the braking mechanism will ensure a high level of safety if and when it is needed.

(B) Techniques for decreasing the number of errors in building internal computer monitoring systems will not be discovered.

(C) Automotive braking mechanisms will not function safely during pumping.

(D) Some method of control other than internal computer monitoring systems will have to be designed.

(E) The safety of automobile braking systems cannot be ensured during pumping.

GO ON TO THE NEXT PAGE.

Questions 9-15

A city planner is planning the layout of exactly six highway exits: Bainbridge, Crescent, Driscoll, Homer, Kimball, and Morrow. They are all to be placed on the same side of a highway, in positions numbered consecutively from 1 to 6. The arrangement of exits is subject to the following restrictions::

The Bainbridge exit must be placed before the Homer exit.
The Kimball exit must be placed before the Morrow exit.
The Crescent exit cannot be placed in position 1.
The Driscoll exit must be placed next to the Bainbridge exit.

9. Which of the following is an acceptable layout of exits, from positions 1 through 6, according to the restrictions above?

   (A) Morrow, Bainbridge, Driscoll, Kimball, Homer, Crescent
   (B) Crescent, Kimball, Morrow, Driscoll, Bainbridge, Homer
   (C) Kimball, Crescent, Morrow, Homer, Driscoll, Bainbridge
   (D) Bainbridge, Homer, Kimball, Morrow, Crescent, Driscoll
   (E) Driscoll, Bainbridge, Kimball, Crescent, Homer, Morrow

10. If the Crescent exit is placed somewhere after the Homer exit, which of the following must be true?

    (A) The Crescent exit is placed somewhere after the Bainbridge exit.
    (B) The Crescent exit is placed somewhere after the Kimball exit.
    (C) The Crescent exit is placed somewhere after the Morrow exit.
    (D) The Homer exit is placed somewhere before the Kimball exit.
    (E) The Homer exit is placed somewhere before the Driscoll exit.

11. If the Homer exit is placed somewhere before the Kimball exit, the Kimball exit could be placed in which of the following positions?

    (A) 1
    (B) 2
    (C) 3
    (D) 4
    (E) 6

12. If the Morrow exit is placed somewhere before the Bainbridge exit, which of the following must be true?

    (A) The Morrow exit is placed somewhere before the Crescent exit.
    (B) The Morrow exit is placed somewhere before the Driscoll exit.
    (C) The Bainbridge exit is placed somewhere before the Crescent exit.
    (D) The Bainbridge exit is placed somewhere before the Driscoll exit.
    (E) The Bainbridge exit is placed somewhere before the Kimball exit.

13. All of the following are possible orderings for the six exits EXCEPT

    (A) Kimball, Morrow, Crescent, Driscoll, Bainbridge, Homer
    (B) Kimball, Crescent, Morrow, Driscoll, Bainbridge, Homer
    (C) Driscoll, Bainbridge, Kimball, Homer, Crescent, Morrow
    (D) Kimball, Homer, Morrow, Driscoll, Bainbridge, Crescent
    (E) Kimball, Driscoll, Bainbridge, Crescent, Homer, Morrow

14. If the Bainbridge exit is placed next to the Morrow exit, which of the following must be true?

    (A) The Kimball exit is placed in position 1.
    (B) The Crescent exit is placed in position 2.
    (C) The Driscoll exit is placed in position 3.
    (D) The Bainbridge exit is placed in position 4.
    (E) The Morrow exit is placed in position 5.

15. If the Kimball exit is placed in position 5, how many logically possible orderings of all six exits are possible?

    (A) 2
    (B) 3
    (C) 4
    (D) 5
    (E) 6

GO ON TO THE NEXT PAGE.

Questions 16-22

A catering company must schedule five different types of events within a seven-day period beginning on a Sunday and ending on the following Saturday. Exactly one event can be scheduled each day. The schedule must conform to the following conditions.

Two banquets are to be scheduled; the second banquet must be scheduled for the fourth day after the day of the first banquet.

Exactly one luncheon is to be scheduled.

Exactly one party is to be scheduled, and the party must be scheduled for either the day before or the day after the day of the first banquet.

Exactly one seminar is to be scheduled, and it must be scheduled on any day before the day of the second banquet.

Exactly one wedding is to be scheduled, and it must be scheduled for the third day after the day of the luncheon.

16. Any of the events could be scheduled for Sunday EXCEPT

(A) a banquet
(B) the luncheon
(C) the party
(D) the seminar
(E) the wedding

17. Which of the following is a possible schedule, including the day off, when no event is scheduled, for the six events from Sunday through Saturday?

(A) banquet, luncheon, party, seminar, banquet, wedding, day off
(B) luncheon, banquet, party, wedding, day off, banquet seminar
(C) party, banquet, luncheon, seminar, wedding, banquet, day off
(D) party, banquet, seminar, luncheon, day off, banquet, wedding
(E) day off, banquet, luncheon, seminar, banquet, party, wedding

18. The day on which the luncheon is scheduled must be no more than how many days after the day scheduled for the first banquet?

(A) 1
(B) 2
(C) 3
(D) 4
(E) 5

19. The party could be scheduled for any of the following days EXCEPT

(A) Sunday
(B) Monday
(C) Tuesday
(D) Wednesday
(E) Thursday

20. If the luncheon is scheduled for Sunday, which of the following pairs of events CANNOT be scheduled for consecutive days?

(A) a banquet and the wedding
(B) the luncheon and a banquet
(C) the luncheon and the party
(D) the party and the seminar
(E) the party and the wedding

21. If no event is scheduled for Sunday, which of the following could be true?

(A) The luncheon is scheduled for the day before the day of the first banquet.
(B) The party is scheduled for the day before the day of the first banquet.
(C) The seminar is scheduled for the day before the day of the first banquet.
(D) The wedding is scheduled for the day before the day of the second banquet.
(E) The wedding is scheduled for the day after the day of the seminar.

22. If the party is scheduled for the day before the day of the first banquet, the days for which the luncheon can be scheduled include

(A) Sunday and Monday
(B) Sunday and Wednesday
(C) Monday and Tuesday
(D) Monday and Wednesday
(E) Tuesday and Wednesday

GO ON TO THE NEXT PAGE.

23. During the past fifteen years, twenty percent of the judges with sufficient experience to be considered for federal judgeships were women, and all of those deemed to have sufficient experience during those years received federal judgeships. Despite this fact, only eight percent of federal judgeships are currently filled by women.

Which of the following, if true, could explain the discrepancy in the percentages cited in the passage above?

(A) Fifteen years ago, it required less experience to be considered for federal judgeships than it does today.
(B) The majority of those holding federal judgeships have held those positions for more than fifteen years, dating back to a time when practically everyone holding that position was male.
(C) The women with sufficient experience to be considered for federal judgeships have tended to specialize in different areas of law than the men considered for federal judgeships.
(D) Men and women holding federal judgeships have received equal financial compensation for the previous fifteen years.
(E) Although women currently hold eight percent of the federal judgeships, they hold only three percent of circuit judgeships.

24. It has been argued that medical researchers would make more impressive strides in their effort to develop cures for certain infectious diseases if they knew more about how cells replicate. This argument, however, could be challenged on the basis that a major advance in pest control has never come from any insight into the reproductive patterns of insects.

The argument above relies on an analogy that assumes that fighting infectious diseases is an endeavor similar to which of the following?

(A) Theories of cell-replication
(B) Efforts at pest control
(C) Conclusions about how researchers make advances
(D) Patterns of infectious disease transmission in insects
(E) Research into the reproductive patterns of insects

25. Rita has more clients than Frank and more clients than Tom. Isabel has more clients than Rita. Sam has no fewer clients than Rita.

If all of the statements above are true, which of the following cannot be true?

(A) Tom has more clients than Sam.
(B) Tom has more clients than Frank.
(C) Isabel has more clients than Tom.
(D) Sam and Rita have the same number of clients.
(E) Frank has fewer clients than Sam.

STOP

IF YOU FINISH BEFORE TIME IS CALLED, YOU MAY CHECK YOUR WORK ON THIS SECTION ONLY.
DO NOT WORK ON ANY OTHER SECTION IN THE TEST.

NO TEST MATERIAL ON THIS PAGE.

SECTION 4
Time—30 minutes
30 Questions

Numbers: All numbers used are real numbers.

Figures: Position of points, angles, regions, etc. can be assumed to be in the order shown; and angle measures can be assumed to be positive.

Lines shown as straight can be assumed to be straight.

Figures can be assumed to lie in a plane unless otherwise indicated.

Figures that accompany questions are intended to provide information useful in answering the questions. However, unless a note states that a figure is drawn to scale, you should solve these problems NOT by estimaing sizes by sight or by measurement, but by using your knowledge of mathematics (see Example 2 below).

Directions: Each of the <u>Questions 1-15</u> consists of two quantities, one in Column A and one in Column B. You are to compare the two quantities and choose

      A   if the quantity in Column A is greater;
      B   if the quantity in Column B is greater;
      C   if the two quantities are equal;
      D   if the relationship cannot be determined from the information given.

Note: Since there are only four choices, NEVER MARK (E).

Common
Information: In a question, information concerning one or both of the quantities to be compared is centered above the two columns. A symbol that appears in both columns represents the same thing in Column A as it does in Column B.

	Column A	Column B	Sample Answers
Example 1:	2×6	$2 + 6$	●ⒷⒸⒹⒺ

Examples 2-4 refer to $\triangle PQR$.

Example 2:	PN	NQ	ⒶⒷⒸ●Ⓔ

(since equal measures cannot be assumed, even though PN and NQ appear equal)

Example 3:	x	y	Ⓐ●ⒸⒹⒺ

(since N is between P and Q)

Example 4:	$w + z$	180	ⒶⒷ●ⒹⒺ

(since PQ is a straight line)

GO ON TO THE NEXT PAGE.

A   if the quantity in Column A is greater;
B   if the quantity in Column B is greater;
C   if the two quantities are equal;
D   if the relationship cannot be determined from the information given.

Column A	Column B

1. The units digit in the number 1,743 — The hundreds digit in the number 5,243

$$1.3 + .6 + .9 + x = 5$$

2. x — 2.3

3. 4^3 — 3^4

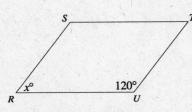

RSTU is a parallelogram

4. x — 45

5. 30 percent of \$150 — 60 percent of \$75

6. $\dfrac{n}{3}$ — $\dfrac{m+n}{3}$

Column A	Column B

7. $\dfrac{\sqrt{27}}{\sqrt{3}}$ — $\dfrac{\sqrt{45}}{\sqrt{5}}$

8. $5\left(\dfrac{x}{5} + \dfrac{y}{5} + \dfrac{7}{5}\right)$ — $x + y + 7$

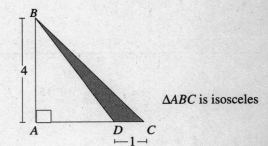

$\triangle ABC$ is isosceles

9. $\dfrac{\text{Area of the shaded region of } \triangle ABC}{\text{Area of the unshaded region of } \triangle ABC}$ — $\dfrac{1}{3}$

The average (arithmetic mean) of two positive integers is equal to 17. Each of the integers is greater than 12.

10. Twice the larger of the two integers. — 44

GO ON TO THE NEXT PAGE.

A   if the quantity in Column A is greater;
B   if the quantity in Column B is greater;
C   if the two quantities are equal;
D   if the relationship cannot be determined from the information given.

Column A	Column B		Column A	Column B

The circumference of a circle having a radius of $\frac{1}{2}$ meter is C meters.

11. C 4

12. $\sqrt{\dfrac{7}{3}}$ $\dfrac{1}{3}\sqrt{7}$

$$\frac{a}{b} = \frac{1}{3} \text{ and } \frac{b}{c} = \frac{15}{4}$$

13. a c

14.   The circumference of a circular region with radius r The perimeter of a square with side r

15. $3^{17} + 3^{18}$ $(4)3^{17}$

GO ON TO THE NEXT PAGE.

Directions: Each of the Questions 16-30 has five answer choices. For each of these questions, select the best of the answer choices given.

16. Which of the following numbers is greater than $-\dfrac{7}{3}$

(A) –7 (B) –3 (C) –2 (D) $-\dfrac{8}{3}$ (E) $-\dfrac{5}{2}$

17. If the cost of a one hour telephone call is $7.20, what would be the cost of a ten minute telephone call at the same rate?

(A) $7.10
(B) $3.60
(C) $1.80
(D) $1.20
(E) $ .72

18. A pie is baked in a circular plate with a radius of 6 inches. If the pie is then cut into eight equal pieces, what would be the area, in square inches, of each slice of the pie?

(A) $\dfrac{1}{8}\pi$ (B) $\dfrac{2}{9}\pi$ (C) $\dfrac{9}{2}\pi$ (D) 6π (E) 36π

19. If $s = 3r$ and $t = 7s$, then, in terms of r, $t - s - r =$

(A) $21r$
(B) $17r$
(C) $10r$
(D) $4r$
(E) r

20. $\sqrt{1.44 - .63} =$

(A) .9
(B) .81
(C) .12
(D) .09
(E) .03

GO ON TO THE NEXT PAGE.

361

Questions 21-25 refer to the following data.

PERCENT CONTRIBUTED TO PROFITS BY EACH OF THE 6 DIVISIONS, *P* THROUGH *U,* OF COMPANY *Y* FOR 1979 AND 1980

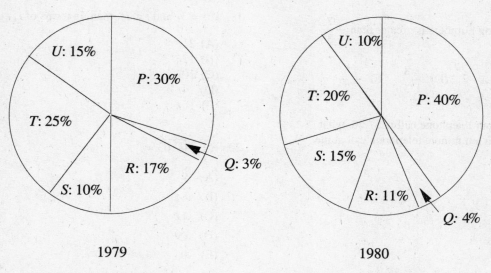

1979

Profits = $20,000,000

1980

Profits = $30,000,000

Note: Figure drawn to scale.

21. In 1979, what was the average of the amounts contributed to profits by Division *P* and Division *S*?

(A) $150,000
(B) $750,000
(C) $2,000,000
(D) $4,000,000
(E) $6,000,000

22. Division *U* contributed how much more to the profits of Company *Y* in 1979 than in 1980?

(A) $500,000
(B) $250,000
(C) $150,000
(D) $100,000
(E) $0

23. In 1980, the greatest contribution to profits by one of the six divisions was what percent of the second least contribution?

(A) 25%   (B) 75%   (C) 175%
(D) 350%   (E) 400%

24. If the six divisions are ranked each year according to their dollar contributions to profits, from greatest contribution to lowest, how many divisions ranked lower in 1980 than in 1979?

(A) None
(B) One
(C) Two
(D) Three
(E) Four

25. How many of the divisions contributed more dollars to profits in 1980 than in 1979?

(A) One
(B) Two
(C) Three
(D) Four
(E) Five

GO ON TO THE NEXT PAGE.

26. In a certain election, 60 percent of the voters were women. If 30 percent of the women and 20 percent of the men voted for candidate X, what percent of all the voters in that election voted for candidate X?

    (A) 18%
    (B) 25%
    (C) 26%
    (D) 30%
    (E) 50%

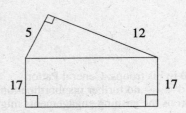

27. What is the perimeter of the figure above?

    (A) 51
    (B) 64
    (C) 68
    (D) 77
    (E) 91

28. If a, b, and c are consecutive non-positive integers and $a < b < c$, which of the following must be true?

    I. $-a < -c$
    II. $abc < 0$
    III. abc is even

    (A) None
    (B) II only
    (C) III only
    (D) II and III only
    (E) I, II, and III

29. If $5a - 3b = -9$ and $3a + b = 31$, then $a + b =$

    (A) −7
    (B) −3
    (C) 6
    (D) 13
    (E) 19

30. 5×10^3 is what percent of $\frac{1}{5} \times 10^2$?

    (A) 2,500%
    (B) 4,900%
    (C) 20,000%
    (D) 24,900%
    (E) 25,000%

STOP

IF YOU FINISH BEFORE TIME IS CALLED, YOU MAY CHECK YOUR WORK ON THIS SECTION ONLY.
DO NOT WORK ON ANY OTHER SECTION IN THE TEST.

SECTION 5
Time—30 Minutes
38 Questions

<u>Directions:</u>   Each sentence below has one or two blanks, each blank indicating that something has been omitted. Beneath the sentence are five lettered words or sets of words. Choose the word or set of words for each blank that <u>best</u> fits the meaning of the sentence as a whole.

1. Many feature films are criticized for their ------- content, even though television news is more often the medium that depicts violent events in excessive detail.

(A) discretionary
(B) graphic
(C) dramatic
(D) artistic
(E) honest

2. The use of alcohol and other drugs, with the exception of tobacco, seems to increase and decrease -------; certain periods are marked by a social inclination toward abstinence, which after a time gives way to drug consumption by some part of society, and eventually to ------- acceptance.

(A) erratically . . partial
(B) cyclically . . widespread
(C) exponentially . . mitigated
(D) criminally . . absolute
(E) simultaneously . . conventional

3. After screenwriter Neil Jordan's most recent work opened in selected urban areas, many theatergoers were -------, but after pundits expressed their -------, appreciation of the film increased and distribution surged.

(A) skeptical . . approbation
(B) apathetic . . diffidence
(C) ebullient . . trepidation
(D) dubious . . disdain
(E) unimpressed . . antipathy

4. The pieces exhibited at many university galleries are chosen to reflect the diverse tastes of the academic communities they serve; the curators avoid ------- in favor of -------.

(A) continuity . . rigidity
(B) variation . . craftsmanship
(C) uniformity . . eclecticism
(D) modernism . . classics
(E) homogeneity . . segmentation

5. The American public venerates medical researchers because the researchers make frequent discoveries of tremendous humanitarian consequence; however, the daily routines of scientists are largely made up of result verification and statistical analysis, making their occupation seem -------.

(A) fascinating
(B) quotidian
(C) recalcitrant
(D) experimental
(E) amorphous

6. In a vitriolic message to his troops, General Patton insisted that he would ------- no further insubordination, no matter how barbarous the ensuing engagements might become.

(A) impede
(B) brief
(C) denote
(D) brook
(E) expose

7. Chang realized that she had been ------- in her duties; had she been more -------, the disaster may well have been avoided.

(A) unparalleled . . careful
(B) irreproachable . . aware
(C) derelict . . vigilant
(D) arbitrary . . interested
(E) neglectful . . insensible

GO ON TO THE NEXT PAGE.

<u>Directions:</u> In each of the following questions, a related pair of words or phrases is followed by five lettered pairs of words or phrases. Select the lettered pair that best expresses a relationship similar to that expressed in the original pair.

8. METEOROLOGY : WEATHER ::
   (A) philology : love
   (B) epistemology : disease
   (C) physiology : mind
   (D) demography : population
   (E) astrology : planets

9. MAELSTROM : WATER ::
   (A) downpour : rain
   (B) wave : current
   (C) cyclone : wind
   (D) tornado : debris
   (E) storm : snow

10. FIX : STABLE ::
    (A) furrow : productive
    (B) mend : torn
    (C) fortify : strong
    (D) deter : active
    (E) captivate : attractive

11. GALL : IRRITATION ::
    (A) accommodate : deception
    (B) beleaguer : felicity
    (C) awe : apathy
    (D) discomfit : confusion
    (E) inculcate : fear

12. PAPYRUS : PAPER ::
    (A) manuscript : book
    (B) hatchet : ax
    (C) cart : wagon
    (D) daguerreotype : photograph
    (E) house : mansion

13. BLACKSMITH : FOUNDRY ::
    (A) farmer : shed
    (B) artist : studio
    (C) physician : laboratory
    (D) teacher : college
    (E) reporter : television

14. ARIA : SONG ::
    (A) covenant : agreement
    (B) fable : story
    (C) monument : sculpture
    (D) prose : poem
    (E) soliloquy : speech

15. LONGING : PINE ::
    (A) remorse : rue
    (B) anguish : seethe
    (C) forbearance : dignify
    (D) concern : intervene
    (E) suffering : inflict

16. CHEVRON : BADGE ::
    (A) caisson : cart
    (B) calcium : bone
    (C) wax : candle
    (D) clothing : uniform
    (E) oration : eulogy

GO ON TO THE NEXT PAGE.

Directions: Each passage in this group is followed by questions based on its content. After reading a passage, choose the best answer to each question. Answer all questions following a passage on the basis of what is <u>stated</u> or <u>implied</u> in that passage.

In *A Room of One's Own*, Virginia Woolf performs a typically stream-of-consciousness feat by beginning with a description of the view from her window: a leaf falls from
Line a tree, and a woman in leather boots and a man in a maroon
(5) overcoat climb into a taxi and glide away. Woolf uses this moment to discuss the unity of the mind, and the effortlessness with which she had invested this ordinary sight with a kind of rhythmic order. She ends with a consideration of Coleridge's remark that a great mind is androgynous.
(10) "What does one mean by 'the unity of the mind?'" Woolf asks.

One of Woolf's theses is that unity, and not repression, is the necessary state for creativity. Woolf describes men's sentences as having a particular shape, natural to men, but
(15) unnatural and clumsy to women. She rightly praises Austen for developing her own rhythm and her own sentence, which is expressive of her genius, her characters, and her history. Woolf suggests that the women's suffrage movement fomented a reaction of threatened male self-
(20) assertion that meant a decline in literary power. "It is fatal," she writes, "for any one who writes to think of their sex . . . it is fatal for a woman to lay the least stress on any grievance; to plead justice with any cause; in any way to speak consciously as a woman."
(25) *A Room of One's Own* exhorts women to reach for a higher, almost religious approach to writing. "Do not dream of influencing other people;" she writes, "think of things in themselves."

17. Which of the following literary projects would Woolf most likely support?

(A) A narrative poem in which a heroine overcomes male challenges through intellectual superiority
(B) A fictional polemic asserting the importance of social equality of men and women
(C) A novel that expresses the unrepressed truth of the author's experience
(D) A short story that responds to the historical injustice in the treatment of women
(E) A critical essay on Coleridge which explains his remark about androgyny in terms of his psychological history

18. The author refers to Woolf's description of the man and women climbing into the taxi in order to

(A) give an example of Woolf's mastery of stream-of-consciousness techniques
(B) show a typically feminine perspective of everyday life
(C) demonstrate how Woolf's writing was unconcerned with changing the social order
(D) refute the notion that Woolf's assertions are anti-female or anti-feminist
(E) begin the discussion of Woolf's conception of the ways in which the mind unifies the world

19. According to the passage, Woolf believes which of the following to be true about Jane Austen's work?

I. Austen's sentences are representative of an androgynous 'unity of the mind.'
II. Austen's syntax and literary form are products of her personal experience.
III. Austen's literary work exemplifies a particular form of well-realized female artistic expression.

(A) I only
(B) II only
(C) I and II only
(D) II and III only
(E) I, II, and III

20. It can be inferred from the passage that Woolf believes that

(A) women should not write about subjects that are specifically female
(B) the women's suffrage movement contributed to a decline in literary quality
(C) Austen created a narrative style that was appropriate for her gender and subject matter
(D) women's sentences should mimic the shape of men's sentences
(E) some readers could misinterpret her statements as being denigrating to women

GO ON TO THE NEXT PAGE.

Because human anatomy does not change (except over long periods of time), knowledge acquired a century ago is still accurate today. Broad functions of any part of the
Line body, such as the skin, are duplicated in different ways by
(5) other organs. One can eventually understand the entire body as a larger system made up of smaller, interdependent systems.

A cross-section of the skin reveals a top layer of epidermis, or cuticle, followed by derma, and finally, subcutane-
(10) ous cellular tissue. Sprouting through all three layers are hairs, with hair follicles and erector pili muscles embedded deep within the subcutaneous tissue. Sweat (sudoriferous glands), fat cells, and sebaceous glands are scattered throughout, while papillae, which are conical and extremely
(15) sensitive, can be found directly beneath the superficial layer.

The skin is the primary organ of the sense of touch. It can excrete substances as well as absorb them, and it plays a vital role in regulating body temperature and in protecting the tissues that lie beneath it.
(20) The epidermis has no veins or arteries and varies considerably both in thickness and in the depth or fineness of its furrows. On the palm, for example, the skin is quite thick, or horny, and is marked by deep furrows or lines. On the back of the hand, however, the skin is less thick, and has
(25) only a faint network of lines crisscrossing it. The pigment found in the epidermis gives whatever color there is to the skin; this pigment is similar to that found in the retina of the eye. One layer down, in the derma, there is similar variation in thickness, mostly to protect underlying tissue.
(30) In the derma lies the vascular system, which includes nerves, blood vessels, and lymphatics. The derma is divided into two sub-layers: the reticular layer and the papillary layer, which is closer to the epidermis. The less sensitive the skin, the fewer papillae reside there; in the most sensi-
(35) tive places, such as the fingertips and the nipples, the papillae are long, large, and grouped closely together to form parallel arcs with ducts to sweat glands lying in between. Under the papillary layer, and conforming to it, is the reticular layer, composed of fibrous bands and elastic
(40) tissue, and interlaced by fat and sudoriferous glands.

The basic functions of muscular contraction, vascular transport, nerve communication, and protection all take place in the various layers of the skin, so that understanding the components of the skin and how they work together is a
(45) helpful step in understanding the complex anatomy of the human body.

21. The author is primarily concerned with

(A) giving an overview of human anatomical functions
(B) describing the layers of the skin to show one example of an anatomical system
(C) concluding that the study of human anatomy must first begin with the skin
(D) discussing how the skin is only one system in a much larger and more complex system
(E) detailing the three layers of the skin: the epidermis, the derma, and the subcutaneous cellular tissue, each of which has its own separate functions

22. The passage suggests that the area of skin most closely associated with skin sensitivity is the

(A) reticular layer
(B) papillary layer
(C) sudoriferous gland
(D) subcutaneous tissue
(E) vascular system

23. The author would most likely agree with which of the following statements?

   I. Extremely sensitive skin is characterized by a minute number of papillae.
   II. Hair can be found in subcutaneous tissue.
   III. Skin and the retina both rely on pigment to give them color.

(A) I only
(B) II only
(C) I and II only
(D) II and III only
(E) I, II, and III

24. The passage supplies information to answer which of the following questions?

(A) What causes the erector pili muscle to contract?
(B) Why is the epidermis covered with furrows?
(C) How quickly do papillae react to sensation?
(D) What do sudoriferous glands and sebaceous glands have in common?
(E) Where in the body can pigmentation be found?

GO ON TO THE NEXT PAGE.

25. The author implies that

    (A) there is a relationship between the thickness of the skin and the number and depth of the skin's furrows
    (B) the reticular layer is the only layer that contains fibrous bands
    (C) the skin is the only part of the body that has a sense of touch
    (D) areas of the skin with sudoriferous glands are extremely sensitive
    (E) both hair and the reticular layer are made up of the same kind of tissue

26. The passage suggests that if the skin were damaged in some way, and unable to perform some of its functions, which of the following might happen?

    (A) The pigmentation would no longer be similar to that found in the retina.
    (B) The deep furrows found on some parts of the skin would disappear.
    (C) The body would regulate its temperature less effectively.
    (D) The fingertips would no longer be characterized by an abundance of papillae.
    (E) The body would lose its sense of touch.

27. The passage states that all the following are found in the skin EXCEPT

    (A) fat cells
    (B) lymphatics
    (C) veins
    (D) pigmentation
    (E) ligaments

GO ON TO THE NEXT PAGE.

Directions: Each question below consists of a word printed in capital letters, followed by five lettered words or phrases. Choose the lettered word or phrase that is most nearly <u>opposite</u> in meaning to the word in capital letters.

Since some of the questions require you to distinguish fine shades of meaning, be sure to consider all the choices before deciding which one is best.

28. CHRONIC:
    (A) intermittent
    (B) healthy
    (C) tardy
    (D) consistently durable
    (E) suddenly available

29. FORK:
    (A) judge
    (B) praise
    (C) agitate
    (D) converge
    (E) impress

30. FANCY:
    (A) ornament
    (B) abhor
    (C) falsify
    (D) reclaim
    (E) stiffen

31. ANIMATE:
    (A) enervate
    (B) frustrate
    (C) regress
    (D) condemn
    (E) distort

32. CARDINAL:
    (A) wholesome
    (B) obscure
    (C) trivial
    (D) impious
    (E) lascivious

33. INCUBATE:
    (A) squelch
    (B) hatch
    (C) assemble
    (D) decide
    (E) sterilize

34. OBSTREPEROUS:
    (A) disciplined
    (B) insubordinate
    (C) predictable
    (D) well-formed
    (E) exhausted

35. CHECK:
    (A) assume
    (B) complete
    (C) disagree
    (D) emulate
    (E) unbridle

36. IMPRECATE:
    (A) evaluate carefully
    (B) uphold forcefully
    (C) bless
    (D) forgive
    (E) confine

37. BEREAVE:
    (A) tear
    (B) collaborate
    (C) solicit
    (D) radiate
    (E) furnish

38. HIE:
    (A) separate
    (B) dawdle
    (C) lower cautiously
    (D) comfort warmly
    (E) leave suddenly

S T O P

IF YOU FINISH BEFORE TIME IS CALLED, YOU MAY CHECK YOUR WORK ON THIS SECTION ONLY. DO NOT WORK ON ANY OTHER SECTION IN THE TEST.

SECTION 6
Time—30 Minutes
25 Questions

<u>Directions:</u>   Each question or group of questions is based on a passage or set of conditions. In answering some of the questions, it may be useful to draw a rough diagram. For each question, select the best answer choice given.

<u>Questions 1-6</u>

A strand of ten lights is to be hung in a store to decorate for the holidays. The bulbs to be used in the strand are three red bulbs, two blue bulbs, two green bulbs, two yellow bulbs and a white bulb. The bulbs are located every three feet on the strand.

The strand has two different colored bulbs at either end.
The red bulbs must all be next to each other.
The white bulb must have a blue bulb immediately on either side of it.
A green bulb and a red bulb cannot be next to each other.
If a yellow bulb is at the end of the strand, then a blue bulb must be next to it.

1. Which of the following is a possible order for the bulbs on the strand?

   (A) Yellow, red, red, red, yellow, green, green, blue, white, blue
   (B) Green, blue, white, blue, red, red, red, yellow, yellow, green
   (C) Blue, white, blue, green, yellow, yellow, green, red, red, red
   (D) Yellow, blue, white, yellow, red, red, red, blue, green, green
   (E) Green, green, yellow, red, red, red, yellow, blue, white, blue

2. If a red bulb is at one end of the strand and a yellow bulb is at the other, which of the following statements must be true?

   (A) The two middle bulbs are both blue.
   (B) The two middle bulbs are both red.
   (C) The two middle bulbs are both green.
   (D) The two middle bulbs are green and blue.
   (E) The two middle bulbs are yellow and green.

3. If the two yellow bulbs are next to each other and the green bulbs are not next to each other, which of the following statements must be true?

   (A) A yellow bulb is next to a red bulb.
   (B) A yellow bulb is next to a blue bulb.
   (C) A blue bulb is not next to a green bulb.
   (D) A white bulb is not next to a blue bulb.
   (E) A yellow bulb cannot be at either end of the strand.

4. If a yellow bulb is at the end of the strand, which of the following statements must be true?

   (A) A green bulb is next to a yellow bulb.
   (B) A white bulb is at the other end of the strand.
   (C) A blue bulb is at the other end of the strand.
   (D) A yellow bulb is at the other end of the strand.
   (E) A blue bulb is next to a red bulb.

5. If a white bulb is next to the bulb at the end of the strand and the two yellow bulbs are next to each other, which of the following statements could be true?

   (A) There is a yellow bulb at the end of the strand.
   (B) There is a red bulb next to a green bulb.
   (C) There is a blue bulb next to a green bulb.
   (D) There is not a yellow bulb next to a green bulb.
   (E) There is a blue bulb next to a yellow bulb.

6. Which of the following is NOT possible?

   (A) A yellow bulb is at one end of the strand, and a green bulb is at the other end.
   (B) A red bulb is at one end of the strand, and a green bulb is at the other end.
   (C) A yellow bulb is directly adjacent to a red bulb and a green bulb.
   (D) There are red bulbs next to a yellow bulb, a blue bulb, and a white bulb.
   (E) There are blue bulbs next to a red bulb, a white bulb, and a yellow bulb.

GO ON TO THE NEXT PAGE.

7. Over the past five years, Clean toothpaste has been advertised as the most effective means of preventing tooth decay. However, according to dentists' records, many patients experiencing severe tooth decay used Clean toothpaste. Clearly, Clean toothpaste is not an effective means of preventing tooth decay.

Which of the following statements, if true, would most seriously weaken the conclusion above?

(A) Of the patients experiencing tooth decay, two-thirds indicate that they would be willing to switch brands of toothpaste.
(B) The advertisements for Clean toothpaste advocate brushing twice a day.
(C) If Clean toothpaste were not available, more patients would experience severe tooth decay.
(D) Dentists continue to recommend Clean toothpaste more than any other brand.
(E) Of those who experienced severe tooth decay, only one-eighth also experienced gum disease.

8. A group of physicians wishing to explore the link between protein and high blood pressure performed a nutrition experiment on a selected group of ten vegetarians. Five of the people were given a high protein, low fat diet. The group given the high protein, low fat diet exhibited the same five percent increase in blood pressure as did the group given the low protein, high fat diet.

Which of the following conclusions can most properly be drawn if the statements above are true?

(A) The physicians did not establish a link between protein and high blood pressure.
(B) The sample chosen by the physicians was not representative of the general vegetarian population.
(C) Some physicians believe there is a link between protein and high blood pressure.
(D) Vegetarians are more likely to eat a high protein, low fat diet than a low protein, high fat diet.
(E) There is a link between protein and high blood pressure.

9. Whenever Joe does his laundry at the Main Street Laundromat, the loads turn out cleaner than they do when he does his laundry at the Elm Street Laundromat. Laundry done at the Main Street Laundromat is cleaner because the machines at the Main Street Laundromat use more water per load than do those at the Elm Street Laundromat.

Which of the following statements, if true, helps support the conclusion above?

(A) The clothes washed at the Elm Street Laundromat were, overall, less clean than those washed at the Main Street Laundromat.
(B) Joe uses the same detergent at both laundromats.
(C) The machines at the Oak Street Laundromat use twice as much water as do those at the Main Street Laundromat.
(D) Joe does three times as much laundry at the Main Street Laundromat as he does at the Elm Street Laundromat.
(E) Joe tends to do his dirtier laundry at the Elm Street Laundromat.

GO ON TO THE NEXT PAGE.

Questions 10-13

A designer is touring five different cities in five days. The first four outfits of each show are either checkered, dotted, striped, or plaid. In every city the models wear these four outfits in a different order.

In successive cities, the first outfits are never the same.
In successive cities, the fourth outfits are never the same.
The plaid outfit is never modeled directly after the striped outfit.
The dotted outfit is never modeled first.

10. Which of the following could be an outfit order on the night following a night when the outfit order is plaid, striped, dotted, and checkered?

   (A) Checkered, dotted, striped, and plaid
   (B) Dotted, checkered, plaid, and striped
   (C) Plaid, dotted, checkered, and striped
   (D) Striped, plaid, checkered, and dotted
   (E) Striped, checkered, plaid, and dotted

11. All of the following could be an outfit order for the evening following an evening in which the outfit order has the checkered outfit fourth and the plaid outfit third EXCEPT

   (A) Checkered, dotted, plaid, and striped
   (B) Checkered, plaid, dotted, and striped
   (C) Striped, dotted, plaid, and checkered
   (D) Plaid, checkered, striped, and dotted
   (E) Plaid, striped, checkered, and dotted

12. If the outfit order on one evening is checkered, plaid, dotted, and striped, and on the next evening the outfit order has the plaid outfit fourth, which of the following must be true of the outfit order on the second evening?

   (A) The checkered outfit is modeled first.
   (B) The striped outfit is modeled first.
   (C) The checkered outfit is modeled immediately before the striped outfit.
   (D) The dotted outfit is modeled immediately before the striped outfit.
   (E) The dotted outfit is modeled directly before the checkered outfit.

13. If on a Monday the outfit order is striped, dotted, plaid, and checkered, and on a Wednesday the outfit order is plaid, checkered, striped, and dotted, which of the following must be true about the outfit order for Tuesday?

   (A) The plaid outfit is modeled second.
   (B) The striped outfit is modeled second.
   (C) The dotted outfit is modeled third.
   (D) The striped outfit is modeled fourth.
   (E) The checkered outfit is modeled first.

GO ON TO THE NEXT PAGE.

Questions 14-18

There are three hiking paths at Miller's Farm Resort in Vermont. The paths are marked by signs on eight tall trees in the woods surrounding the Pine Lodge and the Old Barn: an ash, a birch, a cherry, an elm, a fir, a hemlock, a maple, and an oak.

The Green Mountain Trail goes in a straight line from the Pine Lodge to the ash to the cherry to the maple to the birch and then to the Old Barn.

The Cross Country Trail goes from the Pine Lodge to the cherry to the fir to the hemlock to the birch to the elm and back to the Pine Lodge.

The Bethlehem Trail starts at the Pine Lodge and goes from the oak to the fir to the maple and back to the Pine Lodge.

There are no other routes available. Trails may be travelled in either direction.

14. Which of the following routes must be taken to go from the ash to the elm while passing the fewest trees?

   (A) The Cross Country Trail.
   (B) The Green Mountain Trail, then the Cross Country Trail.
   (C) The Green Mountain Trail, then the Bethlehem Trail.
   (D) The Bethlehem Trail, then the Cross Country Trail.
   (E) The Green Mountain Trail, then the Bethlehem Trail, and then the Cross Country Trail.

15. What is the maximum number of trees one can pass in order to get from the elm to the maple, without reusing any part of a path or passing the Pine Lodge?

   (A) 1
   (B) 2
   (C) 3
   (D) 4
   (E) 5

16. Which sequence of trees is a possible route from the Old Barn to the Pine Lodge?

   (A) Birch, maple, fir, oak
   (B) Birch, elm, ash, cherry
   (C) Birch, maple, fir, ash
   (D) Birch, hemlock, cherry
   (E) Birch, maple, cherry, elm, ash

17. How many different routes are there from the Pine Lodge to the birch which pass exactly three trees and do not reuse any part of a path?

   (A) 2
   (B) 3
   (C) 4
   (D) 5
   (E) 6

18. If a new path is found that connects the fir tree to the Old Barn, what is the fewest number of trees that could be passed on a hike from the Pine Lodge to the Old Barn and back, taking a different route each way?

   (A) 3
   (B) 4
   (C) 5
   (D) 6
   (E) 7

GO ON TO THE NEXT PAGE.

Questions 19-22

Five prints are being arranged in an artist's portfolio. The prints are to be chosen from among the artist's eight best works: M, N, O, P, Q, S, T, and W. The first print is to be on the right hand side of the first two facing pages, opposite a blank page. The second and third prints are to be on the left and right hand sides respectively of the next two facing pages, with the fourth and fifth prints on the left and right hand sides respectively of the last two facing pages.

If print O is selected for the portfolio, print W cannot be included.

If either print P or Q is displayed, the other print must also be displayed, and they must be on facing pages.

Print S must be displayed in the portfolio, but cannot be the first print displayed.

Prints N and T must both be displayed, and can only be displayed on the front and back sides, respectively, of the same page.

Prints M and Q cannot both be displayed.

19. If N is the first print displayed in the portfolio, which of the following statements could be true?

(A)   O is the second print displayed.
(B)   P is the third print displayed.
(C)   Q is the third print displayed.
(D)   W is the fourth print displayed.
(E)   T is the fifth print displayed.

20. If S is the second print displayed, all of the following statements could be true EXCEPT

(A)   M is the first print displayed
(B)   W is the first print displayed
(C)   N is the third print displayed
(D)   N is the fourth print displayed
(E)   Q is the fifth print displayed

21. All of the following prints could be displayed on the first page EXCEPT

(A)   M
(B)   O
(C)   Q
(D)   T
(E)   W

22. If O is the first print displayed, which of the following statements must be true?

(A)   P is the second print displayed.
(B)   W is the third print displayed.
(C)   N is the third print displayed.
(D)   S is the fourth print displayed.
(E)   S and M are both displayed.

23. Collies are the most frequently purchased dogs at dog breeding farms. Clearly, collies' superior performance in dog shows makes them popular dogs to buy as pets.

Which of the following, if true, would most seriously weaken the claim made above?

(A) Collies require less food and care than do most other dogs.
(B) It is because of their glossy fur that collies place well in dog shows.
(C) Public interest in dog shows has been surging in the recent past.
(D) Schnauzers generally place best in show and they are extremely popular dogs to buy as pets.
(E) Dogs that place well in shows invariably are the most popular dogs to buy as pets.

24. There are over fifty furniture stores in Middle Valley and not one of them charges less for furniture than does Green's Furniture Warehouse. It is clear that Green's Furniture Warehouse is the store that will provide the lowest price for furniture in all of Middle Valley.

Which of the following is an assumption on which the assertion made above is based?

(A) Customers do not have the option of shopping somewhere other than Middle Valley.
(B) The other furniture stores in Middle Valley charge more for furniture than does Green's Furniture Warehouse.
(C) The quality of the furniture at Green's Furniture Warehouse is equal to the quality of the furniture in other stores.
(D) Green's Furniture Warehouse is the most cost-effective store in Middle Valley.
(E) Other household items at Green's Furniture Warehouse are also well priced.

25. Unless there is an increase in federal spending, the national book program will fail.

Only if the national book program succeeds will the country escape recession.

There will be no increase in federal spending unless there is an increase in taxes.

If the statements above are true, which of the following must be true?

(A) If there is an increase in taxes, the country will definitely escape recession.
(B) Other programs will lose funding if the national book program succeeds.
(C) If the country escapes recession, the national book program must have succeeded.
(D) If the national book program succeeds, the country will escape recession.
(E) To escape recession, an alternate way of stimulating the economy must be found.

STOP

IF YOU FINISH BEFORE TIME IS CALLED, YOU MAY CHECK YOUR WORK ON THIS SECTION ONLY.
DO NOT WORK ON ANY OTHER SECTION IN THE TEST.

Correct Answers for The Princeton Review GRE Diagnostic Test

Section 1	Section 2	Section 3	Section 4	Section 5	Section 6
1. B	1. A	1. B	1. A	1. B	1. E
2. B	2. D	2. C	2. B	2. B	2. C
3. B	3. B	3. B	3. B	3. A	3. E
4. A	4. C	4. E	4. A	4. C	4. A
5. C	5. E	5. A	5. C	5. B	5. C
6. A	6. A	6. A	6. D	6. D	6. D
7. B	7. D	7. D	7. C	7. C	7. C
8. B	8. B	8. E	8. C	8. D	8. A
9. D	9. B	9. E	9. C	9. C	9. B
10. C	10. B	10. A	10. B	10. C	10. E
11. A	11. E	11. D	11. B	11. D	11. C
12. A	12. C	12. B	12. A	12. D	12. B
13. B	13. A	13. D	13. A	13. B	13. E
14. D	14. C	14. A	14. A	14. E	14. B
15. C	15. E	15. C	15. C	15. A	15. D
16. D	16. C	16. E	16. C	16. A	16. A
17. C	17. E	17. D	17. D	17. C	17. D
18. B	18. B	18. C	18. C	18. E	18. B
19. E	19. E	19. E	19. B	19. D	19. D
20. C	20. C	20. D	20. A	20. C	20. E
21. A	21. E	21. A	21. D	21. B	21. C
22. C	22. D	22. B	22. E	22. B	22. E
23. D	23. E	23. B	23. E	23. D	23. A
24. B	24. C	24. B	24. C	24. E	24. B
25. E	25. E	25. A	25. D	25. A	25. C
26. C	26. A		26. C	26. C	
27. B	27. E		27. B	27. E	
28. E	28. C		28. C	28. A	
29. E	29. E		29. E	29. D	
30. E	30. C		30. E	30. B	
	31. A			31. A	
	32. A			32. C	
	33. E			33. A	
	34. A			34. A	
	35. A			35. E	
	36. A			36. C	
	37. E			37. E	
	38. E			38. B	

Score Conversion for The Princeton Review
GRE Diagnostic Test

Raw Score	VERBAL Scaled Score	% Below	QUANTITATIVE Scaled Score	% Below	ANALYTICAL Scaled Score	% Below	Raw Score	VERBAL Scaled Score	% Below	QUANTITATIVE Scaled Score	% Below	ANALYTICAL Scaled Score	% Below
74-76	800	99					39	430	36	540	45	680	87
73	790	99					38	420	33	530	43	660	84
72	780	99					37	420	33	520	40	650	82
71	770	99					36	410	30	500	35	630	77
70	750	98					35	400	26	490	33	620	75
							34	390	24	480	30	600	70
69	740	98					33	380	22	470	29	590	68
68	730	97					32	370	20	460	26	570	62
67	720	96					31	370	20	450	24	560	59
66	710	95					30	360	16	440	22	540	53
65	690	94											
64	680	93					29	350	14	430	20	530	51
63	670	92					28	340	12	420	18	510	44
62	660	90					27	340	12	400	15	500	42
61	650	89					26	330	10	390	13	490	39
60	640	87	800	98			25	320	9	380	12	470	33
							24	310	7	370	10	460	31
59	630	85	800	98			23	300	6	360	9	440	25
58	620	84	800	98			22	290	5	350	8	430	24
57	610	82	780	95			21	280	4	340	7	410	19
56	590	78	760	93			20	270	3	330	6	400	17
55	580	76	740	89									
54	570	74	730	87			19	260	2	320	5	390	15
53	560	72	710	83			18	250	1	310	4	370	12
52	550	69	700	81			17	240	1	290	3	360	10
51	540	67	680	77			16	230	1	280	2	340	8
50	530	64	670	75	800	99	15	220	1	270	2	330	6
							14	210	1	250	1	310	5
49	520	61	660	73	800	99	13	200	1	240	1	300	4
48	520	61	640	69	800	99	12	200	1	220	1	290	3
47	510	59	630	66	790	98	11	200	1	210	1	270	2
46	500	56	620	64	780	98							
45	490	54	610	62	760	96	10	200	1	200	1	250	1
44	480	51	590	57	750	96	9	200	1	200	1	230	1
43	470	48	580	55	730	94	8	200	1	200	1	220	1
42	460	44	570	52	720	93	0-7	200	1	200	1	200	1
41	450	41	560	50	710	91							
40	440	38	550	48	690	89							

What follows is a detailed explanation for each question in our diagnostic test. Although you will naturally be more curious about the questions you got wrong, don't forget to read the explanations for the questions you left blank. In fact, you should even read the explanation for the questions you got right! Our explanations present the safest, most direct solution to each question. Even though you may have gotten a question right does not mean you analyzed it in the most efficient way.

SECTION 1

1. $4[(3 + 3) + 4]$ 45

1. The best answer is B. Use PEMDAS. $(3 + 3) = 6$. $6 + 4 = 10$. $4(10) = 40$.

    So Column A = 40 and Column B = 45.

a and *b* are each greater than 1.

2. $3ab$ $(3a)(3b)$

2. The best answer is B. Plug in numbers for *a* and *b*. Make $a = 2$ and $b = 3$. Then plug in to the two columns. Column A would be $3(2)(3)$ and Column B would be $3(2)3(3)$. So Column B is greater.

3. $\dfrac{5}{9}$ $\dfrac{4}{7}$

3. The best answer is B. Use the Bowtie to compare fractions! In column A you would have $7(5) = 35$ and in column B you'd have $9(4) = 36$.

4. $4(2^6)$ $6(4^2)$

4.   The best answer is A. For exponents, Expand It Out! In column A you have 4*2*2*2*2*2*2. In Column B you have 6*4*4. Then divide both sides by 4*4. In Column A that leaves 16. In Column B 6 is left.

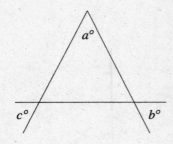

5. $b + c$ $180 - a$

5.   The best answer is C. Plug in on geometry problems with variables. Plug in to the triangle according to the rule of 180. Let's make $a = 50$, and the other two angles make 60 and 70. Because b and c are vertical to the other angles in the triangle, $b + c =$ 130 in column A. 180-50=130 in column B.

Mr. Jones purchased a new bedroom set by using an extended payment plan. The regular price of the set was $900, but on the payment plan he paid $300 up front and 9 monthly payments of $69 each.

6. $23   The amount Mr. Jones paid in addition to the regular price of the bedroom set.

6.   The best answer is A. To find the amount Mr. Jones paid in addition to the regular price of the bedroom set, multiply $69 by the 9 months = $621. Then add the $300 payment. 621 = 300 = 921. So Mr. Jones paid an additional $21. $23 in Column A is larger than $21 in Column B.

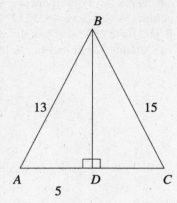

7.   The perimeter of triangle *BCD*   42

7.   The best answer is B. To find the perimeter of triangle *BCD*, first find the length of *BD* using the Pythagorean Theorem. $5^2 + BD^2 = 13^2$. So *BD* = *12*. Then you can find the third side of triangle *BCD*. $12^2 + DC^2 = 15^2$. Notice that this is a 3 : 4 : 5 right triangle. So *DC* is 9. Then add up the sides of triangle *BCD*. 9 + 12 + 15 = 36. 42 in Column B is greater.

8. $\frac{1}{5} + \frac{1}{7}$ $\frac{1}{9} + \frac{1}{4}$

8.   The best answer is B. Use the Bowtie to add fractions. $\frac{1}{5} + \frac{1}{7} = \frac{7+5}{35} = \frac{12}{35}$ in Column A. $\frac{1}{9} + \frac{1}{4} = \frac{4+9}{36} = \frac{13}{36}$ in Column B. The use the Bowtie again to compare fractions. (36)(12) = 432 in Column A. (35)(13) = 455 in Column B.

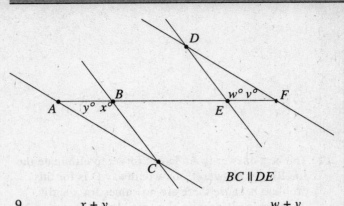

$BC \parallel DE$

9. $x + y$ $w + v$

9. The best answer is D. We know that BC is parallel to DE. According to Fred's Theorem, angle x must be equal to angle w. So the problem really depends on angle y and angle v. The diagram makes it look as if AC is parallel to DF, so Joe Bloggs would assume that they are parallel. That would make angle y equal to angle v. But we don't know that! Try re-drawing the diagram, making AC not parallel to DF.

10. The average (arith-   The average (arith-
     metic mean) of 7, 3,   metic mean) of $2a + 5$,
     4, and 2. $4a$, and $7 - 6a$

10. The best answer is C. To find the average, first find the total (sum) of the numbers you're averaging. Then divide by the number of elements you're averaging. The total in Column A is 16, divided by 4 = 4. The total in Column B is 12 divided by three = 4.

11. $\sqrt{7} + \sqrt{11}$ $\sqrt{3} + \sqrt{15}$

11. The best answer is A. First eliminate answer choice D, because there are no variables. Then eliminate the Joe Bloggs answer, which would be C, because the two columns "look" equal. But remember that you <u>cannot</u> add square roots! To help you estimate, you could use bigger numbers. Try comparing $\sqrt{7} + \sqrt{11}$ in Column A with $\sqrt{30} + \sqrt{150}$ in Column B. $\sqrt{70}$ would be a bit bigger than 8, and the $\sqrt{110}$ would be a bit bigger than 10. So Column A would be a bit bigger than 18. $\sqrt{30}$ would be a bit bigger than 5, and the $\sqrt{150}$ would be a bit bigger than 12. So Column B would be a bit bigger than 17. Column A is greater.

Questions 12-13 refer to the following number line.

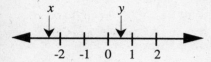

12.   −x   2y

12. The best answer is A. Don't forget to eliminate the Joe Bloggs answers! Joe would say D is for this problem because there are no values for x and y. Another Joe Bloggs choice would be B, because 2y "looks" greater than -x. Now Plug In! Make $x = -2.5$ and $y = .5$. Then Column A = 2.5 and Column B = 1.0.

13.   x + 2y   2y − x

13. The best answer is B. Again Joe Bloggs would choose D because there are no values for x and y. Or Joe might choose Column A, because $x + 2y$ "looks" bigger than $2y - x$. Plug in the same values we used in #12. In Column A $-2.5 + 1 = -1.5$. In Column B $1-(-2.5) = 3.5$.

$$\sqrt{4r} = 6 \text{ and } s^2 = 81$$

14.   r   s

14. The best answer is D. $\sqrt{4r} = 6$ so $4r = 36$ and $r = 9$ in Column A. But if $s^2 = 18$ s could equal either +9 or −9. If s = 9 the two columns would be equal. If s = −9 then Column A is greater.

QUESTIONS	EXPLANATIONS

15. $7^{15} - 7^{14}$ $7^{14}(6)$

15. The best answer is C. Use process of elimination!. Eliminate answer choice D because there are no variables. Then eliminate the Joe Bloggs answers. Joe would say that either Column A is greater, or that Column B is greater. So eliminate answer choices A and B! To see why C is the right choice, factor the expression in Column A.

$$7^{13} - 7^{14} = 7^{14}(7-1) = 7^{14}(6)$$

16. What is the remainder when 117 is divided by 3?

(A) 3   (B) 2   (C) 1   (D) 0   (E) $\frac{1}{3}$

16. The best answer is D. Without doing long division, you can determine whether a number is divisible by 3 by adding the digits of the number. If the sum of the digits is divisible by 3 then the number is divisible by 3. In this case 1+1+7=9. Because 9 is divisible by 3, 117 is divisible by 3. So the remainder is 0.

17. The price of a certain stock increased 8 points, then decreased 13 points, and then increased 9 points. If the stock price before the changes was x points, which of the following was the stock price, in points, after the changes?

(A) $x - 5$
(B) $x - 4$
(C) $x + 4$
(D) $x + 5$
(E) $x + 8$

17. The best answer is C. When you see variables in the answer choices, Plug In! Let's make x=10. That's the starting point. So 10 + 8 = 18. 18 - 13 = 5. 5 + 9 = 14. So 14 is the arithmetic answer we're looking for in the answer choices. Now plug in 10 for every x in the answer choices. 10 + 4 = 14. Bingo!

18. If $x = 1$, then $\left(2 - \frac{1}{2-x}\right)\left(2 - \frac{1}{3-x}\right)\left(2 - \frac{1}{4-x}\right) =$

(A) $\frac{1}{6}$ (B) $\frac{5}{2}$ (C) $\frac{10}{3}$ (D) $\frac{7}{2}$ (E) $\frac{5}{6}$

18. The best answer is B. If $x=1$ then the expression looks like this: $\left(2 - \frac{1}{1}\right)\left(2 - \frac{1}{2}\right)\left(2 - \frac{1}{3}\right)$. Use PEMDAS. Do what's in the parentheses first, then reduce. So you get:

$$(1)\left(\frac{3}{2}\right)\left(\frac{5}{3}\right) = \frac{5}{2}$$

19. If $s = 4r$ and $t = 2s$, then, in terms of r, $3r + 2s + t =$

(A) r (B) $6r$ (C) $7r$ (D) $8r$ (E) $19r$

19. The best answer is E. Variables in the answer choices? PLUG IN! Lets make $r=2$. Then 4r=8, s=8. If s=8 then t=16. So 3r + 2s + t = 6 + 16 + 16 = 38. So the arithmetic answer is 38. Now plug in r=2 in all the answer choices. (19)(2) = 38. Yes.

QUESTIONS	EXPLANATIONS

20. What is the least number r for which $(3r + 2)(r - 3) = 0$?

(A) –3   (B) –2   (C) $-\dfrac{2}{3}$ (D) $\dfrac{2}{3}$ (E) 3

20. The best answer is C. If $(3r + 2)(r - 3) = 0$, then either (3r+2)=0, or (r–3)=0, or both. If $r - 3 = 0$ then r = 3. If $3r + 2 = 0$, then $3r = -2$ and $r = -2/3$. The "least number r" would be –2/3.

21. From 1951 to 1960, the third greatest number of immigrants to the United States were from which region?

(A) Asia
(B) Africa
(C) North and South America
(D) Australia and New Zealand
(E) Other Oceania

21. The best answer is A. The question asks for the <u>third greatest</u> number of immigrants from 1951 to 1960. Europe had the greatest number (1,325.6), North and South America had the second greatest number (996.9), and Asia had the third greatest number (153.3).

22. In 1974, approximately what was the average (arithmetic mean) number of immigrants to the United States per country of Asia that is represented?

(A)   1,050
(B)   5,000
(C)   10,500
(D)   33,000
(E)   130,000

22. The best answer is C. To find the average number per country, take the total and divide it by the number of countries. In 1974 Asia had a total of 127,000 immigrants to the United States. There are 12 countries represented. So 127,000/12 is approximately 10,500.

23. From 1951 to 1960, the number of immigrants to the United States from India was 36 thousand. Approximately what percent of the total number of immigrants to the United States from Asia during that decade were from India?

(A) 10%   (B) 15%   (C) 20%   (D) 25%   (E) 30%

23. The best answer is D. First you need to translate the question into a math equation, $36,000 = x/100(153,300)$, or $36,000/153,300 = x/100$. Approximate! Reduce it to 36/153. Now look at the answer choices. 20% of 150 would be 30. So it's closer to 25%.

24. From 1951 to 1960, approximately what was the ratio of the number of immigrants to the United States from Africa to the number of immigrants to the United States from Australia and New Zealand?

(A) $\dfrac{1}{1}$ (B) $\dfrac{5}{4}$ (C) $\dfrac{4}{3}$ (D) $\dfrac{3}{2}$ (E) $\dfrac{5}{2}$

24. The best answer is B. Don't worry about the thousands. From 1951 to 1960 the number of immigrants from Africa was 14.1, and the number of immigrants from Australia and New Zealand was 11.5. So the ratio would be 14.1/11.5 or a little bit greater than 1/1. Eliminate answer choices (A), (D) and (E). It's easier to evaluate the two remaining answer choices if you round 11.5 to 12. Answer choice (B) would be 15/12, and answer choice (C) would be 16/12. You can see that (B) is closer.

25. Which region had the greatest percent change in the number of immigrants to the United States from 1974 to 1975?

(A) Europe
(B) Asia
(C) North and South America
(D) Africa
(E) Other Oceania

25. The best answer is E. To find percent change, take the amount of change, and relate it to the original amount. You don't actually need to convert the fractions to percents, since a percent is a fraction. The answer choices, approximated as fractions would be: (A) $\dfrac{8}{80}$ or $\dfrac{1}{10}$, (B) $\dfrac{2}{127}$, (C) $\dfrac{4}{178}$, (D) $\dfrac{7}{52}$, (E) $\dfrac{4}{14}$ or $\dfrac{1}{7}$. Eliminate (A), (B) and (C) right away. Then use the Bowtie to compare (D) and (E).

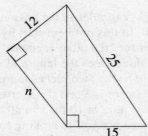

26. What is the value of *n* in the figure above?

(A) 9
(B) 15
(C) 16
(D) $12\sqrt{3}$
(E) 20

26. The best answer is C. To find the value of n, start with the right triangle for which we're given two of the three sides. Use the Pythagorean Theorem: $15^2 + b^2 = 25^2$. Notice that this is a 3:4:5 right triangle, since 15= 3(5) and 25= 5(5). So *b*=20 or 4(5). Now we have two of the three sides of the triangle we're interested in: $12^2 + n^2 = 20$. Once again notice that we've got another 3:4:5 right triangle. 12 = 3(4) and 20 = 5(4). So *n* = 4(4) or 16.

27. If $2 < r < 8$ and $1 < s < \dfrac{5}{2}$, which of the following expresses all possible values of *rs*?

(A) $1 < rs < 5$
(B) $2 < rs < 20$
(C) $\dfrac{5}{2} < rs < 8$
(D) $\dfrac{5}{2} < rs < 20$
(E) $5 < rs < 10$

27. The best answer is B. Break this problem into two parts, and use process of elimination. Which numbers are easier to work with? Since $r > 2$ and $s > 1$, the product of rs must be greater than the product of (2)(1) = 2. Now go to the answer choices and eliminate. The only answer choice in which $2 < rs$ is answer choice (B). End of discussion!

28. What is the perimeter, in centimeters, of a rectangular newspaper ad 14 centimeters wide that has the same area as a rectangular newspaper ad 52 centimeters long and 28 centimeters wide?

    (A) 80
    (B) 118
    (C) 160
    (D) 208
    (E) 236

28. The best answer is E. To find the perimeter of a rectangle you need to know the length and the width. Of course you don't need to worry about the "centimeters." If the newspaper ad with a width of 14 has the same area as another ad 52 long and 28 wide, that means that 14(length) = 52(28). Divide both sides by 14, and you get length = 52(2) = 104. Now to find the perimeter, add up the sides of the rectangle. 104 + 104 + 14 + 14 = 236.

29. A pipe of length x inches is cut into two segments so that the length of one segment is two inches more than three times the length of the other segment. Which of the following is the length, in inches, of the longer segment?

    (A) $\dfrac{x+4}{3}$

    (B) $\dfrac{3x+2}{3}$

    (C) $\dfrac{x-2}{4}$

    (D) $\dfrac{3x+5}{4}$

    (E) $\dfrac{3x+2}{4}$

29. The best answer is E. Variables in the answer choices? PLUG IN! In this problem start by plugging in a number for "the other segment." Let's make that 2. Then "three times the length of the other segment" would be 6. Two inches more than 6 is 8. If the longer segment is 8 and the shorter one is 2, then $x = 10$. Now plug in 10 for x in all the answer choices. Remember you're looking for the length of the longer segment, so you have to solve for 8. $\dfrac{3(10)+2}{4} = \dfrac{32}{4} = 8$.

30. For all real numbers x and y, if $x \star y = x(x - y)$, then $x \star (x \star y) =$

    (A) $x^2 - xy$
    (B) $x^2 - 2xy$
    (C) $x^3 - x^2 - xy$
    (D) $x^3 - (xy)^2$
    (E) $x^2 - x^3 + x^2y$

30. The best answer is E. This function problem is obviously a huge waste of time, but it's not too difficult if you PLUG IN! To find $x * (x * y)$, we have to plug in to the parentheses first. If $x * y = x(x-y)$, let's plug in $x = 3$ and $y = 2$. $3(3-2) = 3(1) = 3$. So if $x = 3$ and $(x * y) = 3$, then the question really is $3 * 3 = 3(3-3) = 3(0) = 0$. So by plugging in $x=3$ and $y=2$ in the answer choices, the right answer will be 0. Choice (E) works:
$$x^2 - x^3 + x^2y = 3^2 - 3^3(2) = 9 - 27 + 18 = 0$$

SECTION 2

1. It is the concern of many ecologists that the "greenhouse effect" is changing many of the Earth's ------- weather patterns into ------- systems, unable to be accurately forecast by those who study them.

   (A) predictable . . erratic
   (B) steady . . growing
   (C) uncertain . . uncanny
   (D) chaotic . . unforeseeable
   (E) weighty . . unbounded

1. The best answer is A. Focus on the second blank. The clue for the second blank is "unable to be accurately forecast." So a good word for the second blank would be "unpredictable." Looking at the second blank only, that eliminates answer choices (B) and (E). The trigger word for the first blank is "changing" so the first blank must be a word that's the opposite of the one for the second blank That eliminates answer choices (C) and (D).

2. Children, after more than a generation of television, have become "hasty viewers"; as a result, if the camera lags, the attention of these young viewers -------.

   (A) expands
   (B) starts
   (C) alternates
   (D) wanes
   (E) clarifies

2. The best answer is D. The clue in the sentence is "Children ... have become 'hasty viewers.'" The trigger words are "as a result." So a good word for the blank would be "wanders." In any case it must be one with negative connotations. The words in answer choices (A), (B), and (E) are positive. Answer choice (C) isn't really negative.

3. Many of the troubles and deficiencies in otherwise thriving foreign enterprises are ------- ignored or diminished by the author of the article in order to ------- the ways in which other businesses might attempt to imitate them.

   (A) unintentionally . . overstate
   (B) deliberately . . stress
   (C) intermittently . . equalize
   (D) willfully . , confound
   (E) brilliantly . . illustrate

3. The best answer is B. The clue for the second blank is "the ways in which other businesses might attempt to imitate them." The trigger words are "in order to." So a good word for the second blank would be "highlight." That eliminates answer choices (A), (C) and (D). The clue for the first blank is "the troubles and deficiencies ... ignored or diminished by the author of the article." So a good word for the first blank would be "intentionally." That eliminates answer choice (E).

4. Frequently a copyright holder's property, published articles for example, is reproduced repeatedly in the absence of ------- for its reproduction, an action ------- by long-standing practice.

   (A) validation . . provoked
   (B) recognition . . forecast
   (C) payment . . licensed
   (D) accommodation . . instigated
   (E) allowance . . aggravated

4. The best answer is C. The clue for the second blank is "reproduced repeatedly ... by long-standing practice." A good word for the second blank would be "approved." Looking only at the word in the second blank, you can eliminate answer choices (A), (B), (D) and (E).

5. The ------- of early metaphysicians' efforts to decipher the workings of the universe led some later thinkers to question the ------- of man's intellectual capabilities.

   (A) strain . . roots
   (B) intent . . superiority
   (C) intricacy . . realization
   (D) prevarications . . deceptiveness
   (E) failings . . adeptness

5. The best answer is E. The clue in the sentence is "led some later thinkers to question." That tells you that there was some problem with the "early metaphysicians efforts to decipher the workings of the universe." So a good word for the first blank would be "problems." That eliminates answer choices (A), (B) and (C). The second blank must be a word such as "workings," or at least one with positive connotations. That eliminates answer choice (D).

6. Being gracious should not be mistaken for a ------- characteristic of men's personalities; it is instead a fundamental virtue, one whose very state of being is increasingly ------- by the fashionable directive to "say what you feel."

   (A) trivial . . imperiled
   (B) pervading . . undermined
   (C) frivolous . . averted
   (D) superior . . renounced
   (E) immaterial . . influenced

6. The best answer is A. The clue in the sentence is "Being gracious ... is instead a fundamental virtue." This tells you that the word in the first blank means the opposite of "fundamental virtue," or at least is one with negative connotations. That eliminates answer choices (B), (C) and (D). The virtue of being gracious would be "threatened" by "the fashionable directive to 'say what you feel.'" That eliminates answer choice (E).

7. While some individuals think that the purpose of sarcastic remarks is to disturb, by turning all communication into -------, other people see sarcastic remarks as a desire for supremacy in miniature over an environment that appears too -------.

   (A) chaos . . perplexed
   (B) equivalence . . confused
   (C) discord . . amiable
   (D) pandemonium . . disorderly
   (E) similarity . . upset

7. The best answer is D. The clue for the first blank is "the purpose of sarcastic remarks is to disturb." So a good word for the first blank would be "disturbances." That eliminates answer choices (B) and (E). The clue for the second blank is "desire for supremacy in miniature over an environment." So a word for how that environment appears must have negative connotations. That eliminates answer choice (C). Answer choice (A) would be a good guess, but remember to check both words. An "environment" can't really appear "perplexed."

8. CHOREOGRAPHER : DANCE ::
   (A) connoisseur : art
   (B) composer : music
   (C) acrobat : height
   (D) athlete : contest
   (E) virtuoso : skill

8. The best answer is B. A good sentence for the stem words would be "A choreographer creates a dance." Answer choices (C) and (D) don't fit that sentence for sure. Maybe you left answer choices (A) and (E) because you weren't sure what "connoisseur" or "virtuoso" meant. But remember the order of difficulty! Easy questions have easy answers, so choices (A) and (E) each would be too hard to be the answer to an easy question.

9. SCOWL : DISPLEASURE ::
   (A) sing : praise
   (B) kiss : affection
   (C) confess : crime
   (D) irritate : anger
   (E) hurl : disgust

9. The best answer is B. A good sentence for the stem words would be "To scowl shows displeasure." This is a very common relationship on the GRE: some action shows or indicates some attitude. The only answer choice that fits this sentence is choice (B).

10. GOGGLES : EYES ::
    (A) tie : neck
    (B) gloves : hands
    (C) elbow : arm
    (D) braid : hair
    (E) cast : leg

10. The best answer is B. A good sentence for the stem words would be "Goggles provide protection for the eyes." The only answer choice that fits this sentence is (B).

11. DRAWL : SPEAK ::
    (A) spurt : expel
    (B) foster : develop
    (C) scintillate : flash
    (D) pare : trim
    (E) saunter : walk

11. The best answer is E. A good sentence for the stem words would be "To drawl means to speak slowly." Answer choices (A), (B) and (D) don't fit this sentence. If you weren't sure of the meaning of "scintillate," ask yourself "Could it mean to flash slowly?" Not likely. And "saunter" does mean to walk slowly.

12. ARBORETUM : TREE ::
    (A) dam : water
    (B) planetarium : star
    (C) apiary : bee
    (D) museum : painting
    (E) forum : speech

12. The best answer is C. If you're not exactly sure what "arboretum" means, work backwards! Make a sentence for each answer choice and see whether the stem words would fit that sentence. For answer choice (A) you could say "A dam holds back the flow of water." Could something hold back the flow of a tree? No way. For choice (B) you might say that "A planetarium is a room where the image of a star is projected." Could something be a room where the image of a tree is projected? Not likely. Perhaps you're not sure what an apiary is — never eliminate an answer choice when you don't know the meaning of one of the words. In choice (D) you could say "A museum is place to exhibit a painting." Could something be a place to exhibit a tree? Possibly. For (E) your sentence might be " A forum is a public place where a person makes a speech." Could something be a public place where a person makes a tree? No chance. #12 is right in the middle of the medium questions, doesn't answer choice (D) seem a bit too easy in comparison with the other choices? A good sentence for the stem words is "An arboretum is a man-made environment where a tree grows." This is another very common relationship on the GRE.

13. SUBTERFUGE : DECEIVE ::
    (A) decanter : pour
    (B) interview : hire
    (C) account : save
    (D) outpost : protect
    (E) film : view

13. The best answer is A. If you're not sure what a "subterfuge" is, go right tot the answer choices and eliminate answer choices that don't have a clear and necessary relationship. Answer choices (B), (C), and (D) aren't clear and necessary. #13 is the hardest medium question. Between answer choices (A) and (E) which is harder? The sentence for the stem words would be "The function of a subterfuge is to deceive." The function of a decanter is to pour.

14. RATIFY : APPROVAL ::
    (A) mutate : change
    (B) pacify : conquest
    (C) duel : combat
    (D) appeal : authority
    (E) tribulate : opinion

14. The best answer is C. First eliminate answer choices that don't have a clear and necessary relationship. That gets rid of choices (B) and (D) for sure. Work backwards on choices (A) and (C). To "mutate is to make a change in nature or form." Could "ratify" mean to make an approval in nature or form? Not likely. For choice (C), "to duel is to have a formal combat, according to rules." Could to "ratify" mean to have a formal approval, according to rules? Yes! Joe Bloggs likes answer choices (D) and (E) because "authority" and "opinion" remind him of "approval."

15. SOPORIFIC : SLEEP ::
    (A) conductor : electricity
    (B) syncopation : beat
    (C) provocation : debate
    (D) coagulant : blood
    (E) astringent : pucker

15. The best answer is E. "Soporific" is a word you need to know for the GRE. "A soporific causes sleep." Using that sentence you can eliminate answer choices (A), (B), (C), and (D). An astringent does cause a pucker. ETS loves this one.

16. METTLESOME : COURAGE ::
    (A) audacious : tenacity
    (B) mediocre : originality
    (C) ludicrous : inanity
    (D) dubious : suspiciousness
    (E) altruistic : donation

16. The best answer is C. Go right to the answer choices and eliminate answer choices that do not have a clear and necessary relationship. Answer choices (A), (B) and (E) are not clear and necessary relationships. Then make sentences for the remaining answer choices, and work backwards to the stem words. For answer choice (C) your sentence should be, "something ludicrous is characterized by inanity." Could something mettlesome be characterized by courage? Sure. For choice (D) your sentence would be, "something dubious causes suspiciousness." Could something mettlesome cause courage? Does <u>anything</u> cause courage? Not really.

Directions: Each passage in this group is followed by questions based on its content. After reading a passage, choose the best answer to each question. Answer all questions following a passage on the basis of what is <u>stated</u> or <u>implied</u> in that passage.

In eighteenth-century France and England, reformers rallied around egalitarian ideals, but few reformers advocated higher education for women. Although the
Line public decried women's lack of education, it did not
(5) encourage learning for its own sake for women. In spite of the general prejudice against learned women, there was one place where women could exhibit their erudition: the literary salon. Many writers have defined the woman's role in the salon as that of an intelligent hostess, but the salon
(10) had more than a social function for women. It was an informal university, too, where women exchanged ideas with educated persons, read their own works and heard those of others, and received and gave criticism.

In the 1750's, when salons were firmly established in
(15) France, some English women, who called themselves "Bluestockings," followed the example of the *salonnières* (French salon hostesses) and formed their own salons. Most Bluestockings did not wish to mirror the *salonnières*; they simply desired to adapt a proven formula to their own
(20) purpose—the elevation of women's status through moral and intellectual training. Differences in social orientation and background can account perhaps for differences in the nature of French and English salons. The French salon incorporated aristocratic attitudes that exalted courtly
(25) pleasure and emphasized artistic accomplishments. The English Bluestockings, originating from a more modest background, emphasized learning and work over pleasure. Accustomed to the regimented life of court circles, *salonnières* tended toward formality in their salons. The
(30) English women, though somewhat puritanical, were more casual in their approach.

At first, the Bluestockings did imitate the *salonnières* by including men in their circles. However, as they gained cohesion, the Bluestockings came to regard themselves as
(35) a women's group and to possess a sense of female solidarity lacking in the *salonnières*, who remained isolated from one another by the primacy each held in her own salon. In an atmosphere of mutual support, the Bluestockings went beyond the salon experience. They traveled, studied,
(40) worked, wrote for publication, and by their activities challenged the stereotype of the passive woman. Although the *salonnières* were aware of sexual inequality, the narrow boundaries of their world kept their intellectual pursuits within conventional limits. Many *salonnières*, in
(45) fact, camouflaged their nontraditional activities behind the role of hostess and deferred to men in public.

Though the Bluestockings were trailblazers when compared with the *salonnières*, they were not feminists.

They were too traditional, too hemmed in by their genera-
(50) tion to demand social and political rights. Nonetheless, in their desire for education, their willingness to go beyond the confines of the salon in pursuing their interests, and their championing of unity among women, the Bluestock-ings began the process of questioning women's role in
(55) society.

17. The primary purpose of the passage is to explain that

   (A) the founding of literary salons was a reaction to reformers' insistence that women be granted more extensive rights.
   (B) literary salons were initially meant to be a meeting ground for male and female reformers, but gradually became a social forum with limited educational value.
   (C) the literary salon provided French and English women with the opportunity to gather and discuss the rationale for free and equal access to higher education.
   (D) due to widespread prejudice against higher education for women, the function of the literary salon, in both France and England, was fundamentally social.
   (E) for women, who unlike men, did not have free access to higher education, literary salons offered an opportunity to pursue alternative forms of education and a chance to challenge some of society's stereotypes about the "proper" place of women.

17. The best answer is E. This question is asking you for the main idea of the passage. Try to get the main idea of the passage first, then use process of elimination on the answer choices. The main idea of the passage would be something like "literary salons were informal educational opportunities for women in 18th century France and England." Eliminate answer choices (A), (B) and (D). Choice (C) is close, but not best because the literary salons were not merely limited to "an opportunity to gather and discuss the rationale for free and equal access to higher education."

18. According to the passage, a significant distinction between the *salonnières* and Bluestockings was in the way each group regarded which of the following?

   (A) The value of acquiring knowledge
   (B) The role of pleasure in the activities of the literary salon
   (C) The desirability of a complete break with societal traditions
   (D) The inclusion of women of different backgrounds in the salons
   (E) The attainment of full social and political equality with men

18. The best answer is B. Look back to the second paragraph, where the distinctions between the *salonnieres* and the Bluestockings were discussed. The answer is a paraphrase of the sentence beginning in line 25: "The English Bluestockings ... emphasized learning and work over pleasure." Also you can eliminate answer choices (C) and (E), because they are extremely disputable statements.

QUESTIONS	EXPLANATIONS

19. The author refers to differences in social background between *salonnières* and Bluestockings in order to do which of the following?

(A) Criticize the view that their choices of activities were significantly influenced by male salon members

(B) Discuss the reasons why literary salons in France were established before those in England

(C) Question the importance of the Bluestockings in shaping public attitudes toward educated women

(D) Refute the argument that the French salons had little influence over the direction the English salons took

(E) Explain the differences in atmosphere and style in their salons

19. The best answer is E. This question is just a repeat of the previous one. Go back to the same place in the passage, the second paragraph. Answer choice (E) is a paraphrase of the sentence that begins in line 21: "Differences in social orientation and background can account perhaps for differences in the nature of French and English salons."

20. It can be inferred from the passage that which of the following statements most accurately represents the principles of the *salonnières*?

(A) It is desirable for women to aim to be both well-educated and autonomous.

(B) Women who have a higher education have a responsibility to be politically active in order to serve as role models for those who are less educated.

(C) A quest for artistic and aesthetic excellence is justified in itself.

(D) In establishing a literary salon, content, rather than form, should be the primary focus.

(E) Only women should be allowed to join groups which seek to establish equal rights for women.

20. The best answer is C. Again, go back to the second paragraph to find the *salonnieres* described. The key sentence begins in line 23: "The French salon incorporated aristocratic attitudes that exalted courtly pleasure and emphasized artistic accomplishments." Answer choice (C) is the only one that mentions anything about art. Answer choice (A) sounds good, but the passage doesn't support it.

21. According to the passage, which of the following factors most likely lessened the impact that the Bluestockings had on society?

(A) The rivalry that existed between the various salons.

(B) The strong emphasis that they placed on fostering individualism.

(C) The fact that the activities in which they participated were limited in depth.

(D) The fact that they patterned their own salons after the model provided by the French.

(E) Their willingness to passively accept many of the conventions of the day.

21. The best answer is E. To answer this explicit question, go to the place in the passage where the Bluestockings impact on society is discussed — the last paragraph. At the beginning of the last paragraph, the passage says that the Bluestockings "were not feminists.... They were too traditional, too hemmed in by their generation to demand social and political rights." Answer choice (E) is a paraphrase of those two sentences. The other answer choices are not supported by the passage.

22. The passage suggests that which of the following could most accurately be characterized as a modern-day counterpart to the literary salons depicted in the passage?

   (A) a literary collective
   (B) a neighborhood center
   (C) a seminar on aesthetics
   (D) a liberal arts study circle
   (E) a forum of political activists

22. The best answer is D. The literary salons are best depicted in the passage at the end of the first paragraph, beginning in line 10: "It was an informal university, too, where women exchanged ideas with educated persons, read their own works and heard those of others, and received and gave criticism."

23. To the pronouncement that the Bluestockings could most accurately be characterized as feminists, it can be inferred from the passage that the author would most likely respond with

   (A) blatant disapproval
   (B) limited misgivings
   (C) absolute acceptance
   (D) qualified indifference
   (E) pointed criticism

23. The best answer is E. Refer back to the last paragraph of the passage. There, in line 48, the author asserts that the Bluestockings "were not feminists." So right away you can eliminate answer choices (B), (C), and (D). Between answer choices (A) and (E) choose the less disputable, less emotional and more "academic-sounding" response.

24. Which of the following titles best describes the content of the passage?

   (A) Eighteenth-Century Egalitarianism
   (B) Feminists of the Eighteenth Century
   (C) Eighteenth-Century Precursors of Feminism
   (D) Intellectual Life in the Eighteenth Century
   (E) Female Education Reform in the Eighteenth Century

24. The best answer is C. This is just another main idea question, asking about the passage as a whole. You should have done this question right after you did question 17. Use process of elimination. Eliminate answer choices (A) and (D) because they don't say anything about women. The first sentence of the last paragraph explicitly claims that the *salonnieres* and Bluestockings were not feminists. Eliminate answer choice (B). You can eliminate answer choice (E) because the passage never mentioned anything about actual educational reform in the 18th century. The last sentence of the passage says that the *salonnieres* and Bluestockings "began the process of questioning women's role in society." That's why they were precursors of feminism.

When the same parameters and quantitative theory are used to analyze both termite colonies and troops of rhesus macaques, we will have a unified science of sociobiology.

Line Can this ever really happen? As my own studies have
(5) advanced, I have been increasingly impressed with the functional similarities between insect and vertebrate societies and less so with the structural differences that seem, at first glance, to constitute such an immense gulf between them. Consider for a moment termites and
(10) macaques. Both form cooperative groups that occupy territories. In both kinds of society there is a well-marked division of labor. Members of both groups communicate to each other hunger, alarm, hostility, caste, status or rank, and reproductive status. From the specialist's point of
(15) view, this comparison may at first seem facile—or worse. But it is out of such deliberate oversimplification that the beginnings of a general theory are made.

25. Which of the following statements best expresses the main idea of the passage?

   (A) A unified science of sociobiology cannot be developed if deliberate oversimplification in the field continues.
   (B) A unified science of sociobiology requires specialized knowledge of both insect and vertebrate societies.
   (C) Human societies offer the most appropriate models for understanding insect and vertebrate societies.
   (D) Most insect and vertebrate societies can best be understood if research continues on termites and rhesus macaques.
   (E) A general theory of sociobiology could begin from a study of the functional similarities between insect societies and vertebrate societies.

25. The best answer is E. You can get the main idea from the first and last sentences of the passage. In your own words the main idea would be something like this, "If we look at termites and rhesus macaques in the same way, we'll start to have a unified science of sociobiology." Answer choices (A) and (C) use extremely disputable language. There's nothing about sociobiology in choice (D). Choice (B) is not supported by what the author states in lines 14-15.

26. The author regards the possibility of a unified science of sociobiology with

   (A) qualified optimism
   (B) unreserved excitement
   (C) neutral distance
   (D) dismission
   (E) displeasure

26. The best answer is A. This is just another version of the main idea. Same question, same answer as #25.

27. The passage implies which of the following about insect and vertebrate societies?

   (A) A well-marked division of labor is a distinctive feature of most insect and vertebrate societies.
   (B) Insect societies have caste structures similar to those found in vertebrate societies.
   (C) Cooperative groups of termites and macaques are formed for the purpose of occupying territories.
   (D) Members of insect societies are able to communicate with members of vertebrate societies.
   (E) There are some important structural differences between insect and vertebrate societies.

27. The best answer is E. This is a paraphrase of the statement beginning in line 5: "... I have been increasingly impressed with the functional similarities between insect and vertebrate societies and less so with the structural differences between them." This implies that there <u>are</u> some structural differences between insect and vertebrate societies.

28. SLUR:
    (A) honor agreements
    (B) settle disputes
    (C) pronounce clearly
    (D) criticize directly
    (E) exclude purposefully

28. The best answer is C. To "slur" means to pronounce indistinctly.

29. MORATORIUM:
    (A) lack of emotion
    (B) discouragement
    (C) savings
    (D) brilliance
    (E) period of activity

29. The best answer is E. A "moratorium is a period of inactivity.

30. DIFFUSE:
    (A) compare
    (B) chill
    (C) concentrate
    (D) blemish
    (E) oscillate

30. The best answer is C. To "diffuse" means to spread out, or disperse.

31. THWART:
    (A) aid
    (B) beseech
    (C) dislocate
    (D) assign
    (E) allege

31. The best answer is A. To "thwart" means to prevent from taking place, or to frustrate.

32 AGITATE:
    (A) relieve
    (B) satisfy
    (C) reject
    (D) condense
    (E) confirm

32. The best answer is A. To agitate means to upset or disturb.

33. AUTHENTICATE:
    (A) sentence
    (B) disseminate
    (C) scrutinize
    (D) theorize
    (E) discredit

33. The best answer is E. To "authenticate" means to establish as being genuine.

34. ACCLIMATION:
    (A) alienation
    (B) adoration
    (C) facilitation
    (D) invigoration
    (E) exaltation

34. The best answer is A. "Acclimation" means an adjustment to a new environment or situation. It's a word with positive connotations. So you can eliminate answer choices that have positive connotations, because the opposite of "acclimation" must be a negative word. Answer choices (B), (C), (D) and (E) are all positive words.

35. TENUOUSLY:
    (A) having a strong basis
    (B) following a formal procedure
    (C) having overall consensus
    (D) with evil intent
    (E) under loose supervision

35. The best answer is A. "Tenuous" means insubstantial or flimsy. So you can eliminate answer choices with negative connotations. That eliminates answer choices (D) and (E) for sure. Answer choice (B) isn't really very positive.

36. FLORID:
    (A) pallid
    (B) vapid
    (C) lucid
    (D) rancid
    (E) candid

36. The best answer is A. "Florid" means flushed, or ruddy. So you could say that it has positive connotations, or at least not negative ones. So you could eliminate answer choices (C) and (E), which are positive words. Answer choices (B) and (D) would be good guesses.

37. FACTIOUS:
    (A) totally generic
    (B) openly welcomed
    (C) closely observable
    (D) seriously rejected
    (E) given to agreement

37. The best answer is E. "Factious" means tending to cause conflict or discord. If you knew that "factious" has negative connotations, you could eliminate answer choices (A) and (D). And you could eliminate answer choices (A) and (C) because they don't have clear, direct opposites. Answer choice (B) is a good guess.

38. MISCIBLE:
    (A) likely to agree
    (B) hard to please
    (C) generous
    (D) desirable
    (E) not capable of being mixed

38. The best answer is E. "Miscible" means able to be mixed. Yeah right. Who's ever heard of this one? Don't worry about it. You can get a few questions wrong and still get an 800 on the Verbal section of the GRE.

3

SECTION 3

1. To send a message from L to G by messenger, it is necessary for the messenger to travel through department

   (A) F
   (B) J
   (C) K
   (D) M
   (E) N

1. The best answer is B. Combine the clues into one diagram. Your diagram might look like this:

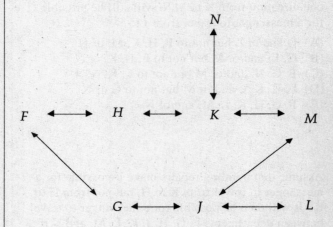

You can see that, to get from L to G, you have to go through J.

2. If a broken elevator temporarily makes the route between H and K unusable, then in order to send a message to F by messenger from N, a messenger would have to go through how many other departments besides F and N?

   (A) 2
   (B) 3
   (C) 4
   (D) 5
   (E) 6

2. The best answer is C. You could use the same diagram, and just cover up the connection between H and K. To get to F from N you'd have to go through K, M, J and G.

3. If the hallway between H and K is being resurfaced, making the route unusable, a messenger would NOT be able to travel from

(A) G to F
(B) G to L
(C) J to M
(D) J to L
(E) K to F

3. The best answer is B. As in the previous question, cover up the connection between H and K. Notice that you can only go from J to G, not from G to J. So you can't go from G to L.

4. If a broken elevator affects the route from K to M, making it possible for a messenger to travel in only one direction from K to M, it will still be possible for a messenger to travel from J to

(A) G and/or L but not to F, H, K, M, or N
(B) G, L, and/or M but not to F, H, K, or N
(C) F, G, H, and/or M but not to L, K, or N
(D) F, H, K, L and/or M but not to G or N
(E) F, G, H, K, L, M, and/or N

4. The best answer is E. This time, cover up the connection between K and M. Then use process of elimination. You can go from J to all of the other departments.

5. Assume that building repairs make it possible for a messenger to travel from K to H, but not from H to K. It will then be possible for a messenger to travel between departments F, G, H, J, K, L, M, and N if which of the following temporary routes is erected?

(A) From F to N
(B) From J to K
(C) From L to K
(D) From L to N
(E) From M to N

5. The best answer is A. You might want to redraw the diagram according to the changed conditions.

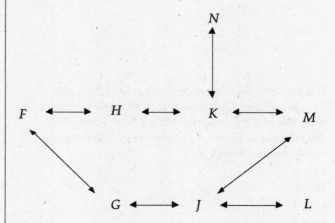

Notice that you need some way to get from the departments on the left side of the diagram (F,G and H) to the departments on the right side of the diagram. The only answer choice that makes a connection between the left side and the right side is (A).

6. For five years, while remodeling the town zoo, the Littleton parks commission has been transferring a large number of animals from the city of Littleton to both the Wambek and Starr King Zoos in the city of Jefferson. It follows that when Littleton's zoo reopens next year, either Wambek or Starr King will have to be closed and their animal populations consolidated.

The author of the statements above assumes that

(A) The removal of the Littleton animals from the Wambek and Starr King zoos will leave one or both of these zoos considerably under-populated.

(B) Littleton's remodeled zoo will not be large enough for the prospective animal population.

(C) The Littleton animals comprise only a small part of the total animal populations at both the Wambek and Starr King zoos.

(D) Incorporation of extra animals from Littleton has placed a tremendous burden on the resources of both the Wambek and Starr King zoos.

(E) Animals will not be sent between the Wambek and Starr King zoos in the next year.

6. The best answer is A. The last sentence of the argument is the conclusion. An assumption must support the conclusion. Answer choice (A) does support it. Answer choices (B), (C) and (E) go against the conclusion. Answer choice (D) is out of the scope of the argument.

7. A man-made plant hormone has been added to a section of a garden in order to ward off insect infestation. The designer of the hormone has asserted that the recent dearth of insects in that section of the garden demonstrates that the man-made plant hormone wards off insect infestation. Which of the following, if true, would cast the greatest doubt on the designer's assertion?

(A) The recent dearth of insects in that section of the garden was not as complete as had been expected given the results derived in controlled experiments.

(B) Because the man-made plant hormone would ultimately be neutralized by soil erosion, more man-made plant hormones would need to be added to the garden every three months.

(C) A man-made plant hormone produced from different chemicals which had been developed by the designer at an earlier period was ineffective in warding off insect infestation.

(D) The recent dearth of insects in that section of the garden is the same as the recent dearth of insects in otherwise very similar sections of the garden without the man-made plant hormone.

(E) The recent dearth of insects in that section of the garden, even though substantial, is not yet sufficient to compensate for the plant loss in that section of the garden in the last year.

7. The best answer is D. The conclusion is that the man-made hormone wards off insect infestation. This assumes that without the man-made hormone, there wouldn't have been a "dearth of insects" in that section of the garden. If it were true that there would be a dearth of insects without the hormone, that undermines the argument.

8. A higher level of safety in automotive braking mechanisms depends upon control by internal computer monitoring systems.

   Automotive braking mechanisms, to be safe, would have to pump in intervals, and determining that the brakes would compensate for all situations is impossible.

   Despite technological advances, every internal computer monitoring system has on use proved to have serious weaknesses which in certain circumstances would bring about significant failure.

   Which of the following can be inferred from the statements above?

   (A) If designers are diligent in planning the internal computer monitoring system to be used for automotive braking mechanisms, there is an exceptionally good chance that the braking mechanism will ensure a high level of safety if and when it is needed.

   (B) Techniques for decreasing the number of errors in building internal computer monitoring systems will not be discovered.

   (C) Automotive braking mechanisms will not function safely during pumping.

   (D) Some method of control other than internal computer monitoring systems will have to be designed.

   (E) The safety of automobile braking systems cannot be ensured during pumping.

8. The best answer is E. Remember that an inference is something that is known to be true, based on what you're told in the argument. For inference questions, go with the safest, least disputable, answer choice that supports the argument. Answer choice (A) goes against the argument. Answer choices (B), (C) and (D) are all too disputable.

9. Which of the following is an acceptable layout of exits, from positions 1 through 6, according to the restrictions above?

   (A) Morrow, Bainbridge, Driscoll, Kimball, Homer, Crescent
   (B) Crescent, Kimball, Morrow, Driscoll, Bainbridge, Homer
   (C) Kimball, Crescent, Morrow, Homer, Driscoll, Bainbridge
   (D) Bainbridge, Homer, Kimball, Morrow, Crescent, Driscoll
   (E) Driscoll, Bainbridge, Kimball, Crescent, Homer, Morrow

9. The best answer is E. Your original diagram should look like this:

   ```
   1   2   3   4   5   6
   –H                  –B
   –C                  –K
   –M
   ```

   B . . . H

   K . . . M

   ⌐BD⌐ ⌐DB⌐

   Then, eliminate answer choices that violate the clues.
   (A) M cannot be in 1.
   (B) C cannot be in 1.
   (C) B cannot be after H.
   (D) B and D cannot be separated.

10. If the Crescent exit is placed somewhere after the Homer exit, which of the following must be true?

    (A) The Crescent exit is placed somewhere after the Bainbridge exit.
    (B) The Crescent exit is placed somewhere after the Kimball exit.
    (C) The Crescent exit is placed somewhere after the Morrow exit.
    (D) The Homer exit is placed somewhere before the Kimball exit.
    (E) The Homer exit is placed somewhere before the Driscoll exit.

10. The best answer is A. If C is placed after H, and B must be before H, then C must be after B.

11. If the Homer exit is placed somewhere before the Kimball exit, the Kimball exit could be placed in which of the following positions?

    (A) 1
    (B) 2
    (C) 3
    (D) 4
    (E) 6

11. The best answer is D. Draw a new picture.
    ```
    1   2   3   4   5   6
    B   D   H   K
    ```

QUESTIONS	EXPLANATIONS

12. If the Morrow exit is placed somewhere before the Bainbridge exit, which of the following must be true?

    (A) The Morrow exit is placed somewhere before the Crescent exit.
    (B) The Morrow exit is placed somewhere before the Driscoll exit.
    (C) The Bainbridge exit is placed somewhere before the Crescent exit.
    (D) The Bainbridge exit is placed somewhere before the Driscoll exit.
    (E) The Bainbridge exit is placed somewhere before the Kimball exit.

12. The best answer is B. Draw a picture that fits the question, then eliminate answer choices that aren't in it.

1	2	3	4	5	6
K	M	D	B	H	C

    Eliminate choices (D) and (E).
    Then redraw the picture to eliminate any remaining answer choices.

1	2	3	4	5	6
K	C	M	B	D	H

    Eliminate choices (A) and (C).

13. All of the following are possible orderings for the six exits EXCEPT

    (A) Kimball, Morrow, Crescent, Driscoll, Bainbridge, Homer
    (B) Kimball, Crescent, Morrow, Driscoll, Bainbridge, Homer
    (C) Driscoll, Bainbridge, Kimball, Homer, Crescent, Morrow
    (D) Kimball, Homer, Morrow, Driscoll, Bainbridge, Crescent
    (E) Kimball, Driscoll, Bainbridge, Crescent, Homer, Morrow

13. The best answer is D. On an EXCEPT question, four of the answer choices are okay, so look for the violation of the clues. In choice (D), H cannot be before B.

14. If the Bainbridge exit is placed next to the Morrow exit, which of the following must be true?

    (A) The Kimball exit is placed in position 1.
    (B) The Crescent exit is placed in position 2.
    (C) The Driscoll exit is placed in position 3.
    (D) The Bainbridge exit is placed in position 4.
    (E) The Morrow exit is placed in position 5.

14. The best answer is A. Draw a picture that fits the question, then eliminate answer choices that aren't in it.

1	2	3	4	5	6
K	M	B	D	C	H

    That eliminates choices (B), (C), (D) and (E).

15. If the Kimball exit is placed in position 5, how many logically possible orderings of all six exits are possible?

    (A) 2
    (B) 3
    (C) 4
    (D) 5
    (E) 6

15. The best answer is (C). Just do it. Draw out the possibilites. If K is in position 5, then M must be in position 6.

1	2	3	4	5	6
D	B	H	C	K	M
D	B	C	H	K	M
B	D	H	C	K	M
B	D	C	H	K	M

16. Any of the events could be scheduled for Sunday EXCEPT

    (A) a banquet
    (B) the luncheon
    (C) the party
    (D) the seminar
    (E) the wedding

16. The best answer is E. Your original diagram should look like this:

    S   M   T   W   Th   F   S
    -W   -W   -W   -L   -L   -L   -S

    B1 - - - B2

    PB1   B1P

    S. . .B2

    L - - W

    If the Wedding is always the third day after the Luncheon, the Wedding can never be on Sunday, Monday, or Tuesday.

17. Which of the following is a possible schedule, including the day off, when no event is scheduled, for the six events from Sunday through Saturday?

    (A) banquet, luncheon, party, seminar, banquet, wedding, day off
    (B) luncheon, banquet, party, wedding, day off, banquet seminar
    (C) party, banquet, luncheon, seminar, wedding, banquet, day off
    (D) party, banquet, seminar, luncheon, day off, banquet, wedding
    (E) day off, banquet, luncheon, seminar, banquet, party, wedding

17. The best answer is D. Use process of elimination to eliminate choices.

    (A) The Party must be the day before or the day after the first banquet.
    (B) The Seminar can never be Saturday.
    (C) The Wedding must be the third day after the Luncheon.
    (E) The Wedding must be the third day after the Luncheon.

18. The day on which the luncheon is scheduled must be no more than how many days after the day scheduled for the first banquet?

    (A) 1
    (B) 2
    (C) 3
    (D) 4
    (E) 5

18. The best answer is C. Draw a picture, trying to make the Luncheon as many days after the first banquet as you can.

    S   M   T   W   Th   F   S
    B1   P   S   L   B2   O   W

19. The party could be scheduled for any of the following days EXCEPT

    (A) Sunday
    (B) Monday
    (C) Tuesday
    (D) Wednesday
    (E) Thursday

19. The best answer is E. Draw a picture using your B1 - - - B2 block.

    S M T W Th F S
    B1 P - - B2

    Notice that the latest the first Banquet can be is Tuesday. Therefore, the latest that the Party could be is Wednesday.

20. If the luncheon is scheduled for Sunday, which of the following pairs of events CANNOT be scheduled for consecutive days?

    (A) a banquet and the wedding
    (B) the luncheon and a banquet
    (C) the luncheon and the party
    (D) the party and the seminar
    (E) the party and the wedding

20. The best answer is D. Draw a picture, trying the answer choices. If the answer choice could be true, eliminate that choice.

    S M T W Th F S
    L P B1 W   B2

    Eliminate choices (A) and (C).

    L B1 P W   B2

    Eliminate choices (B) and (E).

21. If no event is scheduled for Sunday, which of the following could be true?

    (A) The luncheon is scheduled for the day before the day of the first banquet.
    (B) The party is scheduled for the day before the day of the first banquet.
    (C) The seminar is scheduled for the day before the day of the first banquet.
    (D) The wedding is scheduled for the day before the day of the second banquet.
    (E) The wedding is scheduled for the day after the day of the seminar.

21. The best answer is A. Draw a picture, trying the answer choices. If the answer choice could be true, that's it!

    S M T W Th F S
    O L B1 P W S B2

    That works. End of discussion.

22. If the party is scheduled for the day before the day of the first banquet, the days for which the luncheon can be scheduled include

    (A) Sunday and Monday
    (B) Sunday and Wednesday
    (C) Monday and Tuesday
    (D) Monday and Wednesday
    (E) Tuesday and Wednesday

22. The best answer is B. Draw a picture, eliminate answer choices, then redraw the picture to eliminate remaining choices.

    S M T W Th F S
    L P B1 W S O B2

    Eliminate choices (C), (D) and (E).

    P B1 O L S B2 W

    Eliminate choice (A).

23. During the past fifteen years, twenty percent of the judges with sufficient experience to be considered for federal judgeships were women, and all of those deemed to have sufficient experience during those years received federal judgeships. Despite this fact, only eight percent of federal judgeships are currently filled by women.

    Which of the following, if true, could explain the discrepancy in the percentages cited in the passage above?

    (A) Fifteen years ago, it required less experience to be considered for federal judgeships than it does today.
    (B) The majority of those holding federal judgeships have held those positions for more than fifteen years, dating back to a time when practically everyone holding that position was male.
    (C) The women with sufficient experience to be considered for federal judgeships have tended to specialize in different areas of law than the men considered for federal judgeships.
    (D) Men and women holding federal judgeships have received equal financial compensation for the previous fifteen years.
    (E) Although women currently hold eight percent of the federal judgeships, they hold only three percent of circuit judgeships.

23. The best answer is B. Use process of elimination. Answer choices (C), (D) and (E) are out of scope. Answer choice (A) doesn't say anything about women or men.

24. It has been argued that medical researchers would make more impressive strides in their effort to develop cures for certain infectious diseases if they knew more about how cells replicate. This argument, however, could be challenged on the basis that a major advance in pest control has never come from any insight into the reproductive patterns of insects. The argument above relies on an analogy that assumes that fighting infectious diseases is an endeavor similar to which of the following?

   (A) Theories of cell-replication
   (B) Efforts at pest control
   (C) Conclusions about how researchers make advances
   (D) Patterns of infectious disease transmission in insects
   (E) Research into the reproductive patterns of insects

24. The best answer is B. The analogy is between fighting infectious diseases and attempts at pest control.

25. Rita has more clients than Frank and more clients than Tom. Isabel has more clients than Rita. Sam has no fewer clients than Rita.

   If all of the statements above are true, which of the following cannot be true?

   (A) Tom has more clients than Sam.
   (B) Tom has more clients than Frank.
   (C) Isabel has more clients than Tom.
   (D) Sam and Rita have the same number of clients.
   (E) Frank has fewer clients than Sam.

25. The best answer is A. This is a game disguised as an argument. You should symbolize the clues, then combine them into one diagram:

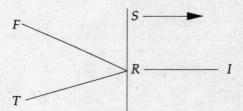

   (B) Could be true.
   (C) Must be true.
   (D) Could be true.
   (E) Must be true.

SECTION 4

1. The units digit in   The hundreds digit in
    the number 1,743   the number 5,243

    1. The best answer is A. The units digit in 1,743 is 3.
        The hundreds digit in 5243 is 2.

$$1.3 + .6 + .9 + x = 5.$$

2. x 2.3

    2. The best answer is B. $1.3 + .6 + .9 = 2.8$ So $x = 5 - 2.8 = 2.2$ in Column A.

3. 4^3 3^4

    3. The best answer is B. In Column A, $4^3 - 64$. In Column B, $3^4 - 81$. .

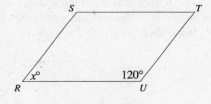

RSTU is a parallelogram

4. $4(2^6)$ $6(4^2)$

    4. The best answer is A. Use Fred's Theorem on parallelograms! opposite angles are equal, and the big angle plus the small angle add up to 180 degrees. So $x + 120 = 180$. $x = 60$ in Column A.

5. 30 percent of $150   60 percent of $75

    5. The best answer is C. Translate percentages into fractions. $\left(\dfrac{30}{100}\right)150 = 45$ in Column A.

        $\left(\dfrac{60}{100}\right)75 = 45$ in Column B.

QUESTIONS	EXPLANATIONS

6. $\dfrac{n}{3}$ $\dfrac{m+n}{3}$

6. The best answer is D. Plug in numbers for variables in Quant Comp. Let's make $n = 3$ and $m = 2$. In Column A $\dfrac{3}{3} = 1$. In Column B $\dfrac{2+3}{3} = \dfrac{5}{3}$.

So you can eliminate answer choices (A) and (C), because Column B is greater when you use those numbers.
Now plug in again. Keep $n = 3$, but let's make $m = 0$. If $m = 0$, the two columns are equal. That eliminates answer choice (B). So, by process of elimination, (D) is the answer.

7. $\dfrac{\sqrt{27}}{\sqrt{3}}$ $\dfrac{\sqrt{45}}{\sqrt{5}}$

7. The best answer is C. Remember, you <u>can</u> multiply and divide square roots!

$$\dfrac{\sqrt{27}}{\sqrt{3}} = \sqrt{\dfrac{27}{3}} = \sqrt{9} = 3 \text{ in Column A}$$

$$\dfrac{\sqrt{45}}{\sqrt{5}} = \sqrt{\dfrac{45}{5}} = \sqrt{9} = 3 \text{ in Column B}.$$

8. $5\left(\dfrac{x}{5}+\dfrac{y}{5}+\dfrac{7}{5}\right)$ $x+y+7$

8. The best answer is C. You should distribute the product in Column

A. $5\left(\dfrac{x}{5}+\dfrac{y}{5}+\dfrac{7}{5}\right) = 5\left(\dfrac{x}{5}\right)+5\left(\dfrac{y}{5}\right)+5\left(\dfrac{7}{5}\right) = x+y+7$ in

Column A and $x+y+7$ in Column B.

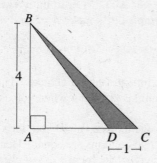

$\triangle ABC$ is isosceles

9. $\dfrac{\text{Area of the shaded region of } \triangle ABC}{\text{Area of the unshaded region of } \triangle ABC}$ $\dfrac{1}{3}$

The average (arithmetic mean) of two positive integers is equal to 17. Each of the integers is greater than 12.

10. Twice the larger of   44
      the two integers.

11. C 4

9. The best answer is C. Joe Bloggs puts answer choice (D). But did you notice that triangle ABC is isosceles? That means that the base and the height are each equal to 4. So the base of the unshaded region is 3, and the base of the shaded region is 1. Then use the formula for area of a triangle $\frac{1}{2}$(base)(height) and you get

$$\dfrac{\frac{1}{2}(1)(4)}{\frac{1}{2}(3)(4)} = \dfrac{2}{6} = \dfrac{1}{3} \text{ in Column A.}$$

10. The best answer is B. Joe Bloggs says (D), because you could have different values for Column A. But if the average of two positive integers is 17, then the total of the two numbers = 34. Since the smallest one of the numbers could be is 13, the largest the other number could be is 21. Twice 21 = 42. That's the largest possible value for Column A. So Column B is <u>always</u> greater.

11. The best answer is B. If a circle has a radius of $\frac{1}{2}$, then its diameter = 1. To find the circumference of a circle, use the formula $2\pi r$ or πd. So the circumference would be $(1)(\pi) = \pi$ in Column A. Remember π is only slightly greater than 3. So 4 in Column B is greater.

| QUESTIONS | EXPLANATIONS |

4

12. $\sqrt{\dfrac{7}{3}}$ $\dfrac{1}{3}\sqrt{7}$

12. The best answer is A. Joe Bloggs would say (C). But if you manipulate the two quantities it's easier to see the difference. $\sqrt{\dfrac{7}{3}} = \dfrac{\sqrt{7}}{\sqrt{3}}$ in Column A and $\dfrac{1}{3}\sqrt{7} = \dfrac{\sqrt{7}}{3}$ in Column B. Remember that $\sqrt{3} \approx 1.7$. When you divide a number by a smaller number you get a bigger result.

$$\frac{a}{b} = \frac{1}{3} \text{ and } \frac{b}{c} = \frac{15}{4}$$

13. a c

13. The best answer is A. Joe Bloggs looks at it too quickly and picks (B). Try to make b the same for both ratios. Let's use 15. Then $\dfrac{a}{b} = \dfrac{1}{3} = \dfrac{5}{15}$ Now that b is the same for both ratios, you can compare a and c. $a = 5$ in Column A, and $c = 4$ in Column B.

14. The circumference of a circular region with radius r The perimeter of a square with side r

14. The best answer is A. Joe Bloggs chooses (D), because he says, "We don't know what r is." But let's plug in some numbers and see what happens.
To start with, make $r = 2$.
Then you get $2\pi r = 4\pi$ in Column A and $4(2) = 8$ in Column B.
So Column A is greater if $r = 2$. So you can eliminate choices (B) and (C).
Now let's plug in a weird number, make $r = 1$.
Then you get 2π in Column A and 4 in Column B. Column A wins again.

Plug in once more, to be sure. Make $r = \dfrac{1}{2}$

Then you get π in Column A and 2 in Column B. Column A wins again.
You can't plug in 0 or a negative number, because r is the radius of the circle and the side of the square.

15. $3^{17} + 3^{18}$ $(4)3^{17}$

15. The best answer is C. Use process of elimination. Answer choice (D) is impossible, because there are no variables in the problem. Joe Bloggs would choose either (A) or (B) because either one or the other "looks" greater. So the right answer must be (C). To see why, factor the quantity in Column A.
$$3^{17} + 3^{18} = 3^{17}(1+3) = 3^{17}(4)$$

16. Which of the following numbers is greater than $-\dfrac{7}{3}$

(A) -7 (B) -3 (C) -2 (D) $-\dfrac{8}{3}$ (E) $-\dfrac{5}{2}$

16. The best answer is C. Use the Bowtie to compare fractions, or change $-\dfrac{7}{3}$ into $-2\dfrac{1}{3}$.

17. If the cost of a one hour telephone call is $7.20, what would be the cost of a ten minute telephone call at the same rate?

(A) $7.10
(B) $3.60
(C) $1.80
(D) $1.20
(E) $ .72

17. The best answer is D. If the cost of a one hour telephone call is $7.20, divide that by 6 to find the cost for a ten minute call, because 10 minutes is one-sixth of an hour. $7.20 ÷ 6 = $1.20.

18. A pie is baked in a circular plate with a radius of 6 inches. If the pie is then cut into eight equal pieces, what would be the area, in square inches, of each slice of the pie?

(A) $\dfrac{1}{8}\pi$ (B) $\dfrac{2}{9}\pi$ (C) $\dfrac{9}{2}\pi$ (D) 6π (E) 36π

18. The best answer is C. to find the area of a slice of the pie, first you need to find the area of the whole pie, then divide the area of the whole pie by 8 to find the area of each slice. If the radius of the pie is 6, then the area of the whole pie would be
$\pi r^2 = \pi 6^2 = 36\pi$. Then divide by 8. $\dfrac{36\pi}{8} = \dfrac{9\pi}{2}$.

QUESTIONS	**EXPLANATIONS**

19. If $s=3r$ and $t=7s$, then, in terms of r, $t - s - r =$

    (A) $21r$
    (B) $17r$
    (C) $10r$
    (D) $4r$
    (E) r

19. The best answer is B. Variables in the answer choices? Plug In! Start with r, because r is the variable in all the answer choices.
Let's make $r = 2$. Then $s = 6$ and $t = 42$. So the question really would be: 42 - 6 - 2 = 34. Plug in $r = 2$ in all the answer choices, to see which one equals 34.

20. $\sqrt{1.44 - .63} =$

    (A) .9
    (B) .81
    (C) .12
    (D) .09
    (E) .03

20. The best answer is A. Remember that you can't subtract square roots. So you have to do the subtraction under the square root sign first.
$\sqrt{1.44 - .63} = \sqrt{.81}$ Then, change the decimal to a fraction to make it easier to find the square root.

$$\sqrt{\frac{81}{100}} = \frac{\sqrt{81}}{\sqrt{100}} = \frac{9}{10} = .9$$

Questions 21-25 refer to the following data.

PERCENT CONTRIBUTED TO PROFITS BY EACH OF THE
6 DIVISIONS, P THROUGH U, OF COMPANY Y
FOR 1979 AND 1980

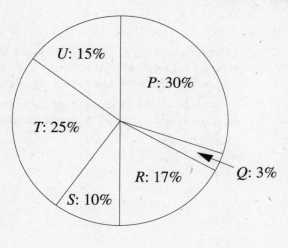

1979

Profits = $20,000,000

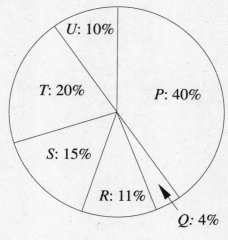

1980

Profits = $30,000,000

21. In 1979, what was the average of the amounts contributed to profits by Division *P* and Division *S*?

   (A) $150,000
   (B) $750,000
   (C) $2,000,000
   (D) $4,000,000
   (E) $6,000,000

21. The best answer is D. Since the question refers to the same year, to find the average amounts contributed by Divisions P and S, you can take the average of the two percentages, and then convert the average percentage into the average amount. The average of 30% and 10% is 20%. Now translate this percentage into a fraction.

$$\frac{20}{100}(20,000,000) = 4,000,000$$

22. Division *U* contributed how much more to the profits of Company *Y* in 1979 than in 1980?

   (A) $500,000
   (B) $250,000
   (C) $150,000
   (D) $100,000
   (E) $0

22. The best answer is E. Division U contributed 15% of 20 in 1979, and 10% of 30 in 1980. Forget about the millions. $\frac{15}{100}(20) = 3$ and $\frac{10}{100}(30) = 3$. So Division U contributed the same amount to profits in each year.

23. In 1980, the greatest contribution to profits by one of the six divisions was what percent of the second least contribution?

    (A) 25%   (B) 75%   (C) 175%
    (D) 350%   (E) 400%

23. The best answer is E. Again, since the question refers to the same year, you don't need to convert the percentages into amounts, just answer the question using the percentages in the pie chart. In 1980, the greatest contribution to profits was from Division P (40%) and the second least contribution was from Division U (10%). You could translate the question this way: "40 is what percent of 10?" In a math equation this would be: $40 = \frac{x}{100}(10)$. Now reduce and solve for x. $400 = x$.

24. If the six divisions are ranked each year according to their dollar contributions to profits, from greatest contribution to lowest, how many divisions ranked lower in 1980 than in 1979?

    (A) None
    (B) One
    (C) Two
    (D) Three
    (E) Four

24. The best answer is C. Write out the ranks of the divisions for each year, and then see how many ranked lower in 1980 than in 1979.
Divisions ranked in 1979: P, T, R, U, S, Q
Divisions ranked in 1980: P, T, S, R, U, Q
Divisions R and U were ranked lower.

25. How many of the divisions contributed more dollars to profits in 1980 than in 1979?

    (A) One
    (B) Two
    (C) Three
    (D) Four
    (E) Five

25. The best answer is D. Clearly, if a division contributed a greater percentage of a greater amount of profits in 1980, then it contributed more dollars. So obviously, Divisions P, S, and Q all contributed more dollars. But this is the hardest question in this set, so the right answer can't be (C), because that would be too easy. So either guess (D) or (E) or check out the numbers for Divisions R and T.

Division R contributed in 1979 $\frac{17}{100}(20) = 3.4$ and in 1980 $\frac{11}{100}(30) = 3.3$. So Division R did not contribute more dollars in 1980. Division T's 1979 contribution was $\frac{25}{100}(20) = 5$ and in 1980 was $\frac{20}{100}(30) = 6$. So Division T did contribute more dollars in 1980.

26. In a certain election, 60 percent of the voters were women. If 30 percent of the women and 20 percent of the men voted for candidate *X*, what percent of all the voters in that election voted for candidate *X*?

(A) 18%
(B) 25%
(C) 26%
(D) 30%
(E) 50%

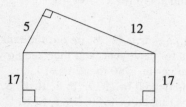

27. What is the perimeter of the figure above?

(A) 51
(B) 64
(C) 68
(D) 77
(E) 91

28. If *a*, *b*, and *c* are consecutive non-positive integers and $a < b < c$, which of the following must be true?

 I. $-a < -c$
 II. $abc < 0$
 III. abc is even

(A) None
(B) II only
(C) III only
(D) II and III only
(E) I, II, and III

26. The best answer is C. What's missing? How many voters there were. Let's say there were 100 voters. Then if 60% were women, 60 were women and 40 were men. If 30% of the 60 women voted for candidate X, then $\frac{30}{100}(60) = 18$ women voted for candidate X. And if 20% of the 40 men voted for candidate X then $\frac{20}{100}(40) = 8$ men voted for candidate X. So out of the 100 voters, 18 + 8 = 26 voted for candidate X, or 26%.

27. The best answer is B. To find the perimeter of the figure, you need to add up all the sides. To find the missing side of the rectangle, solve for the opposite side of the rectangle, using the Pythagorean Theorem: $a^2 + b^2 = c^2$. You may remember that $5^2 + 12^2 = 13^2$. So the missing sides of the rectangle are each 13. Now add up the sides of the figure: 5 +12 +17 + 13 + 17 = 64.

28. The best answer is C. Plug in numbers! You have to plug in consecutive non-positive integers. Let's make a = -2, b = -1 and c = 0. Using these numbers, you can see right away that II is false: (-2)(-1)(0) = 0. So you can eliminate every answer choice that includes II. That eliminates answer choices (B), (D), and (E). Now you only have to check III. Using these numbers, the product is even, because 0 is even, but let's plug in different numbers to be sure. Now make a = -3, b = -2, and c = -1. (-3)(-2)(-1) = -6. That's also even, so III must be true.

QUESTIONS	EXPLANATIONS

29. If $5a - 3b = -9$ and $3a + b = 31$, then $a + b =$

(A) -7
(B) -3
(C) 6
(D) 13
(E) 19

29. The best answer is E. When you have two equations with two variables, usually you can either add or subtract the two equations to solve for one of the variables. When you try that with these two equations, however, it doesn't work with the two equations in their original forms. So you have to manipulate one of the equations to get it into a form that will be useful.

Let's multiply both sides of the second equation by 3, so that we get $+3b$.

$3(3a + b) = 3(31)$ Remember to distribute! You get : $9a + 3b = 93$. Now we can add the two equations to solve for a.

$9a + 3b = 93$

$5a - 3b = -9$

$14a + 0 = 84$

so $a = 6$. Now plug $a = 6$ back into the second equation we started with, in order to solve for b most easily.

$3(6) + b = 31$

$18 + b = 31$

$b = 13$. Finally, we can answer the question. $6 + 13 = 19$. Whew!

30. 5×10^3 is what percent of $\frac{1}{5} \times 10^2$?

(A) 2,500%
(B) 4,900%
(C) 20,000%
(D) 24,900%
(E) 5,000%

30. The best answer is E. Translate into a math equation and expand out the exponents.

SECTION 5

1. Many feature films are criticized for their ------- content, even though television news is more often the medium that depicts violent events in excessive detail.

   (A) discretionary
   (B) graphic
   (C) dramatic
   (D) artistic
   (E) honest

1. The best answer is B. The clue in the sentence is "that depicts violent events in excessive detail." So the word in the blank must mean "depicting in excessive detail." Also, feature films are criticized for some reason, so the word in the blank must have negative connotations.

2. The use of alcohol and other drugs, with the exception of tobacco, seems to increase and decrease -------; certain periods are marked by a social inclination toward abstinence, which after a time gives way to drug consumption by some part of society, and eventually to ------- acceptance.

   (A) erratically . . partial
   (B) cyclically . . widespread
   (C) exponentially . . mitigated
   (D) criminally . . absolute
   (E) simultaneously . . conventional

2. The best answer is B. The clue for the first blank is "certain periods are marked by a social inclination toward abstinence, which after a time gives way to drug consumption." So a good word for the first blank would "periodically." The only answer choice with a first word meaning "periodically" is (B).

3. After screenwriter Neil Jordan's most recent work opened in selected urban areas, many theatergoers were -------, but after pundits expressed their -------, appreciation of the film increased and distribution surged.

   (A) skeptical . . approbation
   (B) apathetic . . diffidence
   (C) ebullient . . trepidation
   (D) dubious . . disdain
   (E) unimpressed . . antipathy

3. The best answer is A. The clue for the second blank is "appreciation of the film increased ...." So the word in the second blank must have positive connotations. Looking only at the second word, you can eliminate answer choices (B), (C), (D) and (E), because the second words in all these choices have negative connotations.

4. The pieces exhibited at many university galleries are chosen to reflect the diverse tastes of the academic communities they serve; the curators avoid ------- in favor of -------.

   (A) continuity . . rigidity
   (B) variation . . craftsmanship
   (C) uniformity . . eclecticism
   (D) modernism . . classics
   (E) homogeneity . . segmentation

4. The best answer is C. The clue in the sentence is "chosen to reflect the diverse tastes of the academic communities they serve." So the word in the second blank must mean "diversity" and the word in the first blank must mean the opposite of "diversity."

5. The American public venerates medical researchers because the researchers make frequent discoveries of tremendous humanitarian consequence; however, the daily routines of scientists are largely made up of result verification and statistical analysis, making their occupation seem -------.

    (A) fascinating
    (B) quotidian
    (C) recalcitrant
    (D) experimental
    (E) amorphous

5. The best answer is B. The clue for the blank is "the daily routines of scientists are largely made up of result verification ...." So the word in the blank must be one meaning "characterized by daily routine." That's what "quotidian" means. Also, since the first part of the sentence is positive, and the trigger word is "however," you know that the word in the blank must be negative. Choice (C) would be a good guess.

6. In a vitriolic message to his troops, General Patton insisted that he would ------- no further insubordination, no matter how barbarous the ensuing engagements might become.

    (A) impede
    (B) brief
    (C) denote
    (D) brook
    (E) expose

6. The best answer is D. The clue for the blank is "no further insubordination...." So the word in the blank must mean "tolerate." That's what "brook" means.

7. Chang realized that she had been ------- in her duties; had she been more -------, the disaster may well have been avoided.

    (A) unparalleled . . careful
    (B) irreproachable . . aware
    (C) derelict . . vigilant
    (D) arbitrary . . interested
    (E) neglectful . . insensible

7. The best answer is C. The clue in the sentence is "the disaster may well have been avoided." So you know that the first word must be negative, and the second word must be positive. Eliminate positive words for the first blank (choices (A) and (B)). Eliminate negative words for the second blank, choice (E). Then choose the most difficult answer you have left.

8. METEOROLOGY : WEATHER ::
    (A) philology : love
    (B) epistemology : disease
    (C) physiology : mind
    (D) demography : population
    (E) astrology : planets

8. The best answer is D. A good sentence would be, "Meteorology is the study of weather."

9. MAELSTROM : WATER ::
    (A) downpour : rain
    (B) wave : current
    (C) cyclone : wind
    (D) tornado : debris
    (E) storm : snow

9. The best answer is C. If you weren't sure what a "maelstrom" is, eliminate answer choices that don't have clear and necessary relationships. Answer choices (B), (D) and (E) aren't clear and necessary relationships. Joe Bloggs is attracted to (A), so eliminate that one!

10. FIX : STABLE ::
    (A) furrow : productive
    (B) mend : torn
    (C) fortify : strong
    (D) deter : active
    (E) captivate : attractive

10. The best answer is C. A good sentence for the stem words would be, "To fix means to make stable."

11. GALL : IRRITATION ::
    (A) accommodate : deception
    (B) beleaguer : felicity
    (C) awe : apathy
    (D) discomfit : confusion
    (E) inculcate : fear

11. The best answer is D. Eliminate answer choices (A), (C), and (E) because they don't have clear and necessary relationships. (D): "discomfit" means to cause "confusion" and "gall" means to cause "irritation."

12. PAPYRUS : PAPER ::
    (A) manuscript : book
    (B) hatchet : ax
    (C) cart : wagon
    (D) daguerreotype : photograph
    (E) house : mansion

12. The best answer is D. A good sentence would be "Papyrus is a primitive form of paper." If you didn't know "daguerreotype" you could use process of elimination. A hatchet is not a primitive ax, it's just a small one. A cart is not a primitive wagon, it's a two-wheeled vehicle and a wagon is a four-wheeled vehicle.

13. BLACKSMITH : FOUNDRY ::
    (A) farmer : shed
    (B) artist : studio
    (C) physician : laboratory
    (D) teacher : college
    (E) reporter : television

13. The best answer is B. If you weren't sure what a "foundry" is, go right to the answer choices and eliminate answer choices that don't have clear and necessary relationships. That eliminates (A), (C), (D) and (E). Work backwards from answer choice (B): "A studio is a place where an artist works." Could a "foundry" be a place where a blacksmith works? You bet. If you thought a college is where a teacher works, make a more specific sentence. You could say that a studio is where an artist <u>makes things</u>.

14. ARIA : SONG ::
    (A) covenant : agreement
    (B) fable : story
    (C) monument : sculpture
    (D) prose : poem
    (E) soliloquy : speech

14. The best answer is E. You might start with the sentence, "An aria is part of a song." Then eliminate answer choices (B), (C) and (D). Then make your original sentence more specific, "An aria is the part of a song performed by one person." Now you can eliminate (A).

QUESTIONS	EXPLANATIONS

15. LONGING : PINE ::
    (A) remorse : rue
    (B) anguish : seethe
    (C) forbearance : dignify
    (D) concern : intervene
    (E) suffering : inflict

15. The best answer is A. Eliminate answer choices (B), (C), (D) and (E). They don't have clear and necessary relationships. Hard questions have hard answers, and answer choice (A) is the hardest answer.

16. CHEVRON : BADGE ::
    (A) caisson : cart
    (B) calcium : bone
    (C) wax : candle
    (D) clothing : uniform
    (E) oration : eulogy

16. The best answer is A. Don't waste too much time on the hardest problem! Answer choices (B), (C) and (D) are awfully easy, don't you think? Choice (D) is a Joe Bloggs trap. Choice (E) would be a good guess, but isn't (A) more difficult?

Directions: Each passage in this group is followed by questions based on its content. After reading a passage, choose the best answer to each question. Answer all questions following a passage on the basis of what is <u>stated</u> or <u>implied</u> in that passage.

In *A Room of One's Own*, Virginia Woolf performs a typically stream-of-consciousness feat by beginning with a description of the view from her window: a leaf falls from
Line a tree, and a woman in leather boots and a man in a maroon
(5) overcoat climb into a taxi and glide away. Woolf uses this moment to discuss the unity of the mind, and the effortlessness with which she had invested this ordinary sight with a kind of rhythmic order. She ends with a consideration of Coleridge's remark that a great mind is androgynous.
(10) "What does one mean by 'the unity of the mind?'" Woolf asks.

One of Woolf's theses is that unity, and not repression, is the necessary state for creativity. Woolf describes men's sentences as having a particular shape, natural to men, but
(15) unnatural and clumsy to women. She rightly praises Austen for developing her own rhythm and her own sentence, which is expressive of her genius, her characters, and her history. Woolf suggests that the women's suffrage movement fomented a reaction of threatened male self-
(20) assertion that meant a decline in literary power. "It is fatal," she writes, "for any one who writes to think of their sex. . . it is fatal for a woman to lay the least stress on any grievance; to plead justice with any cause; in any way to speak consciously as a woman."
(25) *A Room of One's Own* exhorts women to reach for a higher, almost religious approach to writing. "Do not dream of influencing other people;" she writes, "think of things in themselves."

17. Which of the following literary projects would Woolf most likely support?

   (A) A narrative poem in which a heroine overcomes male challenges through intellectual superiority

   (B) A fictional polemic asserting the importance of social equality of men and women

   (C) A novel that expresses the unrepressed truth of the author's experience

   (D) A short story that responds to the historical injustice in the treatment of women

   (E) A critical essay on Coleridge which explains his remark about androgyny in terms of his psychological history

18. The author refers to Woolf's description of the man and women climbing into the taxi in order to

   (A) give an example of Woolf's mastery of stream-of-consciousness techniques

   (B) show a typically feminine perspective of everyday life

   (C) demonstrate how Woolf's writing was unconcerned with changing the social order

   (D) refute the notion that Woolf's assertions are anti-female or anti-feminist

   (E) begin the discussion of Woolf's conception of the ways in which the mind unifies the world

19. According to the passage, Woolf believes which of the following to be true about Jane Austen's work?

   I. Austen's sentences are representative of an androgynous 'unity of the mind.'

   II. Austen's syntax and literary form are products of her personal experience.

   III. Austen's literary work exemplifies a particular form of well-realized female artistic expression.

   (A) I only

   (B) II only

   (C) I and II only

   (D) II and III only

   (E) I, II, and III

17. The best answer is C. The passage tells you that Woolf said not to "dream of influencing other people." So she wouldn't like the literary projects described in choices (A), (B) and (D). The first sentence of the second paragraph stresses "unity, and not repression, is the necessary state for creativity."

18. The best answer is E. See the sentence following the one referred to in the question. The passage states, "Woolf uses this moment to discuss the unity of the mind ...."

19. The best answer is D. Beware of direct repetitions of words from the passage! It was Coleridge, not Woolf, who said that a great mind is androgynous. Eliminate answer choices (A), (C) and (E). You don't have to check II, because it's in both remaining choices. III is true, because in the middle of the second paragraph the author tells you that Woolf praised Austen.

QUESTIONS	EXPLANATIONS

20. It can be inferred from the passage that Woolf believes that

   (A) women should not write about subjects that are specifically female

   (B) the women's suffrage movement contributed to a decline in literary quality

   (C) Austen created a narrative style that was appropriate for her gender and subject matter

   (D) women's sentences should mimic the shape of men's sentences

   (E) some readers could misinterpret her statements as being denigrating to women

20. The best answer is C. Use common sense to eliminate answer choices (B), (D) and (E). Answer choice (A) is close, but it's worded in a way that's too disputable.

Because human anatomy does not change (except over long periods of time), knowledge acquired a century ago is still accurate today. Broad functions of any part of the body, such as the skin, are duplicated in different ways by other organs. One can eventually understand the entire body as a larger system made up of smaller, interdependent systems.

A cross-section of the skin reveals a top layer of epidermis, or cuticle, followed by derma, and finally, subcutaneous cellular tissue. Sprouting through all three layers are hairs, with hair follicles and erector pili muscles embedded deep within the subcutaneous tissue. Sweat (sudoriferous glands), fat cells, and sebaceous glands are scattered throughout, while papillae, which are conical and extremely sensitive, can be found directly beneath the superficial layer.

The skin is the primary organ of the sense of touch. It can excrete substances as well as absorb them, and it plays a vital role in regulating body temperature and in protecting the tissues that lie beneath it.

The epidermis has no veins or arteries and varies considerably both in thickness and in the depth or fineness of its furrows. On the palm, for example, the skin is quite thick, or horny, and is marked by deep furrows or lines. On the back of the hand, however, the skin is less thick, and has only a faint network of lines crisscrossing it. The pigment found in the epidermis gives whatever color there is to the skin; this pigment is similar to that found in the retina of the eye. One layer down, in the derma, there is similar variation in thickness, mostly to protect underlying tissue.

In the derma lies the vascular system, which includes nerves, blood vessels, and lymphatics. The derma is divided into two sub-layers: the reticular layer and the papillary layer, which is closer to the epidermis. The less sensitive the skin, the fewer papillae reside there; in the most sensitive places, such as the fingertips and the nipples, the papillae are long, large, and grouped closely together to form parallel arcs with ducts to sweat glands lying in between. Under the papillary layer, and conforming to it, is the reticular layer, composed of fibrous bands and elastic tissue, and interlaced by fat and sudoriferous glands.

The basic functions of muscular contraction, vascular transport, nerve communication, and protection all take place in the various layers of the skin, so that understanding the components of the skin and how they work together is a helpful step in understanding the complex anatomy of the human body.

5

QUESTIONS	EXPLANATIONS

QUESTIONS

21. The author is primarily concerned with

   (A) giving an overview of human anatomical functions

   (B) describing the layers of the skin to show one example of an anatomical system

   (C) concluding that the study of human anatomy must first begin with the skin

   (D) discussing how the skin is only one system in a much larger and more complex system

   (E) detailing the three layers of the skin: the epidermis, the derma, and the subcutaneous cellular tissue, each of which has its own separate functions

22. The passage suggests that the area of skin most closely associated with skin sensitivity is the

   (A) reticular layer

   (B) papillary layer

   (C) sudoriferous gland

   (D) subcutaneous tissue

   (E) vascular system

23. The author would most likely agree with which of the following statements?

   I. Extremely sensitive skin is characterized by a minute number of papillae.

   II. Hair can be found in subcutaneous tissue.

   III. Skin and the retina both rely on pigment to give them color.

   (A) I only

   (B) II only

   (C) I and II only

   (D) II and III only

   (E) I, II, and III

24. The passage supplies information to answer which of the following questions?

   (A) What causes the erector pili muscle to contract?

   (B) Why is the epidermis covered with furrows?

   (C) How quickly do papillae react to sensation?

   (D) What do sudoriferous glands and sebaceous glands have in common?

   (E) Where in the body can pigmentation be found?

EXPLANATIONS

21. The best answer is B. The main idea of the passage could be expressed: "The skin is an example of one of the systems that work together in the body." Then use process of elimination.

   (A) nothing about the skin

   (C) "must first begin with" is too disputable.

   (D) close, but the word "only" makes this choice a bit harsh

   (E) what about the context? See the first paragraph and last sentence.

22. The best answer is B. See lines 17-18 and 43-45.

23. The best answer is D. If you took the time to get #22 right, it pays off here, because you know that I is false. Eliminate answer choices (A), (B) and (E). Don't check II because it's in both remaining choices. To see why III is true go back to lines 31-33.

24. The best answer is E. A repeat of III in #23! See lines 31-33.

25. The author implies that

    (A) there is a relationship between the thickness of the skin and the number and depth of the skin's furrows

    (B) the reticular layer is the only layer that contains fibrous bands

    (C) the skin is the only part of the body that has a sense of touch

    (D) areas of the skin with sudoriferous glands are extremely sensitive

    (E) both hair and the reticular layer are made up of the same kind of tissue

26. The passage suggests that if the skin were damaged in some way, and unable to perform some of its functions, which of the following might happen?

    (A) The pigmentation would no longer be similar to that found in the retina.

    (B) The deep furrows found on some parts of the skin would disappear.

    (C) The body would regulate its temperature less effectively.

    (D) The fingertips would no longer be characterized by an abundance of papillae.

    (E) The body would lose its sense of touch.

27. The passage states that all the following are found in the skin EXCEPT

    (A) fat cells
    (B) lymphatics
    (C) veins
    (D) pigmentation
    (E) ligaments

25. The best answer is A. See lines 25-26. Answer choices (B) and (C) are too disputable ("the only"), as is choice (E) ("the same kind").

26. The best answer is C. To answer this question, look for the place in the passage which describes some of the normal functions of undamaged skin. See the third paragraph, lines 20-24. Answer choices (B) and (E) go against common sense.

27. The best answer is E. Use process of elimination! Eliminate (D) based on what you learned in the previous questions. Common sense tells you the skin has veins, eliminate (C). Fat cells are mentioned in line 16, as are lymphatics in line 40.

QUESTIONS	EXPLANATIONS

28. CHRONIC: (A) intermittent (B) healthy (C) tardy (D) consistently durable (E) suddenly available

28. The best answer is A. "Chronic" means continuing, or of long duration.

29. FORK: (A) judge (B) praise (C) agitate (D) converge (E) impress

29. The best answer is D. "Fork" means to divide into branches.

30. FANCY: (A) ornament (B) abhor (C) falsify (D) reclaim (E) stiffen

30. The best answer is B. To "fancy" means to be fond of. To "abhor" means to detest.

31. ANIMATE: (A) enervate (B) frustrate (C) regress (D) condemn (E) distort

31. The best answer is A. "Animate" means to give life to. "Enervate" means to deprive of vitality.

32. CARDINAL: (A) wholesome (B) obscure (C) trivial (D) impious (E) lascivious

32. The best answer is C. "Cardinal" means of foremost importance.

33. INCUBATE: (A) squelch (B) hatch (C) assemble (D) decide (E) sterilize

33. The best answer is A. To "incubate" means to maintain in favorable environmental conditions for development. You know that "incubate has positive connotations, eliminate positive answer choices (C), (D) and (E). Answer choice (B) is a Joe Bloggs trap. To "squelch" means to crush completely.

34. OBSTREPEROUS: (A) disciplined (B) insubordinate (C) predictable (D) well-formed (E) exhausted

34. The best answer is A. If you knew that "obstreperous" is a negative word, eliminate answer choices (B) and (E). "Obstreperous" means unruly.

35. CHECK: (A) assume (B) complete (C) disagree (D) emulate (E) unbridle

35. The best answer is E. To "check" means to hold in restraint. To "unbridle" means to remove restraint.

36. IMPRECATE: (A) evaluate carefully (B) uphold forcefully (C) bless (D) forgive (E) confine

36. The best answer is C. If you knew that "imprecate" has negative connotations, eliminate choice (E), because it's negative. Choices (A) and (B) aren't as positive as choices (C) and (D). "Imprecate" means to curse.

37. BEREAVE: (A) tear (B) collaborate (C) solicit (D) radiate (E) furnish

37. The best answer is E. You know that "bereave" is a negative word. Eliminate answer choices (A), because it's negative, and choices (B) and (C), because they aren't really very positive. Choice (D) has no direct opposite. "Bereave" means to deprive of, as by death, but not always.

38. HIE: (A) separate (B) dawdle (C) lower cautiously (D) comfort warmly (E) leave suddenly

38. The best answer is B. Who knew "hie"? Shakespeare did, and he used it a lot. "Hie" means to go quickly.

SECTION 6

1. Which of the following is a possible order for the bulbs on the strand?
    (A) Yellow, red, red, red, yellow, green, green, blue, white, blue
    (B) Green, blue, white, blue, red, red, red, yellow, yellow, green
    (C) Blue, white, blue, green, yellow, yellow, green, red, red, red
    (D) Yellow, blue, white, yellow, red, red, red, blue, green, green
    (E) Green, green, yellow, red, red, red, yellow, blue, white, blue

1. The best answer is E. Your diagram for the set up might look like this:
    1 2 3 4 5 6 7 8 9 10

    1/10 different

    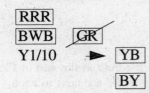

    Use process of elimination .

    (A) If Y is first, it must be next to B.
    (B) 1 and 10 must be different colors.
    (C) G can't be next to R.
    (D) W must have B on either side of it.

2. If a red bulb is at one end of the strand and a yellow bulb is at the other, which of the following statements must be true?
    (A) The two middle bulbs are both blue.
    (B) The two middle bulbs are both red.
    (C) The two middle bulbs are both green.
    (D) The two middle bulbs are green and blue.
    (E) The two middle bulbs are yellow and green.

2. The best answer is C. Draw a picture. The two middle bulbs are in places 5 and 6.

1	2	3	4	5	6	7	8	9	10
R	R	R	Y	G	G	B	W	B	Y

3. If the two yellow bulbs are next to each other and the green bulbs are not next to each other, which of the following statements must be true?
    (A) A yellow bulb is next to a red bulb.
    (B) A yellow bulb is next to a blue bulb.
    (C) A blue bulb is not next to a green bulb.
    (D) A white bulb is not next to a blue bulb.
    (E) A yellow bulb cannot be at either end of the strand.

3. The best answer is E. If the two yellow bulbs are next to each other, then a yellow bulb cannot be at either end of the strand, because if a yellow bulb is at either end, it must be next to a blue bulb. You could draw a picture.

1	2	3	4	5	6	7	8	9	10
B	W	B	G	Y	G	Y	R	R	R

QUESTIONS	EXPLANATIONS

4. If a yellow bulb is at the end of the strand, which of the following statements must be true?
    (A) A green bulb is next to a yellow bulb.
    (B) A white bulb is at the other end of the strand.
    (C) A blue bulb is at the other end of the strand.
    (D) A yellow bulb is at the other end of the strand.
    (E) A blue bulb is next to a red bulb.

4. The best answer is A. Draw a picture.

1	2	3	4	5	6	7	8	9	10
R	R	R	Y	G	G	B	W	B	Y

5. If a white bulb is next to the bulb at the end of the strand and the two yellow bulbs are next to each other, which of the following statements could be true?
    (A) There is a yellow bulb at the end of the strand.
    (B) There is a red bulb next to a green bulb.
    (C) There is a blue bulb next to a green bulb.
    (D) There is not a yellow bulb next to a green bulb.
    (E) There is a blue bulb next to a yellow bulb.

5. The best answer is C. Again, draw a picture.

1	2	3	4	5	6	7	8	9	10
B	W	B	G	G	Y	Y	R	R	R

6. Which of the following is NOT possible?
    (A) A yellow bulb is at one end of the strand, and a green bulb is at the other end.
    (B) A red bulb is at one end of the strand, and a green bulb is at the other end.
    (C) A yellow bulb is directly adjacent to a red bulb and a green bulb.
    (D) There are red bulbs next to a yellow bulb, a blue bulb, and a white bulb.
    (E) There are blue bulbs next to a red bulb, a white bulb, and a yellow bulb.

6. The best answer is D. Look back to the pictures you drew for earlier questions to eliminate answers. The picture for #3 eliminates (C). Then draw pictures to eliminate other choices.

1	2	3	4	5	6	7	8	9	10
Y	B	W	B	R	R	R	Y	G	G

    eliminate choice (A).

R	R	R	B	W	B	Y	Y	G	G

    eliminate choices (B) and (E).

7. Over the past five years, Clean toothpaste has been advertised as the most effective means of preventing tooth decay. However, according to dentists' records, many patients experiencing severe tooth decay used Clean toothpaste. Clearly, Clean toothpaste is not an effective means of preventing tooth decay

   Which of the following statements, if true, would most seriously weaken the conclusion above?
   (A) Of the patients experiencing tooth decay, two-thirds indicate that they would be willing to switch brands of toothpaste.
   (B) The advertisements for Clean toothpaste advocate brushing twice a day.
   (C) If Clean toothpaste were not available, more patients would experience severe tooth decay.
   (D) Dentists continue to recommend Clean toothpaste more than any other brand.
   (E) Of those who experienced severe tooth decay, only one-eighth also experienced gum disease.

7. The best answer is C. Use process of elimination. Answer choices (A), (B), (D) and (E) are out of the scope of the argument.

8. A group of physicians wishing to explore the link between protein and high blood pressure performed a nutrition experiment on a selected group of ten vegetarians. Five of the people were given a high protein, low fat diet. The group given the high protein, low fat diet exhibited the same five percent increase in blood pressure as did the group given the low protein, high fat diet.

   Which of the following conclusions can most properly be drawn if the statements above are true?
   (A) The physicians did not establish a link between protein and high blood pressure.
   (B) The sample chosen by the physicians was not representative of the general vegetarian population.
   (C) Some physicians believe there is a link between protein and high blood pressure.
   (D) Vegetarians are more likely to eat a high protein, low fat diet than a low protein, high fat diet.
   (E) There is a link between protein and high blood pressure.

8. The best answer is A. Answer choices (B), (C) and (D) are out of the scope of the argument. Choice (E) goes against the argument.

9. Whenever Joe does his laundry at the Main Street Laundromat, the loads turn out cleaner than they do when he does his laundry at the Elm Street Laundromat. Laundry done at the Main Street Laundromat is cleaner because the machines at the Main Street Laundromat use more water per load than do those at the Elm Street Laundromat.

Which of the following statements, if true, helps support the conclusion above?
(A) The clothes washed at the Elm Street Laundromat were, overall, less clean than those washed at the Main Street Laundromat.
(B) Joe uses the same detergent at both laundromats.
(C) The machines at the Oak Street Laundromat use twice as much water as do those at the Main Street Laundromat.
(D) Joe does three times as much laundry at the Main Street Laundromat as he does at the Elm Street Laundromat.
(E) Joe tends to do his dirtier laundry at the Elm Street Laundromat.

9. The best answer is B. Answer choices (C) and (D) are out of scope. Choices (A) and (E) go against the argument.

10. Which of the following could be an outfit order on the night following a night when the outfit order is plaid, striped, dotted, and checkered?
(A) Checkered, dotted, striped, and plaid
(B) Dotted, checkered, plaid, and striped
(C) Plaid, dotted, checkered, and striped
(D) Striped, plaid, checkered, and dotted
(E) Striped, checkered, plaid, and dotted

10. The best answer is E. Since the first order is:
P   S   D   C, use process of elimination.

(A) P can never be directly after S.
(B) D can never be first.
(C) P can't be first because it was first in the previous order.
(D) P can never be directly after S.

11. All of the following could be an outfit order for the evening following an evening in which the outfit order has the checkered outfit fourth and the plaid outfit third EXCEPT
(A) Checkered, dotted, plaid, and striped
(B) Checkered, plaid, dotted, and striped
(C) Striped, dotted, plaid, and checkered
(D) Plaid, checkered, striped, and dotted
(E) Plaid, striped, checkered, and dotted

11. The best answer is C. The previous order would be: S D P C.
Now look for the violation of the clues. Choice (C) has S first, and that violates the clue that the first outfits can never be the same.

QUESTIONS	EXPLANATIONS

12. If the outfit order on one evening is checkered, plaid, dotted, and striped, and on the next evening the outfit order has the plaid outfit fourth, which of the following must be true of the outfit order on the second evening?
    (A) The checkered outfit is modeled first.
    (B) The striped outfit is modeled first.
    (C) The checkered outfit is modeled immediately before the striped outfit.
    (D) The dotted outfit is modeled immediately before the striped outfit.
    (E) The dotted outfit is modeled directly before the checkered outfit.

12. The best answer is B. If the order on the first evening is C P D S, and on the next evening P is fourth, C can't be first, and D can never be first, so S must be first. The order would have to be S C D P.

13. If on a Monday the outfit order is striped, dotted, plaid, and checkered, and on a Wednesday the outfit order is plaid, checkered, striped, and dotted, which of the following must be true about the outfit order for Tuesday?
    (A) The plaid outfit is modeled second.
    (B) The striped outfit is modeled second.
    (C) The dotted outfit is modeled third.
    (D) The striped outfit is modeled fourth.
    (E) The checkered outfit is modeled first.

13. The best answer is E. if on Monday the order is S D P C, and on Wednesday is P C S D, then which outfit can be first on Tuesday? S can't be first, because it was first Monday. P can't be first on Tuesday, because it is first on Wednesday. D can never be the first outfit. So, by process of elimination, C must be the first outfit on Tuesday.

14. Which of the following routes must be taken to go from the ash to the elm while passing the fewest trees?
    (A) The Cross Country Trail.
    (B) The Green Mountain Trail, then the Cross Country Trail.
    (C) The Green Mountain Trail, then the Bethlehem Trail.
    (D) The Bethlehem Trail, then the Cross Country Trail.
    (E) The Green Mountain Trail, then the Bethlehem Trail, and then the Cross Country Trail.

14. The best answer is B. for a map game, work off of one diagram.

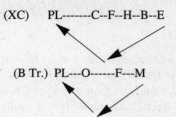

(Gr MT) PL---A---C---M---B---OB

(XC)   PL-------C--F--H--B--E

(B Tr.) PL---O------F---M

The A is on the Green Mountain Trail, then, at B, switch to the Cross Country Trail.

QUESTIONS	EXPLANATIONS

15. What is the maximum number of trees one can pass in order to get from the elm to the maple, without reusing any part of a path or passing the Pine Lodge?
 (A) 1
 (B) 2
 (C) 3
 (D) 4
 (E) 5

15. The best answer is D. From the elm, use the Cross Country Trail go past B, H, F to C. Switch at C to the Green Mt. Trail and go to M.

16. Which sequence of trees is a possible route from the Old Barn to the Pine Lodge?
 (A) Birch, maple, fir, oak
 (B) Birch, elm, ash, cherry
 (C) Birch, maple, fir, ash
 (D) Birch, hemlock, cherry
 (E) Birch, maple, cherry, elm, ash

16. The best answer is A. You can go on the Green Mt. Trail to B and to M. Switch at M for the Bethlehem Trail and go past F and O.

17. How many different routes are there from the Pine Lodge to the birch which pass exactly three trees and do not reuse any part of a path?
 (A) 2
 (B) 3
 (C) 4
 (D) 5
 (E) 6

17. The best answer is D.
 1. Green Mt. Trail from PL past A, C and M.
 2. Cross Country Trail from PL past C, F and H.
 3. Bethlehem Trail from PL past O and F to M, Green Mt Trail to B.
 4. Cross Country Trail from PL past C to F. Switch to Bethlehem Trail at F and go to M. Switch at M to Green Mt. Trail to B.
 5. Bethlehem Trail from PL past O to F. At F switch to Cross Country Trail past H to B.

18. If a new path is found that connects the fir tree to the Old Barn, what is the fewest number of trees that could be passed on a hike from the Pine Lodge to the Old Barn and back, taking a different route each way?
 (A) 3
 (B) 4
 (C) 5
 (D) 6
 (E) 7

18. The best answer is B. With the new connection between F and the OB, you could start at the PL and pass O and F on the way to the OB. That's 2 trees so far. From the OB take the new connection as far as F, then switch to the Cross Country Trail at F. Go past C to the PL. F and C would be 2 more trees. That's 4 all together.

QUESTIONS	EXPLANATIONS

19. If N is the first print displayed in the portfolio, which of the following statements could be true?
    (A) O is the second print displayed.
    (B) P is the third print displayed.
    (C) Q is the third print displayed.
    (D) W is the fourth print displayed.
    (E) T is the fifth print displayed.

19. The best answer is D. Your set up for the game should look like this:

    0 1 2 3 4 5

       -S
    O ——▶ -W, W ——▶ -O
    PQ / QP in 2+3 or 4+5
    NT / TN in 1+2 or 3+4
    MQ

    Then draw a diagram for this question
    0 1 2 3 4 5
      N T

    Eliminate choices (A) and (E). Now the only places to put P and Q would be on pages 4 and 5. So eliminate choices (B) and (C).

20. If S is the second print displayed, all of the following statements could be true EXCEPT
    (A) M is the first print displayed
    (B) W is the first print displayed
    (C) N is the third print displayed
    (D) N is the fourth print displayed
    (E) Q is the fifth print displayed

20. The best answer is E. Draw a new picture. If S is the second print, prints N and T must be on pages 3 and 4.
    0 1 2 3 4 5
    S N T
     T N
    So you have no room to put both P and Q.

21. All of the following prints could be displayed on the first page EXCEPT
    (A) M
    (B) O
    (C) Q
    (D) T
    (E) W

21. The best answer is C. This should have been one of your original deductions. If P and Q must be on facing pages, neither P nor Q can ever be on the first page, because the first page faces the blank page 0.

22. If O is the first print displayed, which of the
following statements must be true?
    (A) P is the second print displayed.
    (B) W is the third print displayed.
    (C) N is the third print displayed.
    (D) S is the fourth print displayed.
    (E) S and M are both displayed.

22. The best answer is E. Again, draw a new picture.
If O is the first print, W cannot be displayed.
Eliminate choice (B). N and T must be displayed
on pages 3 and 4.

```
0   1   2   3   4   5
    O       N   T
            T   N
```

Eliminate choices (C) and (D). And there's no room
for P and Q. Eliminate choice (A).

23. Collies are the most frequently purchased dogs at
dog breeding farms. Clearly, collies' superior
performance in dog shows makes them popular
dogs to buy as pets.

Which of the following, if true, would most seriously weaken the claim made above?
    (A) Collies require less food and care than do most
other dogs.
    (B) It is because of their glossy fur that collies
place well in dog shows.
    (C) Public interest in dog shows has been surging in
the recent past.
    (D) Schnauzers generally place best in show and
they are extremely popular dogs to buy as
pets.
    (E) Dogs that place well in shows invariably are the
most popular dogs to buy as pets.

23. The best answer is A. Use process of elimination.
Answer choices (B) and (E) strengthen the argument. Choice (C) is out of scope, as is choice (D)
— the argument is about collies, not schnauzers.

QUESTIONS	EXPLANATIONS

24. There are over fifty furniture stores in Middle Valley and not one of them charges less for furniture than does Green's Furniture Warehouse. It is clear that Green's Furniture Warehouse is the store that will provide the lowest price for furniture in all of Middle Valley.

Which of the following is an assumption on which the assertion made above is based?
(A) Customers do not have the option of shopping somewhere other than Middle Valley.
(B) The other furniture stores in Middle Valley charge more for furniture than does Green's Furniture Warehouse.
(C) The quality of the furniture at Green's Furniture Warehouse is equal to the quality of the furniture in other stores.
(D) Green's Furniture Warehouse is the most cost-effective store in Middle Valley.
(E) Other household items at Green's Furniture Warehouse are also well priced.

24. The best answer is B. Choice (B) fills the gap between the premise and the conclusion. The other answer choices are beyond the scope of the argument.

25. Unless there is an increase in federal spending, the national book program will fail.

Only if the national book program succeeds will the country escape recession.

There will be no increase in federal spending unless there is an increase in taxes.
If the statements above are true, which of the following must be true?
(A) If there is an increase in taxes, the country will definitely escape recession.
(B) Other programs will lose funding if the national book program succeeds.
(C) If the country escapes recession, the national book program must have succeeded.
(D) If the national book program succeeds, the country will escape recession.
(E) To escape recession, an alternate way of stimulating the economy must be found.

25. The best answer is C. This is merely a re-statement of the second premise. Answer choices (A) and (D) could be true, but also could be false. Choices (B) and (E) are out of scope.

Afterword

ABOUT THE PRINCETON REVIEW COURSE

The Princeton Review GRE Course is a six-week course to prepare students for the GRE.

Students are assigned to small classes (no more than twelve to fifteen students), grouped by ability. Everyone in your math class is scoring at the same math level; everyone in your verbal class is scoring at the same verbal level; everyone in your logic class is scoring at the same logic level. This enables your teacher to focus each lesson on your problems because everybody else in your class has precisely the same problems.

Each week you will cover one math area, one verbal area, and one logic area. If you don't understand a particular topic thoroughly, we won't ask you to listen to audiocassettes, as some other companies do. If you need more work on a particular topic, you can come to an extra help session later in the week. And if after coming to an extra help class, you want still more practice, you can request free private tutoring with your instructor.

Four times during the course you will take a computer-evaluated diagnostic test. Each diagnostic test is constructed according to the statistical design of actual GREs. The computer evaluation of your diagnostic tests is used to assign you to your class, as well as to measure your progress. The computer evaluation tells you what specific areas you need to concentrate on. We know how busy you are. We don't ask you to spend time on topics you already understand.

Princeton Review instructors undergo a strict selection process and a rigorous training period. All of them have done exceedingly well on standardized tests like the GRE, and most of them have gone to highly competitive colleges. All Princeton Review instructors are chosen because we believe they can make the course enjoyable as well as instructive.

Our materials are updated each year to reflect changes in the test design and improved techniques.

ARE YOUR BOOKS JUST LIKE YOUR COURSES?

Since our SAT book first came out in 1986, many students and teachers have asked us, "Are your books just like your courses?"

No.

We like to think that this book is fun, informative, and well-written, but no book can capture the rigor and advantages of our course structure, or the magic of our instructors. It isn't easy to raise GRE scores. Our course is spread over six weeks and requires class participation, diagnostic exams, and some homework.

Moreover, this book cannot contain all of the techniques we teach in our course for a number of reasons. Some of our techniques are too difficult to explain without a trained Princeton Review teacher to explain and demonstrate them. Also, this book is written for the average student. Classes in our course are grouped by ability so that we can gear our techniques to each student's level. A 500-level Princeton Review student learns different techniques from those learned by a 400- or 600-level Princeton Review student.

IF YOU'D LIKE MORE INFORMATION

Princeton Review sites are in dozens of cities around the country. For the office nearest you, call 1-800-995-5585.

About Computerized Testing

INTRODUCTION TO COMPUTERIZED TESTING

ETS, CBT, CAT, GRE—WHAT DOES IT ALL MEAN?

For more than a decade, researchers at the Educational Testing Service have been talking about eliminating paper test booklets and answer sheets, and administering tests by computer. ETS uses machines to score its tests; why not use machines to administer them, too? That's the theory, anyway. But there are many difficulties. In 1990, five ETS researchers published a book called *Computer Adaptive Testing: A Primer,* in which they wrote, "There are . . . several aspects of computerized and adaptive testing that raise new issues in the consideration of validity," and went on to admit, "There is, as yet, very little information available about the validity of computerized adaptive tests."

Despite these reservations, ETS began offering a computer version of the paper-and-pencil GRE just one year later. This computer-based test (or CBT) was exactly the same as the paper-and-pencil GRE, except that it was given on a computer.

We urged our students not to take the CBT GRE, because we believe that a test booklet is a lot easier to deal with than a computer screen. In a paper test booklet you can cross out incorrect choices or do scratch work right on top of a math diagram. On an ETS computer screen you can't. Reading comp is a drag in any form, but it's a double drag when you have to use cursor keys or a mouse to scroll through a passage.

Well, now the CBT GRE is gone and ETS has begun to offer a different computerized version called the computer-*adaptive* GRE (or CAT). Baffling, no?

WHAT GIVES?

The CAT is sort of a virtual GRE. Rather than asking you every question that could be found on a paper-and-pencil GRE—the way the CBT did—the CAT asks you only as many questions as ETS thinks it needs to in order to determine a fair score for you. Here's what happens: the computer begins by asking you a question of medium difficulty. If you get that question right, it asks you a question that's a little harder. Or, if you get the first question wrong, it asks you a question that's a little easier. The computer program *adapts* the test to fit your responses. It uses the first few questions to try to zero in on your approximate scoring level. Then it concentrates on questions at that level. High-scoring students will see very few easy questions; lower scoring students will see very few of the hardest ones.

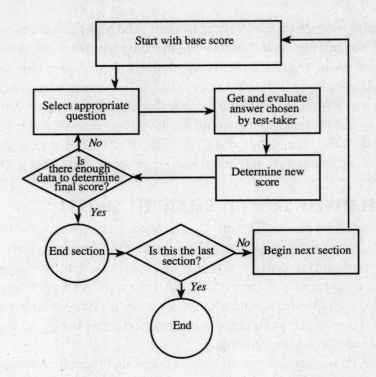

To simplify somewhat, the CAT computer tries to find the difficulty level at which you choose the correct answer about half the time. It looks for the point in the order of difficulty where you begin to lose it. That's how it figures your score.

This probably sounds weird to you. But it's actually not that different from the way the paper-and-pencil GRE works. To test hundreds of thousands of students with a single test—as ETS does with the paper-and-pencil GRE—the test-writers have to include many questions that are too easy for high-scoring students, and many questions that are too hard for low-scoring students. The paper-and-pencil GRE, in other words, is a one-size-fits-all test. It's designed to accommodate both students who score 300 and students who score 800. For every student who takes the test, therefore, most of the questions are essentially irrelevant, because most of them are aimed at students scoring either higher or lower.

Let's say you took the paper-and-pencil GRE last month and scored 600. In order to earn that score, you had to answer a lot of questions, but only a few of them really had a genuine impact on your score. With very few exceptions, you got the easiest questions right and the hardest questions wrong. If ETS had simply left out the easiest and the hardest questions, you would have ended up in about the same place. The real meat of the test, for you, was the medium-difficult and difficult questions where you began to feel shaky.

If ETS didn't have to test everyone with a single version of the GRE, it could

give everyone a substantially shorter test. The highest-scoring students could be given a relatively small number of very difficult questions. The lowest-scoring students could be given a relatively small number of questions from the opposite end of the order of difficulty. Every student, no matter what scoring level, would come away from the test with a sense that it had been pretty hard because what ETS would be looking for would be the wrong answer about half the time.

That's the idea behind the CAT GRE. It's a test that customizes itself to fit the scoring level of an individual test-taker. At any rate, that's what it tries to do.

HOW RELATIVELY SHORT IS RELATIVELY SHORT?

Although ETS researchers are clearly uneasy about the validity of scores from CAT's, they nonetheless also believe that a CAT wouldn't have to ask you very many questions in order to arrive at an acceptable approximation of your likely score on the paper-and-pencil GRE. In theory, a CAT might need to ask you just half a dozen questions, and almost certainly no more than eight or nine. After that, ETS researchers figure, the information provided by each additional question would be mostly redundant.

If ETS researchers are right, you could theoretically take the GRE in about as much time as it takes you to withdraw a hundred bucks from your bank's ATM. You would push a few buttons, a disk drive would whir, and the machine would spit out a printed score report while simultaneously transmitting your results to the graduate schools of your choice. ETS could put GRE machines in bars and video arcades. You could challenge your roommate to a GRE duel, with the loser paying for the beer.

Of course, ETS doesn't want the CAT GRE to seem like a video game. As a result, the CAT GRE contains a lot more questions than ETS researchers believe it absolutely needs to. But the idea is the same. ETS believes that the CAT GRE is a more "efficient" test than the paper-and-pencil GRE. It accomplishes more or less the same thing in less time.

WHAT'S IN IT FOR THEM: CASH AND CONVENIENCE

The paper-and-pencil GRE is administered five times a year. For each administration, ETS must rent thousands of rooms worldwide, hire proctors, transport materials, and register and collect fees from walk-in-test-takers. It must take steps to keep each test secret before it is given, and it must be careful to collect all booklets after it is done. It's a huge operation, with lots of moving parts, and innumerable opportunities for screwups.

For the CAT, in contrast, ETS needs nothing more than a room equipped with a couple of computers, and a single employee to give change and keep an eye on test-takers. No booklets. No proctors. No mobs of nervous test-takers

milling around the halls of a dingy high-school building, waiting for the supervisor to unlock the doors to the testing room. The test can be given at any hour of any day. They don't even need No. 2 pencils.

Another advantage for ETS (and for Sylvan Learning Centers, a company that has a contract with ETS to administer CAT's) is money. The fee for the computer GRE is nearly fifty dollars *higher* than the fee for the paper-and-pencil exam. Given how easy the test is to administer, you'd think the fee would be lower. But ETS wants to recover its development costs in a hurry, and it views the CAT as a major new source of profits. (Or maybe we should say nonprofits.) ETS is not a government agency or a department of Princeton University, as many people assume. It's a major private corporation—though one that is exempt from paying taxes. ETS doesn't call its profits profits. It calls them excess revenues. It needs plenty of excess revenues to maintain its tennis courts, hiking trails, sauna, conference center, baseball diamond, and swimming pool—along with the high salaries of its executives.

WHAT'S IN IT FOR YOU: BIAS, EYESTRAIN, TEARS, AND SWEAT

There are a few possible advantages for test-takers. First, you can take the test virtually any day of the work week. Second, you can have your scores immediately—an advantage if you're applying to graduate school at the last minute. Third, you probably won't need to give up most of a nice Saturday just to have your head kicked in by ETS. Fourth, . . . well, three is probably enough.

Actually, we feel that the disadvantages far outweigh the possible advantages for virtually every test-taker. Here are the main drawbacks:

- CAT test centers are not universally available. You may have to drive a long way to find one, and you may have to take a day off from school or work, since the CAT isn't offered on weekends.

- Because the CAT contains fewer questions than the paper-and-pencil GRE, the impact of any flawed question or any careless mistake is much higher. ETS researchers recognize this problem. In *Computer Adaptive Testing: A Primer*, the authors said, "A CAT makes much more stringent demands on its component items than does its paper-and-pencil counterpart.

Because the CAT tends to be much shorter . . . each item is more critical. If an item is flawed, its impact on the . . . examinee's proficiency [i.e., score] is doubled. Additionally, because not everyone gets the same set of items, a flawed item can affect some examinees and not others. Hence, test fairness, in addition to test validity, can be compromised."

- Computerized testing discriminates against non-nerds. Think about the people you know who spend lots of time with computers or video games. These people have an advantage on the CAT. But who are they? Aren't most of them members of one gender? Aren't most of them members of a specific socioeconomic class—the fancy-hardware-owning class? As ETS researchers have written, "It is conceivable that a CAT may be more vulnerable to problems of [bias] than are conventional paper-and-pencil tests, due to the possibility that differences between ethnic groups or genders in familiarity with computers in general may affect scores on computerized tests." If you don't live on darkness, Twinkies, and Diet Pepsi, you may be in trouble. ETS knows that charges of bias could cause it lots of trouble—so much so that it doesn't even use the word bias anymore. What used to be called "item bias" is now called "differential item functioning," or *dif.*

- Computerized testing discriminates against all the same people that paper-and-pencil tests discriminate against, only more so. To quote again from ETS, "Adaptive tests may be more vulnerable to the effects of *dif* on validity than fixed tests. A fixed test may contain items with counterbalancing *dif* that can 'cancel each other out'; however, in an adaptive testing situation, the presence of such [biased] items in the test pool permits the possibility that an unlucky examinee could be administered several items biased against him or her. The resulting test score would not provide a good indication of proficiency." In other words, according to ETS, a paper-and-pencil test is an equal-opportunity bigot, while a CAT can accidentally tailor itself to discriminate against you specifically.

- Taking a test on a computer is hard and inconvenient. Scratch work can't be done directly on the test booklet (although you are given as much scratch paper as you need). Reading comp is agony. You'll need to redraw math diagrams in order to fiddle with them. ETS's program is cumbersome and—especially to the non-computer-literate—confusing

- Taking the CAT can be a deflating experience for high-scoring students. Remember: the purpose of the CAT is to find the level in the order of difficulty at which you begin to screw up, and then hit you with a number of questions at around that level. If you're used to earning high scores on standardized tests, then you're also used to sailing through most of the questions, confident that you're answering them correctly. On the CAT, though, you'll be thrown a lot more questions that you won't be able to answer. Establishing a good, even rhythm will be harder.

- Some of our techniques will be harder to apply. Because the questions on the CAT are not presented in order of difficulty, Joe Bloggs will be much less helpful than he is on the paper-and-pencil GRE. Instead of seeing questions from an entire spectrum of difficulty, you'll mostly see questions from one narrow band.

- At the moment, you can take the CAT only once a year. The pool of CAT GRE questions is fairly small, and ETS uses a different GRE for each of its five paper-and-pencil administrations, but it can't throw out an entire CAT each time a student goes to the test center. The overlap in questions from one test to another can be as much as twenty or forty percent.

- Test security is a problem. Because the same questions are used over and over, it is theoretically possible for the entire pool to be "lifted." A couple of dozen students with photographic memories would be able to reconstruct the entire pool after a single morning at a test center. Your standing will suffer if other students have scores that are artificially high.

- There is no disclosure. If you take the paper-and-pencil GRE you can order a copy of your test later, and you can complain about unfair questions or scoring errors if you think you find them. The same thing is not possible with the CAT. ETS can't disclose the questions, because it needs to use them again. You have to put your faith in ETS's question writers and scoring formulas.

- There's no going back, and there is no skipping. On the paper-and-pencil GRE, you can circle questions you aren't sure about, and you can skip around each section, tackling the easier questions first. On the CAT, in contrast, you have to answer the questions in the order they are presented, and you can't go on until you have done so. You can't come back to a question you have answered, and you can't skip a question you don't like. The CAT is a one-way roller-coaster ride. Each section lasts until the computer has decided it has enough information to give you a score, or until the allotted time runs out. You are not the one in charge.

- Learning to feel comfortable with the CAT format takes practice, and the time you'll have to spend becoming familiar with the computer program would be better spent learning to tackle GRE questions.

WHAT'S A TEST TAKER TO DO?

Our advice is to avoid the CAT unless you have no choice—as you might if you had to come up with a score in a hurry. The CAT may eventually become the *only* format in which ETS tests are given, but until it does we think you'll probably be better off if you stick with paper-and-pencil.

If you're determined to take the CAT, however, then you need to prepare. That's why we have developed the RevieWare Computer Diagnostic. RevieWare is our own CAT. We have attempted to duplicate precisely the format, style, appearance, and working of ETS's computer tests. Aesthetically, ETS's program is rather unattractive, and it's a bit hard to move around in. So is ours. In mirroring the GRE's look and feel, we made the decision that an accurate reproduction would be more helpful than a fun, attractive test that looked nothing like the barren moonscape of the CAT GRE. They're bland, so we're bland.

Our RevieWare Computer Diagnostic is a useful practice tool even if you're not planning to take the CAT. If you follow the instructions, it will give you a good sense of what your current scoring level is, and show you which areas need work. Using it will help you whether you take the CAT or not.

GET IT BEFORE IT GETS YOU

You've been taking multiple-choice, paper-and-pencil, fill-in-the-bubble tests your whole life. So, while the prospect of taking another one may not be pleasant, it's at least familiar. But imagine walking into something as alien as a test that tries to guess your score before you've had a chance to use Joe Bloggs to eliminate obvious incorrect answers on the hardest geometry problem. You've never seen anything like it before. You haven't been practicing on it since first grade. You feel like Captain Kirk in the *Star Trek* episode where he has to dress up in a toga and be a pawn in a game that super-intelligent beings are playing, but he doesn't know any of the rules.

Well, you don't have to feel that way. RevieWare Computer Diagnostics are here to help. Adaptive testing appears to be the future. If you don't become familiar with it, you'll regret it. Maybe not today, maybe not tomorrow, but soon, and for the rest of your life.

Okay, okay, probably not for the rest of your life. But since you have the option, why not use RevieWare Computer Diagnostics to beat ETS at its own game? Happy testing, and good luck!

NOTES

NOTES

NOTES

NOTES

NOTES

ABOUT THE AUTHORS

Geoff Martz was born in 1956. He attended Dartmouth College and Columbia University, joining The Princeton Review in 1985 as a teacher and writer. Martz headed the development team which designed the Review's GMAT course. He is the author or co-author of *Cracking the ACT, Paying for College, Cracking the GED,* and *How to Survive Without Your Parents' Money.*

Adam Robinson was born in 1955. He graduated from Wharton before earning a law degree at Oxford University in England. Robinson, a rated chess master, devised and perfected the now-famous "Joe Bloggs" approach to beating standardized tests in 1980, as well as numerous other core Princeton Review techniques. A free-lance author of many books, Robinson has collaborated with The Princeton Review to develop a number of its courses.

John Katzman was born in 1959. He graduated from Princeton University in 1980. After working briefly on Wall Street, he founded The Princeton Review in 1981. Having begun with nineteen high school students in his parents' apartment, Katzman now oversees courses that prepare tens of thousands of high school and college students annually for tests, including the SAT, GRE, GMAT, and LSAT.

All three authors live in New York City.

THE PRINCETON REVIEW NETWORK

The Princeton Review wants to provide you with the most up-to-date information you need whether you are preparing to take a test or apply to school. If you are using our books outside of the United States and have questions or comments, or simply want more information on our courses and the services The Princeton Review offers, please contact one of the following offices nearest to you.

- HONG KONG   852-517-3016
- JAPAN (Tokyo)   8133-463-1343
- KOREA (Seoul)   822-795-3028
- MEXICO CITY   011-525-358-0855
- PAKISTAN (Lahore)   92-42-872-315
- SAUDI ARABIA   413-548-6849 (a U.S. based number)
- SPAIN (Madrid)   341-446-5541
- TAIWAN (Taipei)   886-27511293

Need More Practice?

The Princeton Review knows how valuable your time is. That's why we've created software that pinpoints your test-taking strengths and weaknesses and projects your GMAT score—all in about sixty minutes.

We use computer-adaptive technology that allows you to focus on areas where you need the most work. Once you've practiced and improved, the GMAT Computer Diagnostic provides a full-length computer-based

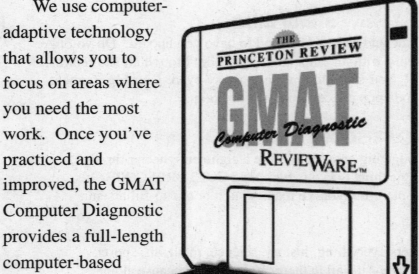

GMAT that gives you the opportunity to apply your new test-taking skills and watch your score go up.

Imagine staring at a monitor, writing with a mouse, and being unable to erase your mistakes. Welcome to the future of standardized testing. The days of #2 pencils are numbered; be prepared.

RevieWare Computer Diagnostic tests are also available for the following tests: GRE, LSAT, MCAT, and SAT.

Call The Princeton Review for more information about computer-adaptive tests.

(800) 995-5565

THE PRINCETON REVIEW

We Score More

CULTURESCOPE

The Princeton Review

Guide to an Informed Mind

Has this ever happened to you?

You're at a party. An attractive person who you have been dying to meet comes over and says, "Man, does that woman have a Joan of Arc complex, or what?" and you, in a tone that is most suave, say "Uh," while your mind races wildly, "*Joan of Arc, OK, France, uh...damn,*" as the aforementioned attractive person smiles weakly and heads for the punch bowl.

No? How about this?

Your boss finally learns your name and says, "Ah, good to have you aboard. Do you like Renaissance painting?" You reply with an emphatic "Yes! I do!" to which she returns, "What's your favorite fresco?" You start stammering, glassy-eyed, your big moment passing you by as visions of soda pop dance through your brain.

CULTURESCOPE can help.

If you have gaps of knowledge big enough to drive a eighteen-wheeler through, The Princeton Review has the thing for you. It's called CULTURESCOPE. It's a book that can make people think you've read enough books to fill a semi, even if you haven't.

CULTURESCOPE covers everything: history, science, math, art, sports, geography, popular culture—it's all in there, and it's fun, because along with all of the great information there are quizzes, resource lists, fun statistics, wacky charts, and lots of pretty pictures.

It's coming soon to a bookstore near you.

You won't go away empty-headed.

THE PRINCETON
REVIEW

Cracking the
GRE®